5th Edition

# Starting & Building a Nonprofit

## A Practical Guide

Peri H. Pakroo, J.D.

| FIFTH EDITION | MARCH 2013 |
|---|---|
| Editor | MARCIA STEWART |
| Cover Design | SUSAN PUTNEY |
| Proofreading | NICOLE THOMAS |
| Index | MEDEA MINNICH |
| Printing | BANG PRINTING |

Pakroo, Peri.
   Starting & building a nonprofit : a practical guide / Peri H. Pakroo. -- 5th ed.
     p. cm.
   Includes index.
   ISBN 978-1-4133-1847-0 (pbk.) -- ISBN 978-1-4133-1848-7 (epub ebook)
   1. Nonprofit organizations--Management. 2. Nonprofit organizations--Law and legislation. I. Title. II. Title:
Starting and building a nonprofit.
  HD62.6.P345 2013
  658'.048--dc23

          2012038393

This book covers only United States law, unless it specifically states otherwise.

**Please note**

We believe accurate, plain-English legal information should help you solve many of your own legal problems. But this text is not a substitute for personalized advice from a knowledgeable lawyer. If you want the help of a trained professional—and we'll always point out situations in which we think that's a good idea—consult an attorney licensed to practice in your state.

# Acknowledgments

Huge thanks to all the Nolo editors who have worked on this book through its various editions, most recently JinAh Lee and Marcia Stewart. Special thanks to Lisa Guerin and Stephanie Bornstein whose crack editing and hard work helped pull the first edition of this book into shape seven years ago.

Thanks to Jake Warner for everything: your ten-minute voicemail messages; your helpful advice when I was stuck; even the swarms of questions scrawled all over the first draft. I'll deeply miss working with you.

Thanks to Janet Portman, Beth Laurence, and the rest of the Nolo editors for welcoming me back on the team during my extended stay in Berkeley. Thanks also to Ilona Bray for sharing her nonprofit fundraising info with me.

Thanks to Betsy Erbaugh, Katayoon Kia, Sara Jamieson, and Melina Salvador for research and all sorts of other help along the way.

Loving thanks to my parents, Kay and Reza Pakroo, my sister Zara Pakroo, and my grandmother Eunice Jones for cheering me on throughout.

Thanks to Sue Moon and Sandy de Lissovoy for warmly welcoming me to Grant St. for my book editing retreat.

Thanks to all the folks who contributed to the book: Randolph Belle, David Dabney, Erika Harding, Michael Hohner, David Kaseman, Giovanna Rossi, and Mona Lisa Wallace. Your real-world experience is a real asset to the book.

Thanks and love to my homegirls, now scattered across red and blue states alike: Alexis Mollomo, Stacey Stickler, Laura Louise Taylor, and Carolyn Nelson. I'd be lost without you. Love also goes to my beautiful friends Inga Muscio and Samantha Campostrini-Medeiros, and to my identical cousin Parisha Pakroo.

Thanks to WFMU (www.wfmu.org) for providing the soundtrack. Freedom is freeform!

Thanks to Flying Star for allowing me to escape my lonely home office and letting me write and edit this book for countless hours in your cheerful café. Juno and I are grateful for the Petio and all the tasty snacks.

Oceans of love and thanks to Turtle, my very best friend. You make my heart swell every day.

## About the Author

Peri Pakroo is a business coach and consultant, specializing in legal and start-up issues for businesses and nonprofits. She has started, participated in, and consulted with nonprofits and for-profit businesses for more than 20 years. She received her law degree from the University of New Mexico School of Law in 1995, and a year later began editing and writing for Nolo, specializing in business and intellectual property issues. She is the author of the top-selling Nolo titles *The Women's Small Business Start-Up Kit* and *The Small Business Start-Up Kit* (national and California editions), and has been featured in numerous national and local publications including *Entrepreneur, Real Simple, Investors Business Daily*, and *Businessweek*.

Peri teaches adult education courses at WESST (www.wesst.org) in Albuquerque, a nonprofit whose mission is to facilitate entrepreneurship among women and minorities in the state of New Mexico. She is active in supporting local, independent businesses and is a co-founder of the Albuquerque Independent Business Alliance. Peri also works as an editor and project manager for web, print, video, and other media projects through her firm P-Brain Media (www.pbrainmedia.com).

For more information and resources for start-ups and nonprofits, see Peri's blog at www.peripakroo.com.

# Table of Contents

# Appendixes

# Your Nonprofit Start-Up Companion

Changing the world is not a one-person job. Of course, one person can make a difference: Committed, motivated individuals are often the seeds of major social movements or the subjects of inspiring stories about how ordinary people, through passion and tireless dedication, can move mountains for a worthy cause. But there is strength in numbers, and those who want to bring about change are most likely to succeed when they come together with like-minded comrades to work toward a common goal. Nonprofit organizations exist to bring together the people and resources necessary to mount these noble efforts. If you're considering trying to bring about change in your corner of the world by starting a nonprofit, this book will help you make your venture a success.

Many people believe—mistakenly—that all nonprofits are underfunded labors of love, kept afloat by the scrappy and tireless efforts of self-sacrificing, long-haired activists. While this description probably fits more than a few nonprofits, there are also plenty of nonprofits that bring in millions of dollars each year, pay hefty salaries to their workers, have swanky corporate offices, and even impose dress codes. In between these extremes, there are scores of nonprofits with varying assets, diverse office cultures, and a wide array of political leanings.

While the volunteer-driven model of nonprofits is alive and well, more and more nonprofits are adopting the entrepreneurial strategies and business models developed in the for-profit world. Many nonprofit managers and staff members have discovered that working for a nonprofit is a satisfying way to meet important community and societal needs and make a living at the same time, which can be more difficult in the for-profit arena. Whether you're driven purely by a passion for your mission or you want to combine your activist aspirations with a solid career, starting and running a nonprofit can be a great way to achieve your goals.

## Who This Book Is For

This book is intended for anyone who is considering starting a nonprofit or reorganizing an existing group.

You may be working with a group in its embryonic stages and coming to realize that you need to organize more formally. (Often, a group's lack of structure makes it ineligible for grants, unprepared to hire paid employees, or simply ineffective in its day-to-day operations.) Or, you may just have a goal or passion in mind and want to learn how to create an organization devoted to achieving that goal. You may be a budding founder of a new group or a staff member or volunteer at an existing group that needs an overhaul. No matter what position you hold or how far along you are in the process of bringing a group together, this book will help you understand the basics— and beyond—of nonprofit organization, planning, structures, management, marketing, and more.

For the most part, this book assumes that the reader is a founder or board member of an existing or future nonprofit group. However, you may be an executive director, manager, staff member, or volunteer who is researching nonprofit management in order to create or improve your group. Where the information in this book is directed not at the board or founder but at the executive director or other manager, it is noted explicitly.

## Nonprofit Basics

The term "nonprofit" is often used loosely to describe all kinds of groups that are bound together by a desire to achieve a mission, rather than to make a profit. By itself, the term "nonprofit" does not indicate any specific type of legal structure. If a nonprofit group incorporates, it is a nonprofit corporation; if not, it is an unincorporated nonprofit association. For example, a group of people interested in keeping a local park litter free would likely be called a nonprofit, as would a group of soccer dads who sell candy bars to fund their children's trips to soccer tournaments around the state. Both groups could be called nonprofits because both are mission driven, not profit driven—but they could have different legal structures. If the park group never did anything to create a formal structure, it would technically be considered an unincorporated nonprofit association. If the soccer dads filed incorporation papers with the state, the group would be a nonprofit corporation.

Before getting into the details of starting and running a nonprofit, here's a brief overview of the legal issues involving corporations in general, and nonprofit corporations in particular, and the various ways that running a nonprofit differs from running a for-profit business.

## Corporations in General

To create any type of corporation, nonprofit or for profit, you must file paperwork with the state government—usually the secretary of state's office. The document you must file with the state to create a corporation is typically called "articles of incorporation." Once you file this document, you have "incorporated" and created a separate legal entity: your corporation.

In the simplest terms, a corporation—whether nonprofit or for profit—is a type of business structure. Other types of business structures include sole proprietorships, partnerships, and limited liability companies (LLCs). Some states also recognize associations: groups of individuals who work together for some common goal but haven't taken steps to create a specific legal entity.

The main differences between the various business structures lie in how they handle two important issues—personal liability and taxation.

### Personal Liability

Some business structures (such as corporations) protect their owners from personal liability, while others (such as sole proprietorships) do not. If the business structure limits its owners' personal liability, the owners' personal assets will be protected if the business is sued or otherwise finds itself in debt. If the business structure does not limit its owners' liability, the owners' personal assets—such as houses, cars, bank accounts, and so on—can be taken to satisfy business debts or a lawsuit judgment.

Many nonprofits choose to incorporate primarily to receive this liability protection.

### Taxation

In some business structures (such as partnerships), business profits are taxed as if they are simply the personal income of the business owners. This is known as "pass-through" taxation—the profits pass through the business to the owners, who report the income on their own personal tax returns. Other business entities (such as corporations) pay and report their own taxes, separate from the owners' personal incomes. The business files its own tax return, as if it were a person. (In fact, you may hear people refer to a corporation as a separate "legal person;" legally, the corporation is a distinct entity that exists separately from its owners.)

Nonprofit corporations are separate tax entities but have different—and more favorable—tax rules than for-profit corporations.

## Nonprofit Corporations

A nonprofit corporation is an organization that has a mission to serve the public interest and has filed incorporation papers with the state. Because the corporation works for the public good, it receives exemptions from state and federal taxes it would otherwise have to pay—which means that these groups are, to a certain extent, publicly subsidized.

The mission-driven nature of nonprofits sets them apart from traditional private businesses, but they're not part of the government, either. (In fact, they are sometimes called nongovernmental organizations or NGOs.) Nonprofits occupy a unique position between the public and private worlds and share some characteristics of each. In exchange for being exempt from many of the taxes that normally apply to private businesses, nonprofits must dedicate themselves to the public interest and govern themselves according to certain rules designed to ensure accountability.

To ensure that nonprofit corporations are, in fact, working for the public good—and earning their tax breaks—state laws require them to establish certain organizational structures. A nonprofit corporation must have a board of directors (sometimes called a board of trustees), which is responsible for keeping the organization on track, working toward its stated nonprofit mission. Other state rules impose legal duties on the board—for example, the duty to act with care and the duty to be loyal to the organization—and ensure that the board does not stand to gain personally from the nonprofit's activities.

The steps you must take to form a nonprofit corporation are similar to the procedures for starting a regular corporation, but a bit more involved. Starting a nonprofit corporation is something like getting a commercial driver's license: The process for getting

a commercial driver's license is very similar to that for getting a regular driver's license, and the same agency grants both licenses, but you must satisfy a few extra rules to gain the additional privileges and responsibilities that accompany the commercial driver's license. Likewise, creating a nonprofit corporation is very similar to creating a for-profit corporation: To do either, you must apply to the same agency and follow a similar process—but to create a nonprofit corporation, you must satisfy a few extra rules.

## Alternatives to Nonprofits: For-Profit and Hybrid Business Models

Some of you reading this may wonder whether it would make more sense to start a regular for-profit business instead of a nonprofit for the work you envision doing. While this book presumes you do in fact want to structure your organization as a nonprofit, it's worth considering whether your goals may be better served with a for-profit business.

When choosing between for-profit or nonprofit structure, there are some new hybrid business structures to be aware of. One such structure is the *low-profit limited liability company*, or L3C. An L3C is similar to a nonprofit in that its primary purpose must be to benefit the public. But an L3C is run and taxed like a regular profit-making business and is allowed to make a profit as a secondary goal. This type of business structure was born so that charitably oriented LLCs could receive seed money (specifically, "program-related investments," or PRIs) from large nonprofit foundations, taking advantage of IRS rules that allow foundations to invest in businesses principally formed to advance a charitable purpose.

A small but growing number of states allow L3Cs, including Illinois, Louisiana, Maine, Michigan, North Carolina, Rhode Island, Utah, Vermont, and Wyoming. L3Cs have also been adopted by the tribal governments of the Oglala Sioux Tribe and the Crow Indian Nation of Montana. If the L3C is an option where you live and you're interested in this structure, contact your state's secretary of state or other office that handles L3C registrations for details. Note that because it's such a new business structure and definitive rulings on various aspects of L3Cs have not yet been issued by the IRS, plenty of questions remain. Keep an ear to the ground as the L3C develops.

Other business forms that are hybrids of the for-profit and nonprofit structures include *benefit corporations* and *Certified B Corps*. A benefit corporation, is a state-conferred legal structure that is currently an option in about 11 states: California, Hawaii, Illinois, Maryland, Massachusetts, Louisiana, New Jersey, New York, South Carolina, Vermont, and Virginia. A Certified B Corp, on the other hand, is a business that has been assessed and certified to meet sustainability-related criteria by B Lab, a nonprofit.

These two structures are quite similar; it's just that benefit corporations are an actual corporate structure recognized by the state, while the Certified B Corp is a certification conferred by a nonprofit. What both have in common is the following:

- The corporation has a purpose to create a material positive impact on society and the environment;
- The corporation is accountable through a fiduciary duty not only to corporate shareholders, but also to workers, community and the environment; and
- The corporation is run transparently, and must publish public annual reports on overall social and environmental performance against an independent and transparent third-party standard.

If you live in a state that does not recognize benefit corporations, you can still seek to be certified as a Certified B Corp. B Lab tracks state legislative activity and adoptions at its Benefit Corp Information Center at www.benefitcorp.net/state-by-state-legislative-status.

## Tax-Exempt Status of Nonprofits

Whether or not you choose to incorporate, you may be eligible for another benefit as a nonprofit organization: tax-exempt status from the federal government. There are several types of federal tax-exempt status, but the most favorable is known as "501(c)(3)" status. This moniker refers to the specific section of the IRS tax code that not only exempts certain nonprofits from having to pay federal income taxes, but also makes contributions to these organizations tax deductible to the donor. Other sections of the federal tax code (such as 501(c)(4) or 501(c)(6)) also offer exemptions from income taxes for nonprofits, but do not allow donors to deduct their contributions. In this way, 501(c)(3) status confers especially favorable tax treatment to organizations that qualify: Tax deductibility is often a crucial factor in attracting donations.

As you can imagine, not just any old group can obtain 501(c)(3) tax treatment. Only groups created for specific exempt purposes—religious, charitable, scientific, educational, or literary purposes that benefit the public—are eligible. Groups that haven't incorporated (often called "unincorporated associations") can still be eligible for 501(c)(3) status as long as they meet all other requirements. Groups that don't qualify for 501(c)(3) status might be eligible for other types of tax-exempt status—for example, social clubs are eligible under Section 501(c)(7), and trade associations are eligible under Section 501(c)(6). See the Organization Reference Chart in Chapter 1 for details.

To obtain 501(c)(3) status, an organization must file an application with the IRS and be approved. The organization must submit documents with the application, such as its articles of incorporation and bylaws, which must show that the entity is, in fact, dedicated to one or more of the specific nonprofit purposes outlined above.

In most states, a nonprofit that obtains an exemption from federal taxes automatically obtains an exemption from state taxes as well, so "tax exempt" generally means exempt from both federal and state taxes. Unless stated otherwise, throughout this book, the term tax exempt refers to federal tax exemption.

**CAUTION**

**The process of filing incorporation papers and applying for 501(c)(3) tax-exempt status is not covered in detail in this book.** Another excellent Nolo title covers these topics in depth, *How to Form a Nonprofit Corporation* by Anthony Mancuso. These processes aren't incredibly difficult, but do involve enough details and subtleties that they really deserve a dedicated book.

The book you are now reading is focused instead on helping readers gain a broader understanding of the many aspects involved in starting a nonprofit organization and getting it on the road to a sustainable and well-planned future. Many folks who are interested and active in community causes have a hard time transitioning to a more formal structure for their organization because they don't understand many fundamental issues such as how nonprofits are structured; roles and responsibilities of the board versus staff positions; basics of strategic planning, budgeting and fundraising; etc. Just because you have a passion for stray animals, fighting pollution or supporting our troops, it doesn't necessarily follow that you have the first clue about how nonprofits are structured or how they operate. This book aims to give activists and community organizers the resources they need to transform their cause into a stable nonprofit with a healthy board and a solid foundation for growing staff.

For a detailed discussion of the process of incorporating and applying for 501(c)(3) status, including step-by-step instructions for filling out the necessary forms, see *How to Form a Nonprofit Corporation*, by Anthony Mancuso (Nolo).

## Running a Nonprofit

Many experienced business owners and managers are surprised to find that running a nonprofit is quite different from running a traditional profit-driven business. Assuming you're an entrepreneurial type, you will probably figure things out quickly—but you should understand up front that running a nonprofit involves different approaches, judgments, and working styles than running a for-profit business.

## Importance of the Nonprofit's Mission

The legal distinction between a for-profit and a nonprofit corporation hinges on the purpose of the corporation's existence: The purpose of a for-profit business is to earn a profit, while a nonprofit exists to further a mission in the public interest. Beyond this legal role, a nonprofit's mission also drives many of the day-to-day operations of the nonprofit.

Because a nonprofit's purpose is to pursue a mission independent of any profit motive, success is measured differently than it is in a for-profit business. A business is considered a success if it makes a profit—and a failure if it doesn't. A nonprofit, on the other hand, is judged by whether it is accomplishing its mission. As you can imagine, success or failure in these terms is not always easy to measure—you can't come up with an answer by running a simple profit/loss analysis, for example.

Of course, just because nonprofits are mission-driven doesn't mean they can ignore financial concerns. In reality, a nonprofit won't be judged purely on how well it's achieving its mission without figuring financial health into the equation. If a nonprofit has achieved success in pursuing its mission—say, in raising literacy rates in a particular city district—but has no money in the bank or financial prospects for the future, it can't be called an unqualified success. Even though many nonprofits are supported by volunteer staff and may be quite adept at making the best use of scarce resources, no organization can run on fumes forever. Because almost every nonprofit faces a delicate balancing act between financing itself and achieving its mission, defining and measuring "success" in the nonprofit sector can be a challenge.

| Characteristics of Various Business Entities | | | |
|---|---|---|---|
| **Entity Type** | **Description** | **Liability** | **Taxation** |
| **For profit corporation** | Legal entity with one or more owners that has filed incorporation papers with the state. Owners (shareholders) of for-profit corporations can reap corporate profits. | Owners/directors are protected from personal liability. | Profits are taxed as corporate income at corporate tax rates. |
| **Nonprofit corporation** | Legal entity with one or more directors that has filed incorporation papers with the state. Directors of nonprofit corporations may not reap corporate profits; profits must stay in the nonprofit corporation. | Owners/directors are protected from personal liability. | May obtain various types of federal and state tax-exempt status, including 501(c)(3) status. If tax exemptions are not obtained, profits are taxed as corporate income. |
| **LLC** | Legal entity with one or more owners working toward a profit that has filed LLC papers with the state. | Owners are protected from personal liability. | Profits pass through to owners and are taxed as personal income (unless the owners elect otherwise). |
| **Partnership** | Legal entity with two or more owners working toward a profit. | Owners can be subject to personal liability. | Profits pass through to owners and are taxed as personal income. |
| **Sole proprietorship** | Legal entity with one owner working toward a profit. | Owner can be subject to personal liability. | Profits pass through to owner and are taxed as personal income. |

## Collaborative Management

For-profit businesses typically place a significant amount of decision-making authority in a few top-level positions—president, CEO, director, and so on—from which leaders may exercise control with little input or interference from others. Nonprofits, on the other hand, are required by law to have a board of directors that oversees operations; as a result, they are typically run in a more collaborative manner.

Board members cannot make unilateral decisions but must vote as a board to approve or nix various proposals for action. If a nonprofit has an executive director, he or she is chosen by and accountable to the board and is not an autonomous decision maker like the head of a private company. For many people who are used to the relative freedom of running a for-profit business, dealing with the collaborative management style of a nonprofit can pose a new challenge.

## Finding and Keeping Qualified Staff

Finding people to work for your nonprofit is likely to be one of the biggest challenges you'll face—particularly in the early days, when your entire organization will probably be on short rations. Many start-up nonprofits lack the resources they need to attract talented, experienced staff people who want to make a good living, which is often measured in competitive salaries and benefits.

Another nearly inescapable reality of the nonprofit sector is that there are never enough volunteers to do everything the nonprofit needs (or wants) to do. You may think that you won't have trouble finding folks to help because your nonprofit mission is so important or you live in a progressive community where everyone likes to pitch in. Unfortunately, people lead incredibly busy lives these days and guard their free time jealously. Much of the volunteer work people do is for well-established organizations and causes with well-defined volunteer needs that can be carried out easily, with little direction. New nonprofits, on the other hand, rarely have needs that are so clear-cut—you may be figuring out your needs through trial and error, which can

put too much responsibility on the casual volunteer. Finding volunteers and staff people is not impossible; you'll just need to be ready for the unique challenges of finding and developing a nonprofit workforce.

## Raising Money

Nonprofit organizations don't typically earn their money by selling products or services, like for-profit businesses do. Instead, nonprofits are supported by grants from public and private foundations, individual contributions, and/or membership fees. As compared to for-profit selling, nonprofit fundraising can be much more complicated and political.

Nonprofit fundraising certainly requires marketing and sales skills, however. You must be able to convince potential funders that your nonprofit is the best or most compelling organization to which they can contribute their hard-earned dollars. If you hate selling and have convinced yourself that nonprofit fundraising will be different, think again.

Fundraising can be difficult and time consuming; as a result, most nonprofits are perennially under-funded. Also, because a nonprofit is bound to a public interest mission and overseen by a board of directors, it doesn't have as much flexibility—or as many options—as a for-profit business would when trying to get out of financial trouble or turn around a cash shortage. In short, nonprofit fundraising isn't for everyone; it requires lots of energy, enthusiasm, and creativity—and the ability to work on a shoestring budget.

## How to Use This Book

Much like starting a typical, for-profit business, starting a nonprofit requires ingenuity, passion, and an entrepreneurial spirit. But nonprofit ventures offer unique rewards that many people find more compelling than the lure of financial gains in the for-profit world. For many socially minded entrepreneurs, starting a nonprofit is an ideal way to maintain a commitment to causes they care about while pursuing a career at the same time.

This book describes the nonprofit organizational model that makes this possible and outlines all the steps and tasks involved in setting one up. It explains all of the practical steps necessary to start and run a nonprofit, from deciding whether to form a nonprofit in the first place, to engaging in strategic planning, managing your finances and taxes, developing a website, and much more. The first chapter explains some of the choices you'll have to face at the outset, such as what to call your nonprofit, whether to incorporate, and whether to apply for a tax exemption. Each subsequent chapter focuses on an issue you will face when launching your nonprofit, such as choosing a board of directors, recruiting and training staff and volunteers, fundraising, and marketing. At the end of each chapter, you'll find a checklist that summarizes the key takeaway points, such as such as tasks for marketing your nonprofit.

When you're finished reading, you'll have a clear understanding of what it takes to run a successful nonprofit, and you'll be ready to pour your efforts into the important work ahead of you. Armed with the information in this book, you'll be ready for the challenges—and rewards—that await you in the nonprofit sector.

---

### More Nolo Nonprofit Resources

Nolo's website (www.nolo.com) offers books, online legal forms, eProducts, a lawyer directory, and free legal information to help nonprofits solve specific legal and practical problems. For example, the Nonprofits section of the Nolo site includes state-by-state details on each state's nonprofit corporation laws, a blog on fundraising tips, and lots of free articles on topics such as green event planning for your nonprofit charity. Here are some of the most popular Nolo titles for nonprofits:

- *How to Form a Nonprofit Corporation*, by Anthony Mancuso. Provides the background information and step-by-step instructions that budding nonprofits need to apply for federal 501(c)(3) tax-exempt status and qualify as a public charity with the IRS. Provides all necessary forms, including nonprofit bylaws, minutes, and tax articles.
- *Effective Fundraising for Nonprofits*, by Ilona Bray. Offers strategies for raising donations from individuals, companies, and institutions, and covers the tools and staff required for the job.
- *The Nonprofit's Guide to Human Resources*, by Jan Masaoka. Covers legal information and best practices for anyone in charge of HR at a small or medium sized organization—from managing volunteers to the board of directors' role in hiring staff.

---

### Get Updates, Forms, and More at This Book's Companion Page on Nolo.com

You can download any of the forms in this book at: **www.nolo.com/back-of-book/SNON.html** When there are important changes to the information in this book, we'll post updates on this same dedicated page (what we call the book's companion page). You'll find other useful information on this page, too, such as a list of each state's charitable solicitation registration offices, author blogs, podcasts, and videos. See the end of the table of contents for a list of forms available on nolo.com.

# Naming and Structuring Your Nonprofit

This chapter explains nonprofit structures in detail and outlines some factors to consider when deciding how best to organize your specific group. It also explains some of the basic decisions you'll have to make at the outset, including what to call your group, whether to formally incorporate, and whether to apply for tax-exempt status from the government. Here, you'll find information on:

- how to choose a name for your nonprofit
- how to decide whether incorporation makes sense for your group, and how corporations rules vary by state
- the different types of tax exemptions available to nonprofits and factors to consider in deciding whether to apply for them, and
- how bringing formal members into your nonprofit will affect its operations.

## Choose a Name for Your Nonprofit

Once you decide to organize a nonprofit, you'll have to figure out what to call your group. This process is a bit more involved than simply picking a name that sounds good. Of course, you'll want to come up with a name that describes your nonprofit's purpose or work, one that the public will understand and remember. But you'll also need to make sure that your name is not already being used by another business or group, either as a trademark or as a domain name. You'll also have to choose a name that complies with your state's legal requirements.

### Avoid Trademark Conflicts

If your name is already being used by another nonprofit or business, trademark laws (and a closely related area of law that prohibits unfair competition) may prevent you from using it. A trademark (sometimes simply called a "mark") is any word, phrase, logo, or other device used to identify products or services in the marketplace. The ins and outs of trademark law are beyond the scope of this book, but this section will quickly review key rules and list some

resources that will help you find out whether the name you want to use is available.

**RESOURCE**

**Nolo has resources on name and trademark issues.** For in-depth information on trademarks (including the legal criteria that determine whether you are infringing on—that is, unfairly using—another business's mark and the process of name searches and registration), the best source of information is *Trademark: Legal Care for Your Business & Product Name*, by Stephen Elias and Richard Stim (Nolo). You can also find lots of free information on trademarks and other business name issues on Nolo's website, at www.nolo. com.

Generally speaking, when a business or nonprofit owns a trademark, it can prevent anyone else from using it in a way that is likely to confuse consumers. If you "infringe" someone else's trademark, the trademark owner can take you to court to try to stop you from using it and even sue you for monetary damages.

Although owners can register trademarks with the U.S. Patent and Trademark Office, you don't have to register to create an enforceable trademark. You are the trademark owner if you are the first to use a name in connection with a business, trade, product, service, or activity. Because use of a name, rather than formal registration, creates trademark ownership, lots of trademarks cannot be found in any local, state, or federal databases. To avoid potential trademark fights later on, you'll have to do some research to find out whether anyone else is already using a name that's identical or similar to the one you want to use.

**CAUTION**

**The potential for name conflicts is much higher than it used to be.** In the pre-Web world, small, local businesses and nonprofits didn't have to worry too much about trademark conflicts as long as no one in their area was using a similar name. Today, however, the Web has created a global marketplace, in which physical location is almost irrelevant. Particularly if you plan to put your nonprofit online, you'll have to worry not only about trademarks used online, but also about names used almost anywhere the Web reaches—which, of course, is just about everywhere.

The good news is that trademark conflicts are far less common among nonprofits than they are in the for-profit world. One legal test for determining whether similar names are likely to cause consumer confusion is whether the entities using the names actually compete with each other. The less the entities compete, the less likely a court is to find a trademark violation. Because most nonprofits aren't heavily engaged in sales or other commerce, the risk of competition is significantly less than it is for commercial businesses.

Nonetheless, you don't want to make the mistake of choosing a well-established trademark for the name of your nonprofit or for any of its programs, services, or products. This is particularly true if you plan to conduct any business activities, such as retail sales. (Chapter 6 explains the rules regarding nonprofits conducting business-type activities and earning unrelated business income.) To find out whether the name you want is already in use, check some or all of the following resources:

- **The Web.** Start with the Internet, which is huge, fast, and free. By using search engines like Google or Yahoo!, you can quickly determine whether (and how) a specific term is in use. You should also check to see whether the name you want is being used as a domain name, which may present a trademark conflict.

- **Phone directories.** Don't overlook the humble phone book (and its increasingly preferred online version) as a valuable source of local name information. If you find that someone is using the name you want in your local area, there's no reason to waste time and money searching further—instead, start brainstorming to come up with another name for your group.

- **Industry sources.** Trade publications and business directories can be great sources of name information. You can also call local trade associations and chambers of commerce to ask whether they provide lists or directories of businesses in your area.

- **Federal trademark database.** If you use a trademark that's registered in this federal database, you can be sued for "willful infringement"—a legal violation that can carry hefty monetary penalties. To start your federal trademark search, go to the free trademark database of the U.S. Patent and Trademark Office (PTO), at www.uspto.gov. Or, you can visit your local Patent and Trademark Depository Library (PTDL)—there's at least one in every state—and use its research materials. You can also use any large public library or a special business and government library, which should carry the federal trademark register, a publication that lists all federal trade and service marks arranged by categories. For more information on trademark searches, see *Trademark: Legal Care for Your Business & Product Name*, by Stephen Elias and Richard Stim (Nolo).

- **State trademark registries.** Contact the secretary of state's office in your state (for a state-by-state list, visit the National Association of Secretaries of State at www.nass.org) to find out which government agency is in charge of trademark registries. Ask that agency for information on how to conduct a search, or you can hire a trademark search firm to do the work for you.

- **County fictitious name databases.** Many counties maintain a database of fictitious business names (FBNs) that have been registered there. An FBN is a business name that does not include the legal name of the entity that owns it—for example, if a nonprofit named Nurses for the Homeless, Inc., ran a clinic called Healthy Horizons, the clinic name "Healthy Horizons" would be an FBN that probably would have to be registered with the state or county. Even if you won't be using an FBN yourself, it's a good idea to check the FBNs used by other businesses in your county or state to see whether the name you want is already in use.

## Consider Domain Name Availability

Assuming that you'll set up a website (see Chapter 11 for information on how to do it), you should make sure that the name you want to use—or some logical abbreviation or acronym—is available as a domain name. Your domain name is part of the address visitors will use to access your site, such as akitarescue. org or cleanourcreeks.org. Most nonprofits use the suffix ".org" instead of ".com" to indicate that they have a noncommercial purpose. Governmental entities use ".gov," while educational entities use ".edu."

Clearly, it will be easier for your supporters to find you if your domain name and nonprofit name are identical. To be in the happy position of using your nonprofit name as your domain name, you'll need to choose a name that isn't already being used, which can be tricky these days—it seems that virtually every word and phrase has already been registered as a .com or .org address. To find out whether a name is available, go to an online registrar such as Namecheap (www.namecheap.com). You can enter the domain name you want and find out immediately whether it's available. If the name you choose for your nonprofit is already being used as a domain name, you will not only have to choose a different domain name for your website, but you may also face claims of trademark violation if you go ahead and use that name as your nonprofit name.

> **EXAMPLE:** A new nonprofit peace group wants to name itself Families for Peace and checks to see if www.familiesforpeace.org is available. They find it is already taken by a group called The Peace Initiative.
>
> Not only will the new group be unable to register the domain name www.familiesforpeace.org, but they might get into trademark trouble by choosing Families for Peace as the name of their nonprofit. By using the www.familiesforpeace.org domain name, the other group (The Peace Initiative) owns some level of trademark rights to the phrase and may be able to prevent the new group from calling itself by that name, even if the new group uses a totally different domain name. The new group

would be wise to choose a different nonprofit name altogether—preferably one that also can be used as its domain name.

Even if a domain name is available, trademark law may prevent you from using it if the name is already being used by another entity. For example, say there's an animal protection organization in Wyoming called Rural Pet Rescue that doesn't have a website. If a different animal rights group in Colorado sees that www.ruralpetrescue.org is available, it should not automatically assume that it can safely register and use that domain name. If it did, the Colorado group would be courting a trademark infringement lawsuit from the original Rural Pet Rescue in Wyoming, which may have been using the name for years. In short, domain name availability is no indicator of whether a name is safe to use under trademark law.

If your nonprofit name is on the long side, you might want to adapt it for your domain name. Consider any obvious abbreviations that the public would likely use. For example, a nonprofit called New York Arts Alliance might try www.nyartsalliance.org. Similarly, the Shawnee Independent Business Alliance might consider www.shawneeiba.org.

## Name Requirements for Nonprofit Corporations

You need to be concerned about trademark conflicts and domain name availability whether you incorporate your nonprofit or not. However, if you decide to incorporate, you will have to follow a few additional state rules. If you don't follow these rules in choosing your corporate name, your state's corporate filing office may not approve your name—and may reject your articles of incorporation. (See "Incorporation Paperwork and Fees," below.)

### Avoid Corporate Name Conflicts

Your state's corporate filing office—often the secretary of state's office—will reject your name if it is already in use by another corporation (nonprofit or for profit) or is confusingly similar to the name of another corporation in your state. Some states will also check your proposed name against other business databases, such as listings of state limited liability companies or limited partnerships. If your proposed name is already in use, you'll be out of luck.

To save time and headaches, do some research before you file your articles of incorporation to find out whether your proposed name is available. You can usually call or write the state filing office (usually the secretary of state) to check on name availability; many states also allow you to check names online. Ask your state's filing office about its search procedures, or check your state filing office's website. You can find a list of secretaries of state nationwide at the National Association of Secretaries of State online, at www.nass.org.

Once you find an available name, reserve it if you can. Most states allow you to reserve a corporate name for a specified period of time, sometimes for a small fee. Reserving a name is a good idea because it prevents someone else from taking your name before you have a chance to file your articles. For more information on selecting and reserving a corporate name, including a sample name reservation letter, see *How to Form a Nonprofit Corporation*, by Anthony Mancuso (Nolo).

### Other Name Requirements

Many states require nonprofit corporations to use—or avoid—certain words in their corporate names. For example, you may have to use the word "corporation" or the abbreviation "inc." in your corporate name, or avoid using words that falsely imply a particular business structure or affiliation, such as "bank," "trust," "cooperative," "federal," or "insurance." Of course, if your nonprofit really is a cooperative or trust, you may be able to use these words in your corporate name. Check with your state's filing office for its specific rules.

If you plan to apply for tax-exempt status (see "Do You Want Tax-Exempt Status?" below), you should also avoid any words implying that your nonprofit might not be eligible for a tax exemption. For example, if you used the words "trade association" or "political action group," you might not sound like the kind of organization that is eligible for certain kinds of tax exemptions. This is not a requirement of state or federal law; instead, it is a commonsense precaution that will prevent possible problems down the road when you apply for your tax exemption.

## Should You Incorporate?

You don't necessarily have to incorporate your group to accomplish your nonprofit goals. (The same goes for obtaining 501(c)(3) or other tax-exempt status, which is covered below.) Many small groups operate perfectly well without incorporating and happily remain what's sometimes referred to as an unincorporated association. In fact, many groups decide to incorporate only when faced with some pressing reason to do so—for example, because the group won't be eligible for a grant unless it incorporates.

When you incorporate as a nonprofit (by filing papers with your state's filing office), you create a separate legal entity that pays its own taxes and protects the people who run it and work for it from personal liability. If an organization does not incorporate, its legal status is fuzzier. As discussed below, unincorporated groups are treated differently from state to state. Some states treat them like corporations in some respects; others don't.

 **TIP**

**You don't have to incorporate to obtain tax-exempt status.** Unincorporated associations can apply for and obtain 501(c)(3) status (and other types of tax-exempt status as well). Keep this in mind if you are considering applying for a grant that is available only to groups that have 501(c)(3) or other tax-exempt status—it's not necessary to incorporate to get 501(c)(3) status and be eligible for the grant. Still, it's often a good idea to incorporate, anyway. A group that plans to seek federal tax-exempt status will likely benefit from the more formal corporate structure.

In the absence of a clear need to incorporate, the members of a nonprofit group may wonder whether incorporating makes any sense at all. Some may think it's the right thing to do based on a vague notion that it will protect board members from personal liability or because it sounds more official. Others may not want to incorporate, fearing the dreaded corporate paperwork or simply feeling that incorporating isn't the best use of time, money, and other resources. While there may be some truth in each of these notions, it's important to get past these generalities and consider specific reasons why your particular group will or won't benefit from incorporating.

Broadly speaking, the main reason most nonprofits incorporate is to protect those who work for the organization from personal liability. In addition to limited liability, other considerations may be important to your nonprofit, such as whether your group plans to obtain federal tax-exempt status, whether it plans to handle large sums of money, whether it seeks to gain credibility by incorporating, or how unincorporated associations are treated in your state. The sections below look at each of these factors in more detail.

people who run the nonprofit. Only the assets of the corporation itself will be vulnerable, not the personal assets of the board and staff.

If your nonprofit is lucky enough to have sizable assets, losing them to debt would of course be devastating. But a more common and serious problem occurs when creditors go after board members or staffers with deep pockets, instead of targeting the nonprofit itself (which may lack cash and other assets). If the group is not incorporated, the people running the organization might find themselves personally liable for the nonprofit's debts. This possibility creates a pretty powerful incentive for many nonprofits to incorporate. But, as discussed below, other laws might protect your members from liability even if you don't incorporate, and your group's actual liability risks may be quite low. In short, not every nonprofit has to incorporate to adequately protect its members from liability.

---

### Are You Sure You Want to Incorporate?

As discussed in this chapter, incorporating allows you to take advantage of sometimes favorable corporate tax treatment and protection from personal liability. But some groups won't realize many benefits by incorporating; for them, there's no reason to spend the time and money required to incorporate. If your liability risks are minimal to nonexistent, and if incorporating doesn't make any additional tax advantages available to your group, it often makes more sense to keep things simple and operate as an unincorporated group until growth or other changes warrant a more formal organizational structure.

---

## Liability Issues

One of the most compelling reasons to incorporate a group is to protect directors, officers, and staff from personal liability. If the nonprofit corporation loses an expensive lawsuit or finds itself in debt, creditors typically won't be able to get at the assets of the

---

### Corporation Rules Vary by State

All corporations—nonprofit and for profit alike—are creatures of state law. Although state laws that govern corporations are, for the most part, similar throughout the nation, there are important differences. For example, states vary on the minimum number of directors required for nonprofit boards, as well as eligibility rules for directors. And corporate tax laws can vary significantly from state to state.

In addition, corporations created in one state are not automatically qualified to do business in others. If you create your nonprofit corporation in Wisconsin, for example, it is technically a "Wisconsin corporation." Other states will view it as a "foreign corporation" and will generally require you to file paperwork and pay a fee before allowing you to do business within their borders. If you do not plan to engage in nonprofit activities in other states, then incorporating in your home state alone is probably sufficient, at least in your early days. If, on the other hand, you expect the scope of your activities or services to extend into other states, you should investigate the requirements for operating as a nonprofit corporation in those other states.

CAUTION

**Corporate protection from personal liability is not absolute.** In some unusual circumstances, individuals may be held personally liable for corporate debts. Often called "piercing the corporate veil," this individual liability is usually reserved for cases of extreme mismanagement or self-dealing. In these situations, the corporate structure may not shield an individual who commits improper, unethical, or criminal activities. (Liability is covered in greater detail in Chapter 7; you'll find information about the duties of nonprofit directors in Chapter 4.)

So, how worried should you be about liability issues? The answer will largely depend on what your activities and potential risks will be, and whether other sources of protection offer enough of a shield to make incorporation unnecessary.

CAUTION

**Incorporating won't shield the nonprofit's assets.** Forming a corporation limits only personal liability—that is, the liability of those who work for the nonprofit. If a successful lawsuit is filed against a nonprofit corporation, the nonprofit's staff and volunteers may not have to pay a penny, but the assets of the nonprofit itself can be wiped out. Taking risk management seriously will help you keep your nonprofit out of financial and legal trouble. (Risk management and insurance are covered in more detail in Chapter 7.)

### Assess Your Risks

Start your risk assessment by reviewing your expected activities. If your group will regularly engage in activities that involve physical or financial risk (including any plans to solicit large amounts of money), incorporating may be the wisest choice. (Or consider changing your activities—see "Other Risk Management Strategies," below.) For example,

a bicycling team, a children's gym, an environmental organization that plans to clean up hazardous waste, or an independent business alliance that holds large conventions would be well advised to incorporate.

On the other hand, if you anticipate very little risk, you may reasonably conclude that avoiding personal liability doesn't justify the time and expense of incorporating. For example, a neighborhood association, a slam poetry group, a gathering of French-language enthusiasts, or a group that wants to improve a rose garden at a local park might not face much liability risk during their activities. If there's little or no risk of injury and everyone reasonably agrees that a lawsuit would be extremely unlikely, operating as an informal, unincorporated group may be an entirely sensible path to take.

Lots of groups will fall somewhere in between, with activities that could pose small to moderate amounts of risk—say, a weekend soccer league or a group that periodically holds food drives for the homeless. Before jumping into incorporating, groups like this should consider some other sources of protection from liability exposure, discussed below.

TIP

**Whatever your true risks are, make sure your volunteers, staff, board members, and others are comfortable with your organizational structure.** If you find that potential directors, employees, or volunteers are reluctant to work for the organization without the protection of the corporate structure, you've got a problem on your hands. If you feel their worries are unwarranted—for example, every player on your softball team is covered by comprehensive insurance provided by the Amateur Softball Association of America—you might try to address their concerns and convince them they are not facing as much risk as they think. On the other hand, their fears may be a sign that it's time to incorporate your nonprofit.

## What's in the Uniform Unincorporated Nonprofit Association Act?

Recognizing that unincorporated groups do much good for the public but can be hampered by their vague legal status, in 1992, the National Conference of Commissioners on Uniform State Laws drafted the Uniform Unincorporated Nonprofit Association Act (UUNAA). The act, a model law for states to adopt, attempts to encourage involvement in small community groups and other organizations that aim to benefit the public but don't want to establish formal corporate structures. The UUNAA was revised in 1996, and a revised act, the RUUNAA, was drafted in 2008. So far, several states have adopted the UUNAA and a few have adopted the RUUNAA.

Under the UUNAA, an unincorporated nonprofit has the legal status of a separate entity for purposes of liability. This means that people who work for an unincorporated nonprofit won't be liable for the actions of the nonprofit or other people working for it merely by virtue of their involvement with the group. The UUNAA definition of "unincorporated nonprofit associations" is broad: "[Two] or more members joined by mutual consent for a common, nonprofit purpose." Members may be individuals, corporations, other associations, or governmental agencies. Both volunteer and paid workers are protected.

The UUNAA gives five benefits to unincorporated nonprofits:

- the legal capacity to receive, hold, and transfer real and personal property
- limited liability for members and managers for personal injury (tort) and contract claims
- the right to sue and be sued as associations
- a procedure for disposing of the property of inactive associations, and

- the right to designate a member of the association to be its "agent for service of process"—the person who has the authority to receive legal papers on the group's behalf.

The RUUNAA is substantially similar to the UUNAA and provides additional guidance, incorporating modern practices and eliminating potential conflicts with other laws.

The states that have adopted the UUNAA or the RUUNAA as this book went to press include:

**RUUNAA (2008):**

Arkansas

District of Columbia

Iowa

Nevada

**UUNAA (1996):**

Alabama

Arkansas

Colorado

Delaware

District of Columbia

Hawaii

Idaho

Illinois

Louisiana

North Carolina

Texas

Wisconsin

Wyoming

The most current version of the act, the RUUNAA, is tracked at the website of the Uniform Law Commission at www.uniformlaws.org. Visit this site for the full text of the law, a legislative summary, and any recent state adoptions.

## Balancing Liability Considerations

Once you've assessed your risks and looked at the various ways to protect your group and its people from liability, you'll be in a much better position to decide whether incorporation makes sense in your situation. Consider the following example.

**EXAMPLE:** The New Mexico Cactus Lovers (NMCL) is a group of about 25 people who get together every other month or so to view and photograph various cactus plants. They post the pictures and other informative material at a small website. Keeping the group organized and planning its activities falls to a group of five people who call themselves the steering committee. The folks on the steering committee plan outings, notify members of the time and place for each outing, and coordinate getting the cactus photos and information from members to post at the website, among other basic tasks.

At the last outing, one member slipped and fell into a prickly pear. She wasn't hurt too badly and has no intention of suing, but it got NMCL's steering committee thinking about their liability risks. Even though people could get hurt during their outings, the steering committee concludes that the chances of a successful lawsuit against the group or its members are small. Because all of the members are friends and outings are not open to the public, there's a low likelihood of a member suing in the first place. Still, a lawsuit is possible and could be expensive to defend, even if it was ultimately unsuccessful. The committee isn't worried about the group's assets, which don't typically exceed $1,000 at any given time; what concerns them are the assets of the group's individual members.

They do a quick search of laws online and learn that New Mexico has not adopted the Uniform Unincorporated Nonprofit Association Act. However, they see that New Mexico's laws do provide some other protections for unincorporated associations and their members. They find New Mexico's Corporations statute, Unincorporated Associations chapter, which states in Section 53-10-6B: "Any money judgment obtained against an unincorporated association shall bind only the joint or common property of the association." They plan to ask a lawyer about this but surmise that it means individual members can't be held personally liable for judgments against the group.

Continuing their research, the steering committee reads about and discusses the Volunteer Protection Act. They note that the VPA applies only to volunteers of 501(c)(3) tax-exempt nonprofits, or those operated "for public benefit and operated primarily for charitable, civic, educational, religious, welfare, or health purposes." After some discussion, they agree that they'll want to keep the primary focus on the Cactus Lovers' educational website and other informative activities (as opposed to purely recreational purposes), so that their group will be covered by the VPA.

After discussing their likely risks and the existing sources of protection available to NMCL and its members, the steering committee decides that the risks to the group's members are minimal, so incorporating doesn't appear to be essential at this point. They plan to look into a general liability insurance policy for the group to protect against accidents that might happen during their outings. They also agree to revisit the issue if their group grows significantly or starts to engage in new activities.

To see how taking on new activities will affect your liability risks—and, in turn, the need to incorporate—consider some different possibilities for the New Mexico Cactus Lovers. The chart below shows how the group's need to incorporate might change as its activities grow. These are just general guidelines, but they show that increasing levels of risk will make incorporation look more and more attractive.

| Low Need to Incorporate | Borderline Need to Incorporate | High Need to Incorporate |
|---|---|---|
| NMCL's loose group of cactus enthusiasts visits public lands to take photographs of interesting cactus specimens, which they post at a website. Everyone who participates in the park outings signs a liability release form each year. | NMCL posts notices in local calendars and other media inviting the public to join in the park outings. Participants must make their own travel arrangements and sign a waiver releasing NMCL from liability. | Two to four trips are offered each month to the public and to NMCL's 100 or so members. NMCL offers transportation to those who want it. Release forms are required. Trips venture into areas with hazards such as steep rocks, rattlesnakes, and extreme temperatures. |

## Other Risk Management Strategies

As discussed in more detail in Chapter 7, there are many different ways that groups of all types and sizes can minimize their liability risks. Be sure to consider these simple, effective strategies:

- **Adapt your activities.** If your group identifies a specific activity that exposes the group and its members to risk, consider changing that activity or eliminating it altogether.

- **Use signed waivers.** When appropriate, get participants to sign waivers releasing the group from liability.

- **Find an umbrella group.** If an umbrella group exists for your type of organization, operating under it can help minimize your liability exposure. For example, sports teams typically play in leagues or enter tournaments sponsored by umbrella groups, which often allow and may require every participant to sign up for the group's insurance plan.

## Insurance

For groups whose principal volunteers and staffers face low (but not entirely negligible) liability risk, basic liability insurance might offer adequate protection, making incorporating unnecessary. A simple, reasonably priced policy can shield members or workers of a group from a wide range of liability risks, from typical trip-and-fall claims to cases of mismanagement or fraud.

Take, for example, the food drive group mentioned earlier. If someone was injured by a falling box of canned goods and sued the organization, there's a good chance that neither the organization nor its individual members would be liable in the first place. But even if a lawsuit was successful, liability insurance coverage would probably protect individual group members from having to pay medical bills or legal damages, even if the group was not incorporated. As discussed in Chapter 7, it's a good idea for any group to consider at least some basic insurance—but

it's especially smart for those that don't have the protection of the corporate structure.

### State Laws Protecting Members of Unincorporated Associations

Some states have enacted laws providing at least some limited liability to people involved with unincorporated groups. Depending on the state, this protection may cover paid and/or volunteer workers; other specifics also vary from state to state. In addition, some states have adopted the Uniform Unincorporated Nonprofit Association Act (UUNAA), which, among other things, limits the liability of members and functionaries of unincorporated associations for personal injury (tort) and contract lawsuits. (See "What's in the Uniform Unincorporated Nonprofit Association Act?" above, for more information on the act's provisions and the states that have adopted it.)

Other states have no laws at all regarding the liability of those associated with unincorporated groups. Even though you probably won't be on the losing end of a lawsuit, it's nevertheless important to recognize that these states offer no personal liability protection to the people who work for unincorporated associations. (But federal law does—see below.)

To find out about your state's laws, you may have to do a little research. A good place to start is at the Nonprofit Risk Management Center's website, where you can download an excellent guide, *State Liability Laws for Charitable Organizations and Volunteers*. This free guide offers state-by-state legal information on liability issues in the nonprofit world. You'll find it at www.nonprofitrisk.org; look in the "Library" section or do a search for "state liability laws."

### The Federal Volunteer Protection Act

In addition to the variety of state laws that protect the people who work for nonprofits, federal law provides some basic protections to volunteers who work for nonprofit groups, whether or not they incorporate. The Volunteer Protection Act (VPA) of 1997 provides limited immunity to unpaid volunteers—including directors, officers, and trustees—for any injuries or damages they cause in the course of their volunteer activities. (42 U.S.C. §§ 14501 and following.) A group must either have federal 501(c)(3) tax-exempt status or be operated "for public benefit and operated primarily for charitable, civic, educational, religious, welfare, or health purposes" to qualify for this protection. (42 U.S.C. § 14505(4).) The group does not have to be incorporated or possess any tax-exempt status to meet the second definition.

Because the VPA is a federal law, it provides what amounts to a mandatory minimum level of protection for nonprofit volunteers in all 50 states. In states that have no law governing volunteers' liability, the VPA will apply. In states that provide even more protection to volunteers, state law trumps the VPA. (For more information on the VPA and liability issues in general, see Chapter 7.)

### CAUTION

**The Volunteer Protection Act does not prevent lawsuits against nonprofit organizations.** The VPA protects only the volunteers who work for a nonprofit, not the nonprofit group itself. Similarly, the VPA does not prevent a nonprofit from suing a volunteer for damages; it just shields volunteers from lawsuits by third parties. But, as mentioned earlier, nonprofits themselves usually aren't sued because they so often have minimal assets. Much more often, it's a volunteer with a fat bank account who faces a lawsuit. This is the situation that the VPA protects against.

## Tax Exemptions

Generally speaking, there are two ways that a nonprofit can enjoy exemptions from federal or state taxes. As discussed in more depth below, a nonprofit that meets federal and state requirements can:

- avoid paying federal and state taxes on income, and
- for nonprofits that qualify under Section 501(c)(3), offer donors the opportunity to deduct the value of their contributions.

These benefits can be quite valuable, but your group doesn't have to incorporate to get them. Your group's eligibility for any sort of tax exemption will depend on your nonprofit's activities—not on whether or not it is incorporated.

If it meets all other requirements, an unincorporated association can obtain tax-exempt status from the IRS (including exemption from taxes and tax deductions for contributors), as long as the group has a written organizational document, often called articles of association. Many states allow unincorporated groups to file articles of association with a state office (usually the secretary of state), in much the same way corporations file articles of incorporation.

### TIP

**Follow IRS rules when filing articles of incorporation or association.** If you plan to apply for federal tax-exempt status, your organizational document must pass IRS muster. For corporations, the IRS says you must provide evidence that the articles of incorporation were filed and approved by the state. You can do this by submitting a copy of the articles that are stamped "Filed" and dated by the secretary of state or you can provide a written declaration from an authorized person stating that the articles submitted are complete and were filed and approved by the state, including the date filed. For unincorporated associations, the articles of association must be signed by two or more people and must be dated. Further, if you plan to apply for 501(c)(3) tax-exempt status—as opposed to tax exemption under other IRS provisions, such as 501(c)(4) or 501(c)(6)—your organizational document must include specific language regarding your tax-exempt purpose and a limitation on political activities, among other things. This applies to associations and corporations alike. If you file your state organizational paperwork without knowing exactly what will be required if you decide to apply for tax-exempt status, you could create a lot of unnecessary trouble for yourself down the road.

Even though you don't have to incorporate in order to pursue tax-exempt status, it can still be a good idea. Adopting the formal corporate structure will force you to be more organized and approach important tasks—like defining your mission, clarifying roles within the organization, and managing your finances—more seriously. These tasks are especially important for groups that plan to seek federal tax-exempt status, because these groups will be legally required to stay true to their mission, keep good records, and carefully manage their finances. In short, you will be in a stronger position to obtain tax-exempt status if you incorporate your group because incorporation forces you to impose and maintain a higher degree of organization.

On the flip side, remember that incorporation alone doesn't automatically make you eligible for the tax-exempt status you want. Your ability to obtain federal tax-exempt status will depend on your nonprofit's activities, which may or may not fall within a specific tax-exempt category. For example, a bridge-playing group probably wouldn't be eligible for 501(c)(3) status, which is generally reserved for charitable nonprofits. If the bridge group incorporated to obtain 501(c)(3) status, it would be out of luck (unless it overhauled its activities substantially).

As for state income taxes, each state follows its own rules as to granting exemptions to nonprofit groups. If your unincorporated group will not be eligible for a state tax exemption, incorporating might be your best option. State rules for income tax exemptions are covered later in this chapter.

 **TIP**

If you plan to incorporate, do it *before* applying for federal tax-exempt status. You should apply for tax-exempt status only after you finalize your business structure. If you decide to incorporate *after* obtaining tax-exempt status, the IRS will require you to go through the tax-exempt application process all over again. By incorporating, you will have created a business entity separate from your prior association—and that new entity will need its own tax exemption.

## Financial Accountability

While nothing prevents an unincorporated association from having well-developed and well-organized financial systems, sometimes the additional formality of the corporate structure helps promote sound financial management. Because a corporation is legally required to fill certain board and officer

positions (and each position has important legal duties), the people working for a nonprofit corporation often have a clearer sense of accountability and how important it is to manage funds with care. In an unincorporated group that doesn't have these built-in legal responsibilities, it's not uncommon for financial systems to be messy or nonexistent. In short, if membership dues, fundraising events, private contributions, or other sources bring in even a few hundred dollars per year to the nonprofit, your group might benefit from the greater financial accountability that comes with incorporation.

Incorporating can also help you show outsiders that your group is a serious endeavor—and convince them that they should support it financially. Potential contributors often want to see financial systems and accountability in place before they commit any funds to a group. In particular, foundations and other large grant providers may not consider giving financial support to unincorporated groups, precisely because the formality of the corporate structure provides additional assurance that the money will be managed in a professional manner. So, when it comes to attracting and securing contributions, incorporating may be a practical necessity.

 **TIP**

**Do you really want to start a for-profit business?** Even though you may feel certain that you want to pursue your goals with a nonprofit, be open to the possibility that your ideas may be better served by starting a for-profit business. You can be as socially progressive with your business as you and your partners want, but will not be bound by the special tax and other rules that govern non-profits. Remember to consider new hybrid business models like the low profit limited liability company (L3C) and the benefit corporation. See the introductory "Companion" chapter of this book for details.

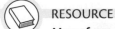 **RESOURCE**

**Many foundations give money only to nonprofit corporations with 501(c)(3) status.** If your potential funding sources don't give money to groups without 501(c)(3) status, you'll obviously want to obtain that exemption. You'll find detailed information on what groups are eligible for this type of tax-exempt status, as well as other kinds of federal tax-exempt status, in "Do You Want Tax-Exempt Status?" below. For line-by-line instructions on filling out the 501(c)(3) application, read Nolo's *How to Form a Nonprofit Corporation*, by Anthony Mancuso.

On the other hand, if your group collects a few bucks from its members every other month to cover photocopying expenses or holds a yearly bake sale to help cover the cost of a trip to the Grand Canyon, incorporating may well be more costly and complicated than it's worth. Unless there are other reasons to incorporate—liability issues, for example—it often doesn't make sense for small groups with minimal funds to take on the formality and complexity of the corporate structure.

**TIP**

**Incorporating may enhance your group's credibility.** Many people are just more inclined to respect an organization that has gone to the trouble to incorporate, whether or not it truly deserves that respect. Of course, credibility and reputation are important for any nonprofit, and you'll build them by running your organization well. But if credibility is a particular concern for your group, you might want to consider incorporating sooner than later to establish your bona fides early on.

## Other Considerations

Besides the big issues of liability and considerations related to taxes and financial management, other factors may affect whether or not you should incorporate. Here are a few to consider.

### Likely Duration

Generally speaking, incorporating is more appropriate for groups that expect to have a lifespan of at least a few years. If your group is short-term in nature—for example, you banded together to prevent a big-box store from moving into the neighborhood—it probably doesn't make sense to incorporate. If the issue will likely be resolved one way or the other fairly quickly, precious time and energy could be better spent on the campaign,

not on building and maintaining the corporation. But if your group sticks together after the initial battle and redefines its mission as creating and maintaining appropriately sized neighborhood shopping areas, it might be a good idea to form a corporation.

Look at your organization's goals and evaluate whether you will be able to meet them relatively quickly, or whether they will require an ongoing, long-term effort. Unless you expect to be pursuing your mission for quite a while, incorporating may be more trouble than it's worth.

**EXAMPLE:** A group of neighbors frustrated with the litter at a neglected local park decides to band together for a Clean Up Our Park Weekend. They organize an event to clean up a lake and a forested area in the park. They take risk management seriously and plan to have all participants sign a release from liability. Beyond that, they don't worry about forming any organizational structure.

The weekend clean-up event is a huge success, drawing dozens of participants from the surrounding neighborhoods. The Clean Up Our Park organizers decide that lots more work could be done at the park if they held similar events regularly throughout the year. They develop new goals, including restoring natural vegetation and aquatic life to the lake, eliminating diseased trees, and improving park trails. With their new mission, they realize that they will need contributions and grants, as well as cooperation from the city and the parks department. Because their planned activities will keep them busy for at least the next two years, they decide that a more formal organization is in order. They make plans to form a nonprofit corporation and seek tax-exempt status.

### Overlap With Similar Groups

Before starting your own nonprofit (whether incorporated or not), you should find out whether any other nonprofit in your area is working toward the same goals. You should certainly figure this out before you incorporate and establish your nonprofit more permanently.

Politically speaking, it's important not to invade another nonprofit's territory—at least, not without communicating first and having good reason to go ahead with your own nonprofit. You may well find that the best way to pursue your goals is by joining forces with the other nonprofit, rather than starting your own and spending time and energy on the incorporation process and other legal and tax issues. The other group may have already made valuable progress in terms of raising money and awareness, forging alliances, and so on.

Instead of incorporating your group, you might:

- study the list of nonprofits already active in the same area and join their efforts as a volunteer, a board member, or an employee
- identify existing groups in your area that are compatible with your ideas and meet with them to explore creating a special project or initiative, or
- explore the list of national organizations in your area of interest and find out whether a local chapter is needed in your geographic area.

**EXAMPLE:** After the successful Clean Up Our Park Weekend, the organizers decide that lots more work at the park could be done if they organized similar events regularly throughout the year. They discuss incorporating the group in order to minimize ongoing liability risks and to develop a strong organizational framework to handle more money and activities.

One of the members suggests that they first do some research to find out whether any other local or regional groups are doing similar work. Sure enough, a quick search of the Web turns up Neighbors Helping Parks, a 501(c)(3) nonprofit in their state that is dedicated to mobilizing neighbors and local businesses to help improve and maintain neglected city parks. Neighbors Helping Parks is set up to work with local groups, just like the Clean Up Our Park folks, and provides insurance, training, and other resources to these groups.

Even better, Neighbors Helping Parks has a simple application process local groups can use to request and receive funds to use in their efforts.

The Clean Up Our Park organizers agree that it makes much more sense to work with Neighbors Helping Parks rather than incorporate on their own and reinvent the wheel.

## Incorporation Paperwork: Articles of Incorporation and Bylaws

To create a corporation of any kind, you must file formal paperwork with the state and pay a filing fee. You will also need to undertake some additional formalities, such as drafting bylaws. And you'll have to keep up with various corporate requirements, including regularly convening meetings of the board of directors, keeping minutes of board meetings, filing annual reports, possibly filing tax returns, and more. Although these tasks aren't overly burdensome, they do make incorporating your nonprofit more costly and time-consuming than simply operating as an unincorporated group.

**RESOURCE**

**Get step-by-step instructions for creating your articles, drafting your bylaws, completing your federal 501(c)(3) application, and much more.** This chapter provides only a brief overview of the paperwork requirements associated with forming a nonprofit corporation. For detailed instructions on completing all of the necessary forms—and all of the information you'll need to make sure that your paperwork complies with your state's rules—see *How to Form a Nonprofit Corporation,* by Anthony Mancuso (Nolo).

### File Articles of Incorporation

Your corporation's legal existence doesn't begin until your state's corporate filing office (usually an agency within the secretary of state's office) accepts your articles of incorporation. The articles simply list basic descriptive information about the corporation, such as the corporation's name and address, the names of the initial directors, and the corporation's purpose. Most states provide downloadable, fill-in-the-blanks articles forms, so you don't have to draft yours from scratch. To get information and a copy of your state's form, contact your state's corporate filing office (often within the secretary of state's office) or visit its website. The National Association of Secretaries of State offers a state-by-state list at www.nass.org.

> **CAUTION**
>
> **If you are planning to apply for federal 501(c)(3) tax-exempt status, your articles must include specific language that satisfies the IRS's requirements.** For example, you should specify a tax-exempt purpose that meets the IRS's criteria and state that your nonprofit's assets will be used for tax-exempt purposes upon dissolution. For detailed information on these requirements and sample language you can use in your articles, see *How to Form a Nonprofit Corporation*, by Anthony Mancuso (Nolo).

State filing fees range from less than $50 to several hundred dollars. While these fees are usually not prohibitively expensive, attorneys' fees may be if you hire a lawyer for help. With hourly rates ranging from $75 to $300 or more, a lawyer's bill can easily reach into the thousands of dollars. It's not uncommon for lawyers to offer a package of incorporation services for a flat fee, ranging from $2,000 to $5,000 for a simple corporation.

### Draft Corporate Bylaws

While the articles of incorporation legally "create" your nonprofit corporation, its bylaws outline basic rules for the corporation's internal operations. Bylaws generally contain standard provisions that set forth the rules for board meetings, elections, compensation, nominating procedures, and officer positions, among other things. Many states regulate these issues, so you'll want to make sure that your bylaws reflect your state's requirements.

You can either draft your own bylaws, using a resource such as *How to Form a Nonprofit Corporation*, by Anthony Mancuso (Nolo), or hire a lawyer to put them together for you.

## Do You Want Tax-Exempt Status?

As you're undoubtedly aware, many nonprofits don't have to pay taxes on much of their income. If a nonprofit is eligible and has obtained the proper tax-exempt status from the IRS and the state, income derived from business activities that are related to the nonprofit's mission will not be taxable as income to the group. In addition, if a charitable nonprofit qualifies under Section 501(c)(3) of the IRS code, contributors to the group can claim a federal tax deduction for the value of their donations.

For many organizations, obtaining tax-exempt status is a top priority. It's easy to understand why— after all, who wouldn't want to get out of paying taxes? Well, slow down for just a second. There are several reasons why it may not be worth your while to apply for tax-exempt status:

- **Unless your organization brings in taxable income, obtaining a tax exemption won't do you much good.** For example, if your animal welfare group is supported solely by contributions and grants, then you don't have income tax issues to worry about, because contributions and grants aren't taxable. It doesn't make sense to jump through hoops to get tax-exempt status if you won't owe any taxes in the first place.

- **Some income-producing activities will be taxable even if you obtain tax-exempt status.** If you raise money through a business activity that's not related to your nonprofit mission, you owe taxes on that income regardless of your tax-exempt status. This is usually referred to as "unrelated business income tax," sometimes abbreviated as UBIT. So if your only income comes from an unrelated business activity, obtaining tax-exempt status won't save you a dime—you'll still owe taxes on that income. (See Chapter 6 for more on UBIT.)

- **Your donors may not be looking for a tax deduction.** Although contributors often expect to be able to deduct their donations, that isn't always the case. For example, a group organized to restore a

## Classifying Membership Fees

It can be tough to figure out whether membership fees should be categorized as contributions or as gross receipts from a business activity. (Remember, contributions are not taxable, whether or not your group has obtained tax-exempt status.) Very generally speaking, a membership fee will be considered a nontaxable contribution if the basic purpose of the fee is to provide general support for the organization. This is true even if the nonprofit does in fact provide services, admissions to events, merchandise, or other things of value to its members, as long as these things are just incidental benefits.

But if the nonprofit solicits membership fees primarily as a way to sell admissions, merchandise, services, or other things of value to members of the general public who don't have any common interest other than wanting the admissions, merchandise, or services, then the IRS will consider the membership fees to be gross receipts from a business activity. This means that they are taxable if you don't have tax-exempt status. They may well be taxable even if you do have tax-exempt status, if the IRS deems the fees unrelated to your nonprofit purposes.

The tax rules regarding membership fees can get a lot more complicated than this. If, for instance, a nonprofit offers a subscription to its monthly newsletter to people who join and pay a membership fee, it will need to grapple with awfully nitpicky IRS rules about whether that membership fee is a contribution (money given without expectation of something in return), or gross receipts from a business

activity (payment in exchange for something of value). For detailed information on how membership fees should be classified in specific situations, consult a nonprofit-savvy accountant or lawyer.

As you can see, the only type of taxation that depends on your tax-exempt status is tax on business income that's substantially related to your nonprofit purposes. Contributions and grants are never taxable, and business income that's not substantially related to your nonprofit purposes is always taxable, whether you have tax-exempt status or not.

| Type of Income | Without Tax-Exempt Status | With Tax-Exempt Status |
|---|---|---|
| Contributions (donations, grants, and so on) | Not taxable | Not taxable |
| Income from a business activity substantially related to the nonprofit's exempt purposes | Taxable | Not taxable |
| Income from a business activity not substantially related to exempt purposes | Taxable | Taxable |

small local rose garden might well conclude that potential contributors won't care whether their donations are tax deductible or not, making 501(c)(3) status unnecessary.

- **Not every nonprofit is eligible for 501(c)(3) status.** Only nonprofits organized to conduct certain activities qualify for 501(c)(3) treatment. You may find that certain aspects of your nonprofit must be changed in order to qualify for 501(c)(3) status, or that you're simply not eligible at all.

 **TIP**

**There are many types of tax-exempt status.** Many groups mistakenly think 501(c)(3) is the only type of tax-exempt status. 501(c)(3) status is certainly the most coveted, because it gives the most favorable tax treatment: It not only offers exemption from income taxes but also allows donors to claim their contributions as tax deductions. But there are plenty of other types of federal tax-exempt status that also offer exemption from income taxes. What these other types *don't* offer is a tax deduction for donors.

This section explains the various types of tax-exempt status the IRS offers and how they can impact a nonprofit's various tax obligations. Understanding what taxes can or can't be avoided by obtaining tax-exempt status will help you figure out which kind of exemption—if any—looks best for you.

## Tax-Exempt Status in General

If a nonprofit is tax exempt, that generally means one or both of the following:

- Tax exemption for the nonprofit itself, so that it does not have to pay taxes on income. Broadly speaking, the main effect of federal tax-exempt status is to relieve the nonprofit of the obligation to pay federal income taxes (and usually state taxes, and possibly other taxes like sales or property tax). This rule applies to all nonprofits that have obtained any IRS tax-exempt status.
- Tax deductibility for donors, so that they can deduct contributions they make to your nonprofit. If a nonprofit has 501(c)(3) status, contributors can claim a tax deduction for any donations they make to the nonprofit. The IRS will grant 501(c)(3) status only to organizations pursuing a short list of specific goals, as discussed below.

As used in this book, the term "tax exempt" generally refers to the basic exemption from income tax given to all tax-exempt nonprofits. To refer specifically to the special exemption enjoyed by 501(c)(3) groups, this book uses terms like "tax deductibility for contributors" or "501(c)(3) tax-exempt status."

This section takes a closer look at the first definition: the general exemption from income taxes that all tax-exempt nonprofits enjoy.

## What Taxes Does Tax-Exempt Status Avoid?

Lots of folks have misguided notions about what it means to be tax exempt, largely because they don't have a clear understanding of what income is taxable for a nonprofit in the first place.

Broadly speaking, the IRS classifies a nonprofit's income as either contributions or gross receipts from a business activity. You generally won't have to pay taxes on contributions, whether or not you have tax-exempt status. Contributions include payments to the nonprofit that were made with nothing expected in return, such as donations from individuals, grants, or some membership fees (though membership fees can get sticky; see "Classifying Membership Fees," above). If your only source of income is contributions, then getting tax-exempt status won't change your tax bill—although it may make a huge difference in your eligibility for certain grants.

> **TIP**
> **Many funding sources will give money only to groups with 501(c)(3) status.** If your potential funders restrict their grants to 501(c)(3) groups, obtaining this status may be a practical necessity.

Gross receipts from business activities, on the other hand, may be taxable; these include payments made to the nonprofit in exchange for something of value. In these types of transactions, the payer expects something specific in return for the payment: admission to an event, merchandise, access to the nonprofit's facilities, and so on. If something is expected in return for the payment, it will likely be considered to be gross receipts from a business activity.

If you don't have tax-exempt status, then all gross receipts from business activities are taxable. But with tax-exempt status, a big chunk of these gross receipts may be exempt from taxation, depending on whether it was earned from:

- a business activity substantially related to the nonprofit's exempt purposes, or
- a business activity not substantially related to exempt purposes.

With tax-exempt status, you will escape paying taxes on income earned from the first category: business activities that are substantially related to your exempt purposes. For example, if your tax-exempt nonprofit is devoted to educating the public about how to use technology for social activism, any money you charge for seminars and classes on that subject will not be taxable, because the classes

## Organization Reference Chart—page 1

### Organization Reference Chart

| Section of 1986 Code | Description of organization | General nature of activities | Application Form No. | Annual return required to be filed | Contributions allowable |
|---|---|---|---|---|---|
| 501(c)(1) | Corporations Organized under Act of Congress (including Federal Credit Unions) | Instrumentalities of the United States | No Form | None | Yes, if made for exclusively public purposes |
| 501(c)(2) | Title Holding Corporation For Exempt Organization | Holding title to property of an exempt organization | 1024 | 990[1] or 990-EZ[8] | No[2] |
| 501(c)(3) | Religious, Educational, Charitable, Scientific, Literary, Testing for Public Safety, to Foster National or International Amateur Sports Competition, or Prevention of Cruelty to Children or Animals Organizations | Activities of nature implied by description of class of organization | 1023 | 990[1] or 990-EZ[8], or 990-PF | Yes, generally |
| 501(c)(4) | Civic Leagues, Social Welfare Organizations, and Local Associations of Employees | Promotion of community welfare; charitable, educational, or recreational | 1024 | 990[1] or 990-EZ[8] | No, generally [2,3] |
| 501(c)(5) | Labor, Agricultural, and Horticultural Organizations | Educational or instructive, the purpose being to improve conditions of work, and to improve products of efficiency | 1024 | 990[1] or 990-EZ[8] | No[2] |
| 501(c)(6) | Business Leagues, Chambers of Commerce, Real Estate Boards, etc. | Improvement of business conditions of one or more lines of business | 1024 | 990[1] or 990-EZ[8] | No[2] |
| 501(c)(7) | Social and Recreational Clubs | Pleasure, recreation, social activities | 1024 | 990[1] or 990-EZ[8] | No[2] |
| 501(c)(8) | Fraternal Beneficiary Societies and Associations | Lodge providing for payment of life, sickness, accident or other benefits to members | 1024 | 990[1] or 990-EZ[8] | Yes, if for certain Sec. 501(c)(3) purposes |
| 501(c)(9) | Voluntary Employees Beneficiary Associations | Providing for payment of life, sickness, accident, or other benefits to members | 1024 | 990[1] or 990-EZ[8] | No[2] |
| 501(c)(10) | Domestic Fraternal Societies and Associations | Lodge devoting its net earnings to charitable, fraternal, and other specified purposes. No life, sickness, or accident benefits to members | 1024 | 990[1] or 990-EZ[8] | Yes, if for certain Sec. 501(c)(3) purposes |
| 501(c)(11) | Teachers' Retirement Fund Associations | Teachers' association for payment of retirement benefits | No Form[6] | 990[1] or 990-EZ[8] | No[2] |
| 501(c)(12) | Benevolent Life Insurance Associations, Mutual Ditch or Irrigation Companies, Mutual or Cooperative Telephone Companies, etc. | Activities of a mutually beneficial nature similar to those implied by the description of class of organization | 1024 | 990[1] or 990-EZ[8] | No[2] |
| 501(c)(13) | Cemetery Companies | Burials and incidental activities | 1024 | 990[1] or 990-EZ[8] | Yes, generally |
| 501(c)(14) | State-Chartered Credit Unions, Mutual Reserve Funds | Loans to members | No Form[6] | 990[1] or 990-EZ[8] | No[2] |
| 501(c)(15) | Mutual Insurance Companies or Associations | Providing insurance to members substantially at cost | 1024 | 990[1] or 990-EZ[8] | No[2] |
| 501(c)(16) | Cooperative Organizations to Finance Crop Operations | Financing crop operations in conjunction with activities of a marketing or purchasing association | Form 1120-C[6] | 990[1] or 990-EZ[8] | No[2] |
| 501(c)(17) | Supplemental Unemployment Benefit Trusts | Provides for payment of supplemental unemployment compensation benefits | 1024 | 990[1] or 990-EZ[8] | No[2] |
| 501(c)(18) | Employee Funded Pension Trust (created before June 25, 1959) | Payment of benefits under a pension plan funded by employees | No Form[6] | 990[1] or 990-EZ[8] | No[2] |

Organization Reference Chart (excerpted from IRS Publication 557, *Tax-Exempt Status for Your Organization*)

## Organization Reference Chart—page 2

| Section of 1986 Code | Description of organization | General nature of activities | Application Form No. | Annual return required to be filed | Contributions allowable |
|---|---|---|---|---|---|
| 501(c)(19) | Post or Organization of Past or Present Members of the Armed Forces | Activities implied by nature of organization | 1024 | 990[1] or 990-EZ[8] | No, generally[7] |
| 501(c)(21) | Black Lung Benefit Trusts | Funded by coal mine operators to satisfy their liability for disability or death due to black lung diseases | No Form[6] | 990-BL | No[4] |
| 501(c)(22) | Withdrawal Liability Payment Fund | To provide funds to meet the liability of employers withdrawing from a multi-employer pension fund | No Form[6] | 990[1] or 990-EZ[8] | No[5] |
| 501(c)(23) | Veterans' Organization (created before 1880) | To provide insurance and other benefits to veterans | No Form[6] | 990[1] or 990-EZ[8] | No, generally[7] |
| 501(c)(25) | Title Holding Corporations or Trusts with Multiple Parent Corporations | Holding title and paying over income from property to 35 or fewer parents or beneficiaries | 1024 | 990[1] or 990-EZ[8] | No |
| 501(c)(26) | State-Sponsored Organization Providing Health Coverage for High-Risk Individuals | Provides health care coverage to high-risk individuals | No Form[6] | 990[1] or 990-EZ[8] | No |
| 501(c)(27) | State-Sponsored Workers' Compensation Reinsurance Organization | Reimburses members for losses under workers' compensation acts | No Form[6] | 990[1] or 990-EZ[8] | No |
| 501(c)(28) | National Railroad Retirement Investment Trust | Manages and invests the assets of the Railroad Retirement Account | No Form | None | No[11] |
| 501(c)(29) | CO-OP health insurance issuers | A qualified health insurance issuer which has received a loan or grant under the CO-OP program | TBD | 990[1] or 990-EZ[8] | No[13] |
| 501(d) | Religious and Apostolic Associations | Regular business activities; Communal religious community | No Form | 1065[9] | No[2] |
| 501(e) | Cooperative Hospital Service Organizations | Performs cooperative services for hospitals | 1023 | 990[1] or 990-EZ[8] | Yes |
| 501(f) | Cooperative Service Organizations of Operating Educational Organizations | Performs collective investment services for educational organizations | 1023 | 990[1] or 990-EZ[8] | Yes |
| 501(k) | Child Care Organizations | Provides care for children | 1023 | 990[1] or 990-EZ[8] | Yes |
| 501(n) | Charitable Risk Pools | Pools certain insurance risks of sec. 501(c)(3) organizations | 1023 | 990[1] or 990-EZ[8] | Yes |
| 501(q) | Credit Counseling Organization | Credit counseling services | 1023 | 1023[12] | No |
| 521(a) | Farmers' Cooperative Associations | Cooperative marketing and purchasing for agricultural procedures | 1028 | 990-C | No |
| 527 | Political organizations | A party, committee, fund, association, etc., that directly or indirectly accepts contributions or makes expenditures for political campaigns | 8871 | 1120-POL[10] 990[1] or 990-EZ[8] | No |

## Organization Reference Chart—page 3

[1]For exceptions to the filing requirement, see chapter 2 and the form instructions. Note: For annual tax periods beginning after 2006, most tax-exempt organizations, other than churches, are required to file an annual Form 990, 990-EZ, or 990-PF with the IRS or to submit an annual electronic notice, Form 990-N (*e-Postcard*), to the IRS. Tax-exempt organizations failing to file an annual return or submit an annual notice as required for 3 consecutive years will automatically lose their tax-exempt status.

[2]An organization exempt under a subsection of section 501 other than 501(c)(3) can establish a charitable fund, contributions to which are deductible. Such a fund must itself meet the requirements of section 501(c)(3) and the related notice requirements of section 508(a).

[3]Contributions to volunteer fire companies and similar organizations are deductible, but only if made for exclusively public purposes.

[4]Deductible as a business expense to the extent allowed by section 192.

[5]Deductible as a business expense to the extent allowed by section 194A.

[6]Application is by letter to the address shown on Form 8718. A copy of the organizing document should be attached and the letter should be signed by an officer.

[7]Contributions to these organizations are deductible only if 90% or more of the organization's members are war veterans.

[8]For limits on the use of Form 990-EZ, see chapter 2 and the general instructions for Form 990-EZ (or Form 990).

[9]Although the organization files a partnership return, all distributions are deemed dividends. The members are not entitled to **pass through** treatment of the organization's income or expenses.

[10]Form 1120-POL is required only if the organization has taxable income as defined in section 527(c).

[11]Only required to annually file so much of the Form 990 that relates to the names and addresses of the officers, directors, trustees, and key employees, and their titles, compensation, and hours devoted to their positions (Part VII of Form 990) and complete Tax exempt status (Item I in the Heading of Form 990).

[12]See section 501(q) if the organization provides credit counseling services and seeks recognition of exemption under section 501(c)(4). Use Form 1024 if applying for recognition under section 501(c)(4).

[13]See section 501(c)(29) for details.

are intrinsically tied to your nonprofit purpose. But if your group also operates an Internet café as a moneymaking enterprise, that activity probably won't be considered substantially related to your exempt purposes, and you will owe taxes on that income.

### IRS Tax-Exempt Categories

The IRS offers tax-exempt status to a wide range of organizations: charitable groups, civic leagues, trade associations, social clubs, fraternal societies, title holding corporations, teachers' retirement fund associations, black lung benefit trusts, veterans' organizations, and cemetery companies, to name just a few. Each tax exemption is authorized under a particular section of the Internal Revenue Code. Recreational and social groups can obtain tax-exempt status under Section 501(c)(7), fraternal societies are eligible for exemption under 501(c)(10), child care organizations are eligible under 501(k), and so on.

Each tax-exempt category has its own requirements and taxation rules. Broadly speaking, however, the essential tax rule for all these categories is much the same: Tax-exempt organizations do not have to pay tax on income earned from activities substantially related to their nonprofit purposes. In other words, as long as a nonprofit has applied for and been granted tax-exempt status, it can earn money, tax free, from its business activities, as long as the activities are substantially related to the group's nonprofit purpose. (Certain categories—such as 501(c)(3) groups—have additional benefits as well.)

**RESOURCE**
**The Organization Reference Chart on the previous pages is from IRS Publication 557, *Tax-Exempt Status for Your Organization*.** You can get a copy of the entire publication, as well as other helpful information and publications, by calling 800-TAX-FORM, visiting your local IRS office, or going to the IRS website at www.irs.gov.

## 501(c)(3) Tax-Exempt Status

What sets 501(c)(3) status apart from the other types is that it not only exempts an organization from

having to pay federal income taxes but also allows donors to deduct contributions to the organization on their personal tax returns. Clearly, being able to offer your contributors a tax deduction for their gifts can be a big help in attracting funds for your organization.

### IRS Criteria

A group is eligible for tax-exempt status under Section 501(c)(3) only if its primary activity is pursuing one or more of the following purposes:

- charitable
- religious
- educational
- scientific
- literary
- testing for public safety
- fostering national or international amateur sports competition, and
- preventing cruelty to children or animals.

This fundamental requirement is known as the "organizational test." If your nonprofit's primary activities include any purposes that aren't on this list, then you will not meet the organizational test and won't be able to obtain 501(c)(3) status. Put another way, if you pursue activities that are not on the list, they cannot make up a substantial part of your nonprofit's work if you want to be eligible for this exemption.

Your nonprofit may engage in more than one of the exempt activities listed above—for instance, it can pursue both charitable and educational activities. But if your nonprofit pursues any nonexempt purposes as a primary activity—social, recreational, or business activities, for example—then it would not be eligible for tax-exempt status, even if it also pursues exempt purposes.

Perhaps you find yourself asking, "What if our nonprofit only occasionally dabbles in social or recreational activities? Does that mean we aren't eligible for 501(c)(3) status?" The good news is that it's okay for a nonprofit to engage in nonexempt activities, as long as they are insubstantial. An occasional social or recreational event is probably fine, as long as your nonprofit's primary activities continue to be related to exempt purposes.

If you expect that nonexempt activities like social and recreational events will be more than an insubstantial part of your nonprofit's work, you should consider pursuing a different type of tax-exempt status. Alternatives include:

- a 501(c)(4) organization—civic leagues, social welfare organizations, and local associations of employees. These groups are allowed to engage in more social and recreational activities than 501(c)(3) groups but cannot have social/recreational activities as their primary purpose.
- a 501(c)(7) organization—social and fraternal clubs. These groups may engage primarily in social activities.

If you intend to apply for 501(c)(3) tax-exempt status, you should take the time before you incorporate to find out whether your nonprofit will be eligible. If it's not eligible, you may decide not to incorporate after all, or you might want to change aspects of your organization to make it eligible. If it is eligible, you'll need to include specific language in your articles of incorporation that states your nonprofit purposes and limits them to allowable 501(c)(3) activities.

**RESOURCE**

**Applying for 501(c)(3) status.** To seek 501(c)(3) status, you must file IRS Form 1023, *Application for Recognition of Exemption Under Section 501(c)(3) of the Internal Revenue Code.* You can get a copy of this form, instructions for filling it out, and helpful IRS publications (such as Publication 557, *Tax-Exempt Status for Your Organization*) by calling 800-TAX-FORM, visiting your local IRS office, or going to the IRS website, at www.irs.gov. Be forewarned, however, that the IRS estimates it will take the average person more than four hours to learn about the form—and another eight hours to fill it in and return it to the IRS! For detailed, line-by-line instructions that will make filling out a federal 501(c)(3) application much easier (and quicker), see *How to Form a Nonprofit Corporation*, by Anthony Mancuso (Nolo). Mancuso's book also provides information on state—as well as federal—tax exemptions.

## Creating a Separate Fund

If your organization is not eligible for 501(c)(3) status but is eligible under a different category, you may still be able to set things up so that you can offer tax deductions to contributors. Some nonprofits set up a separate fund to receive money exclusively for allowable 501(c)(3) purposes (religious, charitable, scientific, literary, or educational purposes; testing for public safety; fostering national or international amateur sports competition; or the prevention of cruelty to children or animals). If it's done right, this fund can obtain 501(c)(3) status and all the benefits that flow from it.

Of course, the money in this separate fund must actually be used only for those purposes—in other words, you can't set up a 501(c)(3) educational fund and use that money for your backgammon club's operating expenses. But you could use that money for an educational website on the history of backgammon or similar educational pursuits. Some nonprofits find that this is a good way to finance certain activities that would be eligible for 501(c)(3) status, even if the organization overall is not eligible.

Because setting up a separate fund requires specialized knowledge of nonprofit tax laws and IRS rules, you should consult an attorney if you're considering this strategy.

## Unrelated Business Income Tax

One type of income that's always taxable—whether your nonprofit has tax-exempt status or not—is income from a regularly operated business activity that is not substantially related to your nonprofit purposes. The shorthand for this is "unrelated business income," and it is subject to income tax (unrelated business income tax, or UBIT) just as if you were running a for-profit business. For nonprofit corporations, corporate tax rates will apply. For unincorporated associations, the way the group will be taxed depends on the laws of your state. (The discussion below assumes that your group is incorporated.)

If your gross receipts from an unrelated business activity exceed $1,000, you'll have to file IRS Form 990-T to report and pay tax on that income. If you bring in less than $1,000, you don't have to file the form. (For more information on filing requirements, see Chapter 12.)

If the business activity is not regular—say, an occasional rummage sale or silent auction—then it is not subject to UBIT. Other types of income that are not taxable as unrelated business income include:

- volunteer operations—income from a business activity in which substantially all the work is performed without pay (such as a volunteer bake sale)
- activities for the convenience of members— income from a business activity that is primarily for the convenience of its members, students, patients, officers, or employees (such as a school cafeteria), and
- sales of donated merchandise—income from a business activity that consists of selling merchandise that the organization received as gifts or contributions (such as thrift shops).

Many other types of income are also exempted from UBIT; these include dividends, interest, royalties, certain rental income, certain income from research activities, and gains or losses from the disposition of property.

**RESOURCE**

**More information on the unrelated business income tax rule.** IRS Publication 598, *Tax on Unrelated Business Income of Exempt Organizations,* provides detailed advice on the subject. Also, see *Every Nonprofit's Tax Guide* by Stephen Fishman (Nolo) for more on UBIT and other nonprofit tax issues.

## State and Other Tax Exemptions

Most states exempt a nonprofit from state income taxes if it has obtained federal 501(c)(3) status. In these states, the state exemption should apply whether the group is incorporated or not, though it's wise to check with your state to be sure. Depending on the state, the exemption may be automatic, or the group may have to submit paperwork showing that the federal exemption has been granted. Some states exempt a nonprofit from state income taxes regardless of whether it has received 501(c)(3) federal tax-exempt status. In other states, a nonprofit must go through a separate process to determine whether it will be exempt from state income taxes, even if it has already obtained federal tax-exempt status.

Similarly, the rules vary as to whether a nonprofit will be subject to other state or local taxes, such as sales tax or property tax. Some states and local governments may grant an automatic exemption if you have obtained 501(c)(3) status; others may require you to jump through some hoops.

Contact your state's nonprofit corporation filing office for information about exemptions from state income tax for nonprofits. For a list of secretaries of state nationwide, visit the National Association of Secretaries of State online at www.nass.org. For other types of taxes, such as state sales tax, contact your state and local tax authorities to find out how they treat nonprofits. To find your state tax agency's website, either search the IRS website at www.irs.gov for its list of state tax sites (use the search term "state links"), or do an online search with Google or Yahoo! using your state name along with the words "tax department" or "tax agency" as your search terms.

## How Important Is Tax Exemption to Your Organization?

Now that you have some basic tax information, give some thought to how important it really is for your nonprofit to be tax exempt or to offer tax deductibility to donors. Ask yourself the following two questions.

**Will your organization bring in enough taxable income to make avoiding taxes a real concern?** If your organization doesn't bring in any income from business activities, it won't owe taxes in the first place. And if the income is from a business activity that's not related to your nonprofit purposes, then that income is taxable with or without tax-exempt status. If, on the other hand, you have (or plan to have) a business activity that's related to your nonprofit purposes, tax-exempt status can save you real money. In this case, obtaining some type of tax-exempt status should be near the top of your "to do" list.

**Will you need 501(c)(3) status to be eligible for grants or to attract contributions?** While some organizations depend on sizable contributions and major grants, plenty of others do just fine with individual contributions in the $10 to $50 range. If eligibility for grants isn't an issue, and if your organization doesn't plan to go after the big bucks, you may find that your group does just fine raising money from folks who don't care about deducting their small donations come tax time. But if your organization's activities depend on obtaining at least some large contributions or grants from foundations or other sources, having 501(c)(3) status is crucial. People or organizations asked to provide $100 or more will usually want to know (or will assume) that their contributions will be tax-deductible. And grant criteria often include having 501(c)(3) status. Put bluntly, without 501(c)(3) status, your chances of attracting large-scale financial support will be significantly hampered.

**EXAMPLE:** The New Mexico Cactus Lovers (NMCL) has grown into a group with approximately 100 members. The group incorporated last year in order to limit its liability and create a more formal organization. It now has a board of directors, plus three paid staffers who maintain the group's website and organize and lead hiking trips. It hasn't yet obtained tax-exempt status but is considering doing so.

When it was a young organization with 25 or so members, the only real money the group handled was $20 contributions from each member, which went toward the costs of its website, gas money for hiking trips, and other minor operating expenses. Its only income was from nontaxable contributions (given by donors who didn't expect anything of value in return), so there wasn't any point in obtaining tax-exempt status. Even when NMCL engaged in unrelated business activities to earn money, the activities weren't regular enough to qualify the proceeds as unrelated business income. If the activities ever had become more regular, taxes would have been due on that money anyway, even if the group had tax-exempt status.

Now, however, the group earns money from several sources, some of which are currently taxable but would not be if NMCL obtained tax-exempt status. Besides a $75 annual membership fee, NMCL charges fees for its hiking day trips. The trips are held fairly regularly, usually every other week. In addition, the group operates a small store from its office where it sells cactus plants to the public. It also has self-published two books on desert ecosystems, which bring in revenues of roughly $4,000 annually.

Currently, all participants must provide their own transportation to the hiking day trips, but NMCL wants to raise money for a vehicle so it can offer transportation to those who want it. They also want to expand the website and add more scientific articles about desert ecosystems. They plan to apply for grants for these larger funding needs.

At a recent board meeting, the directors agree that it is time to seek tax-exempt status. While their membership fees would probably count as nontaxable contributions (because they are used for general operating expenses), the fees for the trips might very well qualify as gross receipts from a business activity which would be taxable without tax-exempt status. Because the trips are substantially related to NMCL's mission of educating the public about cactus plants and desert ecosystems, the income they generate would be tax exempt if the group obtained tax-exempt status. In addition, obtaining 501(c)(3) status will help the group meet eligibility requirements for grant money.

Using the above example, consider the increasing need to obtain tax-exempt status as the NMCL becomes involved in new activities and starts to bring in income that would otherwise be taxable.

| Low Need to Obtain Tax-Exempt Status | Borderline Need to Obtain Tax-Exempt Status | High Need to Obtain Tax-Exempt Status |
|---|---|---|
| The New Mexico Cactus Lovers (NMCL) has about 20 members who pitch in $25 a year each for the group's website, gas and travel expenses for hiking trips, and T-shirts. | NMCL has about 50 members who contribute $45 per year each to the group's general fund. Those who participate also pay $25 for each trip, organized every month or so. The group also earns income from occasional fundraising events, such as cactus sales, art auctions, and concerts, some of which are unrelated to NMCL's mission. | NMCL wants to solicit grant money to expand its website and to offer educational hiking trips to the public. The group organizes hiking day trips every other week and charges fees to participants. NMCL also sells cactus plants and publishes two books on desert ecosystems in New Mexico, which bring in about $4,000 a year. |

## Should You Have Voting Members?

If you incorporate your nonprofit, you'll need to decide another issue: whether to allow people to join your nonprofit as members with voting rights in nonprofit affairs. (This is sometimes referred to as choosing a membership or nonmembership structure, as described below.) Generally speaking, state laws give legal voting rights to members of nonprofit corporations, allowing members to participate along with directors in corporate decision making. Among other rights, voting members of a nonprofit corporation have legal rights to elect board members, to approve or reject changes to the nonprofit's articles or bylaws, and to vote for a merger or dissolution of the nonprofit.

Voting rights and other membership specifics should be detailed in your nonprofit's bylaws. If your bylaws don't address the issue (or you have no bylaws at all), the laws of your state will apply as a default. Some states ask you to specify a membership or nonmembership structure in the standard articles of incorporation. If your state's standard articles ask you to choose a membership structure, make sure that your articles are consistent with your bylaws, which will undoubtedly cover the issue at more length.

**RESOURCE**

**Need help preparing bylaws and articles?** For step-by-step instructions on drafting bylaws and articles, including detailed information on membership provisions, see *How to Form a Nonprofit Corporation*, by Anthony Mancuso (Nolo).

Often, a nonprofit with voting members is called a "membership" nonprofit, and a nonprofit with no voting members is called a "nonmembership" nonprofit (or sometimes a "directorship" nonprofit, reflecting the fact that only the directors have the right to vote). However, this distinction can be confusing, because most states allow nonprofits to have nonvoting members. Instead of framing the question as whether to adopt a membership or nonmembership structure, you may find it clearer to consider whether you want your members to have voting rights in nonprofit affairs.

### Why You Probably Don't Want Voting Members

If your members have voting rights, they can have a major say in steering your nonprofit. If they don't, then only the board will have voting rights—and the legal power to guide the nonprofit. In practice, involving all members in corporate affairs is too burdensome for many small nonprofits. To keep things simple and avoid the hassles involved in allowing members to vote—convening and giving notice of meetings, especially—most nonprofits choose not to give members voting rights. Even though these participants may not have the right to vote, they can be treated like voting members—for example, they can receive benefits like a newsletter or reduced admission to events.

If a nonprofit does not want voting members, it can opt not to have members at all. Or, in most states, it can set up a special class of members with no voting rights. If the nonprofit doesn't have members or if no members are given voting rights, only the board of directors has the power to vote.

However, bear in mind that state laws and processes governing membership rights vary considerably, so proceed with caution if you want to allow people to become members but don't want to give them voting rights. Restricting voting rights from some members doesn't mean that those members have no rights at all under your state's laws. For example, state laws typically establish rules for expelling members, which will generally apply to nonvoting members and voting members alike.

## Practicalities of Having Voting Members

If you do choose to have legal, voting members, you'll need to be ready for the administrative burdens of managing membership. These include maintaining membership lists and processes for joining the nonprofit, which may or may not involve paying dues. Thankfully, most of these practical details are up to the nonprofit and not set in law. What are legally mandated, however, are the procedures you'll need to follow whenever a matter is up for a vote. You'll need to provide adequate notice to all voting members before the vote is held and follow careful rules of order during discussions and the vote itself.

The board president is in charge of running meetings, so he or she will need to have decent skills in order to oversee well-organized meetings and votes involving a general membership. (See Chapter 4 for information on running meetings effectively and using formal meeting procedures such as *Robert's Rules of Order*.)

---

### Checklist: Naming and Structuring Your Nonprofit

☐ Do some research before choosing a name for your nonprofit. Be sure to choose a name that does not infringe on anyone else's trademark rights. Also consider domain name availability when picking your nonprofit name.

☐ Don't jump into incorporating—and assuming the responsibilities of nonprofit corporate management— without considering whether it's really necessary to incorporate. Consider whether incorporating will reduce your liability risks, offer tax benefits, or help establish your nonprofit's credibility or financial accountability.

☐ Understand the different types of federal tax exemptions available to nonprofits, and decide whether tax-exempt status will be a benefit to your nonprofit. If you plan to apply for grants, find out whether 501(c)(3) status is required for the grants you'll seek.

☐ If you decide that you will pursue tax-exempt status now or in the future, decide which type of status you plan to seek, and make sure you set your nonprofit up so it will be eligible for that type of exemption.

☐ Decide whether your nonprofit will have members with voting rights or whether you want only directors to be able to vote in corporate affairs.

# Developing Your Strategic Plan

Once you and your cohorts have committed to your idea for a nonprofit, it's time to sit down and create a strategic plan—the working document that will chart your nonprofit's course through the coming years. A strategic plan identifies your nonprofit's goals for a certain time period (generally one to five years, as described below) and outlines how you will achieve them. While your nonprofit will undoubtedly engage in other planning for specific activities, think of the strategic plan as the "master plan" for your organization.

Translating your hopes and dreams into concrete plans is an essential undertaking for lots of reasons. First and foremost, making specific plans will help you get beyond your idealistic visions to focus on exactly what your group hopes to accomplish—and what you can realistically expect to get done, based on your available resources. Drafting a plan transforms abstract ideas into specific "to do" items, which is a critical step in setting your nonprofit's wheels into motion.

**TIP**

**Your planning process may redefine your basic nonprofit idea.** As your group works on its strategic plan, you may come up with some new ideas or challenges you hadn't yet considered. For example, a group dedicated to preventing teen pregnancy may decide to branch out into AIDS education. Or, it may learn that a local church will loudly boycott any organization that offers explicit sex education for teens. While unexpected options or obstacles can make your collective heads spin, don't panic. Opening your mind to broader opportunities—even if you decide in the end not to embrace them—is always a positive learning experience. And if your planning process reveals such a substantial flaw in your idea that you decide not to start the nonprofit after all, your strategic planning has done its job: helping you realistically assess whether—and to what extent—you can achieve your goals.

Having a clear strategic plan in place will also serve you well when you seek to raise money and/or build community support. People may be mildly interested in your mission and goals, but their main question will always be, "What does your nonprofit *do*?" If you can't clearly describe your planned activities—for example, teaching adult literacy classes, researching endangered fox habitat, or running an after-school music program—it will be hard to win the hearts and minds of potential supporters.

Strategic planning doesn't mean coming up with a 100-page manifesto exploring every aspect of your nonprofit's operations; you just need to nail down some key basics about what your nonprofit actually plans to do. The extent of the planning process will vary from one nonprofit to the next. In a tiny organization with a highly focused goal, members may be able to hammer out a perfectly adequate one- or two-page plan during a couple of hour-long meetings. A bigger operation with a large budget will likely need to devote a number of meetings to the process and produce a more detailed plan.

This chapter will help your group—whatever its size—prepare a solid and functional strategic plan that defines your mission; outlines your goals, objectives, and activities; assesses your resources; and identifies strategies. Unless your fledgling nonprofit is starting out with an enormous budget or plans high-profile activities from the get-go, there's no need for your strategic planning process to be a complicated affair involving outside consultants, board retreats, or review protocols. The information in this chapter will help you come up with a basic plan that will work for your nonprofit without spending all of your time and energy on the planning process.

**TIP**

**Strategic planning is an ongoing process.** While strategic planning is a crucial start-up task, it's also important for existing organizations to revisit their plans every year or so to make any necessary amendments. As your organization grows and brings in more money, people, and other resources, your goals, budgets, and programs may change—and the strategic planning process will necessarily become more complex. The basic approaches to, and elements of, strategic planning that you'll learn in this chapter will give you a solid foundation for your future planning efforts.

---

### Starting a Nonprofit: Why Do Something Like That?

Randolph Belle spent years as the director of information at the East Bay Nonprofit Center in Oakland, California. In his decade of experience in this role, he counseled hundreds of nonprofits in all stages of development, from initial planning to maturity and expansion. He offers the following advice for nonprofit start-ups working their way through the idea stage.

*When people come to me with the pronouncement, "I'd like to start a nonprofit," my first question is "Why?" Sometimes the response is silence, which is not a good sign. For those who dare answer, "Because I care deeply about..." whatever issue, I'm compelled to introduce them to some harsh realities of the world of nonprofits. The truth is, whether your nonprofit will succeed and find support will depend not so much on the fact that you care about your mission, but on whether you've tackled the fundamentals in developing your purpose, planning your organization, and building your community.*

*In developing its purpose, a fledgling nonprofit needs to craft a position of value, understanding that any nonprofit does only one of two things: increases human potential or decreases human suffering. It's important to find the words that explain what it is that you hope to change, not just what activities you plan to do. Your goal is to create a solid, unduplicated program, addressing a pressing community need.*

---

## Strategic Plan Basics

A solid, simple strategic plan for a start-up nonprofit will generally include the following (none longer than a few pages):

- a mission statement
- an outline of goals, objectives, and activities
- an assessment of current resources, and
- a strategic analysis.

Each of these is discussed in more detail in the sections that follow. This section covers some basic issues that apply to the planning process generally.

---

**RELATED TOPIC**

**Planning your fundraising activities.** All new nonprofits will need to take some time to hammer out a plan for raising money. These details will be covered not in your strategic plan but in a separate fundraising plan, as described in Chapter 6.

## Keep It Simple

You'll want to keep your strategic plan short and sweet—a big-picture overview of what your nonprofit will accomplish, not a detailed blueprint showing how you will carry out each and every area of operations. In other words, your strategic plan should outline what you'll do, without going into great detail about how you'll do it. Leave the specifics—such as how often you'll hold board meetings, how you'll approach potential donors, or how many staff members you plan to hire—for other, more narrowly focused planning sessions. Including too many operational details is sure to bog down the strategic planning process and divert your attention away from the big picture, which should be your focus now.

**EXAMPLE:** Robots Care is a nonprofit dedicated to helping disabled people live independently with the help of robotic technology. The group pursues two main activities: developing new robotic technology to provide home care for people with disabilities and donating robots to disabled people who meet certain criteria (its "robot rescue" program).

The strategic plan of Robots Care includes information about its two program areas: technology research and development and the robot rescue program. The plan includes details such as the type of new technology that is the focus of development efforts, what robotic products it plans to develop each year, who will qualify for a free robot, the group's plan for training its clients about using the robots, and how it plans to publicize its programs to reach potential donees. Other operational details—such as where the group will purchase equipment and supplies, who will work at the laboratory, what questions will be included on the application for a free robot, and how the group will deal with donated robots that turn out to be defective—are left out of the plan. These details are addressed separately, as part of developing the programs themselves.

## Choose a Time Frame

While some established nonprofits plan five years in advance, most nonprofits plan for one to three years into the future. When creating a strategic plan for the first time, choosing a period of two or three years usually works well. Planning for more than three years is often a waste of time, because new nonprofits rarely find that their first years go according to plan. Instead, plan for your first couple of years, and then compare your plan to what actually happened as this time period winds to a close. Once you hit years two and three, your plans will likely become more realistic, and you can consider extending your strategic plan for five years or so into the future.

> *Write, write, and keep writing. A plan isn't a plan until it's in writing. If it doesn't pencil out on paper, you probably have more work to do. I've found that when you write, you come up with answers to questions that haven't been asked yet.*
>
> **Randolph Belle—Director of Information
> East Bay Nonprofit Center
> Oakland, California**

## Decide Who Will Participate

Whether you've already incorporated with formal board members or you're still just a loose group of organizers, you'll need to decide who will play a part in the strategic planning process. If your group consists of one committed, passionate person (you), then now is the time to think about bringing in other interested people.

For small nonprofits with up to six or seven organizers or board members, it usually makes sense for everyone to participate. Once ten or more people are involved, however, it can be quite unwieldy and inefficient to include everyone. In this case, it's often more effective to assign parts of the planning process to smaller committees that can more efficiently tackle specific issues or tasks and then present their results to the full group for comment and approval.

A new nonprofit's first strategic planning efforts might feel a bit awkward. The people involved probably don't have defined roles at this early stage. The group may not have incorporated yet, or it may have just the statutory minimum number of board members, with plans to add more in the near future. When a loose group of initial organizers tackles the nonprofit's first strategic plan, they may not know who else will join the board once they incorporate—or even whether they will serve on it themselves.

 **RELATED TOPIC**
**Building your board is covered in Chapter 4.** Chapter 4 explains how to recruit the right people for your board and covers common questions, such as how large your board should be, how often it should meet, and how to run effective board meetings.

No matter where you are in your group's development, however, the initial planning process will be valuable. If your group hasn't yet incorporated or chosen its full slate of formal board members, don't worry—just keep in mind that your strategic plan will have to be acceptable to the board that is eventually selected. Because the folks who participate in the strategic planning will likely end up on the group's board after it incorporates, this usually isn't a problem.

Besides organizers or board members, you may also want to include others in your strategic planning efforts. Potential funders and other supporters are particularly helpful strategic planning participants, at least in some limited way. Their input can help your group fine-tune its activities and goals to keep these supporters interested and willing to help. Of course, you shouldn't design your programs solely to please potential supporters, but keeping the lines of communication open and developing good relationships with your natural allies will make your job easier once you begin fundraising and trying to develop community support.

Similarly, if your group will depend on a specific grant or other donation—for example, a local school has offered you free office space, or you plan to launch your group with a donation promised by a local bank—be sure to keep those key supporters involved every step of the way. The more you will rely on their support, the more you will need to make sure that they approve of your plans.

If you're one of the few new nonprofits that have already hired an executive director at this early stage, then be sure to include him or her in your strategic planning process. Similarly, if you've hired any professionals such as fundraisers or management consultants, they should be included—they can often contribute valuable information and perspectives to your strategic plan. Some nonprofits even hire experts specifically for the planning process. For example, you can hire a strategic planning consultant who is trained to help nonprofits work through the tasks involved in creating a strategic plan. However, most start-up nonprofits won't need, want, or be able to afford to hire outside consultants.

At the end of the day, it's the board of directors (or the people in charge of an unincorporated group) that will need to approve the strategic plan, no matter who generates it—committees, consultants, or anyone else. While it's useful to include a diverse range of voices in the process, you don't want to include so many that the nonprofit's essential direction gets lost in a cacophony of different viewpoints and ideas.

## Develop Your Mission Statement

Every nonprofit needs a mission statement: a clear description of the reason the nonprofit exists. Your mission statement should be the first section of your strategic plan and will set the stage for all that follows. Because all nonprofits are mission driven, you must take care to define your mission clearly. If the group is unclear about its mission, it can easily drift off course. Straying from the mission is an obvious problem for practical reasons, because it can lead to wasted energy, inefficient use of time and resources, and failure to

reach your goals. It can also result in losing your status as a nonprofit corporation under state law or losing tax-exempt status under federal and state laws.

Some people who start nonprofits believe that they already know exactly what needs to be done and that it won't take more than a few minutes to come up with a mission statement. If you're one of them, think again—drafting your mission statement deserves more care and attention. While you shouldn't agonize over your statement, it's important to put some careful thought into articulating the mission that will guide your organization for years to come.

### What Is a Mission?

Essentially, your mission is your broad goal—your reason for being. Why did you start your organization? The short answer to this question will likely be a good first stab at your mission statement.

Here are some clear, concise expressions of nonprofit missions:

- "To create a youth choir for the disabled children of El Paso, Texas"
- "To stop a Wal-Mart from moving into Corrales"
- "To provide veterinary services to the pets of homeless people in Atlanta," and
- "To stop the filling of Johnson Bay and restore its watershed to its natural condition."

Your organization will also undoubtedly have many tactical goals, such as organizing events, raising money, finding volunteers, and more. Although these activities should all be designed to further your mission, they aren't part of your mission per se and should not be included in your statement.

### A Clear Mission Is Critical

While it may not be difficult to define many aspects of your mission, it's not a task that should be approached lightly. Remember, all the activities you'll engage in for at least the next few years should flow from your stated mission. Also, crucial questions of scope and purpose that will almost surely come up in the future will often be answered by revisiting your mission statement.

This section takes a closer look at the benefits of having a well-defined mission.

### A Well-Defined Mission Focuses Your Organization

Taking care to define a clear mission statement will ensure that all of the decision makers in your organization have a role in deciding exactly what your mission should be. You may think your mission is obvious. Once you try writing it out, however, you will probably find that there are unresolved questions or issues that have to be addressed. For example, will your choir for disabled youth include children who are physically disabled, developmentally disabled, or both? If you're fighting to keep Wal-Mart out of your town, what about Home Depot or Ikea? Will your organization to stop bay fill also conduct educational programs about the many valuable ecological attributes of wetlands?

> **EXAMPLE:** A group comes together to form Youth Music, inspired by a common desire to promote music education in a specific school district. What should Youth Music do if a group of parents approaches them asking for help supporting or implementing art programs? At least some Youth Music board members may have sympathy for these parents and may be tempted to assist their cause, especially because it's so similar to the group's original purpose.
>
> If the music organization hasn't taken the time to define its mission carefully, these board members may find themselves in conflict with other parents who believe that focusing solely on music programs makes more sense. But if Youth Music has clearly defined for itself the mission of "promoting music education in the Cibola County school district," then it would be easy for it to decide the issue; absent a formal mission change, visual art education is beyond the organization's scope.

**TIP**

**When in doubt, start with a narrow mission.** Rather than bite off more than you can chew, start your nonprofit with a more tightly defined mission. Later, when you have a few successes under your belt, you can consider whether it makes sense to broaden the mission.

Your mission statement doesn't have to be written in stone. It's fairly common for an organization to broaden or redefine its mission as circumstances change. For example, if a group working to prevent bay fill is offered a major grant to do community education on the value of maintaining healthy wetlands, it might wisely decide to expand its mission statement to include bay-related environmental education. But even if particular circumstances don't cause you to change your mission statement, it makes sense to formally revisit it every few years. Situations change, organizations grow and evolve, and you may find that your group has begun to take on new challenges that call for a careful reexamination of its mission and goals.

Whether your mission evolves or stays the same, it must be defined—and understood—by the people involved in the organization. This will give you a point of reference to use not only in planning your activities, but also in resolving disagreements about your group's scope. Your mission statement is at the heart of your enterprise, so any ambiguity or flaws in it will almost certainly result in a less effective organization.

### A Well-Defined Mission Can Attract People and Resources

Besides helping to focus your organization internally, a clear mission provides another crucial benefit: It can attract people and resources to your cause. Your mission statement can and should clearly communicate to outsiders what your nonprofit is all about. The more compelling your mission statement, the better you'll be able to appeal to like-minded folks and get them on board. This doesn't mean you should pander to potential funders or the public. On the contrary, trying to create a trendy program is almost sure to fail, as popular tastes change quickly. But a clear, compelling mission statement plays the important public relations role of explaining exactly what your nonprofit does—which will help you communicate your purpose and goals to those who may wish to get involved in your work.

When you speak to people about the nonprofit—whether they are potential funders, reporters, government officials, or anyone else—you should be able to state your mission in just a few simple sentences.

EXAMPLE: Wild Horizons is a nonprofit created to bring children from poor urban neighborhoods in Wisconsin to national forests and wilderness areas. In the very early days of the nonprofit, before the board of directors sat down to carefully define the group's mission, they weren't effectively communicating the purpose of their nonprofit to others. Many people mistakenly believed the main focus of Wild Horizons was to teach the children outdoor survival skills, when in fact the goal was simply to introduce kids from often troubled urban neighborhoods to the great outdoors as a healthy point of reference.

The volunteers that Wild Horizons tended to attract were almost exclusively outdoor adventure enthusiasts eager to teach the kids skills like rock climbing, long-distance backpacking, and river kayaking. But Wild Horizons also wanted to attract social workers, outdoor educators, and counselors who understood the issues of at-risk youth—and these folks were conspicuously absent. While camping and backpacking trips were part of the plan, the Wild Horizons directors really wanted the group to focus on the special needs of at-risk youth, not on the outdoor skills themselves. They realized that they needed to do a better job of communicating that their group had a social work focus so that they'd attract the people with the crucial youth-counseling skills they lacked.

Once it realized the problem, the board decided to draft a clear mission statement. They prepared by surveying people in the field for input on how Wild Horizons could best meet the needs of the at-risk youth they wanted to help. After receiving and considering that input, they drafted the following mission statement:

"Wild Horizons is dedicated to introducing children from low-income urban neighborhoods in the state of Wisconsin to national parks, forests, and wilderness areas. Our primary goal is to address the issues of at-risk youth through outdoor education, wilderness experiences, self-expression, and counseling. Our activities will encourage personal growth and broaden the experiences of Wisconsin's at-risk urban children by providing them the opportunity to spend time in beautiful, natural, nonurban environments."

## A Well-Defined Mission Can Help You Get 501(c)(3) Status

When drafting your mission statement, remember that your mission will be of crucial importance if you decide to apply for 501(c)(3) or another type of tax-exempt status. As discussed in Chapter 1, the IRS has criteria for each type of tax-exempt status, and it will look closely at your nonprofit's mission to make sure that you meet the requirements.

To obtain 501(c)(3) status, your nonprofit's mission must be charitable, religious, educational, scientific, literary, testing for public safety, fostering national or international amateur sports competition, or preventing cruelty to children or animals. Other types of status have different criteria. If you intend to apply for tax-exempt status, you should make sure that your mission statement meets the eligibility requirements of the type of status you plan to obtain.

RESOURCE

**Need details on IRS criteria?** For detailed information on the criteria for each type of tax-exempt status, see IRS Publication 557, *Tax-Exempt Status for Your Organization*.

## Defining Your Mission

How you come up with your mission statement will depend on the circumstances of your organization. A group of concerned citizens whose goal is to prevent a huge megastore from moving into their neighborhood will probably not have to spend much time developing the finer points of their mission, which is fairly well defined from the start. By contrast, a nonprofit group designed to educate the public on the relationship between the mass media and big business surely needs to define a tighter focus. Its mission statement writing process will be much more involved, and it may take weeks of meetings, drafts, and revisions to arrive at a statement that everyone can support.

Although there are no hard and fast rules for writing mission statements, here are some tips that will help make the process as effective and efficient as possible.

### Bring In Multiple Perspectives

Start the process by bringing in a diverse range of voices. The more input you obtain from the community you intend to serve, as well as from your board, staff, and volunteers, the easier it will be to create an organization that will enjoy a broad base of support.

Depending on your organization's location, purpose, and scope, you might consult experts in the field, representatives of potential funding organizations, or members of the general public. You could invite them to an informal meeting, talk to them individually by phone, ask them to fill out a survey, or use another method of gathering information. Ask them what needs or concerns they have regarding your general area of interest. Of course, only your group's decision makers will decide exactly what the mission statement says in the end, but you should make a real effort to obtain informed input so that you don't define your mission in a vacuum—and, therefore, miss important

opportunities to further your goals and better serve the issue or community that your group hopes to address.

**EXAMPLE:** Before drafting their mission statement, the board members of Wild Horizons created a brief survey that they emailed to about 50 people selected from their contact list. The survey recipients included social workers who work with at-risk youth, teachers and counselors from local schools, nature guides from area parks and forests, and outdoor education professionals. The survey asked for input on what goals and activities would best serve low-income urban kids and what other related needs were not being met.

About half of the survey recipients filled out and returned the survey, giving the Wild Horizons board members valuable perspectives and ideas. This input helped the board refine the group's mission and draft a statement that reflected a balance between the group's two primary activities: outdoor activities and counseling.

### Allow Enough Time

Give yourselves enough time to consider various options and perspectives, write an initial draft, allow all key participants to review it, and incorporate any necessary changes. As mentioned, some organizations with a potentially broad mission or lots of people to satisfy may need significant time and several rewrites to arrive at a statement that really works. But even if your organization is small and your goals seem straightforward, be sure to set aside at least a few days to come up with your final mission statement.

### Be Open to New Ideas

Everyone involved in defining the mission should keep their minds open to new ideas, different interpretations, and fresh perspectives. This is

## Sample Mission Statements

As a point of reference, consider these real-life mission statements from several nonprofits.

### Human Rights Campaign
**Our Mission Statement**

The Human Rights Campaign is America's largest civil rights organization working to achieve lesbian, gay, bisexual and transgender equality. By inspiring and engaging all Americans, HRC strives to end discrimination against LGBT citizens and realize a nation that achieves fundamental fairness and equality for all.

HRC seeks to improve the lives of LGBT Americans by advocating for equal rights and benefits in the workplace, ensuring families are treated equally under the law and increasing public support among all Americans through innovative advocacy, education and outreach programs. HRC works to secure equal rights for LGBT individuals and families at the federal and state levels by lobbying elected officials, mobilizing grassroots supporters, educating Americans, investing strategically to elect fair-minded officials and partnering with other LGBT organizations.

### Progressive Technology Project
**Mission**

The Progressive Technology Project (PTP) seeks to raise the scope and scale of technology resources available to grassroots community organizing groups working for environmental, economic, and social justice in low-income communities and communities of color. PTP provides training, technical assistance, and grants to develop the capacity of grassroots organizing groups through the use of information technology.

### Michael Reese Health Trust
**Mission**

The Michael Reese Health Trust seeks to improve the health of people in Chicago's metropolitan communities through effective grantmaking in health care, health education, and health research. The Trust will focus a portion of its funding on Jewish institutions and issues to fulfill the 110-year legacy of Michael Reese Hospital, founded and supported primarily by the Jewish community. The Trust, in fulfilling its Jewish responsibilities to participate in the arena of general community needs and problem solving, will strive to serve the health care needs of vulnerable and underserved Chicagoans of all races and ethnic origins.

### NativeWeb
**Mission Statement**

NativeWeb is an international, nonprofit, educational organization dedicated to using telecommunications including computer technology and the Internet to disseminate information from and about indigenous nations, peoples, and organizations around the world; to foster communication between native and non-native peoples; to conduct research involving indigenous peoples' usage of technology and the Internet; and to provide resources, mentoring, and services to facilitate indigenous peoples' use of this technology.

particularly true for the group's founders. Sometimes those who have invested the most time and energy planning the organization have the hardest time considering new or different possibilities. Some may simply have tunnel vision; others may be blinded by ego. But whatever the reason, if some participants resist an open and creative writing process, the final statement won't be as thorough and as carefully considered as it could be.

To head off any possible resistance at the pass, urge everyone involved to agree at the outset that all ideas will be encouraged and discussed. One way to help set this tone is to set aside your first meeting exclusively for brainstorming, with no hard-and-fast decisions to be made until a later time. Asking one person to lead the meeting and write down ideas on a big board for the group to consider is a good way to conduct a brainstorming session.

 **TIP**

**Brainstorming helps generate good ideas—and eliminate bad ones.** Turning the idea faucet on full strength at the beginning of any planning process is a great way to get good ideas to flow. Just as important, it allows ideas that won't work to surface and be dismissed early in the process, so your later meetings can be devoted exclusively to refining your best proposals.

### Write Only as Much as You Need

The best mission statements are short and state the obvious. For example, the mission statement of a medical clinic in a low-income area might be, "To help the sick recover and to keep the healthy well." If the need that your nonprofit will serve will be clear to funders, volunteers, and others—for example, providing emergency health care for homeless people—a sentence or two may be all you need. If the purpose or role of your nonprofit isn't so readily apparent—for example, studying migrating patterns of desert toads—you will probably want to say more.

For example, you might want to explain how your toad research nonprofit will attempt to fund studies that will add to existing information about the toad's

mating behavior, food sources, and natural enemies so that a comprehensive habitat protection and species restoration program can be designed. Your mission statement's length and detail will depend on the circumstances of your nonprofit, but always try to keep it as brief as possible, considering the complexity of your group's purpose.

## Outline Specific Goals, Objectives, and Activities

In addition to stating a well-defined mission, your strategic plan should outline more specifically what your nonprofit plans to do. In this section, you'll refine the overall purpose and direction of your nonprofit, as set out in your mission statement, into more specific goals and objectives, which should go a long way toward defining your activities and program areas.

With only a broad, "big picture" mission statement to guide you, your nonprofit wouldn't have much of a road map to follow and would almost surely get sidetracked or lost on its way to accomplishing its mission. Identifying more specific goals helps break down your broad mission into individual elements, which you can then pursue with even more specific planning, as discussed below. For example, if your broad mission is to create economic opportunities for teenagers in a certain city or district, you might have specific goals of publicizing job opportunities for teens, mentoring teens in career development, and nurturing teens' leadership and entrepreneurial skills.

Getting even more specific, you can identify objectives, which are closely related and similar to goals but more concrete and measurable. For example, if the above nonprofit's goal was to mentor teens in career development, an objective might be to implement a mentoring program in a certain city or district, by a certain date. It's often hard to judge whether a nonprofit has successfully accomplished a broad mission or even a narrow goal but much easier to determine whether it has achieved a well-defined, concrete objective.

| Mission | Goals | Objectives/Activities/Programs |
|---|---|---|
| To create economic opportunities for teenagers in Sparks, Nevada | To publicize job opportunities for teens<br><br>To mentor teens in career development<br><br>To nurture select teens who demonstrate leadership or entrepreneurial skills | Create and maintain an online jobs database by July 2013<br><br>Establish a mentoring program with local business owners and teens by November 2013<br><br>Hold a Teen Leader weekend retreat in July 2013 |
| To provide veterinary care for the pets of homeless people | To provide annual, free preventive vaccinations for cats and dogs<br><br>To offer free emergency care for cats and dogs in life-threatening situations<br><br>To offer free spaying and neutering for cats and dogs | Hold quarterly vaccination clinics beginning January 2014<br><br>Finalize agreement with local emergency veterinarian by January 2014<br><br>Finalize agreement with local veterinarian by January 2014 |
| To help disabled people live independently with the help of robotic technology | To research and develop new robotic technologies to help disabled people<br><br>To provide free robots to low-income disabled people | Equip and open research and development laboratory by August 2013<br><br>Launch the Robot Rescue program by March 2014 |

Some nonprofits go a step further and outline planned activities and programs separately from objectives. This step may be unnecessary if you find that your list of objectives offers a complete picture of the activities you plan to undertake. If you decide to list activities separately, they should flow fairly naturally from your list of objectives.

TIP

**Tailor your planning approach to best suit your needs and mindset.** For example, some nonprofits use the goals, objectives, and activities categories, while others use a different breakdown—"strategic vision" or "program goals," for example. The purpose of this section is not to force you into rigid planning categories, but to help you understand how the planning process can break down into useful components. If creating separate subsections for goals, objectives, and activities works for you, great. But if you prefer to merge these categories or create your own divisions, that's fine, too.

When describing objectives, activities, or program areas, it can be tricky to figure out how much detail to include. You want to be detailed enough to give a full picture of the activity, but not so specific that you get mired in logistical details. One good approach is to describe the activity in your strategic plan in as much depth as you would give to an interested outsider—for example, a prospective funder or a newspaper reporter—but not as much detail as you would provide to the staffers who will be running the activities.

For examples of the distinctions between missions, goals, and objectives (including activities and programs), see the chart above.

**EXAMPLE:** Wild Horizons outlines its list of goals, objectives, and activities for the next year, as follows:

| Goals | Objectives | Activities |
|---|---|---|
| • Encourage personal growth of at-risk youth in selected cities and neighborhoods in Wisconsin through outdoor education and wilderness experiences | • Organize and lead wilderness trips for at-risk youth<br>• Provide resources for at-risk youth to encourage them to enjoy wilderness experiences on their own | • A total of five day trips to Nicolet National Forest, each trip taking 45 students from one of five target schools<br>• Two overnight camping trips to Nicolet National Forest, each trip taking a mix of 30 students from all five target schools; camping trips will include canoeing or a similar activity<br>• Publish a two-page map and guide to national parks and forests in Wisconsin, tailored to at-risk youth<br>• Fundraising dinner and silent auction |

TIP

**Strategic planning can be circular.** Because so many aspects of a strategic plan are interrelated, you may have to go back and make changes to earlier sections as you go through the process. For example, you may find it necessary to slightly broaden your mission statement once you start outlining planned activities and realize that a key program doesn't quite fit within your initial statement. Similarly, you may find it awkward to develop a list of goals or activities without first assessing your resources or drafting a budget. It often makes sense to start by focusing on what you reasonably *hope* to do—to let your dreams and aspirations motivate you and inspire you to be resourceful, to do more with less. Although you may need to scale back your list of plans after you assess your limited resources (discussed in the next section) or draft your budget (discussed in the next chapter), at least you'll have these plans simmering on the back burner, ready to go when you have the means to achieve them.

## Assess Your Resources

Now it's time to take a look at the resources your nonprofit has at its disposal to help get its activities rolling. If yours is like most nonprofits, you won't have lots of cash on hand to pay for all of the great things in your plan. But a fact that many new nonprofits overlook in their worry about funds is that money is only one of many types of resources that will be essential to your enterprise—and it may not even be the most important one. For example, even if your nonprofit lacks cold, hard cash, it may possess other key assets, such as volunteers committed to the cause,

people with expertise in a given field, a network of community relationships, a positive reputation, or access to influential people.

In this section of your strategic plan, you should include an assessment of all of your resources, including money, people, expertise, skills, and other intangibles, that are currently available to your nonprofit. Your goal here isn't to detail your fundraising plan—no matter how much it may be on your mind—but simply to develop a realistic understanding of the assets you have in hand. Because it forces you to look honestly at the resources available to implement your planned activities, assessing your current resources might feel like taking a cold shower. But you can't evaluate your nonprofit's current position and identify strategies for pursuing your goals, covered in the next section, without a clear idea of what you have to work with.

Below is a list of things you'll want to consider when assessing your nonprofit's resources. The list is divided into "hard" assets, like cash and equipment, and people assets. You'll find categories that are often used in common nonprofit activities, but you may not need to use all of them—what you have on hand will obviously depend on your specific situation.

### Cash and Equipment Resources
- cash
- office space
- computer equipment and printers
- office supplies
- desks, file cabinets, and other office furniture

- vehicles, especially trucks
- chairs and tables (for seminars and events)
- public address equipment: microphone, microphone stand, amplifier, and so on
- photo and video equipment, and
- presentation equipment: projector, projection screen, and so on.

**People Resources**

- interested volunteers
- the skills or expertise of key people
- miscellaneous contacts: bankers, government regulators, businesspeople, and so on
- access to private or institutional funding sources
- contacts in the media for publicity
- celebrity or famous supporters
- volunteers with technical skills (database development, website building, graphic design, and so on)
- political allies: city council members, the mayor, state representatives, officials at government agencies, and so on
- service sponsors: printers, caterers, transport services, and so on, and
- board members who are famous, experts in their fields, or highly visible, or who otherwise enjoy a good reputation.

Of course, the above list merely suggests possibilities to point you in the right direction when making your own lists. Just remember to think broadly—you probably already possess several resources that you had never considered as such.

 **RELATED TOPIC**

**Budgeting is covered in Chapter 3, and fundraising in Chapter 6.** The budgeting chapter explains how to estimate income and expenses for your planned activities. When you do your first budget, you may find that your available resources won't be adequate to accomplish your planned activities as outlined in your strategic plan. This is where fundraising comes in, which is covered in detail in Chapter 6.

## Develop Strategies

With goals, objectives, and activities identified and your current resources assessed, you're ready to get started on the "strategic" part of your strategic plan. In broad terms, a strategy is a plan for working towards your goals that takes into account your existing situation and resources. A good word to keep in mind as you work on developing strategies is "leverage"—as in, how can you leverage what you've got in order to achieve what you want? The answer to this is essentially your strategy.

 **TIP**

**Lots of folks writing a strategic plan for the first time find it difficult to express strategies in writing.** Concisely describing how you'll get from Point A to Point B can be challenging. But tackling this task is at the heart of the strategic plan. Do your best to focus on step-by-step actions your nonprofit will take, describing both (1) how they take advantage of opportunities and (2) how they will help achieve your goals.

Because it can be tricky to distill so many elements of your nonprofit's operations into clear strategies, many nonprofits use a tool called a "SWOT" analysis. SWOT is an acronym for strengths, weaknesses, opportunities, and threats, which are defined as follows:

- Strengths are positive assets within your organization. Examples might include highly respected board members, a talented group of volunteers, or ownership of valuable intellectual property, such as a book or software.
- Weaknesses are negative aspects within your organization. Examples might include a shortage of volunteers or outdated technology.
- Opportunities are positive elements outside your organization. Examples might include a high demand for your services or availability of a grant in your topic area.
- Threats are negative elements outside your organization. Examples might include a competing nonprofit or the demise of a major funder.

The key to doing a SWOT analysis is to identify these elements accurately, and then think about ways to maximize the positive and minimize the negative elements. Brainstorm about ways to use your strengths to take advantage of existing opportunities and to overcome threats you've identified. Also focus on how you will minimize your weaknesses to make your group less vulnerable to threats. This process of assessment and analysis is the essence of strategic thinking and will help you chart a realistic course for success.

A SWOT analysis is sometimes called other things, such as a "situational assessment" or an "environmental analysis," but all use the same basic approach.

EXAMPLE: In doing a SWOT analysis, Wild Horizons outlines the following strengths, weaknesses, opportunities, and threats:

**Strengths**
- experienced board members and staff
- unique program in the state
- close ties with administrators at target schools

**Weaknesses**
- lack of reputation or recognition by the public or target community
- lack of fundraising experience
- lack of computer experience or database skills

**Opportunities**
- openness by school districts to try innovative programs to help at-risk youth
- large number of granting institutions with at-risk youth as a funding priority
- increased awareness and media coverage of outdoor education and its benefits

**Threats**
- risk of personal injury claims
- competition with other groups for funding
- resistance or apathy from parents and families

Looking over its list, the board members identify various strategies to best take advantage of their strengths and opportunities and to minimize the weaknesses and threats faced by Wild Horizons. For example, the board plans to leverage its close ties with school administrators to remedy its lack of recognition in the community. Similarly, it will take advantage of the large number of funding institutions with a focus on the issues of at-risk youth to minimize its weakness in fundraising experience.

## Edit and Finalize Your Plan

Once you've drafted your mission statement; outlined your goals, objectives, and activities; assessed your resources; and identified strategies, you've completed all the essential elements of your initial strategic plan. All that's left to do is to put it together into a final document.

Let your plan sit for a day or two before beginning a final review. Putting it down for a couple of days will allow the planners to clear their brains and look at it from a fresh perspective. It's a good idea at this point to establish a firm deadline for incorporating any final edits, to keep everyone in "wrap-up" mode and prevent endless rounds of tinkering with the work you've already done. Of course, if people feel strongly that major changes should be made, substantial rewriting may be unavoidable. By the time you've reached this point, however, all the planners should be more or less on the same page.

TIP

**Get community input.** It's not a bad idea to have someone you trust from your community look over a near-final draft of your plan and make edits or suggestions. It's all too common for the people working most closely in the planning process to develop mild cases of tunnel vision and group-think, which sometimes result in the group overlooking issues, opportunities, or flaws in the strategic plan. Having an outsider look it over helps avoid this risk—and helps forge ties with the community as well.

Once your final edits have been incorporated, you may be finished. Or, if you plan to submit the strategic plan to potential funders, you may want to spiff it up and package it into a professional document, perhaps with photos, illustrations, graphs, and the like. (You'll find more on producing professional fundraising materials in Chapter 6.) Package the information as necessary for your intended purposes—an internal working document can be much less formal than a package you send to potential major donors.

---

### Checklist: Developing Your Strategic Plan

☐ Decide who will participate in the strategic planning process—typically, the founders of an unincorporated group or the board of directors of an incorporated nonprofit. Consider others who might have valuable input, including community activists or professionals in your field.

☐ Draft a concise and compelling mission statement describing your nonprofit's overarching goals.

☐ Outline your nonprofit's specific goals, objectives, planned activities, and program areas.

☐ Assess your nonprofit's current and potential resources—including both tangible items, such as cash and computer equipment, and intangibles, such as expertise and community support.

☐ Identify strategies and practical ideas for how your nonprofit will best use its resources to achieve its goals. Use a SWOT analysis, in which you evaluate your nonprofit's strengths, weaknesses, opportunities, and threats.

☐ Have someone you trust from your community look over your plan and make edits or suggestions.

☐ Edit your plan and assemble its various sections into a final document.

# Developing Your Initial Budget

The term "budget" strikes fear in the hearts of many, evoking grim images of counting pennies, tightening belts, and generating complicated spreadsheets filled with endless columns of numbers. But developing a budget doesn't have to be scary—and coming up with a reasonable estimate of your expected expenses and anticipated funds will help you start your nonprofit on stable financial ground.

Budgeting is the process of estimating how much money you'll need to pursue your goals and carry out planned activities and how much money you expect to collect from fundraising, events, sales, and so on. You'll need to draft an initial budget early in your start-up days to get a clear sense of what specific activities will cost and to help you determine how much money you'll need to keep your group afloat.

At its most basic level, a budget is simply a list of:

- estimated income, including how much you think you'll reap in grants, contributions, activity fees, sales, and so on, and
- estimated expenses, including what you expect to spend on day-to-day expenses like postage and office supplies, capital expenses like computers and office furniture, and start-up expenses.

Once you tally up your expected income and expenses, you'll be able to see whether your nonprofit will have enough money to cover all of your future activities, or whether you'll have to scale back your plans and/or figure out a way to bring in more money to make the numbers work.

It's easiest to draft an initial budget after creating your strategic plan. With a strategic plan in place that outlines your activities in detail, making estimates for components of those activities should be pretty straightforward. If, like some nonprofits, you are already engaged in activities and haven't yet created a strategic plan, you might want to draft a budget right away, to keep you on track financially until you do write a strategic plan. Once your strategic plan is in place and your activities are more carefully defined, you can amend your budget accordingly.

While you don't absolutely need special financial software to draft a budget, you'll find that making a budget is easier if you use spreadsheet software such as Microsoft *Excel*. Spreadsheets are essentially rows and columns into which you can enter figures and formulas, allowing you to enter estimated income and expenses and quickly see how different numbers add up. Note that most bookkeeping software such as *QuickBooks* includes budgeting functions, but it's usually considerably easier to use a spreadsheet when drafting a budget. Bookkeeping software is excellent at tracking actual financial data, but spreadsheets offer more flexibility when crunching estimated numbers.

This chapter explains how to draft a budget, including the following components:

- estimated income, including both restricted and unrestricted income (this distinction is explained below)
- estimated program and administrative expenses, divided into categories that will work for accounting and tax preparation purposes
- estimated capital expenses, for long-term assets like computers or vehicles, and
- estimated start-up costs.

**RELATED TOPIC**

**For information on managing and tracking money once it comes into your nonprofit, see Chapter 12.** That chapter discusses basic bookkeeping and accounting principles, including how to generate financial reports that will help you track the financial health of your nonprofit.

**TIP**

**Don't put off preparing your first budget.** Many fledgling nonprofits tend to procrastinate when it comes to budgeting, often because they are intimidated by the process or afraid of the financial realities it will reveal. In fact, budgeting is not difficult—it simply involves breaking down your activities into individual components, then making estimates of what each component will cost. Budgeting is an essential step in getting a handle on the financial resources you'll need to make your group successful. Remember the saying, "Knowledge is power." Understanding exactly how the numbers break down will allow you to make informed decisions that will help you keep your core programs up and running.

FORM

**A blank budget is included in the forms section (Appendix B) in the back of this book, and the Nolo website includes a downloadable copy of this form.** See Appendix A for the link to the forms in this book.

## Set Up Your Budget

Your goals in budgeting are to ensure (1) that the nonprofit is in the black overall, and (2) that each individual program has adequate funding to keep running. To achieve both goals in one budget, you should set the budget up to track both overall funds and funds for specific programs. You'll also need to track any income that must be used for a specific purpose; such income is called "restricted income." This section explains how to set up and manage your budget to accomplish these goals.

### Distinguishing Program Funds From Administration Funds

Administrative expenses (roughly equivalent to "fixed costs" or "overhead" in the for-profit world) are costs associated with keeping your nonprofit running, such as office rent or telephone service. Administrative costs exist independently of any activities or programs your nonprofit conducts. Small nonprofits that begin in a supporter's living room and are headquartered in another volunteer's garage may have very few administrative costs. On the other hand, if you plan to rent office space, hire a part-time coordinator, have a separate phone line, or operate a dedicated vehicle for your nonprofit, you will have fixed costs to consider.

Program costs (much like "variable costs" in the for-profit realm) are associated with specific program activities, such as the price of textbooks purchased for your literacy program or salaries for the nurses who staff your health clinic for the homeless.

Your budget should tell you, at a glance, how much of your income and expenses are attributable to each of your programs and how much are attributable to general nonprofit administration. It's important to divide your budget this way for several reasons:

- You need to know what your individual programs will cost and how much of your overall budget is dedicated to those programs. To make informed decisions about funding, you need to have a clear sense of how much each of your activities and programs costs and how much money each brings in. Allocating your income and expenses by program will let you see how each program is doing financially and make any adjustments necessary to keep important projects up and running.

- You won't be able to make precise overall estimates unless you look at each program and activity separately. Instead of guessing how many total dollars you expect to bring in and spend, you should make separate estimates for each of your planned program areas and for general administration. Making separate estimates will help you generate a more accurate overall result.

- Many funders want to see a high proportion of a nonprofit's funds go toward programs and a low proportion toward administration. Grant-giving organizations in particular want to know that you will spend their money to do good works, not to pay for a receptionist or office rent. Although this may seem a bit arbitrary (after all, you can't carry out your mission without some basics like office space and help), it is a fact of nonprofit life. You won't know how your funds and expenses divide between programs and administration—and you won't be able to provide these funders with the information they demand—unless you make this distinction in your budget.

One good way to distinguish program from administration funds in your budget is to create a separate vertical column for each program, plus a column that you call "Administration" to capture all of the income and expenses that are not directly tied to a specific program. Use the horizontal rows for specific types of income and expenses, and enter the amounts you expect to bring in or spend for each program in that program's column. At the bottom, create a total row to record the overall expenses and income for each program area. The sample budgets throughout this chapter use this basic structure.

---

### Program Cost or Administrative Cost?

Dividing expenses between programs and administration is often more of an art than a science. Sometimes, you'll just need to use your best judgment to decide how to attribute an expense. For example, office rent is usually attributed to general nonprofit administration, but you could also spread the expense of office rent across a nonprofit's program areas. You could divide the cost of rent evenly among all of your programs or allocate rent costs based on the overall percentage of the nonprofit's resources devoted to each program.

As you make these distinctions, remember that the way you divide your expenses may have important consequences when your nonprofit applies for grants or institutional funding. Some funders will provide funds only for program budgets, not administration (or, less commonly, vice versa). Other funders may limit the types of program expenses that they'll fund—they'll only fund educational activities, for example. And many grantors keep a careful eye on your ratio of program to administrative costs. Grantors may turn down your funding requests if your budgets show that you are spending too much money on nonprofit administration—and not enough on worthwhile programs.

---

### Tracking Restricted Income

Restricted income is money that may be used only for particular purposes specified by the donor. For example, some funding groups and individual donors make contributions on the condition that the funds be used only for a specific program—this is restricted income. If there are no conditions on how you can use the funds, the money is unrestricted and may be used for any legitimate expense of your nonprofit.

Accounting rules for nonprofits require you to track restricted income carefully, to make sure that it is spent only on the project(s) specified by the donor. Although this requirement applies only to actual contributions (and not to the anticipated contributions that you'll be using to prepare your budget), it's still a good idea to note whether any of your income is likely to be restricted. That way, you'll have a better sense of how much money will be available to allocate as you wish and how much will have to remain attached to particular programs.

When you draft your budget, list any restricted income you expect to receive in the column for the program for which it will be earmarked. You should also mark these funds in some way—with an asterisk, for example—as a reminder that they are restricted.

Donations from individual contributors are usually unrestricted. Even if your nonprofit has one high-profile flagship program, do not automatically consider regular contributions to be attached or restricted to that program for accounting purposes. However, if you solicit contributions for a particular purpose (for example, to aid the victims of a particular disaster), the resulting donations should be considered restricted income.

### Estimate Income

Start your budget by estimating expected income: how much money you plan to bring in from various sources. As discussed in more detail in Chapter 6, nonprofits typically earn income from membership fees, individual contributions, grants, and special events. Create rows in your budget for each type of income you expect.

Here's a simple approach to follow:

1. Attribute all expected unrestricted income to nonprofit administration, not to any specific program.
2. Attribute any anticipated restricted income to the specific program or programs as specified by the donor. Put an asterisk by any restricted income so you can easily identify it.

To illustrate this process, let's look at a nonprofit dedicated to supporting AIDS patients (see below). The chart shown above budgets for two program areas: a meals-on-wheels program and an AIDS education program. The nonprofit expects restricted income for these programs, so it enters those amounts in the appropriate program column and puts an asterisk by the income as an additional reminder that the income will be restricted. Otherwise, it enters all expected income in the "Administration" column.

For simplicity's sake, many nonprofits assume that all projected income reflected in their initial budgets will be unrestricted unless they have good reason to believe otherwise. Once you've been in operation for a while, you'll be better able to estimate how much restricted income you'll receive—and to include that information in your budgets. But for your initial budget, you can decide for yourselves whether to make this distinction.

**EXAMPLE:** Wild Horizons' list of its income estimates for its first year is shown below. It does not expect any restricted income, so all estimates are entered into the "Administration" column.

## Estimate Expenses

Once you've estimated your income, you'll have to figure out how much your nonprofit plans to spend. You'll need to divide these expenses into basic categories: regular (day-to-day) expenses, capital expenses, and start-up expenses. These divisions will help you prepare your tax returns and balance your books, as explained in Chapter 12. In addition, you'll need to allocate each of your expenses either to an individual program or to administration.

### AIDS Nonprofit Estimated Income

|  | Meals-on-Wheels Program | AIDS Education | Administration | Total |
|---|---|---|---|---|
| **INCOME** |  |  |  |  |
| Individual contributions |  |  | $8,000 | $8,000 |
| Institutional donations | $5,000* | $5,000* | 3,000 | 13,000 |
| Foundation grants | 2,000* |  | 3,000 | 5,000 |
| Special event revenues |  |  | 3,500 | 3,500 |
| **Total income** | $7,000 | $5,000 | $17,500 | $29,500 |

* Restricted funds

### Wild Horizons' Estimated Income

|  | Day Trips (5) | Overnight Trips (2) | Publishing (Map and Guide) | Administration (Unrestricted) | Total |
|---|---|---|---|---|---|
| **INCOME** |  |  |  |  |  |
| Individual contributions |  |  |  | $2,000 | $2,000 |
| Community sponsorships |  |  |  | 2,500 | 2,500 |
| Grants/institutional donors |  |  |  | 5,000 | 5,000 |
| Special events revenues |  |  |  | 2,500 | 2,500 |
| **Total income** | $0 | $0 | $0 | $12,000 | $12,000 |

## Regular Expenses

A nonprofit's regular or day-to-day expenses include costs for anything that you will use in a year or less, such as salaries, rent, utilities, postage, and office supplies. (In contrast, capital expenses like computers last longer than a year; they are discussed next.) Most nonprofits will spend a good part of the budgeting process coming up with figures for these regular expenditures.

List specific types of expenses in each row. To make your budget as clear as possible, it's a good idea to organize your regular expenses into two groups: one set of rows for program-related regular costs, and another set of rows for regular costs spent on administration (or fixed costs). In the program costs group, create a row each for all the specific things you'll purchase for your programs. And in the fixed costs group, create a row each for typical fixed costs, such as rent, salaries, office supplies, and postage. Then enter your estimates for each type of expense. Remember to enter the amounts in the appropriate column; program costs go in a program column, and fixed costs go in the administration column. It's also a good idea to throw in a little extra (10% or so) for administrative costs, to cover miscellaneous expenses that you can't predict.

**EXAMPLE:** A list of Wild Horizons' estimated regular costs for its programs and administration is shown below.

### Wild Horizons' Estimated Regular Costs

| | Day Trips (5) | Overnight Trips (2) | Publishing (Map and Guide) | Administration (Unrestricted) | Total |
|---|---|---|---|---|---|
| **REGULAR EXPENSES** | | | | | |
| **Program costs** | | | | | |
| Food | $1,125 | $600 | | | $1,725 |
| Transportation—gas | 250 | 100 | | | 350 |
| Transportation—van rental | 375 | 300 | | | 675 |
| Insurance | 125 | 150 | | | 275 |
| Day use/campground fees | 50 | 50 | | | 100 |
| Equipment rental | 0 | 200 | | | 200 |
| Printing | | | $500 | | 500 |
| **Program Costs Subtotal** | $1,925 | $1,400 | $500 | $0 | $3,825 |
| **Fixed costs** | | | | | |
| Office rent | | | | $1,800 | $1,800 |
| Salaries | | | | 600 | 600 |
| Utilities | | | | 600 | 600 |
| Telephone service | | | | 600 | 600 |
| Office supplies | | | | 600 | 600 |
| Postage | | | | 300 | 300 |
| Website hosting | | | | 120 | 120 |
| Fundraising costs | | | | 600 | 600 |
| Liability insurance | | | | 1,200 | 1,200 |
| Professional services (accountant, etc.) | | | | 600 | 600 |
| Miscellaneous | | | | 600 | 600 |
| **Fixed Costs Subtotal** | $0 | $0 | $0 | $7,620 | $7,620 |

RELATED TOPIC

**Your budget should track your strategic plan.**
The purpose of your budget is to cost out the specific programs you identified in your strategic plan. If you haven't already outlined your programs, you should do so before starting the budgeting process. See Chapter 2 for detailed information on developing a strategic plan.

TIP

**Keep fixed costs low.** Like many small businesses, too many nonprofits spend too much, too soon. Rather than committing yourself to high overhead, do everything you can to keep expenses low, allowing increases only when your successful fundraising justifies spending more. For example, few nonprofits really need to rent office space in a prominent building. Instead, operating from a low-cost warehouse district, an older office building, or even your garage may work just fine. Not only will this help your bottom line, but it will also impress funders, who like to see organizations operate frugally and are more likely to give money to organizations that stretch their dollars.

## Capital Expenses

In financial terms, "capital assets" (sometimes referred to simply as "assets") are items that have a useful life of more than one year. Common examples include vehicles, computers, and furnishings. The expenses associated with purchasing these assets are called capital expenses and are subject to different tax treatment than regular, day-to-day expenses. (In a nutshell, capital expenses are depreciated, which means their costs are deducted over a number of years, instead of being deducted in full in the year the expenses were incurred.) Even if your nonprofit is tax exempt, it should conform to standard accounting rules and list capital expenses separately. Chapter 12 discusses bookkeeping and accounting in more detail.

Another reason to count capital expenses separately is that they are typically large and often put an otherwise balanced budget in the red. Including these large, sporadic expenses in your fixed or program costs might result in a somewhat misleading picture of your regular costs in those categories. Listing capital expenses separately helps clearly identify these large expenses and facilitates the process of budgeting and planning fundraising efforts. For more details on the treatment of capital expenses, see Chapter 12.

**EXAMPLE:** A list of Wild Horizons' estimates for capital expenses is shown below.

## Start-Up Costs

Start-up costs include expenses for things you'll need to buy in order to get your nonprofit up and running. Estimating them is simple: Just list them and add them up. Include items like incorporation fees, application fees for federal tax-exempt status, initial office supplies, and anything else you'll have to pay for before your group can open its doors for business. Don't include capital expenses, however.

### Wild Horizons' Estimates for Capital Expenses

|  | Day Trips (5) | Overnight Trips (2) | Publishing (Map and Guide) | Administration (Unrestricted) | Total |
|---|---|---|---|---|---|
| **CAPITAL EXPENSES** |  |  |  |  |  |
| Camping equipment |  | $750 |  |  | $750 |
| Computer equipment |  |  |  | $500 | 500 |
| Telephone/fax equipment |  |  |  | 250 | 250 |
| Office furniture |  |  |  | 150 | 150 |
| **Capital Expense Subtotal** | $0 | $750 | $0 | $900 | $1,650 |

TIP

**Capital expenses are not classified as start-up costs.** When doing your initial budgeting, you may find yourself wondering whether the computer or furniture you need for your nonprofit's launch really belongs in the capital expense or the start-up cost category. According to rules known as "generally accepted accounting principles" (or GAAP), any expenses for assets should be allocated to the capital expenses category, even if they're necessary to start your nonprofit. (GAAP rules are further discussed in Chapter 12.)

**EXAMPLE:** Wild Horizons makes a list of the start-up expenses it expects to pay before it begins its first major fundraising drive. The list is shown below.

## Assemble Your Budget

Once you've estimated all of your income and costs, your final task is to compile them into one master budget. This budget will allow you to see whether your nonprofit will be able to carry out all the programs and activities you want to tackle. If your budget shows that your expenses will exceed your income, you'll need either to scale back your plans or to figure out how you'll make up the shortfall.

If you decide you must make cuts, do so only after giving careful thought to your priorities and what you can reasonably put on the back burner. For example, if you really need a part-time paid staffer to coordinate volunteers but have no crucial need for an office, it might make sense for everyone to keep working from their homes (or set up shop in someone's garage) and cut your budget for office space, freeing up some money to pay for the staffer. In other words, think before you cut.

**EXAMPLE:** Wild Horizons puts together all its various estimates into an initial budget, shown below.

Reviewing its initial budget, the board of directors immediately sees that it faces a shortfall of $1,755. While this is certainly a concern, the board is relieved to see that the difference is not so huge as to require radical cutbacks in its planned activities. The board plans to review its program and administrative budgets to see where expenses can be cut back or covered by noncash donations. For example, it hopes to cut the cost of purchasing food for the trips by finding food sponsors willing to donate food. If necessary, it will find ways to raise more funds—however, the board starts by trying to cut expenses, because it doesn't want to raise its income estimates without some solid basis for expecting additional funds.

CAUTION

**Be realistic when comparing resources to planned activities.** If your estimated income won't support your planned activities, don't ignore the problem. If you proceed without sufficient resources, you run the risk that your nonprofit won't be able to follow through with its announced plans. As you can imagine, this could very well result in a loss of credibility and respect in the community, clouding your nonprofit's future. It's much better to scale back your activities and build a strong reputation for success than to overextend yourselves and fail.

### Wild Horizons' List of Start-Up Expenses

| | Day Trips (5) | Overnight Trips (2) | Publishing (Map & Guide) | Administration (Unrestricted) | Total |
|---|---|---|---|---|---|
| **START-UP COSTS** | | | | | |
| Printing—brochures, etc. | | | | $300 | $300 |
| Website creation | | | | 250 | 250 |
| Telephone set-up | | | | 75 | 75 |
| State fees (incorporation, etc.) | | | | 35 | 35 |
| **Start-up Costs Subtotal** | $0 | $0 | $0 | $660 | $660 |

## Wild Horizons' Initial Budget

| | Day Trips (5) | Overnight Trips (2) | Publishing (Map and Guide) | Administration (Unrestricted) | Total |
|---|---|---|---|---|---|
| **INCOME** | | | | | |
| Individual contributions | | | | $2,000 | $2,000 |
| Community sponsorships[1] | | | | 2,500 | 2,500 |
| Grants/institutional donors | | | | 5,000 | 5,000 |
| Special events revenues | | | | 2,500 | 2,500 |
| **Total Income** | $0 | $0 | $0 | $12,000 | $12,000 |
| **REGULAR EXPENSES** | | | | | |
| **Program costs** | | | | | |
| Food | $1,125 | $600 | | | $1,725 |
| Transportation—gas | 250 | 100 | | | 350 |
| Transportation—van rental | 375 | 300 | | | 675 |
| Insurance | 125 | 150 | | | 275 |
| Day use/campground fees | 50 | 50 | | | 100 |
| Equipment rental | 0 | 200 | | | 200 |
| Printing | | | $500 | | 500 |
| **Program Costs Subtotal** | $1,925 | $1,400 | $500 | $0 | $3,825 |
| **Fixed costs** | | | | | |
| Office rent | | | | $1,800 | $1,800 |
| Salaries[2] | | | | 600 | 600 |
| Utilities | | | | 600 | 600 |
| Telephone service | | | | 600 | 600 |
| Office supplies | | | | 600 | 600 |
| Postage | | | | 300 | 300 |
| Website hosting | | | | 120 | 120 |
| Fundraising costs[3] | | | | 600 | 600 |
| Liability insurance | | | | 1,200 | 1,200 |
| Professional services (accountant, etc.) | | | | 600 | 600 |
| Miscellaneous | | | | 600 | 600 |
| **Fixed Costs Subtotal** | $0 | $0 | $0 | $7,620 | $7,620 |
| **CAPITAL EXPENSES** | | | | | |
| Camping equipment | | $750 | | | $750 |
| Computer equipment | | | | $500 | 500 |
| Telephone/fax equipment | | | | 250 | 250 |
| Office furniture | | | | 150 | 150 |
| **Capital Expenses Subtotal** | | $750 | $0 | $900 | $1,650 |
| **START-UP COSTS** | | | | | |
| Printing—brochures, etc. | | | | $300 | $300 |
| Website creation | | | | 250 | 250 |
| Telephone set-up | | | | 75 | 75 |
| State fees (incorporation, etc.) | | | | 35 | 35 |
| **Start-Up Costs Subtotal** | $0 | $0 | $0 | $660 | $660 |
| **TOTAL EXPENSES** | $1,925 | $2,150 | $500 | $9,180 | $13,755 |
| **NET ANNUAL REVENUES** | | | | | ($1,755) |

[1] Five community sponsorships of $500 each are anticipated.

[2] Most tasks will be handled by volunteers, mainly board members. One part-time office worker will be paid $8/hr for a total of 75 hours during the year.

[3] Two fundraising events are anticipated with costs of $300 each.

Raising the additional money or other resources you need to accomplish your plans is another option. Of course, you'll need to be realistic when considering whether you can acquire more money or resources. Rather than simply upping the income estimates listed in your plan to match your needs, raise your estimates only if you have some realistic basis for doing so. And remember that bringing in more resources often comes at a cost. For example, if you decide to add an extra fundraiser to your plans to bring in an extra $5,000, be sure you'll have enough resources to pull off that event. Even if the venue, food, and drinks for the fundraiser are donated, you shouldn't overlook the commitment of time that events always require.

**TIP**

**Stretch your existing resources.** Instead of forging ahead and hoping you'll be able to raise the funds and corral the resources you're lacking, a less risky way to proceed is to figure out how to stretch the resources you already have. In other words, focus on making your existing resources go farther rather than on expanding those resources.

---

### Tips for Structuring Your Budget

Remember that your budget should present your nonprofit's financial picture as clearly and accurately as possible. In particular, you want your budget to communicate your expected financial situation to potential supporters who will not know the first thing about your nonprofit's funds. To that end, here are some tips for structuring your budget:

- **Use a budget narrative to explain specific budget items.** Some of your income or expenses may warrant a short explanation. For instance, you may want to describe what staff you plan to hire to justify the salary figure in your budget, or state what fundraising activities will cost the figure for fundraising noted in your budget. A good way to do this is with what's called a "budget narrative." Simply insert a footnote-style notation next to the line item in question, and at the bottom of the budget include a short explanation for each noted item. The sample budget for Wild Horizons contains an example of a budget narrative with notes for the line items Community sponsorships, Salaries, and Fundraising costs.

- **Account for donations of goods and services.** Most nonprofits are able to cut their cash expenses by wrangling donations of goods and/or services, otherwise known as "in-kind donations." These noncash gifts can make a real difference to your bottom line, so it's smart to include them in your budget if you know in advance that any such donations are likely. There are a number of ways to accomplish this; one way is to include an additional column after the Totals column where you record the value of the goods or services donated, and another column after that where you adjust the cash total by subtracting the amount of the in-kind donation.

Here's an abbreviated example, with a budget narrative:

| | Music Lessons | Newsletter | Administration | Total | In-Kind Donations | Adjusted Total (Cash) |
|---|---|---|---|---|---|---|
| **Program Costs** | | | | | | |
| Teacher salaries (a) | $5,000 | | | $5,000 | $2,500 | $2,500 |
| Piano rental | 1,200 | | | 1,200 | | 1,200 |
| Printing costs (b) | | $1,000 | | 1,000 | 1,000 | 0 |
| **Program Costs Total** | $6,200 | $1,000 | | $7,200 | $3,500 | $3,700 |

(a)  All music teachers have agreed to cut their fees in half.

(b)  Printing for the newsletter will be donated by Main Street Printing.

## Adjusting Program Budgets

Separating your program expenses from administrative expenses allows you to see whether individual programs have enough funds to survive and, if not, to make adjustments. Consider the following example of a nonprofit to support AIDS patients.

As you can see, the budget shows an overall surplus of $1,700, but the program budgets are short of funds. The good news is that there's enough unrestricted income in the administration category to allocate to the programs to make up the deficits. By reallocating $500 to the meals-on-wheels program and $1,300 to the AIDS Education program, those programs will break even—and there will still be a $1,700 surplus, allocated to the administration category.

| | Meals-on-Wheels Program | AIDS Education Program | Administration | Total |
|---|---|---|---|---|
| **INCOME** | | | | |
| Individual contributions | | | $8,000 | $8,000 |
| Institutional donations | $5,000* | $5,000* | 3,000 | 13,000 |
| Foundation grants | 2,000* | | 3,000 | 5,000 |
| Special event revenues | | | 3,500 | 3,500 |
| Total Income | $7,000 | $5,000 | $17,500 | $29,500 |
| **REGULAR EXPENSES** | | | | |
| **Program costs** | | | | |
| Food | 3,000 | | | 3,000 |
| Gas | 1,000 | | | 1,000 |
| Insurance | 1,000 | | | 1,000 |
| **Fixed costs** | | | | |
| Office rent | | | 4,000 | 4,000 |
| Office supplies | | | 2,000 | 2,000 |
| Postage | | | 750 | 750 |
| Printing | 500 | 2,000 | 500 | 3,000 |
| Salaries | 2,000 | 2,300 | 1,750 | 6,050 |
| Telephone service | | | 2,000 | 2,000 |
| Website hosting | | | 1,500 | 1,500 |
| **CAPITAL EXPENSES** | | | | |
| Computer equipment | | 750 | | 750 |
| Telephone/fax equipment | | 250 | | 250 |
| **START-UP COSTS** | | | | |
| Website creation/setup | | 1,000 | 1,500 | 2,500 |
| **TOTAL EXPENSES** | $7,500 | $6,300 | $14,000 | $27,800 |
| **NET REVENUES** | ($500) | ($1,300) | $3,500 | $1,700 |

* Restricted funds.

## Checklist: Developing Your Initial Budget

☐ Tackle your initial budget early in the life of your nonprofit—ideally, right after you finish your strategic plan.

☐ Set up your budget to list expenses for individual programs and expenses for ongoing administration in separate columns.

☐ If you expect some income to be restricted to certain programs, track it in your budget. Otherwise, put all income in your administration column.

☐ List your estimated expenses in three categories: (1) day-to-day expenses, (2) capital expenses, and (3) start-up expenses.

☐ If you need to buy assets to get your nonprofit started, such as a computer or office furniture, list them as capital expenses, not as start-up expenses.

☐ If your budget shows that you'll be short on funds, focus on stretching existing resources rather than increasing estimates of income.

# Your Board of Directors

One of the fundamental tasks facing the founders of any nonprofit is choosing a board of directors to oversee the organization. The board plays an essential legal and practical role in any nonprofit, even if others (such as an executive director, paid staff, and/or volunteers) handle the organization's everyday affairs.

Nonprofits receive favorable tax treatment and other benefits precisely because they are created to serve the public interest. And, as you'll remember, the nonprofit's board must shoulder the legal duty to keep the organization true to its public service mission so that it continues to deserve its tax-favored status. (This "public trust" role explains why nonprofit directors are sometimes called trustees.)

The board's role of setting policies and maintaining the nonprofit's overall direction serves more than just a legal function. By defining the mission of the nonprofit, establishing priorities, crafting strategies, and ensuring that plans and programs are implemented, a good board serves an immensely practical role as well. Without a committed board to tackle these tasks, a nonprofit can all too quickly run adrift, without clear goals or any specific plans to achieve them. True, an executive director can and should provide day-to-day management and decision-making skills, but the board has the legal duty and authority to set policy.

Another area in which board members are typically involved is fundraising efforts. You should be able to count on your board members to spread the word about your good work, use their connections to gain access to potential donors, actively participate in fundraising campaigns, and—when financially feasible—make their own donations. As discussed later in this chapter, there are many ways that board members can participate in fundraising. Whether a board member is more comfortable planning behind the scenes or asking for money directly, there should be a way for the whole board to get involved.

Nonprofit board members often go beyond the traditional directorial tasks of setting policy and defining a nonprofit's goals. Especially in small all-volunteer nonprofits (and even in those with a small paid staff), board members often roll up their sleeves and do much of the nonprofit's actual work, be it feeding the hungry, helping the unemployed, or cleaning the forests. In other words, it's not uncommon for board members to go beyond nonprofit planning and steering and get involved in the actual execution of the nonprofit's objectives.

Think of your board as the heart of your nonprofit. At the legal level, your organization can't live without one, and, practically, your group's mission, key strategies, and policies all flow from the board's decisions and leadership. This chapter will help you select and manage a board that will steer your nonprofit in the right direction. It covers:

- qualities to look for in your board members
- the *board's* legal duties and activities
- how to create policies and develop procedures for your board
- how to recruit board members
- how to hold effective board meetings, and
- the role of board committees.

## What Makes a Good Board

Most great boards share some common traits and qualities that enable them to lead their groups creatively and effectively. The members of an ideal board of directors:

- share a passion for and commitment to the nonprofit's mission
- are willing to roll up their sleeves when necessary to help with the practical work of the nonprofit
- have strong ties to their communities
- are diverse—in age, gender, race, religion, occupation, skills, and background, and
- are willing to support efforts to raise money.

The sections that follow look at these various qualities in a bit more detail.

### Passion and Commitment

The very best prospects for your nonprofit's board will be people who share a passion for, and commitment to, the nonprofit's mission. No matter what name recognition or professional credentials particular people may have to offer, they will not be assets to your nonprofit's board unless they care enough about what you do to involve themselves actively in helping you pursue your goals. If yours is a small nonprofit that doesn't have the resources to hire staff or pay for outside services, it's even more important that board members be committed to the cause and willing to contribute their time to get nonprofit tasks done.

Unfortunately, the best prospects in terms of professional achievement and influence in the community are often the very people who have the least amount of time to help. Finding people who are both professionally accomplished and willing to pull an oar isn't easy. Here are some brief tips on the types of people who might make good recruits. (For strategies that will help you attract and approach people to serve on your board, see "Recruiting Board Members," below.)

- **Young professionals eager to make a difference and expand their skills.** While established professionals at the top of their fields will often have zero time to spare, eager and talented up-and-comers may have more time to commit to your cause. Particularly for those in their 20s and 30s, being invited to participate on a board can be quite an honor and will often be viewed as an exciting opportunity for professional development and career advancement.
- **Recently retired people.** People who have recently retired often have fresh skills, good contacts, and time. And, just as important, they are often looking for ways to stay active in the world beyond playing golf or mah-jongg.
- **Businesspeople in related fields.** For instance, if your nonprofit aims to feed the homeless, you should consider not just community leaders and social activists, but also restaurant and grocery store owners. Similarly, a group wanting to provide sports opportunities for the disabled might contact owners of local sports equipment stores or architects who design recreational facilities for the physically impaired.
- **Local media people.** Reporters, editors, and others from local media—newspapers, television and radio stations, and others—are good candidates because they're typically both well informed and well connected. Reporters often cover certain beats that may make them particularly well suited for your board—for example, a local reporter who covers energy markets might be a good addition to your energy conservation nonprofit. (However, keep in mind that in some cases the opposite might be true—reporters might not want to put their journalistic objectivity in question by becoming involved in issues they routinely cover, particularly in controversial fields.)
- **Professors, scholars, and researchers.** Anyone who studies issues in your nonprofit's subject area is a natural candidate for your board. For a nonprofit dedicated to promoting urban green space, for example, an urban planning professor (or landscape architecture professor, among others) would be a natural. College professors also tend to have flexible schedules, so they may be more likely to have time to serve.
- **New moms or dads.** Working professionals who take a year or more off to raise a young child may be looking for ways to stay involved in the world. Sometimes, serving on a board for a cause they care about is an ideal way to stay active.

## Willingness to Help Raise Money

The most successful nonprofits have boards that are willing and able to help with fundraising efforts. Of course, most board members are likely to be driven by an interest in the nonprofit's main cause—not by an interest in raising money. But no matter what your nonprofit's core mission and priorities are, it will have to generate some income in order to survive. As the leaders of the nonprofit, board members are in a particularly strong position to promote it to potential funders. It's important to find people who understand the importance of their fundraising role and are willing to lend a hand.

There are lots of different ways for board members to be involved in fundraising. Board members who aren't comfortable directly soliciting funds can be involved in organizing events or developing membership drives. Other board members might be natural networkers or salespeople who would excel at contacting potential donors and actively soliciting contributions. And all board members should expect to help generate ideas for raising money, identify good donor prospects, and otherwise develop fundraising strategies.

In addition to helping raise funds from others, board members should also be willing to support your nonprofit financially. Some board members might not be able to contribute more than $50 per year; others might comfortably give $5,000. More important than how much money board members give is their willingness to demonstrate some level of financial commitment to the organization. Outside funding sources will want to see this level of faith and commitment from the board; its absence will be taken as a sign that all is not well within the organization. In addition, contributions from board members are often a godsend in a nonprofit's early start-up days, when you will need cash up front for incorporation fees, a phone line, or other expenses before your fundraising machine is up and running.

Some nonprofits require board members to donate a certain amount each year; others suggest a contribution amount and leave it up to the individual members to decide how much to give. Your nonprofit will have to decide for itself what, if any, contribution requirements you'll impose on board members. Keep in mind that there may be excellent potential board members who don't have a lot of cash but more than make up for it with valuable skills or connections in the community.

> **TIP**
>
> **Don't require contributions that your prospective board members can't afford.** Don't make the mistake of overlooking or alienating potential board members with more to offer in expertise and connections than in cold, hard cash. While some nonprofits require board members to contribute financially, such a requirement might be a turnoff to

those with limited funds. Remember that access to influential people, management expertise, and cachet in your field or community may be even more crucial than money in your early start-up days—and will certainly lead to a broad base of financial contributors down the road. In short, a committed board member with a fat Rolodex can be at least as valuable to your fledgling nonprofit as one with a fat wallet.

No matter how your nonprofit chooses to handle this issue, you must let prospective board members know before they agree to serve on the board what, if any, financial commitment will be expected of them. (How to define and communicate board members' responsibilities is explained in "Board Policies and Procedures," below.)

## Connection to Many Communities

Many nonprofits are started by groups of people who think a lot alike—they might even look a lot alike in terms of skin color, age, class, or gender. This isn't a problem in itself; it's often just the natural way that people come together to promote an issue they care about. But when you choose your board, you should consider who isn't at the table and whose voices aren't included in your start-up group. There may be people of other races, ages, or communities who care deeply about your issue and whose perspectives could greatly strengthen your board—and, by extension, your organization.

Going out of your way to build diversity in your board is not just an exercise in political correctness. Rather, by incorporating a range of viewpoints on your board, your group will be more likely to truly serve the public interest—not just a small slice of it. The goal is not simply to have a diverse board, but to translate the perspectives of your diverse board into a nonprofit that offers services broadly.

In addition, having a diverse board will help you forge ties to a wider range of the community and broaden your base of support. When you build your board inclusively, you increase the board's natural networking power.

**EXAMPLE:** Inga and Steven are the initial incorporators of Peace Through Understanding, a nonprofit dedicated to promoting peace by educating the American public about other cultures worldwide. In putting together a list of prospective board members, they have included religious leaders from local churches, synagogues, mosques, and other places of worship. Also on their list are university professors who teach about international issues and activists from several local antiwar groups. But then, thinking more broadly, Inga suggests some activists from the sizable gay and lesbian community in the area who have been in the forefront in the fight against hate crimes.

Besides diversity, it's important that the people you choose have strong ties to the communities you're trying to reach. Remember, it's not enough to have a diverse board—you ultimately want to reach diverse communities through that board. To achieve this, you should choose people who are connected to—and influential in—their communities. Examples include prominent businesspeople and others who are successful in their fields, community activists, politicians, religious leaders, and noted academics.

## Diverse Viewpoints

In addition to having board members who are connected to diverse communities, you want at least some board members who represent different points of view. While you obviously don't want a board member who is hostile to your overall mission, it can be extremely advantageous to include people who have independent or unusual perspectives. For instance, a nonprofit dedicated to improving opportunities for minorities in newspaper journalism should try to include representatives from different aspects of the newspaper industry on its board. A diverse board would include not just newspaper editors and reporters, but also photographers, copy editors, circulation managers, and publishers, all of whom will typically have different perspectives and concerns than editors and reporters. Again, your ultimate goal is always to serve the public, which is usually best achieved with an open-minded board that engages in healthy debate.

## The Board's Duties and Tasks

Clearly, the nonprofit's board plays an important legal, leadership, fundraising, and ideological role. But how, exactly, does a board translate these broad responsibilities into everyday actions and decisions? How should a board function, day to day and meeting to meeting? And what legal duties must board members observe as they handle the nonprofit's business? This section answers these important questions by explaining the legal duties—and practical tasks—board members must take on.

### Board Members' Legal Duties

New or prospective board members often are concerned about what the law requires of them in their board roles. Here's the deal: Under state laws, members of the board of directors have two main duties to a nonprofit corporation: the duty of care and the duty of loyalty.

 **TIP**
**Board members typically aren't personally liable for mistakes.** Don't let directors lose sleep worrying about violating these duties and being sued personally. As discussed in more detail in Chapter 7, directors are rarely held personally liable for errors committed in steering the nonprofit, unless the acts (or failures to act) were fraudulent or extremely careless. In addition, most states have laws protecting directors from personal liability, and a federal law protects volunteers as well. (See Chapter 7 for more on liability issues.)

### Duty of Care

The duty of care requires board members to act with reasonable care in making decisions and taking actions on the nonprofit's behalf. Board members can go a long way toward fulfilling this duty simply by being informed. Board members should attend meetings, be in the loop on matters under consideration, and take care to look into any relevant and important information that's available before making a decision or taking action. Before voting to approve a new program area, for example, board members should have a clear understanding of important issues like what the program will cost, whether there is money in the budget to pay for it, and whether it involves any activity that might expose the nonprofit to risk.

A common (if slightly legalistic) definition of "reasonable care" is the level of care that an ordinarily prudent person in the same circumstances would reasonably believe is appropriate. A more basic formulation is that directors will satisfy the duty of care if they act rationally and in good faith.

### Duty of Loyalty

The duty of loyalty—sometimes called a "fiduciary duty"—requires board members to always put the interests of the nonprofit ahead of their personal interests. This duty is often expressed in other ways, too: as a rule against self-dealing or against conflicts of interest, for example. With some subtle differences (explained below), all of these rules require much the same thing: Board members must always make decisions that are in the best interests of the nonprofit.

Examples of self-dealing might include a director voting for the nonprofit to rent an office in a building that the director owns or to make a purchase from a company owned by the director. In both cases, the director stands to realize a personal financial gain from the nonprofit transaction. A conflict of interest might exist if a director sits on the boards of two nonprofits that pursue the same funding sources. Even though the director does not stand to personally gain, the dual directorships raise a potential violation of the director's duty of loyalty to each group.

In cases such as these, state laws generally require that the director disclose all the relevant facts about the potential conflict (including any personal interest the director has in a transaction) and that only non-interested directors participate in the vote. If these two requirements are met, then the conflict will have been avoided (in legalese, the conflict will have been "discharged").

### Board Roles Versus Staff Roles

Generally speaking, the board is not in charge of the day-to-day affairs of the nonprofit. Taking care of the many details involved in running the organization is the responsibility of the nonprofit's staff, including the executive director, paid workers, and volunteers.

Of course, many nonprofits—especially new and small ones—have no staff and are run almost entirely by the board and other volunteers. Plenty of micro-nonprofits operate this way, which can make the distinction between the board role and the staff role quite confusing. The key is to understand that the same person may sometimes play a board member's role, and sometimes an activist or volunteer staff role. Board members should be clear on this: Although they may take care of all the nonprofit's day-to-day details, they are not doing so in their capacity as board members.

For example, if a board member dons galoshes to help with a Clean Up the Wetlands day, helps stuff envelopes, picks up chairs for an event, or teaches a seminar, the member is wearing a "staff hat"—not a "board hat." When a board member is discussing whether certain programs fit into the nonprofit's overall mission, on the other hand, that member is wearing a board hat. Keeping this distinction in mind will help you understand the board/staff relationship and the breakdown of roles that is so important to a nonprofit's effective functioning. Clearly recognizing these different roles is especially essential when a nonprofit has paid staff, so that board members refrain from interfering in day-to-day staff duties. Nothing irritates competent nonprofit staffers more than having board members meddle where they're not wanted (or needed).

### Typical Board Activities

The types of activities that nonprofit boards typically handle tend to break down into the following categories:

- defining the organization's mission and ensuring that the nonprofit stays on course

- outlining the nonprofit's main programs designed to accomplish its mission, usually on an annual basis
- establishing and managing financial systems by developing budgets, monitoring finances, and implementing accounting controls
- leading and helping with fundraising efforts
- dealing with internal board management, such as electing officers and finding new board members to replace outgoing ones
- establishing and overseeing committees to handle special issues, such as membership, special events, or fundraising
- hiring and managing an executive director (if the nonprofit plans to have one), and
- helping promote the nonprofit and its activities to the public.

Keep in mind that the tasks and scope of work outlined above will change somewhat as the nonprofit grows and hires paid staff. Generally, the more paid staff you have, the less board members will be involved in day-to-day tasks.

Nonprofit boards typically create committees to focus on specific areas or complicated issues. Once the committee makes progress, these issues are brought back to the board as a whole for approval or other guidance. Sometimes a subgroup of the board sits as an "executive committee," which can convene and act with the full authority of the board. As with other types of committees, an executive committee can be particularly useful when a nonprofit has a large board, making it logistically difficult to meet often. But executive committees should be used judiciously, not as a regular substitute for full board involvement. Committees are discussed in "The Role of Committees," below.

## Board Meetings

The main way the board functions is by meeting to discuss issues and make decisions about how to get things done. These decisions are passed on to the nonprofit's staff (if there is one). Boards generally have regular meetings—monthly, bimonthly, or quarterly—and call special meetings if issues arise that need immediate attention.

Keeping board meetings efficient and focused is an important issue for all nonprofits (and just about every other type of business, for that matter). This means that the board should develop a clear sense of priorities, including what to cover at meetings and what to leave for others to handle. While the board has a legal duty to set policy and keep the nonprofit on course, there's little legal guidance about what specific matters the board must address. As a practical matter, board meetings should not get mired in the minutiae of nonprofit operations. (As discussed below, specific tasks are often managed by committees, which may include nonboard members, leaving the board to focus on higher-level steering issues.)

> **CAUTION**
> **Save valuable meeting time for important issues.** Although day-to-day details may ultimately end up on board members' plates, they shouldn't become a main topic at your board meetings. If a board member will be in charge of buying office supplies or designing letterhead, that doesn't make discussions of the pros and cons of various types of paperclips or letterhead font sizes appropriate subjects for lengthy board discussion.

## Board Officers

The people who head boards of directors are referred to in the law as officers—typically president, vice president, secretary, and treasurer. Having leaders in place obviously helps the board function more effectively by designating responsibilities to specific people, which helps ensure that things actually get done. In practice, board officers often also serve as a principal point of contact between the board and staff. For example, in organizations with paid staff, the president usually works closely with the executive director and other key workers to make sure staff and board are on the same page.

While board officers legally lead or govern the board, which in turn governs the nonprofit, board officers themselves do not run the nonprofit as a whole. This is a subtle but crucial distinction. The officers are in charge of keeping the board functioning smoothly so that it can consider issues and make decisions, which are then passed to the staff to execute. The executive director, who is hired by the board, is in charge of running the nonprofit, which typically includes hiring and firing other staff.

Officer duties are spelled out in the nonprofit's bylaws and generally are pretty similar from one nonprofit to the next. Typical officer positions and duties are:

- **President.** The president's main duty is to preside over meetings, including drafting the agendas beforehand. The president is usually also in charge of appointing committees and generally making sure that board projects are proceeding as planned. Many nonprofits also require the president to compose an annual report to be presented at the nonprofit's yearly meeting, although the executive director often handles this task in larger organizations. In smaller nonprofits that rely entirely or primarily on volunteers, the president usually has the authority to sign contracts and checks (a responsibility often shared with the treasurer).

- **Vice president.** Of all the officer positions, the vice president generally has the fewest specific formal responsibilities. By custom, the vice president is expected to help the president with various tasks, fill in for the president as necessary, and generally put a shoulder to the wheel when important work needs to be done. Legally, if the president needs to vacate office, the vice president assumes that role until the next officer elections.

- **Secretary.** A nonprofit's secretary keeps minutes of board meetings and manages the nonprofit's records, such as articles of incorporation, bylaws, and other official documents (these tasks may be delegated to staff in larger groups). Under the terms of the nonprofit's bylaws, the secretary usually has the legal duty to give notice of meetings and file any state-required paperwork.

- **Treasurer.** The treasurer is generally responsible for keeping track of the nonprofit's funds, including maintaining the books, handling bank transactions, and preparing any financial reports that may be necessary. The treasurer often shares check-signing authority with the president. In larger groups, the treasurer's duties may be delegated. (Bear in mind that failing to pay required payroll and other taxes may subject the treasurer to personal liability—see Chapter 7 on liability issues for your nonprofit and its board, staff, and volunteers.)

## Board Policies and Procedures

Nonprofits have wide legal latitude to decide for themselves how big their boards will be, how long board members' terms will last, and how often the board will meet. Obviously, you should nail these details down before recruiting people to serve. Some of these issues should be addressed in your bylaws, others in separate policies, and some in both. This section explains what specifics you'll need to define and where they should be set forth.

### Number of Directors

There's no simple formula for calculating how many members should be on a nonprofit's board. Some groups function well with as few as five members; others with as many as 25. Generally, you need enough members to ensure the nonprofit's mission is carried out, but not so many that members feel superfluous. But in figuring out how to apply this rule, all sorts of factors come into play. For example, a nonprofit that has a small budget or operates in a limited geographical area shouldn't necessarily have a small board. In fact, the opposite is often true—a small nonprofit that can't afford paid staff may have to rely on committed board volunteers to carry out its basic programs. There may also be political reasons to have a slightly larger board. For example, if your nonprofit is established to build a hiking and biking trail that will run through a dozen communities in two counties, you might want your board to be large enough to accommodate a representative from most of the affected neighborhoods.

Once the organization grows and brings in more money, you may be able to bring in paid staff to take over many of these duties, which will reduce the need for board members to volunteer their time and allow the board to function well with fewer members. Of course, the more programs and services a nonprofit offers, the more policy making, budgeting, fundraising, staffing, and other issue wrangling the board will have to tackle.

In deciding how large your board should be, keep in mind that most state laws establish a minimum number of board members, usually one or three. And, in practice, you should have an odd number of members to avoid tie votes. It's also best to establish a size range rather than a firm number of members, as directors tend to come and go. If you're committed to having five, nine, or 17 members, for instance, it can seem like a never-ending task to keep the board at full strength. A range of five to nine members seems to work well for many small- to medium-sized nonprofits; larger ones might use a range of nine to 15; only nonprofits that are quite large have more than 15 board members, typically.

State laws generally require you to list the number of directors or size range in both the articles of incorporation and the bylaws.

 **RESOURCE**
**Need to know more about these essential nonprofit documents?** For detailed information on drafting articles of incorporation and bylaws, be sure to read Anthony Mancuso's *How to Form a Nonprofit Corporation* (Nolo).

## Terms and Term Limits

Every board should adopt a set term for board membership—two or three years is a common term length—and should consider a limit on the number of consecutive terms a member can serve.

Putting a time limit on board terms has several benefits. First, it helps members focus on the need to get things done in a certain time frame. Second, it creates an incentive for the members to do their jobs conscientiously, knowing that they'll have to face an election or appointment process to stay on the board once their term is up. Third, it gives busy board members who might otherwise be reluctant to serve—or possibly be tempted to resign early—a clear understanding of the length of their commitment. Finally, it offers a clean path to remove troublesome board members eventually, without the unpleasantness of purging them from office in the middle of their terms. Although midterm removal might still be necessary in extreme circumstances, most board member problems aren't quite that severe. When a board member is ineffective, inert, absent, or just garden-variety difficult, it's often easiest to simply wait out his or her term and let the elections take care of the problem.

You may also want to limit how many consecutive terms board members can serve. Term limits ensure that a board will periodically have new members and fresh energy. They also allow you to gently remove long-time members who have lost effectiveness because of declining interest, health problems, or other personal issues.

But term limits are a double-edged sword. Limiting consecutive terms means that even your best board members will have to step down at some point, which can seriously impact the momentum of the board's work. If you do impose term limits and lose a valuable board member, you can try to keep that person involved by appointing him or her to one or more committees that don't require board membership. And, like most nonprofits that impose consecutive term limits, you can allow the member to run again after having been off the board for at least one year. But if you don't want your most valuable board members to be forced off the board by term limits, then simply don't use them. After all, in our busy world, you're more likely to have a problem finding and keeping good board members, not getting rid of them.

Any term limits you adopt should be spelled out in your bylaws. You may also want to summarize this information and include it in your board guidebook, described below.

TIP

**Create staggered board terms.** ~~It's a good idea to stagger your board terms so that everyone's term doesn't expire at the same time.~~ This will help you ensure board member continuity—and avoid having to round up an entire slate of new members when elections roll around. To create staggered terms, simply establish different term lengths for your initial board. For example, for a five-person board, you could appoint three members for two-year terms, and two members for one-year terms. All subsequent elections would be for terms of two years, and every year some (but not all) of your board's seats would be up for election.

## Board Member Responsibilities

Just as employers often use job descriptions to outline exactly what will be expected of an employee, nonprofits should take care to define the tasks and responsibilities of their board members. The previous section outlined the general types of activities that are common to most boards, including defining policy, creating financial systems, and managing the executive director or other staff. But these broad responsibilities should be broken down into more specific tasks that board members will be expected to tackle. Outlining these tasks as specifically as possible creates accountability and lets everyone know what is expected of them—thereby improving the chances that the board's work will actually get done.

It's a good idea to put these job descriptions into a written document and include them in a board guidebook, as discussed below.

RESOURCE

**Need help writing job descriptions?** *The Job Description Handbook*, by Margie Mader-Clark (Nolo), provides step-by-step instructions on drafting a legal, effective description for any position. It also explains how to use job descriptions in hiring, orientation, evaluating performance, and more.

---

### Deciding Where to Record Your Rules

It can be tough to figure out whether certain rules, policies, or other information should be included in a board member's guidebook or in your nonprofit's official bylaws. One way to handle this question is to include your bylaws in the handbook. But because even conscientious people don't always read the often stilted language of legal documents, it makes sense to repeat important information and rules in plain English. For example, rules regarding term limits definitely belong in the bylaws, because they're essential to the nonprofit's legal operation. But they should also be included in the "Board Affairs" section of your board guidebook; that section's purpose is to inform directors about key issues, including election rules.

As a general rule, you should put detailed housekeeping-type information in a board handbook, not your bylaws. There's a practical reason for this—any changes you want to make to your bylaws must be done by formal board vote at a meeting for which proper notice is given and a quorum achieved. By contrast, rules that aren't included in the bylaws can be adopted and changed much less formally. Information about the length or locations of meetings, committee lists, job descriptions, or personnel policies are best kept out of the bylaws. The time and expense of amending bylaws isn't prohibitive, but there's no reason to make extra work for your board.

---

## Performance Practices and Removal Policies

Virtually every nonprofit has to deal with problem board members from time to time, such as members who regularly miss meetings or who simply aren't contributing sufficient time, energy, or, in some cases, money to the organization. Having performance expectations and removal policies in place before these potential problems arise makes it a whole lot easier to solve them.

Failing to attend meetings is one of the most common problems that arise with board members; thankfully, it's also an easy one to measure and correct. All nonprofits should have a policy stating that attendance at board meetings is mandatory (without a compelling reason to be absent). Some may decide to implement tougher standards—for example, that two unexcused absences per year constitute resignation from the board. (Removal policies are discussed further below.)

Other board-related performance issues are more subjective and, therefore, trickier to measure and enforce. For instance, what (if anything) should you do about a board member who shows up at every meeting but rarely participates in discussions or other activities? The best answer is probably nothing, beyond thinking about ways to help the person become more engaged. If those efforts go nowhere, the member should not be appointed or recommended for election to another term.

Fortunately, in addition to formal policies and penalties, there are informal ways to keep your board members in line and, hopefully, steer wayward members back on track. Some ideas include:

- In a meeting agenda, include a discussion of how everyone can be more effective. This is a good way to focus on performance without singling anyone out. It's not a bad idea to do this regularly—say, once a year.
- Organize a board retreat day. It can be hard to get busy people together for a day or weekend. But because events like this help build morale, fight burnout, and reenergize members, it's worth the time and effort every year or two.
- Ask experienced board members to mentor new ones. When new members join the board, assign an experienced and willing board member to work with each one for a couple of months. Encourage the new members to actively use their mentors as a resource. This works well as a preemptive practice to help avoid problems in the first place.

Performance policies are generally not included in a nonprofit's bylaws, which shouldn't contain such detailed, practical information.

The process for removing a director, on the other hand, should be covered in your bylaws, to help avoid further conflict and confusion during what is sure to be a difficult time. The main issues you'll need to address are what type of vote will be required—for instance, a majority, two-thirds, or unanimous vote of other board members—and whether directors can be removed without cause.

Each state has legal rules for removing a nonprofit board member from office. Some states give the nonprofit complete discretion to determine the procedure for removing a director; others set certain standards—for example, some states do not allow nonprofits to remove a member without cause. Be sure that the policy you adopt for removing board members meets any requirements imposed by your state. Laws governing nonprofits (including rules for removing board members) are generally found in the corporations code of your state's statutes. (Chapter 13 offers a brief overview of how to do legal research online.)

In addition, you may want to summarize the review and removal policy in a board guidebook.

## Creating a Board Guidebook

It's a great idea for every nonprofit to have a guidebook that contains important reference information for board members. A nonprofit board guidebook might include a:

- legal basics section, including the articles of incorporation and bylaws of the nonprofit
- board affairs section, with concise information about board member duties, review and removal policies, and other rules for board members
- directory section, listing the names and contact information of board members, staff, and volunteers
- committees section, with descriptions and membership rosters of committees
- programs section, with detailed information about current programs (plus the current strategic plan, if you have one), and
- background section, providing basic information about the organization's mission and history.

Besides giving you an opportunity to present information in a more user-friendly way, a board guidebook also allows you to cover information in more detail than you would want to include in your articles or bylaws.

## Recruiting Board Members

You will probably have to appoint your nonprofit's very first board members as part of the process of incorporating in your state. Nonprofit corporations (and for-profit ones, too) are created at the state level, most commonly by filing papers known as articles of incorporation with the secretary of state's office. Those articles generally ask for the names of the nonprofit's initial board of directors. If your state requires a minimum number of directors (many do, and three is a common minimum), you'll need to name at least that many in your articles. (For in-depth information about drafting and filing articles and bylaws, consult Anthony Mancuso's *How to Form a Nonprofit Corporation*, published by Nolo.)

In practice, fledgling nonprofits often consist of a few people who have come together over a particular cause or issue. Once the group is ready to incorporate, part or all of this core group may opt to be named in the articles of incorporation as the initial board. Often, the group will dispense with formalities such as nominating candidates or voting; those willing to volunteer for a board position are appointed to serve. Sometimes, only some of the core group will choose to be on the board. This might be the case if the core group is large, or if the group simply (and sensibly) wants to think carefully about the board's composition and size once they're up and running.

In established nonprofits, appointing board members is generally a more formal process. Often, a nominating committee of existing board members evaluates the current board situation and its needs, gathers names of prospective new members, and recommends candidates to the full board, which then votes on whether to elect the new member(s). (In nonprofits that give members the legal right to elect directors, the members vote, rather than the board. See Chapter 1 for more on this issue.)

While the board-building process you use will depend on your nonprofit's situation, all nonprofits need to know how to recruit excellent board members. If your nonprofit is young and has just one or a small number of committed people, you obviously aren't in a position to use a nomination committee or a highly structured process to recruit new members to your board. However, you shouldn't let this prevent you from taking a careful and methodical approach to the board-building process—your efforts will pay off in the long run.

Whether new board members are chosen by a formal five-person nominating committee or by two newbie incorporators meeting at a coffee shop, the following guidelines will help you focus on your ultimate goal: building an effective board.

---

### Board Recruitment "Don'ts"

Here's a short list of tactics to avoid when recruiting members for your board:

- **Don't appease busy prospects by downplaying a board member's duties.** It's easy to see how this can come back to haunt you. Make it clear up front that an active, engaged board is vital to your organization and that board members will be expected to participate.
- **Don't approach your "dream" prospects until your nonprofit is up and running.** The folks you'd most like to have on board probably won't be swimming in extra time. Rather than inviting the busiest prospects right away, focus instead on building a smaller board of committed, lower-profile members and achieving a success or two to make you more attractive to other potential board members. Once you move a few hills with your initial board, it will be easier to line up the types of heavier hitters who can help you move mountains.
- **Don't invite a high-profile board member based solely on his or her name.** All board members must have a sincere commitment to your mission and be willing to actively participate in running the nonprofit. If a high-profile board member doesn't share that commitment or willingness to work, you can count on resentment and bitterness from the rest of your board.

## Evaluate Your Needs

The board's function is to serve the nonprofit, not the other way around. That's why it doesn't make sense to recruit a slew of interesting, inspiring, or well-connected people to your board unless your nonprofit needs what they have to offer. For instance, if you already have one or two board members with good accounting skills, it probably doesn't make sense to appoint another board member with similar talents, even if you know an excellent candidate who would agree to serve. Better to inventory the other expertise you'll need, such as media relations or fundraising experience, and look for board members who can help with these needs.

Besides seeking board members with specific skills, it's also important to find members who are well-known, respected, or influential in your core communities. Having successful activists, professionals, or other reputable people on your board will lend credibility to your group—which is particularly essential in your early days, before your group has made a name for itself. If you can recruit influential people who also have helpful skills, you've hit the jackpot.

With this advice in mind, start your board building not with a list of prospects, but with an evaluation of your current situation and needs. Focus on any skills or strengths that prospective or current board members lack. Once you've outlined the missing pieces that would be valuable to your group, then you can focus on generating a list of prospects who would fill those gaps.

## Make Sure Recruiters Understand Board Members' Responsibilities

Everyone involved in the recruitment process must understand exactly what board members will be expected to do. For example, is a board member expected to attend a half-dozen meetings a year to help with policy and fundraising, or do you want worker bees who will take on much of the day-to-day work of your organization? It's important to nail down these expectations early in the process, before any board prospects are considered. It goes without saying that if the recruiters don't have a clear understanding of what new members will actually be doing on the board, they won't be in a good position to choose people with the right skills and experience. Not only is this likely to waste time, but it also risks signing up people who can't meet your real expectations.

As described above, most nonprofit boards have fairly similar realms of responsibility, including defining policy, managing finances, and working with an executive director. While these categories are common, each nonprofit will also have its own unique list of board responsibilities. Make sure that everyone on your

---

### Useful Skills for Board Members

While the specific skills your board will need depend on your nonprofit's purpose, there are some skills that are valuable to just about every nonprofit. These include:

- **Fundraising and grant writing.** No surprise here; people who know how to raise money are major assets for nonprofits.
- **Database, website, or other technical skills.** A database is a great way to keep track of mailing lists, financial supporters, members, and more. And most nonprofits should have at least a simple website. A database- or Web-savvy board member can provide lots of help here.
- **Accounting and bookkeeping.** You'll want to look for a few board members who have some financial expertise; if a board member has experience managing nonprofit finances, so much the better.
- **Employee and volunteer management.** Keeping a staff motivated and efficient doesn't happen by itself—skilled managers are key.
- **Public speaking.** Having an effective speaker on your board will open up opportunities to promote your group and its work.
- **Media relations.** A board member who knows how to get coverage in newspapers, radio, television, and other media will help enormously in building recognition and credibility for your group.
- **Graphic design and production.** Putting together media kits, brochures, and other materials will help your nonprofit get the word out about its work.

## Create a Board Candidate FAQ

One way to tell prospective board members what you expect is to create a "board candidate FAQ" that communicates all of the important facts in a simple one-page question-and-answer format. Here is an example of the types of questions that might be included in an FAQ for prospective board members for a homeless assistance nonprofit.

**What is Welcome Home?**
Welcome Home is a 501(c)(3) nonprofit dedicated to serving the needs of the homeless in the greater Oakland area. We offer meals and shelter to those in need and educate the public on the social issues related to homelessness.

**As a board member of Welcome Home, what will I be responsible for?**
As a member of the Welcome Home board of directors, you will help define policy and guide the nonprofit so that it stays true to its mission and achieves its goals effectively. You will be expected to attend and participate in monthly board meetings. You may have additional responsibilities if you join committees or become active in certain areas.

It is expected, though not required, that you will occasionally participate in events as a volunteer.

**How long will I serve on the board?**
Board members serve a two-year term.

**As a board member of Welcome Home, are there any legal issues I need to worry about?**
Under state law, board members are expected to use reasonable care when making decisions or taking actions (called a "duty of care"). In addition, state law establishes a duty of loyalty on board members, which means that you must always act in the best interests of Welcome Home.

In general, board members are not personally liable for their work on the board. You won't face personal liability unless you act fraudulently or with gross negligence.

**Are board members expected to contribute financially to Welcome Home?**
Board members are encouraged, but not required, to contribute financially to the organization. If you choose to contribute, any amount that is comfortable for you is welcome. Contributions from current and past board members have ranged from $50 to $500.

recruiting team knows—and can communicate—what you expect from your board members.

 **CAUTION**
**Don't alienate your prospects.** Before a recruiter approaches a prospective board member, make sure that your current board or core group approves of the choice. Even if you're only planning a preliminary discussion, it's much better to wait and make sure that everyone agrees on the prospect than to jump right in and extend offers you might later have to rescind.

## Educate Prospects and Incoming Board Members

Once someone has expressed a willingness to consider joining the board, the recruiter(s) should make sure the prospect knows everything he or she needs to know to make an informed decision. This includes not only basic information about the nonprofit and its activities, but also what will be expected of board members. For example, if you expect each board member to make a significant financial contribution, it's best to make this clear up front. Otherwise, board members might quit in a huff when they learn how much you expect them to fork over.

You should give incoming board members copies of your articles of incorporation and bylaws, as well as any other materials you have developed to guide the board. You may also want to assign an experienced board member to mentor the new members.

In addition, new board members should go through some sort of orientation process that provides information about the organization's policies and procedures. The length, complexity, and format of the orientation will vary from one nonprofit to the next, depending on the organization's size, activities, history, and other factors. A simple orientation—say, an hour or so of presentations by the nonprofit's founders, current board members (if you have them), president, executive director, committee chairs, or some combination of these folks—will work fine for most new nonprofits. If your nonprofit is larger and more complex, you may want to divide your orientation sessions into a series of presentations, perhaps over a couple of days.

Common topics to cover in an orientation include:
- the nonprofit's mission and goals
- the organization's history
- a financial assessment and overview
- current and planned programs
- the responsibilities of board members
- the responsibilities of the executive director and staff, and
- committee assignments.

Besides offering an orientation program, you might also want to hold some type of informal get-together, to allow new board members to get to know each other in a more relaxed social environment. For example, the entire board could go out for lunch as a group, attend an event related to the nonprofit's mission, or have a potluck at a board member's home.

### Elect Officers

When you establish your initial board, you'll need to elect officers. Most nonprofits choose a president, vice president, secretary, and treasurer (as described above). Officers are chosen and voted in by board members. Often, this is the first item of business at the first board meeting, with the founder temporarily taking the lead and asking for nominations for president. Once elected, the new president takes over the rest of the meeting and asks for nominations for the other officer positions, which are then voted on in turn.

Particularly in new nonprofits, the officer "election" process may be less formal. For example, someone may suggest that the nonprofit founder should serve as president, and a quick show of hands confirms the decision. In some cases, there may not be anyone who is eager to serve as president, and someone will have to be drafted by the rest of the board.

Elections may be a more competitive affair, with two or more board members fighting for the presidency. This isn't common with new nonprofits. If it does occur, however, it's important to conduct a fair election process. After board members are nominated, you should conduct a vote with written ballots and have several board members count the votes.

---

### Use Committees to Avoid Board Burnout

It's very common for new nonprofits to have frequent board meetings due to the flurry of activity that generally happens in a nonprofit's early days. This is especially true for nonprofits that are run by a hands-on board, in the absence of other volunteers or staff. For example, when an event is being organized, the website is under development, the logo is being designed, and a fundraising campaign is being developed, it may seem like the board needs to meet every week to keep everything moving forward. Unfortunately, this can easily lead to overwhelmed, burned-out board members.

The first step in avoiding this common scenario is to remember that when board members help conduct the nonprofit's activities, they are doing so not in their role as board members but as volunteers. In turn, meetings to discuss specific activities (like event planning or logo design) should not be considered board meetings—and attendance by the full board shouldn't be required. Instead, a smaller committee of the people directly involved in a specific activity should meet as necessary, and the full board should meet only for true board meetings, to focus on policy and direction of the nonprofit as a whole. The smaller, specific committees can report on their progress at these board meetings, taking up much less of the full board's time.

Committees are discussed below, in "The Role of Committees." The point here is that hands-on boards need to remember that not everything they do is truly a board issue. Freeing board members from having to attend every meeting regarding every logistical issue is a great way to help prevent burnout.

---

## Holding Effective Board Meetings

Meetings that are unproductive, disorganized, boring, contentious, or poorly attended will seriously undermine the effectiveness of your board—and, by extension, the nonprofit as a whole. Despite this obvious fact, thousands of truly awful board meetings are held every day, leaving tens of thousands of board members shifting in their seats and wondering, "How did I get stuck with this job?" There's no better way to drain the energy from a nonprofit than to let this go on. While it may not be possible to make your board meetings as entertaining as a good Broadway show, you certainly can maximize their effectiveness by following some simple rules.

## Meet Regularly

Adopting a regular meeting schedule is a good way to build momentum for the board's activities. If meetings are held at random or infrequently, it will be hard for members to stay focused on what's going on and push business forward. Depending on your agenda, it's often best to meet monthly, or at least quarterly. If issues come up between board meetings that require immediate attention, you can call a "special" meeting, which simply means a meeting in addition to the board's regular meeting schedule. (Procedures for special meetings should be included in your bylaws.)

> **TIP**
>
> **Keep meetings short.** Your board will need to decide for itself how often and how long to meet, in order to maximize the board's efficiency and productivity. Very generally speaking, meetings of about two hours are optimum; no meeting should last longer than three hours. As long as agendas are planned carefully and time limits are set in advance for each item, the president should be able to keep the meeting on schedule.

## Invite Staff and Outsiders When Appropriate

It's perfectly appropriate, and often a good idea, to invite people other than board members to attend meetings. If, for example, you plan to evaluate the progress of a certain program, then you may want to invite the staffer who runs that program to speak at your board meeting. Similarly, it often makes sense to invite the executive director, who is usually involved in many aspects of the nonprofit's operations. Some nonprofits invite the executive director as a matter of course, whether or not a specific agenda item requires his or her input. However, you shouldn't invite the executive director to be a board member or to vote on board decisions. (See Chapter 5

for more information on the relationship between the board and the executive director.)

You should also feel free to invite guests from outside the organization to attend board meetings from time to time. This is a great way to forge connections to your community and bring new perspectives to the board. For example, your nonprofit dedicated to keeping an urban river clean could invite a prominent local architect who is involved in eco-friendly loft developments along the river. Opening your board meetings to guests in this way lets the board and your guests learn about each other, stay on top of developments in areas of mutual interest, and figure out how to support each other's work.

## Give Notice of Meetings

If you want board members (or others) to show up at board meetings, you'll have to tell them when and where the meetings will be held. For regular meetings, it's best to do this well in advance—for example, you might want to set all the meeting dates for the following year at the annual meeting. For special meetings (those that are held in between regular meetings), most nonprofit bylaws require seven or ten days' notice (although this can be shortened or waived altogether if all board members consent).

The secretary is usually responsible for giving notice of meetings, although the vice president or a designated staff member sometimes takes on the job. Phone calls are the most common way to give notice of special or changed meetings, but many organizations use email. Although a voice message doesn't meet the written notice requirements set out in many nonprofit bylaws, it should work out fine as long as no one objects. But when a special meeting is called to discuss and vote on a contentious issue, you'll want to closely follow the rules set out in your bylaws.

In today's busy world, even if your board meeting has been set well in advance, it's a good idea to make a follow-up call or send a reminder email a week or a few days before the meeting. You should also send board members a copy of your agenda (discussed next), if possible.

## Rules of Order for Meetings

The first time you participate in a board meeting with rules of order, you might feel a little awkward, perhaps even silly. But as arcane as they may seem, rules of order (sometimes called "parliamentary procedures") serve an important purpose: They provide procedures for raising issues to be discussed and making decisions about them. Rules cover how to make motions, second motions, refer motions to committee, call for votes, and so on.

While there are a few different systems out there, the Cadillac version is *Robert's Rules of Order*. Believe it or not, these rules—for "smooth, orderly, and fairly conducted meetings"—were first written in the late 1800s by General Henry M. Robert and continue to be used today by boards of all types, for profit and nonprofit alike. With sections like "Secondary Motions as an Underlying Concept," "Conditions That May Impede Renewal at a Later Session," and "Taking Up Business Out of Its Proper Order," it's clear that General Robert had more than a passing interest in all things orderly.

While rules of order can be fairly technical, the good news is that most nonprofits don't follow them to the letter. Board members should at least be familiar with the rules so that they understand what is going on at any given point in a board's proceedings. A quick search of Amazon.com will yield several titles besides the official *Robert's Rules*; some are "plain English" versions that may offer a livelier read.

**TIP**

**Give board members the previous minutes a week before the meeting.** Because most meetings begin by approving the minutes of the previous meeting, giving board members a chance to review the minutes in advance is a good way to save time at the meeting. Providing the previous minutes ahead of time also reminds board members of any tasks they promised to do before the next meeting. Assuming the minutes have a section outlining action items (they should), this reminder will give board members a chance to take care of anything they may have forgotten about.

## Draft a Solid Agenda

If there's one key to a successful board meeting, it's the meeting agenda. Typically, the president drafts the agenda (and makes sure members stick to it during the meeting). A meeting agenda outlines the topics to be covered at the meeting and sets time limits for the discussion of each. Without an agenda, it's all too easy for a meeting to devolve into unproductive chit-chat— or to be commandeered by one person who's eager to take advantage of a captive audience.

When drafting a meeting agenda, it may be a good idea to ask other board members if they have any items they'd like to add. If your board is email-friendly, you can do this via email a week before the meeting. Another approach is to ask for additional agenda items at the beginning of the meeting, but this can backfire. If too many people want to add agenda items, or if the suggested items are just ill-considered, it can be awkward to nix them in front of the assembled board. A better approach is to make clear that items must be added in advance absent some urgent reason to consider an issue right away. Most agendas include some or all of these items:

- **Welcome and introductions.** The president calls the meeting to order and introduces any guests. If you will allow any last-minute additions to the agenda, now is the time to ask whether anyone has agenda items to add. If they do, set a time limit for each item, with any further discussion postponed to a subsequent meeting. The opening of the meeting is also a good time to remind everyone that the president will enforce the time limits.

- **Guest speakers.** If any guests will make presentations, it's a good idea—though certainly not a hard-and-fast rule—to schedule them near the beginning of the meeting, as a courtesy to the speaker.

- **Approval of previous meeting minutes.** Members typically vote to formally approve the minutes from the previous meeting, which then become part of the corporate records. If any board member has corrections or additions to the minutes, they'll be added before approval. The secretary should distribute the minutes a week or so before the meeting so members have time to review them and note any changes.

> **TIP**
>
> **Limit corrections to the minutes.** Most board members never read the minutes of previous meetings. But a few do so obsessively and insist on raising a laundry list of inconsequential suggestions that waste everyone else's time. If this becomes a recurring problem, the president could announce that the minutes should be corrected only if they contain obvious errors or omissions. To take this a step further, the president could explain this rule to the offending member one on one, emphasizing that meeting time is valuable and that corrections should therefore be limited to truly important issues.

- **Committee reports.** If your board has active committees that have met since the last board meeting, each committee typically summarizes any progress made on its projects. (If routine, these reports are often best submitted in a short written memo.) If any committee is involved in a major or controversial project, you may want to schedule a special slot for that report. Otherwise, reports should be quick and efficient summaries of committee work. If these reports threaten to take up too much time, schedule them toward the end of the meeting, when people want to leave and are likely to be less chatty.

- **Budget/finance committee report.** You may want to address this item separately because budget and money issues are so important for many nonprofits. Depending on your board's size and committee structure, you may want to have a detailed discussion of finances with the whole board, or a budget/finance committee may present a report to the group. You don't have to schedule this separately from the other committees, but it is an option.

- **New business.** The president introduces any new business and gives the floor to whoever will speak in detail about it. Once new business items

are discussed, a specific person or committee is often put in charge of following up and reporting on progress at the next meeting.

- **Review new action items.** It's good practice to do a quick recap of action items that board or key staff have committed to during the course of the meeting. Board members should recount which (if any) tasks they've agreed to do, such as phone calls to make, memos to draft, and so on. The secretary should outline these commitments in the minutes, preferably in a separate section called "Action Items."

- **Adjourn meeting.** If you haven't already scheduled all of your meetings for the year, you should set the time and place for the next meeting before calling the meeting to a close.

## Start on Time

All board members should understand that meetings will start on time, every time. Waiting for latecomers only reinforces their behavior and wastes the time of those who arrive on schedule. If certain board members habitually show up after the meeting has begun, the president may want to privately but explicitly ask them to be more punctual.

## Understand Decision-Making Methods

The most common way that boards make decisions is by taking a vote. Most nonprofits use majority rule for most matters, although some require a two-thirds majority or even a higher plurality for certain unusual issues, such as amending the articles or removing a board member. Your voting rules should be included in your bylaws. (Anthony Mancuso's *How to Form a Nonprofit Corporation* (Nolo) offers in-depth information about voting, quorums, and other rules that you should spell out in the bylaws.)

Because close, contentious votes often produce lingering resentment, it can be a mistake for the president and other leaders to allow a vote on an important item if there is strong disagreement among board members or between board members and senior staff. When this is the case, other decision-making methods can help break the impasse. Techniques that are often used to avoid a divisive vote include:

- **Refer an issue to a committee.** This way, the committee can grapple with the vexing issues and look for ways to find compromise. The committee can then present the issue at the next board meeting, perhaps with a new recommendation.
- **Schedule a discussion and straw vote.** A straw vote is a nonbinding vote, taken to gauge the support on both sides of an issue. When debating controversial issues, the president may call a straw vote just so everyone can see who is on each side. Knowing where things stand can help leaders steer the discussion toward compromise and resolution before a final vote is taken.
- **Build consensus.** Sometimes, it's best for a board to discuss an issue until consensus is reached. Purely applied, this model requires everyone to be in agreement for a decision to be made. Making decisions by consensus can be quite time-consuming; it's often wise to follow this approach only when the issue really is divisive and you need the entire board's support for the resolution.

### Deal With Problem Board Members

Troublesome people come in all shapes and sizes, and some of them may, despite your best efforts, find their way on to your board. Common types of problem board members include those who are argumentative, bullying, rude, or just prone to talking too much. Sometimes a board member who has worked collegially and productively in the past suddenly encounters a personal problem (such as a crumbling marriage or substance abuse) that impairs his or her ability to contribute effectively to the board's activities.

Whatever the underlying reason, it's important not to ignore a problem board member. Difficult as it may be (and it usually is), you must confront the issue quickly in order to save the rest of the board from foundering. Again, there's no one-size-fits-all solution. Gentle coaxing might work best for some, while a

"candor without guilt" type of confrontation may be the only way to get through to others.

Depending on how serious the problem is—and, sometimes, on how important the individual is to the organization—the president should try to figure out which approach seems most likely to resolve the situation. If diplomatic suggestions or stronger admonishments don't work, the person should be dropped from the board as soon as possible. If the next election is too far away, and the board member is seriously impeding the nonprofit's work, removal may be in order. Having removal procedures clearly spelled out in your bylaws will prove to be essential in this situation.

## The Role of Committees

Especially for larger boards, an effective way to break down the board's governance duties is to subdivide board members into committees. Some may be permanent (sometimes called "standing") committees to handle ongoing issues such as finance, program development, membership, or the like. Other issues that come up can be handled by creating a special (sometimes called "ad hoc") committee. Don't worry about what they're called; just keep in mind that nonprofits typically use both kinds of committees to handle regular needs and new issues as they arise.

Committees help maximize the board's productivity in several ways:

- **They make it easier for boards to handle complex issues.** The smaller committee can research and break down complex issues and present its findings to the board, which can then move forward to making decisions.
- **They match board members with particular expertise to appropriate areas.** Forming a committee is a great way to assign specific responsibilities to the people best able to handle them.
- **They can engage with an issue more deeply and consistently than the board as a whole could.** The finance committee, for instance, can and should maintain thorough and ongoing management of the nonprofit's finances between meetings,

so that the whole board can deal with this key concern (based on the reports of the finance committee) at board meetings.

- **They help divide the board's workload.** Having separate committees is a simple way to distribute responsibility for the many tasks boards typically need to tackle.
- **They can attract and involve newcomers.** In some nonprofits, specialized committees often include people who aren't on the board of directors. For example, a nonprofit that promotes physical fitness for diabetic children might have a doctor on one of its program committees to help design fitness activities. That doctor might be happy to be involved in this way but not interested in taking on the additional responsibilities and time commitments required to serve on the board.
- **They serve as a training ground for new board officers.** Chairing or just being involved in a committee is a good way for inexperienced board members to increase their involvement, develop confidence, and learn leadership skills. These people often move on to board leadership or officer roles.

> ! CAUTION
>
> **Don't set up unnecessary committees.** Before you establish a committee, ask what the committee will do that the board can't do just as well. If you have a good answer, set up a committee and get the ball rolling. If not, don't bother setting up a committee that will have to meet and generate projects simply to justify its existence.

---

### Checklist: Your Board of Directors

- ☐ Aim to build a board of directors made up of individuals who are committed to your mission and connected to a wide range of communities.
- ☐ Understand the legal duties of care and loyalty that board members owe to the nonprofit.
- ☐ If board members will also help with the day-to-day tasks of the nonprofit, as either paid staff or unpaid volunteers, make sure everyone understands the distinction between "board" roles and "staff/volunteer" roles.
- ☐ Define board specifics in your bylaws, including the number of board members you will have, any term lengths and/or term limits applicable, and the responsibilities of the board members and officers. Establish performance expectations and removal policies for board members. Include these in a board guidebook. Deal with problem board members when necessary.
- ☐ Educate board prospects and incoming board members about board responsibilities as well as your organization's mission and activities.
- ☐ Hold regular, efficient, focused board meetings. Draft solid meeting agendas and stick to them. Give advance notice of meetings, and start meetings on time.
- ☐ Create board committees to focus on specific tasks and activities when necessary. These committees may contain both board members and other, nonboard, members who are part of your nonprofit (for example, staff or volunteers).

# Your Workforce: Staff and Volunteers

This chapter will help you understand how to hire and manage your nonprofit's workers, including paid staff and volunteers. As discussed in Chapter 4, the board of directors has the legal and institutional responsibility to implement the nonprofit's policies and make sure that it is working toward its mission. However, the board should not be responsible for the day-to-day operations of the organization—those duties should fall to the nonprofit's staff and volunteers.

In nonprofits with a paid staff, the top staff position is traditionally the executive director, a senior-level staff member who is hired by the board to oversee any other staff and volunteers. In small, all-volunteer nonprofits, the board president often plays this role. The executive director is responsible for evaluating the nonprofit's needs; creating a management structure; and recruiting and managing staff, volunteers, and contractors—all with an eye to efficiently carrying out the mission and policies set by the board. The executive director sits at the top of the management hierarchy, with authority over all managers and staff, whether paid or volunteer.

In real life, however, many nonprofits operate with far less formality. Lots of small nonprofits have no staff other than the board members, who don "staff" hats and take care of the nonprofit's day-to-day affairs themselves. Even if there are a few volunteers or part-time staffers, many young nonprofits don't bother with the position of executive director or a rigid management hierarchy. Typically (but certainly not always), an executive director position is created when the paid staff grows to about three to five people, necessitating the imposition of at least some degree of managerial structure.

This chapter explains how to hire and manage the people who work for your nonprofit, whether you're a small grassroots collective or a larger staff-run operation. Here, you'll find information on:

- developing a management strategy
- hiring an executive director
- hiring and managing staff and volunteers

- deciding whether to hire employees or independent contractors, and
- complying with paperwork and tax requirements for employers.

**RESOURCE**

**For more information on hiring and managing employees and volunteers in a nonprofit organization,** see *The Nonprofit's Guide to Human Resources,* by Jan Masaoka (Nolo).

## Developing a Management Strategy

"Management" is a fairly vague word, and one that is used to describe a vast array of decisions and actions. As used in this book, the term "management" refers to the practice of assessing, organizing, and leveraging your nonprofit's available resources in the most efficient and useful way to reach your goals. It follows that a good manager is one who gets the most out of staff, money, and other assets—without overtaxing the nonprofit's resources or stretching them too thin.

The key to coming up with a good management plan is to use an approach that will work for your situation right now, not where you hope to be some time in the future. Perhaps you dream of someday having a well-funded nonprofit with 150 employees. It's fine to think big, but you should start by managing your existing staff well. If you currently rely on a handful of dedicated volunteers and one half-time employee, you won't need the formal hierarchy of departments and lines of authority that a larger group might require. Your tiny nonprofit can probably operate just fine if one or two board members are responsible for giving day-to-day direction to the volunteers and paid assistant—and the rest of the board stays out of the way. Of course, if your organization already has several paid workers and a large cadre of volunteers, you'll need a more formal management structure right from the start.

This section explains some issues to consider when deciding what type of management strategy will work best for your nonprofit.

*I like to impress the value of team building. If you get one person on your team, you can get ten. Ten carefully selected people can accomplish a great deal in the way of the diverse, specialized skills critical to running a nonprofit. I also suggest collaboration for brand-new groups. If incorporation isn't a "must," working with or under the umbrella of another established nonprofit will allow you to test the waters without the full burden of running your own incorporated organization.*

**Randolph Belle—Director of Information
East Bay Nonprofit Center
Oakland, California**

## More Activities Require More Staff and Structure

The main difference between managing a large operation and managing a small one is in the level of formal structure imposed on staff and volunteers. The more activities a nonprofit undertakes, the more staff (both paid and volunteer) it will need and the more structure will be necessary to keep the staff working efficiently. In other words, the type and number of programs and services you plan to provide will largely determine how much staff you'll need, which in turn will suggest an appropriate management structure and strategy.

For example, if your nonprofit's main activity consists of running one prestigious conference each year on landscaping and water conservation, your staff needs would be far smaller than a group that runs a walk-in health clinic for homeless people. Providing health care on a daily basis would surely require full-time staff (say, ten or more volunteers and paid workers), which would also necessitate a fairly formal management structure, with clear lines of reporting and responsibility. The water conservation group, on the other hand, might require only a part-time office helper and a few volunteers (except during the week of the conference, when it would need more) and, therefore, might not need much of a management hierarchy.

As Chapter 2 explains, outlining programs and services is part of drafting your nonprofit's strategic

---

### Main Street Reborn: A Small Nonprofit Run by Its Board

Main Street Reborn is a (fictional) nonprofit dedicated to preserving historical main street districts in Florida's small towns. Main Street Reborn was founded by Melissa and Vincent, who were concerned about decaying town centers throughout Florida. Melissa and Vincent soon found three other interested people—Spencer, Jill, and Damon—and incorporated as a nonprofit, with all five sitting on the initial board.

After a couple of strategic planning meetings, the board decided to pursue the following activities: (1) compiling historical information about chosen main street districts; (2) educating the public through published materials and media relations efforts; and (3) helping building owners get their properties listed on the state historical property registry and research available rehabilitation grants.

The board discussed how to structure things in order to accomplish their list of tasks. They decided that the board could handle their activities for the time being, making paid staff unnecessary. Each board member took on certain tasks: Jill was in charge of doing historical research; Vincent created brochures and fact sheets based on the research; Melissa wrote press releases and letters to the editor to get media exposure; Spencer and Damon focused on the state historical property registration process and grant research. They each expected to contribute approximately ten hours of work per month.

Because each board member would essentially be self-managing, the group decided to have monthly meetings to report on their progress and revisit their priorities and goals. They also decided to look for a part-time volunteer with an interest in historical preservation to help with administrative tasks. They agreed that if the workload exceeded their expectations, they'd either curtail some activities or look into raising enough money to hire a part-time staff person.

After a year of operations, the workload more or less matched the expectations of all the board members, and, none of the tasks were too burdensome for the board members to handle. The board decided to look for an additional volunteer or two to help with the historical property registration applications but to keep its overall minimal management structure for the next year.

plan. If you've already tackled the strategic planning process, you should have a pretty good idea of how extensive your year's activities will be—and how many people it will take to get them done. (Hiring paid staff and volunteers is covered in more detail below.)

## Provide Clear Direction

Nonprofits typically owe their existence to the passion and commitment of a small number of people. Sometimes—especially when the people running the nonprofit don't have much experience in managing others—the founders fail to appreciate that the volunteers and paid staff they bring on board may not share the founders' sense of mission. Although your nonprofit will tend to attract staff and volunteers who are genuinely interested in your goals, this does not necessarily mean that they will be as self-motivated (or, in some instances, as maniacally committed) as the people who got the nonprofit started.

What this means, practically speaking, is that you may have to find two (or three) volunteer staffers

---

### Domestic Comfort Foundation:
### A Medium-to-Large Nonprofit Run by an Executive Director

Domestic Comfort Foundation is a (fictional) nonprofit dedicated to providing financial support to families of military personnel away on active duty. The nonprofit started as a group of military families who met on an informal basis for a couple of years, then decided to organize a nonprofit foundation to raise money for military families in need. When the group incorporated, seven people sat on Domestic Comfort's first board, and it fell to them to figure out how to manage the nonprofit's work.

The initial board saw that their Aid to Families program would involve several components: developing program criteria and procedures, publicizing the program, soliciting applications, reviewing applications, accepting or rejecting the applications, and fulfillment (generating checks and sending them to the families). The board also decided that the program should include sending care packages to the military personnel of families whose applications are accepted. This would involve purchasing and packaging the items for the care packages and shipping them. Finally, they knew that fundraising would be a major ongoing activity.

The initial board decided that board members should focus primarily on fundraising efforts, while a few volunteers and paid staffers handled the tasks involved in the Aid to Families program. The board figured that three paid, part-time staff and five regular volunteers would be sufficient. Because board members would be engaged in fundraising efforts, they decided to hire an executive director to manage the staff and volunteers. After a few months of fundraising, Domestic Comfort had enough funds to hire staff. The group started by hiring an executive director, Sara, who in turn hired three part-time paid employees and recruited five volunteers.

In Domestic Comfort's first year of operation, Sara directly managed all of the staff and volunteers in running the Aid to Families program. At board meetings, Sara reported to the board on every aspect of the program's operation.

In its second year, Domestic Comfort was deluged with applications to the Aid to Families program. The board decided that it was time for the nonprofit to grow, hire more staff, and raise more money in order to meet the needs of the community it wanted to serve. They approved a new budget and charged Sara with recruiting enough staff to increase the number of accepted applications by 30%. Sara promoted the three current part-time employees to full-time staffers, hired five additional part-time paid staff, and recruited eight more volunteers.

To handle this many staff and volunteers, Sara created a more complex management structure: She divided the workers into a marketing division, an application processing division, a fulfillment division, a care packages division, and a fundraising division, each with one person in charge. With this new structure in place, Sara interacted with the division heads instead of managing all workers directly. Division heads were sometimes invited to board meetings to report more detailed information than Sara could readily provide. Creating an additional management layer added a bit more complexity, but it also allowed the nonprofit to run much more efficiently.

to do the same work that one super-committed, mission-consumed founder might accomplish. Because newcomers probably won't be as far along on the learning curve, you also will need to provide appropriate training and guidance to staff and volunteers alike. In other words, directors will have to actually direct. As enthusiastic and energetic as new staff or volunteers may be, they shouldn't have to figure out what their jobs are or what you expect them to do.

On the flip side, don't create an environment where you don't make good use of the inspiration and initiative of those who do want to get more involved. If you sense that someone wants an active role in the organization, be open to it. Make sure everyone knows that ideas, insights, and suggestions about the way things are or should work are welcome. The last thing you want to do is shut out those who can be the most valuable to your organization: motivated, creative people who want to take an active role in building your organization and working toward its mission.

## Issues With Founders

For new nonprofits especially, the close relationship between the nonprofit and its founders can become problematic. In an extreme case, a nonprofit becomes so closely identified with its founders that it might not be able to exist without them. In a nonprofit's earliest start-up days, this may be unavoidable and shouldn't cause too much concern. But before long, the nonprofit must begin to develop an independent identity. Certainly this separation process must begin before the nonprofit loses key founders and risks a loss of momentum—or outright failure.

One practical way to cope with overreliance on a founder is to distribute management duties so that others are clearly responsible for important operations. If the founder is on the nonprofit's board, part of the solution is to make sure that the board is diverse, balanced, and regularly infused with new blood. (Building your board is covered in Chapter 4.) Especially if the nonprofit relies primarily on its board members to manage the group, make sure that the founders don't monopolize too

many key responsibilities. Do your best to disperse management power evenly across the board and make sure everyone—including the founders—honors this division of power.

Founders who serve as executive directors need to understand the proper role of an executive director—in particular, that the executive director is accountable to the board, not the other way around. While the founder/executive director will undoubtedly have plenty to contribute in terms of maintaining and defining the nonprofit's course, the founder/executive director must acknowledge that policy decisions are ultimately up to the board, and the executive director's role is to put those policies into action. More than a few founders who have taken the role of executive director have learned the hard way that there is indeed some loss of power by taking the executive director position. In some cases, founders have even been fired by the board when differences of opinion (or outright conflict) couldn't be resolved.

Even when they intellectually understand the proper roles within a nonprofit, some founders just can't resist the urge to try to control everything. Sometimes dubbed founder's syndrome or "founderitis," this condition can be difficult to treat because staff and board members tend to defer to the founder and are reluctant to criticize a founder's actions. But it's critically important that a nonprofit's board members and staff be left to fulfill their roles and duties without the founder's constant meddling.

*Marie Nord founded Erda Gardens as a community organization and a functioning farm. While a small group of people were involved with the farm along with Marie, it was pretty much a one-woman show—Marie was not only the founder but also the farmer. After her sudden death we were left without any structure, any man- or womanpower, and without much hope. We held a half-memorial, half-business meeting and a "core group" of volunteers emerged. This group was made up of people who had been with the farm for years but who played only minor roles or no role at all while Marie was alive.*

## Tips for Founders: Diagnosing and Curing Your Founderitis

All you founders out there, listen up. Take a good look at the way you interact with your nonprofit, including the board members and any staff and volunteers. Do you have a clear sense of where your job ends and another position begins? Do you feel that the nonprofit could run okay without you for a month or two? Do you give staff or volunteers space to do their jobs without undue interference? If you answer "no" to any of the above questions, you may have a touch (or maybe even a raging case) of founderitis.

If you find yourself afflicted, here are some tips for clearing it up:

- **Educate yourself on your proper role.** Reading books like this one is a good way to learn the distinctions between different roles at a nonprofit. Knowing the boundaries between roles is a first step toward observing them.
- **Let others do their jobs without interference.** While you undoubtedly have a wealth of good ideas, don't drown the staff and volunteers in your brainstorms instead of letting them work independently. If you have a management position over certain workers, constantly peppering them with your ideas about how they could do their jobs better is sure to be an annoyance. Unless an issue is truly pressing or glaring, save your critiques for official performance reviews. If you don't have a management role, then keep your ideas to yourself or pass them to the person who does have management authority—and let that manager decide what to do with your suggestion.
- **Embrace situations in which you aren't the boss.** For example, if you're helping as a volunteer during an event—say, a Clean Up the Beach Day— be sure to let the person who's running the event actually be in charge. By making it clear to the event coordinator that you're willing and eager to take direction, you'll help build trust and respect between you and staff, and in turn help nurture a healthy and efficient staff hierarchy.

## Seek Sustainability

Mona Lisa Wallace, Esq., is a California attorney who has played a key role in several successful nonprofit and socially responsible start-ups. She served as the executive director of the East Bay Nonprofit Center, providing management support for Bay Area nonprofits. She offers the following advice on how to maintain balance during your start-up days.

*Nonprofit leaders are driven by a focus on their mission. Often profoundly more personally committed than for-profit entrepreneurs, many nonprofit founders make exceptional sacrifices financially, temporally, and spiritually. Of course, saving the planet, sheltering the needy, and empowering the disenfranchised are noble justifications for working long hours, skipping workouts, and missing meals. But burnout, family conflict, substance abuse, and social isolation are real risks that can creep up unnoticed during periods of intense work. It's essential to protect your nonprofit's sustainability by protecting its key resource: you.*

*Learning to prioritize and compartmentalize can help you retain balance in your work and personal life. I suggest starting by making four lists:*

1. *Important now: For example, finish proposal by tomorrow's deadline.*
2. *Important later: For example, relocate to a larger office.*
3. *Less important now: For example, repair the copier.*
4. *Less important later: For example, pay parking tickets (just kidding).*

*Also, practice putting your work away periodically. One helpful visualization is to picture empty cubbyholes where you can stash the incomplete brochure, the proposal deadline, or whatever else is foremost on your four lists. With your tasks cleared off your mental plate, you can take off your manager hat and just be yourself for a while. Take mental and physical time for yourself, your family, and loved ones so you can continue your good work long into the future.*

*The group has evolved, and we have all shouldered tremendous responsibilities. Now we remain an all-volunteer organization, with the exception of our farmer and a few apprentices. We have created a much stronger structure and identity as an organization and have developed ties with many members of the community. People used to know Marie, now they know the farm. We document everything, and we are slowly building an organization in which none of us is essential. I think Marie would be very proud.*

**Erika Harding—Core Group member, Erda Gardens and Learning Center, Inc. Albuquerque, New Mexico**

Painful as it may be, a founderitis problem must be confronted, usually by other board members. The best way to address a problem founder will depend on the founder's personality—some might need gentle handling while others will need a kick in the pants. In most cases, you'll want to start by having a rational conversation with the founder, pointing out the problem behavior and explaining the importance of distributing power and responsibilities throughout the organization. It always helps to recognize the founder's good intentions and to avoid an accusatory tone.

## Hiring an Executive Director

One of the board's primary tasks is to hire and manage the organization's chief executive, commonly called the executive director. While the board's role is to establish and guide the organization's overall direction, the executive director is in charge of carrying out the programs and other plans outlined by the board.

### Are You Ready for an Executive Director?

In a nonprofit's early days, the president or another board member often fills the role of an executive director. Many new nonprofits don't have the cash to pay an executive director's salary; others simply aren't ready for the responsibility of hiring and managing an executive director. And many fear—often justifiably—that hiring senior staff may disempower the president or other volunteer leaders. Even when nonprofits can afford paid staff, they may be better served by hiring an office manager rather than an executive director.

*The Santa Fe Alliance grew dramatically in the first 18 months of its existence, due primarily to dedicated volunteers and a very clear mission/vision statement. It is our belief that as soon as you hire an executive director, you take the chance of losing some—or maybe even a lot—of your momentum. In most nonprofits I have been associated with, everyone looks to the executive director for everything. Unless you have a very experienced person in this role who can keep volunteer momentum going, your nonprofit becomes very vulnerable. You take the chance of losing the efforts of many dedicated volunteers working feverishly toward your vision, for the efforts of one.*

*So take your time developing your core group of volunteers to make sure they'll stay involved when you do add an executive director. Also, make sure the new executive director has strong abilities and experience in the areas of leadership. Do not expect a miracle from any executive director. Any executive director is just one person with the ability to do only a certain amount of work. Your executive director should focus on being a leader and stay out of the trenches.*

*Good luck, now go change the world!*

**David Kaseman—Cofounder, Santa Fe Alliance, a New Mexico 501(c)(3) nonprofit dedicated to promoting independent business and community**

A good rule of thumb is that if you have no paid staff, you don't need an executive director. Even if you have one or two office workers or volunteers, bringing in an executive director to manage them may be excessive; a board member may be able to do the job just fine. But as the number of paid staffers increases—say, to three or more—it is probably time to consider hiring an executive director. This is especially true if the staffers are involved in tasks beyond office management, such as executing the nonprofit's programs and services.

**CAUTION**

**Hiring an executive director can be traumatic.**
When an executive director is hired, the president and any other board members who had been managing staff and calling the shots day to day will have to pull back from daily management and restrict themselves to their board roles. This can sometimes be a touchy and territorial issue, but it's important to resolve it right away. Having the president or other board members stepping on the executive director's toes is a very common source of friction and conflict. Before hiring an executive director, define the position clearly and make sure all board members understand their new roles and responsibilities.

## The Executive Director's Role

Before hiring an executive director, you need to understand what this position is all about. Chapter 4 discusses the role of the board—specifically, that once senior staff is on board, it's not the board's job to oversee the day-to-day affairs of the nonprofit. Instead, this is the domain of the executive director. Once the board has established plans and policies for the nonprofit, it's the executive director's job to implement them—to put the "execute" in "executive director."

The specifics of an executive director's job will vary quite a bit from one nonprofit to the next. In a large, complex nonprofit, the executive director may manage several departments with dozens of people on staff; in a fledgling nonprofit, the director might be in charge of overseeing a simple program or two without any permanent employees. And in a nonprofit's early days, it might not even have an executive director at all.

While there's enormous diversity in what nonprofit executive directors do, their work generally falls into the following categories:

- implementing the board's plans and policies
- managing programs, activities, and general operations
- hiring and supervising staff
- monitoring and managing finances and accounting
- reporting information about the organization's activities to the board
- advising the board on policy and program issues

- assisting committees with program and fiscal policy development
- serving as a liaison between staff and the board, and
- communicating with the nonprofit's constituency.

### Should the Executive Director Sit on the Board?

It is generally not considered a good idea for an executive director to be a voting member of the board of directors. Perhaps the primary reason for this is that the board is responsible for managing and evaluating the executive director, so having the executive director on the board creates a conflict of interest. In addition, you risk serious tension if the executive director votes against other board members. Particularly if the board votes on a tightly divided, contentious issue, an executive director with board voting power faces a lose-lose situation no matter how he or she votes and is likely to have strained relations with the other board members who voted differently.

In addition, some state laws limit how many staffers may sit on a nonprofit board. In California, for example, at least half of a nonprofit's board must be made up of people who are neither paid staff (including the executive director, which is a staff position) nor family members of paid staff. (California Corporations Code § 5227.)

Some nonprofits allow the executive director to attend all board meetings as if he or she were a board member but do not give the executive director voting rights. This is sometimes called serving on the board ex officio—legal speak for "nonvoting."

## Hiring Criteria

Whether your nonprofit is large or small, the executive director's job is extremely important. This person generally plays a high-profile role in the inner workings of your organization and often becomes its public face as well. And, because the executive director is in charge of hiring staff, he or she will have an enormous impact on the overall character and quality of the organization. With this in mind, the board should be careful to choose an executive director who not only is qualified for the job, but also reflects its shared values and goals. Because most young nonprofits can't offer a salary that's anywhere near what a similar job in a for-profit organization would command, finding a skilled and dedicated executive director can be a real challenge.

Board members (often, a hiring committee) should begin the process of looking for an executive director by drafting a job description that outlines what they expect from their chief executive. While some of the director's responsibilities will likely be broad, the job description shouldn't speak entirely in generalities. Important tasks should be defined in detail, so applicants will know exactly what the job requires. For example, if the executive director will be expected to spearhead various fundraising initiatives, make sure the job description states this clearly. Or, if the board expects the executive director to attend all public hearings held by a city planning agency and issue press releases on the agency's decisions, say so in the job description—don't just list "public relations activities."

**TIP**

**Be clear about fundraising expectations.** Fundraising often becomes a contentious issue when the board and the executive director don't have the same expectations. It's a good idea to estimate what portion of the executive director's job should be devoted to fundraising. This can be expressed either as a percentage of the job (say, 25% or 50% of the director's time) or a number of hours per week or month.

Besides outlining basic job responsibilities, the board should also make a list of any specific skills, experience, or qualifications they want to see in an executive director. For instance, an educational nonprofit might want its executive director to have teaching experience. A nonprofit dedicated to promoting green space in urban centers might want someone who has a degree in urban planning and at least three years' experience in the field.

The board should also at least discuss the more subjective traits that they desire in their executive

director. Do you want an out-front cheerleader or a more thoughtful, policy type? Although these "softer" qualifications may be harder to define or to agree upon, it's a good idea to get them on the table for discussion before interviewing candidates. The more groundwork the board lays before seeking prospects, the easier the evaluation process will be. When you have a solid job description in hand, you'll be in a good position to draft a job announcement. While the detailed job description will be used internally, the announcement will be shorter and lighter on detail.

**RESOURCE**

**Need help writing job descriptions?** *The Job Description Handbook*, by Margie Mader-Clark (Nolo), provides step-by-step instructions on drafting legal, effective descriptions for any position. It also explains how to use job descriptions in hiring, orientation, evaluating performance, and more.

## Developing a Review Procedure

Every nonprofit should have some type of process in place to review the performance of the executive director, generally on an annual basis. The incoming executive director should be informed about the evaluation process upon taking office—what it will involve, when it will occur, and who will do it—which means that the board should come up with a process ahead of time.

Because the executive director is accountable to the board as a whole, all members of the board are typically involved in the process of evaluation. Often, an evaluation committee will spearhead the process. A common system is for each board member to fill out a survey evaluating the executive director's performance. The evaluation committee or one board member then compiles the surveys and goes over the results in a review meeting with the executive director. The outcome of the review will typically depend on the substance of the evaluation. For example, a salary raise might be in order if you can afford it and the executive director is going well beyond the call of duty. On the other hand, an executive director who is having trouble with his or her job might benefit from a list of areas that need improvement and a detailed discussion of what it will take to get back on track.

> ! CAUTION
>
> **Don't make promises you're not prepared to keep.** When you develop your review process, try to leave your options open. Don't guarantee that a good review will lead to a raise or promotion unless you are ready, willing, and able to follow through. If your director gets a great performance evaluation and asks for that promised raise, you'll have to give it—even if your nonprofit is struggling financially—or risk a lawsuit for breach of contract. The better course of action is to simply state that you will review the director's performance annually, without going into detail about what rewards might follow.

## Hiring and Managing Staff and Volunteers

Whether the people who work for your nonprofit are paid staffers or volunteers, the executive director (or whoever else fills this supervisory role) must hire and manage them with care. Obviously, it's important to hire only those people who can achieve the goals set for them. (Again, this presumes that goals have been set for workers before you start the hiring process—as discussed in more detail, below.) These workers will also need ongoing management to make sure they're doing a good job and dealing with any obstacles along the way.

Many nonprofits start off with all-volunteer help, including board members. Dedicated volunteers who are willing to carry out tedious but essential tasks are often critical to a nonprofit's survival in its early days, when budgets don't allow for paid staff. When a young nonprofit is able to afford paid staff, it's undoubtedly an exciting day—even if just a few part-timers are brought on board to stuff envelopes or help with office work.

This section outlines a simple, systematic approach to recruiting people to work for your nonprofit. The focus of this approach is on creating clearly defined positions and organizing them into an efficient

### Hire and Manage Your Volunteers Carefully

For many nonprofits, building a staff starts with recruiting volunteers. Thankfully for organizations all over the country, Americans are a charitable bunch. According to a U.S. Department of Labor survey, 64.3 million people— or 26.8% of the population—did volunteer work between September 2010 and September 2011, for a  median of 51 hours total. ("Volunteering in the United States, 2011," U.S. Bureau of Labor Statistics, February 2012.)

Don't make the mistake of thinking that you can be cavalier about recruiting and managing volunteers just because you're not paying them any wages. All staff— paid or not—have the potential to expose the nonprofit to liability, so it's essential that you hire only competent, responsible people. Liability issues aside, some volunteers may represent your organization to the public, putting your nonprofit's reputation at stake. You'll certainly want to recruit only those volunteers who demonstrate good judgment and people skills to be your public face.

For your day-to-day success, you'll want to recruit capable, hardworking volunteers to get the work done. Although it's not realistic to demand as much time or expertise from unpaid volunteers as you would from paid staffers, they certainly must be competent to do the work. It may be difficult to turn away eager but inappropriate volunteers, but you should just say no if they don't offer the skills or experience you need. Remember, volunteers never really come free; the costs of managing them—and fixing their mistakes, if necessary— can really add up. Getting rid of a troublesome volunteer will almost surely take more time and cause more headaches than never hiring him or her in the first place.

The good news is that developing even a small volunteer workforce offers nonprofits a great opportunity to develop effective management habits. Especially if the board members of a new nonprofit have little or no management experience, this is a good way for them to learn basic skills such as creating clear job descriptions, interviewing prospects, and monitoring performance. When it's time to hire paid staffers, this experience will be invaluable.

---

### Personal Issues ... er, I Mean Personnel Issues in a Small Nonprofit

- Giovanna Rossi served as the Executive Director of NARAL Pro-Choice New Mexico (www.prochoicenewmexico.org) and knows first-hand the challenges of hiring staffers for a small nonprofit. She offers the following perspective and advice on how to rise to the challenge.

  *If you've mastered the art of dating, you're well on your way to understanding the personnel puzzle. Finding and hiring qualified staffers that fit well with your organization is surprisingly similar to the dating game: You identify your needs and then attempt to find someone qualified and able to meet them. Of course, neither hiring staff nor dating is easy. Here are my answers for the questions that will likely haunt you at night as you tackle the staffing game.*

- When is it right for me to enter into a relationship with someone?

  *You'll know you're ready when you can't imagine spending another 14 hours alone in that office. However, you should never rush into something just because you're desperate (that's so unattractive). A good interview process should include a minimum of two meetings and a written exercise—not just a writing sample, but an exercise directly related to the position you're filling and your organization's work.*

- Why is it so difficult to find someone who fits what I'm looking for?

  *By the very nature of being a small organization, staff must be multitalented (able to write a research report and use Excel spreadsheets), flexible (as in, "Yes, I know we said we'd do that today, but one of our big donors just called and wants to have lunch"), and have compatible*

  *personalities (you don't want five introverts in the same office together).*

  Now that the timing is right, how do I know if he/she is "the one"?

  *Trial and error is the best policy; put her/him on a three-month probation period, with clear, measurable goals and a weekly reporting system so you can evaluate as you go.*

- What if it doesn't work out?

  *While it's disappointing and can throw you off track for a little while, don't be too rattled. Minimize the negative impact and get right back into the game by hiring a temp or going through the file of resumes that made it to the second interview but did not get picked the first time.*

- When it's a good fit, how do we develop a lasting relationship?

  *If you demonstrate your willingness to commit by offering positive feedback, more responsibility, and leadership opportunities, you will find she/he will rise to the challenge. And be sure to complete the six-month and one-year evaluations on time—do not put this off.*

- Why not avoid the pain and go it alone?

  *Well, that would just be plain stupid.*

  *Carefully selecting a staff person, and cultivating and managing that relationship so that it's mutually beneficial, is perhaps the most challenging part of running a small nonprofit organization. But the payoff is huge: Having quality staffers is a major asset to your organization. Remember, love at first sight is very rare; it can take several attempts to find what you're looking for.*

---

structure. Remember, a common scenario is for the board to hire an executive director or top manager, who in turn hires staff, sometimes with the advice and consent of a few key board members. Other times, the board may want to hire a more entry-level position like a part-time office assistant or volunteer. The following information will help in hiring for any position.

### Determine What Tasks Need to Be Done

The first step in recruiting volunteers or hiring staff is to clearly define what needs to be done. Do you need help answering phones? Keeping databases current? Organizing events? Planning the year's work schedule? Raising funds? The clearer the executive director or other manager is about what needs to be done, the easier it will be for workers to meet these expectations.

When outlining tasks, focus on those that really help accomplish the goals and objectives outlined by the board. The task list should be realistic and achievable based on the resources available, not a massive laundry list that includes every activity ever contemplated by the nonprofit. If the executive director feels that the board is asking for too much, too soon, or for some other reason finds the list getting out of control, he or she may need to consult the board and explain that its plans are unrealistic based on the resources at hand.

---

### Resources for Recruiting Volunteers

When looking for volunteers, make sure to tap into the many resources and communities online created just for this purpose.

Several national websites offer networks and databases that nonprofits and volunteers can use to connect with each other. At sites like HandsOnNetwork.org, Idealist. org, VolunteerMatch.org, and Craigslist.com, for example, nonprofits can advertise volunteer opportunities and browse listings of available volunteers. Many colleges, nonprofits and other organizations, including local chapters of the United Way, offer similar online networks at a local level.

Third-party volunteer placement organizations are another source of volunteers. For example, AmeriCorps (a program of the Corporation for National and Community Service, see www.americorps.gov) manages a broad set of programs that organize and place volunteers with nonprofits big and small nationwide. Similarly, the Retired Senior Volunteer Program (RSVP, see www.seniorcorps. gov/about/programs/rsvp.asp) is a federal program that places senior-citizen volunteers (those who are 55 or older) with nonprofits.

Also remember to look into local organizations like Rotary Clubs, churches, trade associations and other community-oriented groups who are often willing to volunteer for community causes.

For more ideas, be sure to read *The Nonprofit's Guide to Human Resources: Managing Your Employees & Volunteers* by Jan Masaoka (Nolo). It offers a wealth of ideas for recruiting and managing a solid crew of volunteers.

---

## Create Positions and Job Descriptions

With a solid and realistic task list in hand, the next step is to group tasks together for each staff or volunteer position. Certain activities will fall together naturally. For instance, the tasks of answering phones, updating membership databases, managing office supplies, and doing very basic bookkeeping might combine well into one position. Hiring and managing volunteers might similarly fall into a distinct task set. Handling event details—such as setting up and breaking down events and signing in event participants—is another set of tasks commonly handled by the same person or team.

Once tasks are grouped together, you can create job positions to handle those areas. The office tasks mentioned above, for instance, could go to an office manager. Tasks such as hiring and managing volunteers might well be headed by a volunteer coordinator. Event assistance (set-up, break-down, participant sign-in, and so on) might not warrant a permanent, specific position, but could be handled by one or more "event specialist" volunteers. Obviously, how you define specific positions for your group will depend on many different factors, including budgeting considerations.

You should write a formal job description for each permanent position. Creating a job description for each position not only will help in the hiring process but will also be valuable when it's time to review the worker's performance. Fortunately, writing job descriptions should be easy if you have created the position from a task-based to-do list; the job description can simply restate the list in a slightly more polished form.

Another good reason to have formal, written job descriptions relates to liability issues. If a staff member or volunteer accidentally injures someone or otherwise causes damage, it can sometimes be unclear whether the accident happened while the worker was doing nonprofit business. A formal job description will indicate which activities are, in fact, part of the worker's duties. If the accident occurred outside the scope of the worker's job, then the nonprofit generally won't be liable for the accident. (Chapter 7 covers liability issues in detail.)

## Develop Staff Hierarchies

If your nonprofit will have five or more regular staffers (either paid or volunteer), it's important to take the time to designate clear lines of authority and accountability. In small groups, this often means that everyone reports to the executive director (or the board president, in all-volunteer groups). As the organization grows, you'll probably want to add a second layer of managerial accountability—for example, to require the volunteers who run your Canoes in the Creek program to report to the program director, not directly to the executive director. Creating departments with department heads can also be a good way to organize a larger staff.

## Create Review Procedures

As discussed above in the section on hiring an executive director, your nonprofit should have an evaluation procedure in place before hiring anyone. That way, new employees and key volunteers know what to expect from the very first day. The review procedure needn't be complex; it might simply identify who will participate in reviews, when they will occur, and the criteria by which staff and volunteers will be measured.

## Create a Staff/Volunteer Handbook

Like the board guidebook discussed in Chapter 4, a handbook for staff and volunteers serves a vital role. A handbook gives everyone ready access to important information about their jobs. Even more important, creating a staff and volunteer handbook is a powerful way to minimize the risks posed by any paid or volunteer staffer that works for your nonprofit. As discussed in more detail in Chapter 7, a nonprofit's potential risk of a liability or contract lawsuit go way up as soon as you bring on even one employee or volunteer. Not only can that worker potentially harm someone and expose the nonprofit to a lawsuit, but

### Rules for Volunteers

In the eyes of the law, volunteers are neither fish (employees) nor fowl (independent contractors). This murky legal status can be treacherous: If a worker is determined to be an employee and not actually a volunteer, a whole host of workplace laws (minimum wage laws, overtime laws, and workers' compensation coverage, for example) and various taxes may apply to that worker.

Courts that have considered whether a worker is truly a volunteer have used an "economic reality" test. This test considers factors such as to what degree the worker is dependent on the employer, and whether the worker had any reasonable expectation of being compensated for doing work, either at the time the volunteer began working or in the future.

While volunteers can be reimbursed for out-of-pocket expenses and can even receive "nominal" benefits, they cannot retain their status as volunteers if they depend on this compensation as a basic necessity. If a court finds that a worker is dependent on food, lodging, reimbursements for miscellaneous expenses, or other compensation, a court may determine that the worker is not truly a volunteer but rather an employee. This is definitely a situation you want to avoid, at the risk of having to pay back wages, taxes, and penalties.

Workers that qualify as true volunteers will not be subject to many laws and taxes that apply to employees. However, volunteers may be protected by some laws, such as federal or state workplace safety regulations. Some states extend federal Occupational Safety and Health Administration (OSHA) regulations to volunteers, and others protect volunteers with their own safety laws. In addition, some states protect volunteers from workplace discrimination and/or impose other requirements on those who employ volunteers. To find out your state's requirements, contact your state labor department.

he or she also could sue the nonprofit for a host of discrimination, wrongful termination, or other claims.

Creating a guidebook that outlines clear policies for employees and volunteers will go a long way toward minimizing these risks. To create a handbook, the executive director or top manager will have to spend some time coming up with a set of rules for workers to follow and procedures the nonprofit will use in dealing with workers. Facing and answering these questions will help ensure that your employment practices are sound. And compiling these policies in a guidebook promotes positive staff relations by demonstrating your nonprofit's commitment to fair treatment for all workers, according to the same set of rules. By offering clearly stated expectations and procedures for treating workers consistently, a handbook provides a powerful deterrent to future workplace trouble.

A staff/volunteer handbook might start with the nonprofit's mission and history, then outline the policies and procedures that apply to the staff and volunteers. Your handbook can be much like the ones typically used in for-profit companies, except that yours will also specifically address volunteers. Employee handbooks typically include information on:

- hiring
- hours and flex time
- sick and vacation leave
- parental leave
- employee benefits
- performance review procedures
- workplace behavior
- health and safety
- employee privacy
- conflicts of interest
- discrimination and harassment
- grievance procedures, and
- termination.

 **RESOURCE**

**Resources for creating your staff/volunteer handbook.** While the details of creating a staff/volunteer handbook are beyond the scope of this book, all nonprofits with any paid or volunteer workers would be wise to take this task seriously. An excellent guide is Nolo's *Create Your Own Employee Handbook,* by Lisa Guerin and Amy DelPo. This book walks you step by step through creating an employee handbook, explaining the issues and offering sample language you can modify to fit your workplace.

Lots of new nonprofits find the prospect of creating a staff/volunteer handbook too overwhelming in their harried early days. While this is understandable, it's a good idea to tackle the task earlier rather than later. Of course, it will be easier to create a handbook before the staff grows large and complex. Also, remember that while the articles of incorporation and bylaws cover basic personnel issues for the board of directors, they typically don't address detailed staff management issues. It's simply unwise to have more than a few workers without a written policy manual.

## Orient New Workers

When staffers or volunteers come on board, it's important to take some time to introduce them to your world. For efficiency's sake, it's a great idea to create a standard orientation process—it could be a video shown in a conference room, a short meeting at a local café, a walk-through of the nonprofit's office, or a get-together at a board member's house—to explain the ins and outs of working for the nonprofit. If and when you have several workers coming on board at once, you can save time by orienting them as a group.

While all new workers should receive basic information about the nonprofit's mission and activities, you'll want to provide a more extensive orientation for higher-level positions. For example, the board may want to spend a significant amount of time with the executive director—say, a series of meetings over a few days—to make sure he or she really understands what the nonprofit is about and how the board wants it to be run. This might include discussing the nonprofit's history and any past problems that the board does not want to see repeated. For regular staffers or volunteers, on the other hand, this much information would be overkill. The point here is to keep those whom you are orienting in mind when deciding what information to include in your orientation sessions.

A good starting point is to provide each new worker with a copy of your staff/volunteer handbook. Beyond that, the type of orientation may well depend on how many staffers or volunteers are involved. If you're starting out with just a handful of staff or volunteers, perhaps a couple hours of orientation followed by lunch might work. (Keep in mind that it generally makes sense to have separate orientation sessions for paid staff and volunteers.) As your staff grows, you may want to have new workers attend presentations by the executive director and possibly others. Pairing new staffers with experienced ones for a mentorship period is also a good way to bring newcomers into the group.

## Employees and Independent Contractors

There are two different types of paid workers: employees and independent contractors (ICs). Different legal and tax rules apply to each, so it's essential that you understand the difference between the two. If your workers fit the description of employees, you'll be subject to a number of state and federal laws that must be strictly observed and taxes that must be paid. If, on the other hand, your workers can be characterized as ICs, you'll be spared many—but not all—of these requirements.

### Laws and Taxes

The law puts all paid workers, whether at for-profit or nonprofit firms, into one of two categories: employees or independent contractors. (Unpaid workers fall into another category, "volunteers," whose status is less firmly established in law. See "Rules for Volunteers," above, for an overview.) In some situations, you may have some flexibility to place paid workers in one category or the other. For the most part, however, the law decides for you.

In a nutshell, an employee is someone who works for you, on your site, with your tools and equipment, and according to your rules and procedures. ICs, on the other hand, are in business for themselves; they work on their own time with their own tools and often perform services for a number of different clients.

This distinction is very important because anyone who hires an employee (again, whether you're a nonprofit or for-profit company) is subject to a number of taxes, such as payroll tax and unemployment tax, plus many state and federal legal requirements governing pay, hours worked, time off, and so on. By contrast, when you hire an IC, you have fewer rules to follow and taxes to pay. If you treat a worker that the law clearly regards as an employee as an independent contractor, you risk subjecting yourself to a huge back tax bill, plus interest and other state and federal penalties.

### IRS Criteria

To stay out of trouble with the IRS, you should understand how it decides whether a worker is an employee or an IC. Keep in mind, however, that your state may have its own rules about classifying workers, which might be stricter than or otherwise different from the IRS rules. Because state penalties can be at least as harsh as those imposed by the IRS, make sure you also understand the rules in your state. An experienced accountant should be able to help you with this. Or contact your state's agency in charge of worker status rules—generally your state's labor (or unemployment) agency or tax department.

The IRS has some guidelines it uses to decide whether a particular worker should be treated as an employee or an IC. As a general rule, the IRS says a worker is an employee if you have the right to control how the work gets done. The IRS considers a worker to be an employee when he or she:

- works only for you and not for any other nonprofit or business
- works on your premises
- uses your tools and equipment
- follows work hours set by you
- follows your instructions on how to complete a job
- receives reimbursement for expenses incurred in doing a job
- can be fired at any time, with or without good cause

- supervises any of your other workers, and/or
- receives any employee benefits, such as holiday pay, vacation time, or health insurance.

On the flip side, the IRS says your worker should probably be considered an independent contractor if you "have the right to control or direct only the result of the work done … and not the means and methods of accomplishing the result." (IRS Publication 15-A, *Employer's Supplemental Tax Guide*.) The IRS considers workers to be independent contractors when they:

- work for a number of different nonprofits, businesses, or clients
- are incorporated as independent businesses
- have their own office, studio, garage, or other permanent place to work
- use their own equipment and tools
- set their own hours
- use their own judgment as to how best to complete a job
- don't get reimbursed for expenses incurred in doing a job, and/or
- advertise their services to the public.

If a worker you hire displays some characteristics of both categories, it can be hard to figure out how that worker should be classified. Ultimately, you'll need to consider the factors outlined above, weigh them against each other, and possibly get expert advice to decide whether a worker should be classified as an employee or as an independent contractor.

EXAMPLE: Debbie does a lot of freelance writing and editing for a nonprofit health care foundation, The Health Trust. She works quite a bit for The Health Trust, editing about six big projects per year, but also does four or five jobs per year for other nonprofits and for-profit businesses. Debbie always works at home, receives minimal instructions as to how to do her work, and does her writing and editing according to her own schedule. Debbie can probably be categorized as an independent contractor.

Another worker, Sascha, holds the title of Editorial Writer at The Health Trust. He works pretty much exclusively for the nonprofit, though occasionally he takes on an outside project, such as writing an article for a health care magazine. Sascha works from home a couple of days per week but has a desk and computer at The Health Trust's office. He works closely with the editorial staff at The Health Trust and has some management responsibility over a couple of editorial assistants. The government is likely to see Sascha as an employee. It would be risky to try to treat him as an independent contractor.

In borderline situations, it's safer to treat a worker as an employee than to risk the penalties that may result if the IRS or your state decides you've misclassified an employee as an IC. The IRS and most states tend to disfavor independent contractor status: They'd much rather see borderline workers treated as employees—so that their employers can withhold taxes from their paychecks—than as ICs who are responsible for reporting and paying their own taxes.

The IRS offers more information online and in printed guides about how to distinguish employees from independent contractors. Publication 15-A, *Employer's Supplemental Tax Guide*, offers more specific information on classifying workers as employees or ICs. IRS Publication 1779, *Independent Contractor or Employee*, is a short fact sheet with useful tips. Another source of information is the IRS internal training manual, "Independent Contractor or Employee?" While this guide is not legally binding, it's a useful window into how auditors determine worker status. All these guides can be downloaded from the IRS website at www.irs.gov (look in the "Small Business and Self-Employed" section).

If you still can't decide how one of your workers should be classified, there are a few ways you can proceed. One is to consult a lawyer or an accountant who understands business tax laws. Another option is to go straight to the horse's mouth and ask the IRS or your state agency to tell you how it would classify a certain worker. The IRS will classify your worker for you if you file Form SS-8, *Determination of Worker Status for Purposes of Federal Employment Taxes and Income Tax Withholding,* to request a formal ruling on a worker's status. You can get this form from an IRS office or from its website, at www.irs.gov. (Don't be surprised if the IRS says your worker is an employee!)

For a state determination, contact your state employment or other agency that governs worker classification and find out what procedure it uses. Like the IRS, it's common for state agencies to classify workers as employees rather than independent contractors. You'll have to decide for yourself whether to leave the determination up to these agencies or decide how to classify your workers on your own.

## Required Paperwork, Filings, and Taxes

When hiring any workers—employees or independent contractors—you'll need to deal with some bureaucratic tasks. As described below, you'll have more work to do when hiring employees than ICs, but hiring independent contractors does trigger a requirement or two as well. This section outlines some tasks to anticipate when hiring either type of worker.

### Rules for Employers

A raft of legal and tax requirements kick in when you hire your first employee. Most of these apply to all employers, whether nonprofit or for profit. Not only will you have to pay a number of employment taxes, but you'll also need to register with several government agencies, buy certain types of required insurance, and comply with various federal and state laws, such as those requiring you to keep a smoke-free workplace and to post certain notices at your nonprofit's premises.

While the details of the many laws that apply to employers are beyond the scope of this book, the major requirements are listed below. If your needs can't be met by hiring an independent contractor and you must hire an employee, you'll need to consult additional resources to make sure you comply with the many state and federal laws governing employers. (Some excellent sources of information are listed below.)

In general, nonprofits with one or more employees are required to do the following:

- Comply with state and federal wage and hours laws. The federal Fair Labor Standards Act establishes a federal minimum wage (currently $7.25 per hour as of July 2009) and rules for paying overtime. Many states also have their own wage and hour laws, and some impose a higher minimum wage or more generous overtime rules than the federal government.

- Obtain workers' compensation insurance and follow rules on notifying employees of their right to workers' compensation benefits. You may typically purchase this insurance from a state fund or from a private workers' compensation insurance company.

- Comply with state and federal job safety laws, administered by the federal Occupational Safety & Health Administration (OSHA) and the agency in your state that governs workplace safety. Among other things, these laws require you to file an illness and injury prevention plan, report work-related injuries and illnesses that result in lost work time, and keep a log of all work-related injuries and illnesses. For more information about OSHA regulations, visit the OSHA website at www.osha.gov, or call OSHA at 800-321-OSHA (6742).

- Withhold federal income taxes and FICA taxes (Social Security and Medicare taxes) from employees' paychecks and periodically report and send these withheld taxes to the IRS.

- Report wages and withholding to each employee and to the IRS with Form W-2.

- Pay the employer's portion of Social Security and Medicare tax for each employee, based on the employee's wages.

- Withhold state income taxes from employees' paychecks and periodically deposit them with your state income tax agency.

- Pay federal unemployment taxes. It's the sole responsibility of the employer to pay the Federal Unemployment Tax (FUTA) directly to the IRS; you may not deduct it from employees' paychecks. You must report FUTA taxes paid annually on IRS Form 940, *Employer's Annual Federal Unemployment Tax Return.*

- Pay state unemployment taxes (not in all states). Most states require employers to pay unemployment taxes, which go into a state unemployment insurance fund. Generally, you can take a credit against your FUTA tax for amounts you paid into state unemployment funds. A list of state unemployment tax agencies is available in IRS Publication 926, *Household Employer's Tax Guide*, available from the IRS's website at www. irs.gov.

If you're overwhelmed by this list, you may want to consider whether you can meet your needs with a combination of paid independent contractors and volunteers. At the very least, you shouldn't jump into hiring employees without having a very good reason to do so.

**RESOURCE**

**Additional resources on hiring employees.** Nolo publishes several books and other resources on hiring employees (see Nolo Resources on Employment Issues in Chapter 7). For hiring issues related specifically to nonprofits, see *The Nonprofit's Guide to Human Resources*, by Jan Masaoka (Nolo) .

## Rules When Hiring ICs

While hiring independent contractors is generally much simpler than hiring employees (and avoids several taxes), it does trigger some legal requirements. One of the main rules is that if you pay any independent contractor more than $600 in a year, you need to report those payments on Form 1099, which you must send to the worker and the IRS. If the IC is doing business as a corporation, you don't have to file a 1099 (unless the IC has formed a medical corporation).

When hiring an IC, be sure to get basic information for your records, both for reporting purposes and to have as documentation in case of an audit. At a minimum, make sure you get the IC's business name, address, and federal taxpayer ID number. The easiest way to obtain this is to have the IC fill out and sign IRS form W-9, *Request for Taxpayer Identification*

*Number and Certification.* You'll keep this form in your files; you don't have to submit it to the IRS. ICs who operate as sole proprietorships without any employees may simply use their Social Security numbers as their taxpayer IDs. Other ICs will have obtained employer identification numbers (EINs) from the IRS for their businesses. Either one is fine.

If you can't or don't obtain the IC's taxpayer ID number, you may need to withhold payments from the IC and deposit them to the IRS. Called "backup withholding," this is required if you do not have the IC's taxpayer ID number and you pay the IC $600 or more during the year. For more information on backup withholding, see the instructions for IRS Form 945, *Annual Return of Withheld Federal Income Tax.*

**TIP**

**Put your IC agreements in writing.** While it may not be legally required, it's always a good idea to use a written contract when you hire an IC. Besides helping to avert garden-variety conflicts over the terms of the job, having a contract in place will also help you prove that the worker is an independent contractor, not an employee. By stating in your agreement that the worker is an independent contractor, you are establishing an intent to create an independent contractor relationship. This may turn out to be helpful evidence in the case of an audit. If all other evidence demonstrates that the worker is an employee, however, that's how the IRS and your state will probably classify him or her. Remember, the only true test of a worker's status is how the worker is actually treated. If you treat workers as employees—require them to work on site, define their hours, closely supervise their work, and so on—merely calling them independent contractors in your contracts won't magically change their status.

**RESOURCE**

**More resources on independent contractors.** For detailed information about hiring independent contractors and sample IC contracts, see *Working With Independent Contractors,* by Stephen Fishman (Nolo). Also check out Nolo's website at www.nolo.com for free information and other resources on hiring independent contractors.

## Checklist: Your Workforce—Staff and Volunteers

☐ Decide what type of management strategy will work best for your nonprofit. In general, the more activities and workers you have, the more structure you'll need to manage them.

☐ Outline the tasks that need to be done, group them into logical sets, and create staff positions.

☐ Write out a job description for each position.

☐ Outline a hierarchy of positions within the organization, indicating who reports to whom.

☐ Create policies for performance reviews.

☐ Create a user-friendly handbook for your staff and volunteers containing information about the nonprofit and all important workplace policies.

☐ Orient new workers soon after hiring them.

☐ Familiarize yourself with the legal differences between employees and independent contractors. Don't try to avoid the obligations of having employees by misclassifying your workers as independent contractors.

☐ Make sure you're ready to take care of all the legal, bureaucratic, and tax requirements that apply to employers *before* you hire your first employee.

# Fundraising

Once you've developed your strategic plan and initial budget, and brought in some people to get your organization up and running (with the help of the previous chapters), it's time to figure out how to raise the funds you will need to reach your goals. This chapter will help even the least-experienced fundraiser understand how to approach the fundraising process, from overall strategies to specific methods for bringing in money from special events and membership drives to using social media and crowdfunding. Even if you've already thought about how and where your organization will get funding—or, better yet, you've already lined up donors who are willing to provide the necessary start-up money—this chapter will help you turn your preliminary ideas into a solid fundraising plan for your organization.

**RESOURCE**

**Want detailed information on fundraising strategies?** This chapter provides the basic information you'll need to know about fundraising as you get your nonprofit off the ground. Once you're ready to kick your fundraising machine into gear, however, you will want more detailed information on fundraising strategies, methods, budgeting, planning, and more. You'll find everything you need in *Effective Fundraising for Nonprofits: Real-World Strategies That Work*, by Ilona Bray (Nolo). Another useful guide authored by Ilona Bray and published by Nolo is *The Volunteers' Guide to Fundraising*, a book that offers special fundraising strategies for nonprofessional fundraisers.

## The Golden Rules of Successful Fundraising

Before you can begin drafting a fundraising plan, you'll need to know some fundamental fundraising rules. Whether you're trying to raise a few hundred dollars or a few hundred thousand, following these five tried-and-true strategies will help you stay focused on your best prospects and improve your chances of success.

## Relationships Are Everything

Any professional fundraiser will tell you that the most successful fundraising efforts are built upon ongoing relationships with donors. Just as repeat customers are crucial to the success of most small businesses, committed supporters are essential to a nonprofit's success. The average American is asked for money dozens, if not hundreds, of times per year, to which he or she will almost always respond "No." As you well know, converting this "No" to a "Yes" is not an easy task; even the most persuasive canvasser or telemarketer probably won't be able to change your mind if you're just not willing or ready to donate. But once you donate to an organization for the first time, your mindset has changed. All of us are much more inclined to support an organization we have come to know and trust.

Because these ongoing relationships are so important, you should make every effort to build strong connections with your first-time donors so they continue to support your organization in the future. A prompt thank-you note is an obvious starting point for building this relationship; other methods of recognizing and encouraging supporters will vary from one organization to the next. But your fundamental goal is always the same: to nurture a strong, positive relationship with your supporters, so they find it a pleasure to support your group. If your supporters feel appreciated and believe the organization is doing good work, they gain something, too: pride and goodwill from contributing to your nonprofit's efforts (and perhaps a tax write-off as well).

**TIP**

**Contributors can provide more than just money.** Besides the valuable funding they provide, long-term contributors may offer many other means of support for your organization, including positive word of mouth, willingness to volunteer, and networking opportunities with their own contacts.

## Target the Best Potential Donors

It's important to focus your fundraising efforts on your most likely supporters, not on the whole wide world of people and groups who might possibly contribute to your organization. Few nonprofits have the resources to send out hundreds of direct mail appeals or blanket the television or radio airwaves with requests for support. Asking the right people—and using the right appeal for the people you approach—is key to cost-effective fundraising.

The best fundraising uses an "inside out" approach, focusing on those closest to the organization first and then widening the scope to target additional prospects. The board of directors and their close contacts, for example, should be the first people you solicit for funds, not the last. There may be great prospects "out there," some of whom might turn out to be deeply committed and generous supporters, but it makes more sense to begin spending your limited fundraising resources on the contacts closest to home.

Once you identify your targets, it's also important to spend some time figuring out what type of appeal is most likely to resonate with them before you ask them to donate. The better you understand the interests and motivations of your prospective donors—individuals, corporations, and foundations alike—the better you'll be able to tailor your fundraising appeals to reach your target audience. (Finding prospects is discussed in greater detail below.)

## Build a Compelling and Detailed Case

When you ask potential donors for money, you must have an absolutely compelling reason why they should support your organization. Why should donors reach into their pockets and give your group money they could spend on themselves or give to thousands of other good causes? As countless failing nonprofits have learned, just stating that your organization works for a worthwhile cause is unlikely to result in a pledge of support. To get people to donate now, it's best to convey a pressing need, a sense of urgency, and a specific program or project for which their donations are needed.

**EXAMPLE:** FoodAid, a nonprofit dedicated to sending food to drought-stricken developing countries, is creating a fundraising brochure. The office manager drafts the following text:

"FoodAid's mission is to provide food to starving people in underdeveloped areas stricken by drought. To carry out its mission, FoodAid needs your support. Please consider a tax-deductible donation of $50 to help us feed the hungry."

One board member (who happens to be a marketing copywriter) suggests that the brochure would be much more powerful if it conveyed a sense of urgency and provided specifics. He rewrites the draft to read as follows:

"FoodAid is committed to providing food shipments to starving people in underdeveloped areas stricken by drought. Without our food shipments, hundreds of children and adults will starve to death each year. We are currently in need of funds for a Spring food shipment to Brazil's drought-plagued Nordeste region, which is home to one-third of Brazil's population. Your tax-deductible donation of $50 will help us get the next shipment of food to those who desperately need it."

Many nonprofits have a variety of fundraising drives in any given year, some tailored to meet specific needs and some more general in nature. No matter what type of campaign you're planning, it's important to convey more than just your overall mission to potential donors. They want to know why you need money. By conveying a sense of urgency in your appeal, you are more likely to engage potential supporters and convince them to help.

*Fledgling nonprofits should test the merits and effectiveness of their program early on—aim to create a success story. It's much easier to raise money when you can point to specific things that you've done and successes you've achieved, rather than merely talking about what you have a mind to do.*

**Randolph Belle—Director of Information**
**East Bay Nonprofit Center**
**Oakland, California**

## Put Your Board of Directors to Work

A nonprofit's directors should be crucial players in the fundraising process. By agreeing to join the board, each member has made a commitment to keep the organization on track, which includes maintaining sound finances. At a minimum, board members should help locate and contact prospective donors in your community. This is especially important for fledgling nonprofits that haven't had the chance to develop relationships through their accomplishments. When a nonprofit has a short or nonexistent track record, its fundraising efforts depend largely on its board members' relationships in the community. All board members must understand this important role before they join the board so they will be active in forging relationships with key fundraising targets.

**TIP**

**Board members can take different fundraising roles.** While some board members will be better rainmakers than others, all should be involved in some aspect of the fundraising process. If a board member is very uncomfortable asking people for money, he or she could focus on creating fundraising materials or planning an event. No matter how they choose to participate, all board members should play a part in fundraising, whether behind the scenes or leading the charge.

Board members also typically help with fundraising by donating their own money to the organization. While you never want to exclude talented people from your board simply because they can't donate at a high level, board members should be among the first to contribute their own money to the nonprofit, in an amount they can afford. This not only provides crucial start-up money in a nonprofit's early days, but it also demonstrates to other potential donors that the board members are strongly committed to the organization.

In fact, foundations, government agencies, and other institutional donors commonly ask how much money the board contributes to the organization. Ideally, all members of the board should contribute at a level higher than your standard suggested contribution. Of course, this may not always be possible, but the closer you can get to this ideal, the better.

## Focus on the Big Picture

Always develop your fundraising goals with the big picture in mind, not just your group's immediate needs. Fundraising is an ongoing process, not a one-time event. The most effective fundraising plan will consider factors beyond immediate expenses; it will anticipate upcoming events or expected accomplishments and plan appropriate fundraising activities to support and capitalize on those events. Your fundraising efforts and your strategic plan should dovetail neatly so that you raise enough donations to fund your activities, and your activities, in turn, create opportunities for future fundraising.

Also keep in mind that it's easier to raise money with an impressive success story under your belt. For example, a fledgling nonprofit with minimal funds might plan to accomplish some meaningful (yet inexpensive) tasks early on so that it can point to those accomplishments when embarking on its first large-scale fundraising activity.

## Your Fundraising Plan

Because successful fundraising involves a swarm of large and small details (from deciding on fundraising tools to determining who will design the brochure and update the mailing list), it's crucial to establish a solid and clear fundraising plan: a prioritized list of tasks you'll need to accomplish to fund your activities successfully. The list below outlines some basic steps you'll have to take to develop a fundraising plan. Of course, each organization is different and your approach may vary somewhat, but most nonprofits will need to tackle the following tasks in one way or another:

1. **Determine your needs and your fundraising budget.** Before you can decide *how* to raise funds, you'll need to decide how much you must raise and how much you are willing and able to spend to execute your fundraising efforts.

2. **Compile a detailed list of prospects.** You'll need to identify who should be at the center of your fundraising efforts and who should be lower-priority targets. Most nonprofits seek funds from individuals, businesses (big and small), foundations, government agencies (local, state, and federal), and any other entities that may be interested in funding their efforts.

3. **Define your overall campaign.** Decide how many and what type of fundraising "pushes" you'll hold each year. For instance, a nonprofit may develop a plan to hold one membership drive, apply for three grants, and hold one fundraising event, supplemented by two issue-oriented special appeals each year.

4. **Choose your fundraising tactics.** Decide how you'll reach your potential contributors—for example, through social media, email, crowdfunding, street fairs, direct mail, or door-to-door canvassing.

5. **Research corporate and government funders and learn their applications processes.** If you plan to apply for grants, you'll need to learn about the funding priorities of the grant-givers and their rules and deadlines for applying for funds.

6. **Assign duties.** Once your plan is well defined, you'll need to delegate the various tasks to your staff and volunteers.

7. **Raise those funds!** Planning only takes you so far—at some point, it's time to roll up your sleeves and get to work.

The rest of this chapter looks at each of these tasks in greater detail.

*I have worked in the nonprofit field for more than 30 years—the last ten as a fundraising consultant—so I have worked with dozens and dozens of nonprofits in education, health care, social services, and the arts. To be successful in fundraising, it's important to start with a good plan and to involve talented and connected people in executing it.*

*Fundraising works best when it is mission driven. Make certain your staff, volunteers, and donors all know and believe in your organization's mission. Then, you can't fail.*

> **Michael D. Hohner—Fundraising consultant and President of Hohner & Company, LLC**
> **Oak Creek, Wisconsin**

## Define Your Fundraising Targets and Budget

Start your fundraising plan by figuring out how much money you need to raise and how much you can spend on your fundraising efforts. The amount of money you need will greatly influence the strategies you use to raise it. Raising $5,000 to feed the pets of homeless people will require a vastly different approach from raising $5 million to build a center to care for homeless people themselves.

Remember that you won't pocket every penny you raise—you'll need a reasonable budget to carry out your fundraising campaign. Printing costs, postage for mailings, and rental fees for special events are a few typical fundraising costs you may face. Unfortunately, you will probably have to pay at least a portion of these costs up front, before you've brought in your first dime of donations.

*Remember to create a sound model for success. Don't base your initial budgeting and planning on giving everything away for free. Draft a budget by accounting for all anticipated expenses and possible revenue; the difference is your fundraising goal.*

> **Randolph Belle—Director of Information**
> **East Bay Nonprofit Center**
> **Oakland, California**

### Fundraising Targets

Start your planning with the most basic question: How much money are you trying to raise? Chapter 3 explained how to draft an initial budget, which should give you a pretty good idea of how much money you need to raise. If your budget includes an expected

$5,000 in membership revenues, $10,000 in grants, and $2,500 in special events, then a portion or all of these amounts may be your fundraising target. How much you'll seek in any given fundraising campaign will depend on how many and what types of campaigns you plan to have each year.

For example, say your nonprofit has budgeted an expected $3,500 in membership fees and $7,500 in sponsorships. If you plan to have two membership drives per year, you might set a target of $2,000 for your first drive—more than half of the total budget in order to jump-start the membership income—and $1,500 for the second. Similarly, if you plan four sponsorship solicitations per year, you could set equal targets of $1,875 for each. If your first fundraising campaign of the year included a membership drive and a sponsorship solicitation, the overall target for the campaign would be $3,875.

How to define and execute your fundraising campaigns is discussed later in this chapter. The goal here is simply to come up with your fundraising targets, which will depend largely on your overall budget. Your budgeted income estimates will be the foundation for your fundraising targets.

Sometimes a nonprofit suddenly needs to raise money for something specific that wasn't included in the budget, such as the cost of defending a lawsuit or the cost of a new computer to replace one that was stolen. In this case, your fundraising goal is defined for you: You'll have to raise enough money to cover your pressing financial need.

## Fundraising Budget

Once you've estimated how much money you'll need for your start-up costs, programs, overhead, and capital expenses, you'll need to figure out another piece of your budget puzzle: how much money you can and should spend on your fundraising efforts. While creative planning can keep fundraising costs low, most nonprofits will need to spend at least some money in order to make money. This section will help you assess your resources and come up with an efficient and realistic fundraising budget.

---

### Fundraising Resources Online

The Association of Fundraising Professionals (www. afpnet.org) offers extensive resources for nonprofits at all levels of experience in fundraising. Paid membership is required for some articles, but there are several free blogs covering topics such as fundraising laws and regulations, and nonprofit technology.

**The Chronicle of Philanthropy** (http:// philanthropy.com) is a magazine focused on the world of philanthropic giving. The online version of the magazine is free, though paid subscribers also have access to premium content. The content is wide-ranging including feature stories, how-to articles, podcasts, searchable grants and jobs listings, and more.

**The Foundation Center** (www.foundationcenter.org) is the go-to source of information on foundations and grants nationwide. Besides publishing the Foundation Directory (both in print and online) which offers updated, comprehensive information on grantmakers and their funding activities, the Foundation Center's website offers other searchable databases and tools such as standard grant application forms and downloadable worksheets to help you track and manage your fundraising activities.

**The National Council of Nonprofits** (www. councilofnonprofits.org) offers informative articles and special reports on fundraising (among many other topics) and subtopics such as charitable registration, fiscal sponsorships, fundraising laws, and ethics in fundraising. In addition, there are member state nonprofit associations in most states, which often offer even more targeted resources, including information about any fundraising opportunities or issues unique to your state. Look up your state nonprofit association at the National Council of Nonprofits website.

**The Network for Good Learning Center** (www. fundraising123.org) also offers free articles, ebooks, webinars and more at its site. Premium subscribers have access to additional resources such as fundraising plan templates, worksheets, and access to expert advice.

**TechSoup** (www.techsoup.org), "the technology place for nonprofits," has a learning center with dozens of articles about using technology, including articles specifically about using technology for fundraising both online and off. It also has a program for nonprofits to register and obtain discounted software, including database and donor management software.

## Evaluate Your Resources

Most fledgling nonprofits don't have the luxury of simply deciding how much to spend on fundraising. Rather, their fundraising budgets will be defined by the cold, hard reality of their limited resources. For example, if your nonprofit needs to raise $1,000 for its 501(c)(3) application fee and a computer, you're in no position to launch a direct mail campaign that could cost thousands of dollars to implement.

One way to keep costs down when developing a fundraising budget is to recognize and use non-monetary resources. When you have limited cash, focus on the other resources available to you, including nonmonetary resources and in-kind donations. For example, your group might have a volunteer who can attract other volunteers, a personal connection to a journalist, or a supporter who owns a printing business and will donate the production of your first brochure. Ideally, this grassroots style of fundraising will allow you to achieve some noteworthy results, attract more funds, and put you in a better position to launch a bigger, more expensive fundraising campaign the next time around.

> **EXAMPLE:** The Citizens for a Green Downtown (CGD) is a new nonprofit that needs money to buy computers and printers for its offices. The board of directors puts together a fundraising plan and budget centered on a direct mail campaign. No matter how conservative the board is with its estimates, the costs of producing the direct mailing—including graphic design, printing, and postage—are discouragingly high.
>
> The board decides to change course and puts together a list of resources they have or are confident they could get to offset the cost of the direct mailing. One board member knows basic graphic design, so he volunteers to create a simple brochure to use when approaching prospective donors. Another board member, who has a high-quality color photocopier at her business, offers to copy and fold 100 brochures.
>
> Several board members have close connections with the director of a downtown farmer's market, who might let them use a booth for free for one month to promote the nonprofit and solicit funds from shoppers. This would allow CGD to reach the public without having to send a mailing. One board member offers to organize volunteers to staff the booth during the market. While such exposure would normally be cost prohibitive, the group can pull this one off without laying out any cash.

## The Cost of Fundraising

You should do everything you can to keep your fundraising costs low. It's important for your budget, and for public perception, that your fundraising costs don't eat up a huge chunk of the total amount of money you raise. Although there is no legal rule, your fundraising costs should be no more than about 25% of your funds raised. This is especially true if you plan to approach foundations, governments, or other sophisticated major donors, who will want to see that most of the money you raise goes toward your nonprofit's mission and not toward more fundraising.

The cost-effectiveness of fundraising methods varies greatly. Holding a special event is an expensive way to raise money, as the cost of putting one on can eat up 30%, 40%, or even 50% of the funds it generates. At the other end of the spectrum, asking ten well-connected supporters to fire up their cell phones and call likely contributors can bring in a significant sum at almost no cost to the organization. In the middle of the spectrum, a targeted direct mail campaign to a carefully selected mailing list can be cost efficient if you can keep printing costs low.

When pricing proposed fundraising efforts, be sure you account for all of the costs involved. Obvious costs include postage, printing, paper, packaging, telephone bills, and mailing lists. Other costs you may not anticipate include fees for writers, graphic designers, website developers, consultants, and accountants.

## Find Prospective Donors

Even the most creative fundraising pitch won't raise a dime if nobody hears it. A key step in every fundraising campaign is to build a list of names and contact information for the individuals, businesses, foundations, and organizations you will ask for donations. While this sounds simple enough, many new nonprofits don't know where to start or how to prioritize. This section discusses some simple ways to develop lists of prospective donors.

A whole profession has grown around nonprofit fundraising, including nonprofit consulting businesses that focus exclusively on developing prospect lists. As you can imagine, these services don't usually come cheap. Similarly, renting mailing lists from other groups has evolved into a profitable industry of its own, one that can be prohibitively expensive for new nonprofits. This section leaves these topics for other resources to cover and, instead, focuses on cost-effective, grassroots methods of finding potential financial supporters.

**TIP**

**Start with individual donors.** Statistics consistently show that the vast majority—roughly 80%—of charitable dollars given in the United States comes from regular individuals, *not* from wealthy corporations or foundations. This is good news for new organizations with minimal contacts or institutional clout, which often find it tough to attract contributions from large organizations. Of course, if you have such contacts, go ahead and solicit the big guys. But never overlook the giving power of individual donors—and make the most of their generosity by making your appeals to them a priority in your fundraising plan.

### Start With Your Closest Contacts

When developing your prospect lists, it's best to start with those closest to your organization and branch out from there. Ideally, your board members will have many contacts in the community and will be able to provide most of the names for your initial list. Staffers and volunteers are also likely to know people interested in your cause, so be sure to consult them when you gather names.

**RELATED TOPIC**

**The best board members are those with contacts in the community.** Your board members should take an active role in hunting for prospective donors by collecting contact information, asking their contacts for additional names, and otherwise shaking leads from the trees. Refer to Chapter 4 for more information on how to build a strong board with members who are both well connected and willing to pitch in with fundraising efforts.

One way to jump-start your quest for prospects is to ask every board member, staff person, and volunteer to provide the names of ten people who might be willing to donate to your organization. Start by including anyone who would be likely to contribute a minimum amount—perhaps $50 or $100. Later, you can identify anyone on your list who might be willing to make a larger contribution, put those names on a separate list, and tailor a separate appeal to these high-dollar prospects.

For example, once you've generated a list from everyone's ten contacts, you might notice that it includes a few successful and prominent business leaders who could likely afford at least a $500 gift. If you send them a regular appeal letter, they may donate $50.

But if you create a separate appeal for potential large donors asking for $500, $1,000, or $2,500, you may find that they open their wallets much wider.

While your most well-connected sources might be able to supply 50 good leads, others may be hard pressed to come up with ten. If so, encourage them to think broadly. Thinking creatively about who might support your group is a good way to build bridges to new communities that you might not have considered otherwise.

### Know Your Prospective Donors

People give money to charitable causes for numerous reasons. Some may share a passion for your ideals or a commitment to your goals, but others may have different motivations. A local business owner may think donating to your organization will generate good public relations or free advertising that will increase customers. Other donors may give because it makes them feel important or proud. And, of course, some donors contribute because they want a tax write-off. Even the giving decisions of foundation, government, and corporate grant givers may be swayed by factors such as internal politics and personal connections.

So how do you figure out what will make your potential funders open their wallets? With individual donors, it's often a matter of keeping your ears open and tuning into the issues that drive them to give. With corporations and funding institutions, a bit of research can yield valuable information. There are countless resources, both online and in print, that contain information on where foundations give their money; even your local newspaper might publish reports of grants given by corporations in your area. Most foundations publish their own reports or provide public information on their priorities and interests.

Networking is another good way to gather this kind of information. For example, ask a program officer at a foundation to which you are applying about the foundation's interests and criteria. Talk to other organizations that have dealt with the funder you're researching—you can get useful information from others who have gone down the path ahead of you. The more you know about your potential funders' giving habits, the better you can tailor your approach.

For many fledgling nonprofits, asking initial supporters to compile lists of people and businesses to solicit will often generate enough prospects to get you started. If you are short of prospects, it may be a sign that you could use an extra member or two on your board—preferably ones whose contacts lists are overflowing with names of potential supporters.

## Use Networking Techniques

If you need more leads beyond those generated by people close to your group, some simple networking techniques may do the trick:

- **Attend community events, particularly those related to your mission.** Talk with people about your group and get contact information from anyone who seems genuinely interested. Bear in mind that many people may be annoyed if your only follow-up is to ask them for money. Instead, stay in touch with them about other issues, invite them to a meeting, or ask for their input on your strategic plan.
- **Ask those who run other nonprofits in your area whether they know people who might be interested in your cause.** Other groups often have valuable contacts or large memberships of proactive people. While they might not freely hand over their membership lists, they might be happy to allow you to make a presentation at their next meeting, where you could meet good contacts and possible donors.
- **Organize a small, informal get-together.** You can easily arrange informal social events by sending out an email invitation to your group and encouraging people to forward the invitation to others they think might be interested. Set up coffee at a board member's house or a happy hour gathering at a local pub. It's a fun, inexpensive way to make new contacts and introduce them to what your group does. Many of these new contacts might turn out to be great fundraising leads.
- **Use social media to expand your world of contacts.** Online networks—particularly social media

sites like Facebook and Twitter—offer the opportunity to reach like-minded people and begin building relationships with them. You can also interact with other groups and businesses and start building a network of alliances online. We discuss fundraising using social media and crowdfunding sites in more detail later in this chapter.

RELATED TOPIC

**Need more information on networking and marketing?** Chapter 9 explains how to get the word out about your nonprofit effectively and inexpensively. Because fundraising depends on having good contacts in the community, effective networking and marketing will really boost your fundraising efforts.

## Keep Your Lists Organized and Updated

It's important to continually update and organize your prospect lists as you pursue your fundraising goals. When you execute a membership drive or a phone-a-thon to raise funds, you must keep careful records of whom you contacted, what methods you used, and what results you achieved. Obvious items to track are whether a prospect gave money (and, if so, how much) and whether the prospect asked not to be contacted again. You should also keep track of more subjective information, such as whether the prospect expressed interest in a certain program area or offered to volunteer.

The best way to keep track of your prospects is to use software, such as general database software like *FileMaker Pro,* customer relationship management (CRM) software like *SalesForce,* which was created for for-profits but is often used by nonprofits, or specialized applications like *CiviCRM* or *The Raiser's Edge,* which are specifically geared towards fundraising and donor management. Donor management software (also sometimes called "fundraising software," "constituent relationship management software," or similar names) is specialized database software that facilitates storage and management of key information about existing and prospective

donors, members, and other contacts and allies. Fundraising software also typically handles functions such as online fundraising, event registration, membership renewals, and mailing list generation, both for direct mail and email campaigns.

Because full-featured donor management software can be expensive to purchase and to maintain, it may be feasible only for large organizations. Fledgling nonprofits can get by using basic versions that are quite inexpensive or even free. Alternatively, your group can keep track of prospects (and many other types of information, for that matter) in basic spreadsheets, using software such as Microsoft *Excel.* Google spreadsheets are a good option, because multiple people can access and edit the spreadsheets collaboratively. While spreadsheets can help you organize your lists, their sorting, grouping, and reporting functions are more limited than full-featured databases. Any true database application—whether or not geared specifically for nonprofit fundraising—will greatly streamline your data managing tasks.

While most of the software described in this section is quite user-friendly, don't underestimate the time necessary to keep your data current and accurate. Make sure you designate a computer-literate board member, volunteer, or staffer to be responsible for this important task.

TIP

**Look into hosted versions of donor management software.** Software geared towards nonprofits is increasingly appearing online—to be used online. Working this way is known as "cloud" computing or using a "hosted" solution. Instead of installing software on your computers (called an "installed" solution), you use the service via a Web browser, either for free or for a periodic fee. You don't need to deal with the technical details of installing, maintaining, or upgrading software on your own computer. Technical support is often available for paid versions. For many small nonprofits with few or no tech-savvy people on staff, maintaining their databases is a huge issue, and hosted services can offer a big advantage over installed software.

RESOURCE

**For in-depth information on researching and developing prospective donors,** check out *Successful Fundraising,* by Joan Flanagan (McGraw-Hill).

*Fundraising is never easy, because thousands of nonprofits pursue many of the same donors for contributions. Beyond identifying the people who could become potential donors to your organization (individuals, corporations, foundations), it's essential to learn all you can about them. Cultivate them by teaching them about your organization and involving them in some meaningful way. Ask them for a specific dollar amount, and then thank them profusely for their talents and treasures.*

**Michael D. Hohner—Fundraising consultant and President of Hohner & Company, LLC Oak Creek, Wisconsin**

## Define Your Fundraising Campaign

A coherent, coordinated approach to raising money will always be more effective than a scattered series of individual solicitations. Defining a fundraising campaign means choosing an overall concept to guide your specific fundraising activities. For example, rather than having board members schedule ad hoc lunch meetings with representatives of local businesses that might contribute, coordinate such meetings as part of an annual fund drive. Besides yielding a more efficient fundraising machine, a coordinated approach will help you avoid duplicating efforts and annoying potential donors by soliciting them more than once.

TIP

**Never ignore a fundraising opportunity.** While it's best to coordinate your fundraising efforts into one or more campaigns each year, don't fail to pursue leads just because they're not part of your overall fundraising plan. For example, if a board member happens to talk with an officer of a local bank who expresses interest in supporting the organization, by all means jump at the opportunity—don't wait until the next fundraising drive to pursue this lead.

One of the most common fundraising campaigns is an annual membership drive and renewal program that seeks dues-paying members. Some nonprofits prefer not to have members and simply solicit donations instead of membership fees. Other types of fundraising campaigns include capital campaigns (to pay for major expenses) and planned giving programs (to encourage donors to include an organization in their wills), although start-up nonprofits rarely use such campaigns due to the considerable time and expense they require.

Within any type of fundraising campaign, a nonprofit can use several different fundraising tools. For example, a nonprofit holding an annual membership drive might use direct mail, telephone solicitations, and special events to execute the campaign. Fundraising tools are covered below; this section focuses on some common types of fundraising campaigns.

### Can a Nonmembership Nonprofit Have a Membership Drive?

As discussed in Chapter 1, you have the right to decide whether to give your group's members the right to vote in corporate affairs such as electing board members or amending bylaws. A group whose participants have voting rights is sometimes called a "membership" nonprofit, while a group with nonvoting participants is often called a "nonmembership" nonprofit.

These labels can be confusing, however, because they imply that a nonprofit cannot have members unless it gives them voting rights. In fact, this is not true. A nonprofit may have members who do not have the power to vote as long as the nonprofit follows state rules and includes specific language in its corporate paperwork.

When discussing membership drives as a fundraising tool, this chapter uses the term "members" to refer to those who pay annual dues and get some sort of benefit in return, regardless of whether they have voting rights. You'll find more information on the legal issues raised by membership in Chapter 1.

## Membership Drives

You've probably been asked to become a member of a nonprofit organization such as your neighborhood association, a business trade group, the AAA auto association, or an environmental group. Offering memberships in your group is a great way to develop a relationship with your supporters—and collecting membership dues is also a tried-and-true way to bring in funds. However, it also implies that you will offer benefits to members, which may not be possible with your current resources.

### Defining Membership Benefits

When you ask people to join your group, you convey a different message from when you simply ask them for a donation. Asking people to join—as a member, sponsor, supporter, or whatever you name it—implies that your nonprofit will offer them something in return. Offering some sort of benefit to attract dues-paying members can be particularly useful for smaller groups without a proven track record. As you decide whether to have members, think about what benefits you could offer members and how you will involve them in your group's activities.

The benefits and types of involvement that will resonate with your members vary greatly from one organization to the next. You could, for example, offer something of value to your members, such as a tote bag, a discount card for local restaurants, a free email account, or a free newsletter subscription. Or, you could offer members the opportunity to be included in the strategic planning process each year or invitations to members-only events. No matter what type of incentive you offer, you should be sensitive to the fact that members will expect to feel included in your work; make sure your members feel rewarded and inspired by their participation.

**TIP**

**Pay attention to members' comments.** In addition to deciding what benefits and involvement in your group you will offer members, you should work out a system to solicit feedback from members. Because they are interested in your cause and familiar with your group, members can offer valuable input on a variety of topics, such as how to reach additional supporters, how to tailor your solicitations to particular groups of donors, or what style T-shirts make the most desirable membership gift. Members will appreciate your interest in their concerns, and you could gain some important insights that will help you better appeal to your current and potential supporters.

Of course, you'll need adequate resources to follow through with membership benefits. Some people may not expect any benefits upon joining and paying dues, but this usually applies to members of large, well-established groups (such as the ACLU, Planned Parenthood, or the National Rifle Association), who join simply because of their desire to support the cause. If you lack the resources to offer membership benefits, you may decide it's more realistic simply to ask prospects for a donation to your group, instead of asking them to "join."

### Planning and Preparing for a Membership Drive

If your group chooses to solicit paid memberships, be sure to get your ducks in a row before you approach or accept your first new member. Because successful fundraising is based on ongoing relationships, it's easier to convince existing members to renew their memberships than it is to sign new members up in the first place. So, you should have your benefits in place and be in a position to treat members well from the get-go. Don't disappoint your members with a poorly planned membership program.

At a minimum, make sure you deal with the following tasks prior to starting your drive:

- **Create materials clearly outlining membership benefits.** Most prospective members of a new nonprofit group will want to know what they get in return for becoming a member. While the worthiness of your group's cause and its need for funds are, of course, important, make sure that all of your solicitation materials clearly outline the material benefits of joining. These materials could be in print form, online, or (ideally) both.

- **Create a solid database to manage member information.** Countless nonprofits have learned the hard way that managing memberships can become a nightmare without some sort of efficient tracking system (and a well-outlined process for using it; see below). Managing members will require a database or at the very least a well-developed spreadsheet to keep track of critical information, such as member names, contact information, and renewal dates. Databases are preferable to spreadsheets because they facilitate more automation—for example, you'll easily be able to generate an email list for members who meet certain criteria or generate a monthly report showing which members are up for renewal.

- **Develop a system outlining who will handle various tasks, including database maintenance.** Even the most robust database won't help your nonprofit be efficient if you are disorganized about maintaining it. You'll need to define a clear system for accepting and managing members, such as specifying how the application process will work (by online registration or a paper form, for example), who will be in charge of maintaining the database, who will deposit checks, who will answer questions, and more. Without a system in place, you run the risk of befuddling or annoying current or prospective members and possibly losing their support.

### Executing a Membership Drive

Most nonprofits that offer paid memberships have at least one annual membership drive to attract new members and renew expiring memberships. One common approach is to identify specific fundraising tools—mail, email, telephone calls, door-to-door canvassers—and draft a schedule. Most membership drives last for a period of two to four weeks, during which the group uses its chosen tools in a coordinated effort. Between membership drives, the nonprofit can and should continue to solicit memberships, just not as intensely as during the drive.

Here are some tips that will help you execute a membership drive effectively and affordably (you'll find more information on specific fundraising tools—and how best to use them—below):

- **Create incentives to bring in new memberships.** For example, you could ask a local hotel to donate a suite for the weekend, which you could offer to the staffer, volunteer, or board member who signs up the most new members.

- **Hit the streets.** Send volunteers armed with membership materials to places where they're likely to find your constituency. For instance, a nonprofit that promotes organic farming could set up a table outside a local food co-op, where it would be seen by plenty of health-conscious shoppers.

- **Avoid costly mass mailings.** While sending an inexpensive mailer to a list of close contacts can be an effective way to drum up members, don't waste your money on expensive mailing lists or elaborate direct mail campaigns to people who aren't familiar with your group. The return on mass mailings rarely justifies the cost.

- **Make it easy for your members to renew.** Allowing your members to renew their memberships online is an increasingly common practice that is convenient and efficient for both members and nonprofits. For non-wired members, mailing a notice that their membership is about to expire (along with a self-addressed, stamped envelope) is a simple, inexpensive way to encourage renewals.

**TIP**

**Watch your pennies.** Overly enthusiastic or poorly planned membership drives can cost a lot without generating much in the way of donations. Be thrifty: Don't spend a small fortune on promotional materials that will often be thrown away—or that may turn off cost-conscious donors.

## Gifts Versus Pledges

Unlike a gift from a donor—for example, a $100 check during your annual fund drive—a pledge is a promise to give a certain amount to your group over a period of time. Soliciting pledges is a great way to increase the amount of money donors give you, as they'll often be willing to promise more over time than they would give in one lump sum. For example, a donor might not consider giving more than $50 at one time but might be willing to pledge $10 per month for the next year, for a total gift of $120. With this in mind, consider soliciting pledges as well as outright gifts in all of your fundraising efforts.

Pledges can be paid in installments either by check or by credit card. For credit card pledges, you'll need to set up a credit card processing system, which generally is paid for with a percentage of your revenues (usually less than 5%). This fee is often worth the convenience for your donors and your nonprofit, as you won't need to send invoices or otherwise track down each payment promised to you by a donor. For the best deals on credit card processing services, ask your bank and other banks in your community. Also check online: Search for "credit card processing" or "credit card merchant services" and you'll find plenty of options.

## Fund Drives

Unlike a membership drive, a fund drive simply seeks donations—not members who will pay dues. A nonprofit can hold a fund drive whether or not it solicits paid memberships. For example, one nonprofit may decide not to seek members and instead raise funds through an annual fund drive, while another nonprofit may hold an annual membership drive and an annual fund drive six months apart.

If you do not offer membership benefits, it's especially important to build a strong case about why you need donor support. This is even more true when you're asking your dues-paying members for additional funds—you will truly need to justify asking your members to dig into their pockets again. As described earlier in this chapter, the strongest appeals are urgent and specific. Your fund drive solicitation must make your organization's needs clear and explain how the funds will be used. It's also a good idea to mention how your group has used any funds raised previously to further its mission.

## Capital Campaigns

A capital campaign is a fundraising drive to raise a significant amount of money for a big project, such as buying real estate or starting a capital-intensive new program. The goal is a coordinated effort that will rally major donors and other funding sources and bring in significant income for a specific purpose.

Fledgling nonprofits typically do not launch capital campaigns because these campaigns depend on an established base of major donors—not to mention dedicated volunteers and staff. Because large amounts of money are involved, it's essential that you have responsible managers to run the campaign and handle the money raised. It's common to hire fundraising professionals for these types of campaigns.

RESOURCE

**Recommended reading on capital campaigns.** *Preparing Your Capital Campaign*, by Marilyn Bancel (Jossey-Bass), is a practical workbook that shows how to organize a capital campaign and walks readers through the process step by step. *Conducting a Successful Capital Campaign*, by Kent E. Dove (Jossey-Bass), is a thorough (if lengthy) guide to the process, and offers a resource section with sample strategic plans and financial reports.

## Planned Giving

Generally speaking, the term "planned giving" refers to a strategy that seeks to merge the fundraising interests of a nonprofit with the estate planning interests of its donors. In a planned giving program (also called a "gift planning" program), a nonprofit asks its supporters to transfer assets to the nonprofit when they pass away, as an estate planning technique.

While it may seem inappropriate to ask supporters for their money upon their demise, planned giving is a rapidly growing source of philanthropy—in large part because of the financial benefits it offers to donors. Depending on the types of assets and the specifics of the transfer, planned giving arrangements can offer donors a significant reduction, or even elimination, of taxes on their estates, gifts, capital gains, and income. Another benefit, of course, is that donors get the satisfaction of giving significant support to a cause they care about and leaving a legacy in their name.

Creating and running a planned giving program is not for beginners, however. In addition to offering information on how to name the nonprofit in a will or real estate transfer, planned giving programs typically help donors set up financial instruments, such as trusts, gift annuities, and other tax-favored funds. Creating and managing these funds requires expertise that most new nonprofits lack. A planned giving program is probably something to consider a few years down the road, when you can afford to hire a consultant to help your organization set it up.

## Fundraising Tools

Once you've decided what type of fundraising campaign (or campaigns) you plan to undertake, you'll need to choose the specific tools you'll use to bring in donations. If you want to conduct an annual membership drive, for instance, how exactly will you go about contacting your potential members? If you need funds right away for a pressing and unexpected emergency—say, to defend a lawsuit or replace a stolen computer system—how will you get them?

The next section introduces the tools nonprofits typically use to raise funds, from email to direct mail to in-person appeals. As explained below, you can use any one or a combination of these tools to carry out whatever fundraising campaigns your nonprofit undertakes.

## Asking for a Gift by Phone or in Person

Once you've identified your prospects and organized them into appropriate categories as discussed earlier (for example, separating regular donors from major donors), you'll need to develop an effective pitch and train your staff and volunteers on how to deliver it.

Here are some tips for making your solicitations as effective as possible:

- **Identify the best people in your organization to do the asking.** Asking for money—especially large amounts of it—takes confidence and the right attitude. If certain staffers or volunteers are shy or inarticulate, assign them to other duties, such as managing mailing lists.
- **Train your fundraisers and lead practice sessions.** Your staff, volunteers, and board members need to learn how to request donations in a straightforward, respectful way, without fear of rejection. Training sessions that address common fears and provide practice asking for gifts will help your fundraisers improve their delivery, anticipate common questions, and refine their pitches.
- **Ask for a specific amount.** Asking for a specific dollar amount tends to steer the discussion toward how much the donor can give, as opposed to whether they'll give. Of course, this doesn't guarantee a gift. But a request like, "We're hoping you could support our work with a $50 (or $500, or $5,000) donation" is always a better approach than, "We're hoping you'll be able to support us."
- **The best fundraisers don't just recite a script—they listen and respond.** People rarely give money to someone who simply recites a canned appeal, isn't able to engage in a discussion about the nonprofit's work, or can't provide meaningful answers to questions. One way to ensure that your fundraising team can speak about the nonprofit convincingly is to make sure they understand and feel personally committed to your organization's mission. Your fundraisers should be responsive and able to think on their feet.

### Do-Not-Call Rules for Nonprofits

In 2003, federal rules went into effect creating a national do-not-call registry. In addition, some states have their own do-not-call rules. Generally speaking, both the state and federal do-not-call rules establish lists of people who have asked not to be called by telemarketers and prohibit telemarketers from contacting people on those lists.

The federal do-not-call rules do not apply to tax-exempt nonprofits (as long as staff or volunteers make the calls), meaning that nonprofits with any type of federal tax-exempt status (not just 501(c)(3) groups) are free to do phone solicitations without having to consult the do-not-call registry. There are a couple of complications, however:

- State rules may have different exemptions and may *not* have exceptions for tax-exempt nonprofits. In other words, some states' do-not-call rules may apply to tax-exempt nonprofits just like for-profit telemarketers.
- Any state do-not-call rules will apply only to calls made within your state. Any interstate calls (made from one state to another) will be governed by the federal do-not-call rules, which do not apply to tax-exempt nonprofits. In other words, if your state prohibits nonprofits from calling people on the do-not-call list, this prohibition will only apply to calls you make within your state—any calls made out of state will be governed by the more lenient federal rule.

In addition, if a tax-exempt nonprofit uses professional telephone solicitors, it will be subject to a few extra rules.

Professional solicitors must make certain disclosures about the nonprofit and the nature of the call, must not make repeat calls to people who indicate they do not want to receive calls, and must not misrepresent the nonprofit's mission or the purposes for the contribution, among other rules.

Before you worry too much about digesting all that law, consider this: Even if your nonprofit does not have to comply with do-not-call rules, it's wise to comply with them anyway. People who have taken the step of adding their names to the do-not-call registry probably don't want any intrusive phone solicitations, whether from nonprofits or for-profit telemarketers. Rather than irritating them and alienating them from your nonprofit, it's better to take the time to review the federal do-not-call registry (and any registry in your state) and avoid calling anyone whose name appears on the list. See www.donotcall.gov for information on the national registry.

Some nonprofits will skip reviewing the registry, reasoning that they're exempt from the rules and so don't have to worry about violating the law. Here's a tip if you decide to take this course: If your callers reach people who say they are on the do-not-call registry, the best response is to apologize and promise not to call them again (and, of course, to live up to that promise). Don't respond by saying, "Nonprofits are exempt from 'do-not-call' rules." This defensive response is sure to turn off potential supporters.

## In-Person Appeals

Making a direct request for money in person is the most basic—and one of the most effective—tools of fundraising. The idea here is to approach someone who is already acquainted with someone in your organization and might be interested in supporting your group (canvassing and other appeals to strangers are discussed below).

One reason why in-person appeals tend to be effective is that nonprofits use the technique with people who are somehow connected to the group—business associates of the board president, for example.

These prospects are naturally more likely to contribute than strangers you contact out of the blue.

But in-person appeals tend to be effective for another reason as well: If the right person makes the pitch, there's no more powerful way to convey your group's urgent needs and the emotion behind its mission. Also, potential donors have a harder time turning someone down face to face than they do over the telephone.

In-person requests for money are particularly appropriate when soliciting major donor prospects. Those who are considering giving a major gift to your group often have more questions and may want to know more about your organization than your regular donors. Taking the time to sit down with them for lunch, coffee, or a meeting at their office is a good way to give them the appropriate personal attention and convince them that your group is worthy of a large gift.

The nonprofit's directors should be heavily involved in setting up and carrying out in-person solicitations. If your group has an executive director, he or she should actively set up meetings and ask for gifts. If, like most start-ups, you have a board of directors but not an executive director, your board members should set a strong example by cultivating relationships with donors, particularly those likely to make substantial contributions.

 **CAUTION**

**Printed materials can hinder an in-person appeal.** It can often be helpful during an in-person solicitation to provide your prospective donor with literature about your nonprofit, such as a brochure outlining goals and planned activities or (better yet) early accomplishments. But do not offer your prospects a thick stack of information. Doing so will encourage them to put off making a decision until they can read through your lengthy materials. Instead, limit the materials you give your potential funders to simple, concise publications tailored to their concerns.

## Telephone Solicitations

Although the pervasiveness of telemarketing has given telephone solicitations a bad reputation, calling your prospects by phone and asking them for money can be a very effective fundraising method. Beware, however, that national do-not-call regulations may affect your nonprofit, as discussed in "Do-Not-Call Rules for Nonprofits," above. Although you must use caution regarding the do-not-call registry, telephone appeals can be an efficient way to solicit funds.

Unlike in-person appeals, which can be time-consuming, you can call a large number of potential donors within a short amount of time. And, unlike emails, social media, or direct mail, speaking with a prospect over the phone creates a personal connection and allows a fundraiser to respond to any questions or concerns the prospect might have.

A good approach to fundraising via telephone is to organize a group of people to get together at a scheduled time to make calls from one or more lists of prospects. For example, you could organize an annual two-day phone drive: two evenings in a row when trained volunteers spend three hours calling prospects to ask for donations. At the end of the second day, you can thank your volunteers with a wrap-up party or night out.

Because your nonprofit probably does not have enough telephone lines to accommodate more than a few volunteer callers, you will need to figure out where you can hold a phone drive. If all of your volunteers have cell phones, you could ask them to use their own phones. Or, you could ask another nonprofit or business if your group could use its office for your drive and spread volunteers out among the telephones in different cubicles. You should schedule your phone drive in the evening after business hours (6 p.m. to 9 p.m., for example) or on a weekend, so it won't be hard to find some empty office space.

Contests and incentives can be useful motivators for your volunteer telephone fundraisers. For example, ask a fancy restaurant if it will donate a dinner for two, and give it as a prize to the person who raises the most money that evening. Local businesses are often happy to sponsor your efforts by donating a small prize that doesn't cost them much—and these incentives can really light a fire under your fundraising team.

Be sure to keep careful records of whom you called, whom you reached, whom you couldn't reach (and whether you left a message), who gave money and how much, who declined, and—most important— who asked not to be called again. Unless prospects specifically say that they're not interested in your organization, they may still be willing to donate, just not over the telephone. Be sure to respect their wishes and avoid annoying them (and looking unprofessional) by calling after they've asked you not to.

## Door-to-Door Canvassing

Sending out a troop of volunteers to solicit door to door can be a great way to build a base of support in a particular community. Unlike other types of fundraising, door-to-door canvassing does not start with a list of prospects; rather, it blankets an entire area to build a list of interested people. Going door to door is especially useful when your cause is tied to a specific community, as would be true of a group dedicated to replanting trees in a blighted neighborhood or building a community center.

The main difference between door-to-door canvassing and in-person appeals is that canvassing involves contacting new people without introduction, while in-person appeals should be reserved for people with whom your organization already has some connection. Of course, contacting people you don't know will usually result in a lower success rate. But making a personal pitch to someone face to face can be much more powerful than appealing to someone over the telephone or through the mail. For the best chance of success, the canvassers you send out must be clear on your organization's mission and enthusiastic enough to engage the people they meet. Your canvassers' energy is the key to a successful door-to-door fundraising campaign.

When sending volunteers to request donations door to door, you obviously need to be concerned about their safety. Don't send them into dangerous neighborhoods, and don't send them anywhere after dark. Always team canvassers up in pairs or small groups so that, even if they split up within a neighborhood, they can meet up regularly to check on each other. If possible, make sure each canvasser carries a cell phone.

## Email Appeals

It's no wonder that email appeals are an increasingly popular fundraising method: You can email an appeal for donations to your whole prospect list with no printing or postage costs. If you want to change your wording or tailor different appeal pitches to different lists, changing an email is far easier and cheaper than revising print materials. And, you don't need to catch your prospects at home, as you do for a telephone solicitation—they can read your email at their convenience.

On the other hand, some people get so much email these days that your solicitation may get buried in their inboxes or filtered out as spam (junk email). Even worse, recipients might get annoyed if they consider your email to be spam and hold this against your organization.

All things considered, the potential benefits of email fundraising outweigh the potential downsides, as long as you do it right. Here are some tips for using email effectively in your fundraising efforts:

- **Include your group's name in the subject line and in your email address.** In your early days, identifying your organization as the sender of an email might not convince a recipient to read it. But, as you develop name recognition, those receiving your fundraising email will be more inclined to read it if they know it is from your organization, rather than from someone they don't know trying to sell them something they don't want. Try to include your nonprofit name, or an abbreviation of it, in the subject line. Also send any fundraising email from an address that contains your nonprofit's domain name—for example, janejohnson@savethewhales.org (rather than janejohnson@yahoo.com).

- **Always include information about how recipients can remove themselves from your email list.** Offer clear instructions for those who want to unsubscribe, such as: "To remove your name from this email list, please reply with 'Remove' in the subject line or body of the email." If you use an email outreach service as recommended below, it will include an unsubscribe option.

- **Encourage people to forward the email.** Asking recipients of your email to forward it to others who might be interested is a great way to spread the word about your group and potentially gain more supporters. This is especially effective if there's urgency behind your email message—for example, if a corporation promises to match any funds you raise in the next two weeks. The more urgent the message, the more inclined people will be to pass it on.

- **Include a link to your nonprofit's website.** As explained in Chapter 11, you should create at least a simple website for your nonprofit as soon as possible. Once your site is live, include your website address in all your email correspondence as a way to drive traffic to the site.

- **Keep recipients' email addresses private by suppressing the names on the email list.** Many people want to keep their email addresses private and don't appreciate receiving an email to a large group that shows everyone's email addresses, including their own. Depending on your email program, there are various ways to hide recipients' email addresses when you send an email to a group. One way to hide recipients' addresses is to put each address in the "Bcc" address field instead of the "To" or "Cc" address fields, so everyone receives a "blind copy," without any names on it.

---

### Use an Email Outreach Service

There are a number of online services that can help you manage your email communications. Services like Campaign Monitor (www.campaignmonitor.com), Constant Contact (www.constantcontact.com), or MailChimp (www.mailchimp.com) are inexpensive and make it easy to create professional-looking email appeals. Perhaps the most compelling reason to consider these services is that they are an enormous help in managing email lists. Managing hundreds or thousands of email addresses—including dealing with returned mail, address change requests, and unsubscribe requests—is no easy task. Using an email outreach service will help you avoid mistakes that could otherwise cost you goodwill among your supporters.

Be careful when choosing an online service. Some are really just spam companies eager to lay hands on your mailing list. The safest bet is to stick with well-known, trusted service providers like the ones listed above.

---

## Crowdfunding and Social Media

Crowdfunding refers to a specific method of raising money online that harnesses the power of social media to spread the word about your campaign. For the uninitiated, social media sites allow users to connect with others online and form networks of contacts variously called "friends," "followers," "circles," etc. Users—who can be individuals or entities like nonprofits or for-profit businesses—interact and share things with their social media networks, usually by posting text, photos, videos, or links. Facebook and Twitter are two of the most high-profile social media sites, but there are tons of others: Google+, LinkedIn, Yelp, YouTube, and Pinterest, to name just a few.

Crowdfunding sites are essentially social media sites that are geared towards enabling users to raise money for various types of projects (more on that in a moment) from other folks online. To raise money through crowdfunding, you typically choose a crowdfunding site (more on that below), create a campaign with information about your project and why it needs funding, set a dollar amount goal and a deadline, and promote your campaign using social media and email outreach. The site will typically keep a percentage of the funding raised, generally 5% to 10%.

The most prominent crowdfunding site, Kickstarter (www.kickstarter.com), is not aimed at nonprofits—in fact, its terms of use prohibit using Kickstarter to raise general funds for charities. However, nonprofits can and do use Kickstarter for specific projects like putting on a festival or producing a video, which do fall within its project guidelines. As long as the money is being raised for a definable "project"—something with a beginning, middle, and end—Kickstarter is an option. Other sites like IndieGoGo (www.indiegogo.com) and Crowdrise (www.crowdrise.com) are more geared specifically towards nonprofits and are more flexible in terms of allowable fundraising goals.

When choosing which crowdfunding site to use, besides knowing which types of projects are allowed, another important detail to understand is whether the site is an "all-or-nothing" model or a "keep what you raise" model. For example, Kickstarter uses an all-or-nothing model, so if you don't meet your fundraising goal by the deadline, then your backers don't pay and your nonprofit doesn't get anything. IndieGoGo, on the other hand, offers a "flexible funding" option that allows you to keep what you raise, even if you fall short of your fundraising goal. If you choose this option and do in fact fall short, you will be charged a fee of 9% of the total raised, compared with 4% if you meet your goal.

Crowdfunding typically works best for nonprofits that already have a strong social media presence. If your nonprofit has hundreds or thousands of followers on Facebook and interacts with them daily, you'll be likely to get a lot of mileage from a crowdfunding campaign that you promote appropriately on Facebook. If, on the other hand your nonprofit rarely uses social media, it will be harder to get traction with a crowdfunding campaign, even one that's well-crafted and compelling.

Apart from crowdfunding, remember that social media in general can be used to great effect in promoting traditional fundraising methods—say, holding a special event or driving traffic to a website that's running a fundraising marathon.

Here are some general tips for using social media in your fundraising efforts.

- **Use social media in combination with other traditional fundraising tools.** Social media is great for spreading the word about offline fundraising events or sharing links to press coverage or other information. When used as a component of a multi-channel fundraising push (which may or may not include a crowdfunding campaign), social media can dramatically expand the reach and exposure of your message.

- **What's hot might not be effective, and what's effective one day may be old news the next.** For example, in 2007 a Facebook application called Causes was launched which allowed Facebook users to indicate which causes they cared about and donate money through an easy-to-use link. The popularity of the Causes application skyrocketed as tens of millions of Facebook members used it to show their support for at

least one organization—but within a few short years the application was obsolete. (According to a 2010 study by M+R Strategic Services, Nonprofit Social Media Benchmarks Study, only a fraction of the hundreds of thousands of organizations on Facebook raised more than $1,000.) Kickstarter and IndieGoGo are hot crowdfunding options today, but in a year or two they may have fallen out of favor. The bottom line is that you have to constantly stay on the lookout for what's new, innovative, and effective in social media fundraising, and be ready to switch courses if your methods become outdated.

- **As with networking in the real world, the payoff from networking online isn't usually immediate or direct.** Keep a broader, longer-term perspective when engaging in social media. Networking isn't the same as direct solicitation, and you shouldn't expect every "friend" to rain funds on your organization. But over time, the exposure, relationships, and goodwill you generate through your social media efforts will undoubtedly pay off in some measure.

## Direct Mail

People often perceive direct mail campaigns to be complex and expensive, and they can be both. However, direct mail campaigns can also be simple, targeted mailings that are effective without costing a fortune. Start-up nonprofits do not need to pay for expensive mailing lists or produce high-end packages of printed materials; they can, instead, minimize costs by adopting a simple, thrifty approach.

### Develop and Categorize Lists

The mailing list business is a profitable industry in which businesses and nonprofits pay for (or "rent") access to databases of names grouped according to certain demographic characteristics. Instead of taking this expensive route, use the methods listed earlier in this chapter to develop your own targeted lists of

## Reduced Postage Rates for Nonprofits

Many nonprofits are eligible for reduced postage rates when they send bulk mail. The U.S. Postal Service calls this its "Nonprofit Standard Mail" rate. To get the reduced rate, your organization must meet the eligibility requirements, submit an application, and receive an authorization at the post office where you will be taking your mailings. The mail you send must also meet certain requirements.

### Eligibility

Only certain types of nonprofits are eligible for reduced postage, including agricultural, educational, fraternal, labor, philanthropic, religious, scientific, and veterans groups. Automobile clubs, business leagues, chambers of commerce, citizens' and civic improvement associations, individuals, mutual insurance organizations, service clubs (for example, Rotary or Lions clubs), social and hobby clubs, and rural electric cooperatives and associations are not eligible.

The rules for political groups are slightly complicated; some are eligible (state and national committees of political parties, for example) but most are not. For detailed eligibility rules, see the U.S. Postal Service's Publication 417, *Nonprofit Standard Mail Eligibility*. (Information on how to get all publications and forms is at the end of this section.)

A nonprofit need not have 501(c)(3) or other tax-exempt status to be eligible.

### The Application Process

To start the process, you must submit an application form, PS Form 3624, *Application to Mail at Nonprofit Standard Mail Prices*, and supporting documents to the post office you will be mailing from. The required supporting documents include:

- your organization's "formative papers"—its articles of incorporation, constitution, or charter, and
- evidence of nonprofit status—either a tax exemption letter from the IRS showing 501(c)(3) or other federal tax-exempt status, or a financial statement from an independent auditor such as a certified public accountant.

Also, submit as many as possible of the following documents along with your application:

- a list of your organization's activities during the past 12 months

- a financial statement detailing your organization's receipts and expenditures for the past fiscal year, and your organization's budget for the current year, and
- other documents, such as your organization's bulletins, minutes of meetings, brochures, and similar papers that show how your organization operates.

### Qualified Mailings

The Postal Service and the IRS have strict guidelines on what types of mail can be sent using the Nonprofit Standard Mail rate. Among other requirements, the mail must:

- contain at least 200 addressed pieces or 50 pounds of addressed pieces
- be prepared according to postal standards in the *Domestic Mail Manual*
- include only your own organization's mail—you may not use nonprofit rates to send mail on behalf of any unauthorized organizations or entities, nor "rent" your nonprofit rate authorization to anyone else
- not contain certain types of advertising
- be accompanied by an appropriately signed postage statement certifying that the mailing is eligible, and
- identify the authorized organization.

Details on these and other requirements are outlined in Publication 417.

### Where to Get Publications

Information, publications, and application forms are available for download at the Postal Service's website at www.usps.gov. Publication 417, *Nonprofit Standard Mail Eligibility*, outlines the eligibility rules, application procedures, and other information about bulk mail rates for nonprofits. The application form, PS Form 3624, *Application to Mail at Nonprofit Standard Mail Prices*, is also available online, is included in Publication 417, and can be obtained at any post office. Other helpful publications available at the Postal Service's website include Publication 177, *Guidelines for Optimizing Readability of Flat-Size Mail*, and Publication 28, *Postal Addressing Standards*.

In addition, the Postal Service's Postal Explorer website, at http://pe.usps.gov, offers additional publications, including the *Domestic Mail Manual* with extensive mailing information tailored for businesses and nonprofits.

prospective donors. Once you have a list of names and have grouped them into categories, you may wish to develop customized sets of printed materials to send—for example, one package for regular donors and another tailored to potential major donors. While most materials, such as your brochure and copies of any press coverage your group has received, can be the same for both groups, you may want to include a different appeal letter and response card (with checkboxes for suggested donation amounts) for each list. (See "Create Printed Materials," below.)

As with all fundraising tools, be sure to track your direct mail appeals and update your mailing lists with information about what was sent to whom and with what result. When you send a direct mail solicitation to a prospect, indicate that in your prospect database. Also code the response cards so that you know which mailing generated the response. Develop a system that works for you based on the information you want to track. For example, you could put in small type in the corner of a response card "GS13" or "MS13"—"G" for general list or "M" for major donor list and "S13" for a spring 2013 mailing.

## Create Printed Materials

Creating the printed materials for your mailing can be more affordable than you might expect. You don't need to produce a direct mail package like the ones you get in your own mailbox, printed in full color on heavy paper with special die-cut shapes and other frills. Instead, focus on creating simple layouts of text and graphics on standard-sized pages. Many of your potential supporters may be pleased to receive modest printed materials instead of a slick, glossy package that obviously cost a lot of money to produce.

If someone at your nonprofit wants to design your materials in-house, relatively inexpensive software (such as Adobe *InDesign* or Microsoft *Publisher*) can create professional-looking documents fairly easily. Alternatively, a professional graphic designer can be immensely helpful, particularly if no one in your organization has graphic design skills.

The trick to using a graphic designer affordably is to do some of the work ahead of time. Sketching out what you want, even in rough form, will make the designer's work easier and save you money. As much as you can, define the materials you want to produce, write some text for the designer to work with, collect any photos or graphics you have that might work well in the materials, and give the designer ideas and direction rather than leaving the designer to start from scratch. You should, of course, remain open to your designer's ideas—after all, he or she has experience on how to best present information. But, by providing your designer with content and direction up front, you can save money and have more input in the final product.

*Dealing with a commercial printer can be a daunting task. The seemingly simple task of getting a price quote often involves technical jargon that can be intimidating to the uninitiated—and with all the options available it can be difficult to know if you're getting a good deal. While you may be able to save money by dealing with the printer directly, it's often wise to let the designer handle this, even if you pay the designer extra (15% is typical). Of course, if you will rely on your designer to handle choosing and working with the printer, you need to choose a designer who has this experience. Be sure to ask prospective designers specifically what their experience is in working with printers if you intend for them to handle this task.*

**David Dabney, Principal of Red Rooster Creative, a graphic design firm Santa Fe, New Mexico**

## Common Components of a Mailing

A fundraising mailing should include at least the following components:

- a letter directly asking for donations and explaining why the nonprofit needs and deserves the support
- a brochure, flyer, or other piece of literature describing the nonprofit and its work
- a copy of articles or other press coverage your nonprofit has received (if any), and
- a response card on which donors write their names, their contact information, and the amount of their donations.

When drafting your materials—particularly the letter asking for support—it's smart to address the issues that commonly concern potential donors. For example, many people worry about how their money will be used, so state specifically how you will spend the money or point out that a high percentage of donations goes directly toward program costs.

## Special Events

Holding a special event can be a fun way to raise money and build name recognition for your nonprofit. A special event can also attract new supporters, improve staff morale, and generally inject a dose of energy into your nonprofit.

On the other hand, producing a special event eats up lots of time and labor, which makes it one of the least cost-effective methods of fundraising. Depending on its size and complexity, a special event can cost more than half of the total funds raised. When compared to other fundraising methods that often cost 10% to 25% of the total funds raised, special events are just plain expensive.

Yet, it is possible that a special event could bring in a larger amount of money than other fundraising efforts—enough money to make it worth the cost of putting the event together. For example, if a fundraising dinner and concert brings in $50,000 at a cost of $25,000, you'll net $25,000, even though your costs ate up 50% of the money raised. In contrast, you may find it difficult to raise more than $10,000 with other fundraising tools, even the most cost-efficient ones. Given the ultimate net gain in funds, it may be worth the time and effort you put into your event.

If you do decide, after weighing all of the factors, to hold a special event as a way of raising funds, keep the following tips in mind:

- **Informal events can be just as effective as fancy fundraising dinners.** If you have a limited budget, consider holding an inexpensive event like a group yard sale at a local park or a karaoke marathon at a venue that will donate the space for the night. Forget about holding a black-tie gala, at least in your early days.
- **Piggyback on someone else's event.** It's much easier to put up a booth at a local street fair than to organize the street fair yourself. Find out what events are scheduled in upcoming months and see if there's a way to involve your nonprofit.
- **Think creatively about how your event will generate cash.** Selling tickets to the event is just one way to bring in funds. You could also hold an auction or a raffle drawing and ask local businesses or supporters to donate the auction items or raffle prize. Or, you could place contribution baskets on tables at the event (under someone's watchful eye, of course) or distribute brochures and donation envelopes. Selling food and drinks or other items (such as T-shirts or mugs) could be an additional source of revenue.

There are countless ways to use a special event to raise funds. While some nonprofits may succeed at hosting a formal, $200-a-plate dinner, most new organizations will do better with a grassroots event, like a dance party or an artists' bazaar. With a realistic budget firmly in mind, let your imagination be your guide.

## Sell Products or Services

Many nonprofits bring in significant income by selling products or services to their members or the public. Prime examples include the Girl Scouts' cookie sales and Goodwill's thrift stores, which are major sources of funding—and the most visible activity—of each group. While nationwide cookie sales or thrift shops are bigger operations than most fledgling nonprofits would want to tackle, these examples show that selling is a common and often lucrative nonprofit fundraising activity.

While starting a sales operation requires many practical considerations, any nonprofit considering a business activity must also understand some important legal and tax rules, discussed below.

## Related Versus Unrelated Activities

The IRS distinguishes between income a nonprofit earns from activities that are "substantially related" to its mission and income it earns from activities that are not. Money earned from substantially related activities is generally not taxed and won't subject the nonprofit to undue IRS scrutiny. Income from unrelated activities, however, will be subject to income taxes—and may jeopardize the nonprofit's tax-exempt status.

To determine whether your business activity is "substantially related" to your organization's tax-exempt purpose, the IRS considers whether the activity "contributes importantly" to accomplishing your mission. The IRS won't find that an activity is "substantially related" solely because it generates income that helps you pursue your laudable work. The business activity itself must be related to the mission—for example, a nonprofit orchestra for disabled people selling CDs of its concerts, a scientific nonprofit selling its research reports, or an archaeological nonprofit selling paid tours to excavated sites would all qualify as substantially related activities.

If your unrelated business activities start to eclipse your related business activities and become the focal point of the organization, you risk losing your tax-exempt status altogether. Unfortunately, the IRS does not offer a clear test to tell when you're at risk of losing your tax-exempt status, such as a maximum percentage of time spent or amount of money derived from unrelated activities. If your programs are shrinking while your unrelated business activity is going strong, you certainly have cause for concern. In that case, you may want to pay a visit to a lawyer, accountant, or nonprofit consultant.

The importance of this rule cannot be overstated: While your nonprofit can freely engage in activities that are substantially related to its mission, you must approach any unrelated business activities with caution, or you could put your tax-exempt nonprofit status at risk.

## Unrelated Business Income Tax (UBIT)

Despite a nonprofit's tax-exempt status, revenue from ongoing business activities that are not substantially related to its mission is subject to unrelated business income tax (UBIT), unless an IRS exemption applies. (Exemptions are discussed below.) UBIT is similar to regular income tax owed by for-profit businesses; its special name reflects the fact that a tax-exempt nonprofit does not normally owe tax on income from its related activities.

A nonprofit's income is subject to UBIT if the income results from a "regularly" conducted "trade or business" that isn't substantially related to the exempt purpose of the organization. "Trade or business" means selling goods or services in order to generate income. Unless you're selling items below their market value, the IRS will likely characterize any sales-generating activity as a trade or business.

Whether a business is carried on "regularly" depends on whether it is run like other similar businesses. If you publish and sell books, for example, do you produce roughly as many titles each year as other publishing companies, and do you have a bookstore that's open during business hours? If so, the IRS would likely consider your business to be carried on regularly. If, on the other hand, you have only published two books in the past five years and you sell them only at events, your publishing operation would likely not qualify as regular and, therefore, your bookselling income would not be taxable.

## Exemptions From UBIT

Even if your income would be taxable under the UBIT criteria described above, your activity or income might fall under an IRS exemption. And, if an exemption applies, you won't have to pay UBIT. First, any activity that results in an annual earned income of less than $1,000 is tax free: Even if the business activity was clearly outside of your mission, you are not required to file a tax return if your income doesn't reach the $1,000 threshold.

Second, the IRS has created UBIT exemptions for income derived from unrelated business activities if any of the following are true:

- Substantially all of the work of providing the services or creating the products is done by volunteers.
- The products or services are primarily for the convenience of the group's members, students, patients, officers, or employees.
- The nonprofit accepts money from a company that sponsors an educational, fundraising, or other event and displays the company's name or logo in return—as long as the nonprofit does not provide other advertising space for the company or allow the company to use the nonprofit's logo in company periodicals.
- The nonprofit sells merchandise that was donated to it.
- The nonprofit uses bingo games as fundraisers —but only if bingo is legal in the nonprofit's area, and the games are not played in a hall that's also used for commercial bingo gaming.
- The nonprofit exchanges or rents its membership list with another nonprofit.
- The nonprofit provides entertainment to attract people to a fair or exposition that promotes agriculture or education.

Third, in addition to exempting certain kinds of activities from UBIT, IRS regulations also exempt certain types of income from UBIT, including:

- dividends, interest, annuities, and other investment income
- royalties earned from allowing use of the nonprofit's trademark, trade name, copyrighted material, or other valuable rights (but not personal appearances or services)
- income from research grants or contracts, and
- gains and losses from selling property.

RESOURCE

**Recommended reading on unrelated business income.** The IRS has many more rules regarding taxation of nonprofit business activity income. If you are considering pursuing any business activities that are not substantially related to your nonprofit's mission, be sure to read IRS Publication 598, *Tax on Unrelated Business Income of Exempt Organizations.* This and other IRS publications are available online at www.irs.gov or can be ordered by calling the IRS at 800-829-3676. Consult an attorney if anything remains unclear.

CAUTION

**Paid advertising is considered unrelated business income.** Many nonprofits make the mistake of assuming that all aspects of their newsletters or websites— including paid ads—are related to their mission. However, the IRS doesn't see it that way and may impose UBIT on money you earn by selling ads. An easy way to avoid this is to forgo paid ads entirely. To make up the lost income, you could increase your subscription price or try to boost paid circulation. Unlike advertising income, subscription income from a newsletter about your nonprofit's activities would not be subject to UBIT, because informing people about your work is substantially related to your mission. For detailed information on creating a newsletter or other publishing vehicle for your nonprofit, see *Every Nonprofit's Guide to Publishing,* by Cheryl Woodard and Lucia Hwang. (Nolo).

**Sales Tax and Other State Requirements**

If your nonprofit will sell goods to the public, the federal government isn't the only tax collector you have to satisfy. You may also need to obtain a seller's permit from your state and pay state sales tax. Nonprofits are not automatically exempt from these types of general business requirements. While nonprofits may be eligible for exemptions for certain types of transactions, they must usually go through an application process to obtain that exemption. Make sure you understand and comply with your state's rules before selling goods, or you risk being charged back taxes and penalties.

Many states require nonprofits to obtain a seller's permit before they may begin selling goods. Later, you determine whether any of your sales were actually taxable under the state's rules and calculate any taxes you owe the state. Typically, you'll pay any taxes you owe at the end of the year, but you may have to pay taxes quarterly if your sales volume is high. Even if you end up owing no tax at all, many states require you to get a seller's permit in order to make the sales in the first place.

In most states, seller's permits are required and sales taxes due only for sales of tangible goods—such as books, shirts, or coffee mugs—to the public. Sales of services, such as counseling or educational assistance, are often exempt from seller's permit requirements and from state sales taxes. However, the rules vary widely from state to state, and each state's rules are riddled with exceptions. To find out more about your state's rules, contact your state sales tax agency.

A few states—including Alaska, Delaware, Montana, New Hampshire, and Oregon—don't impose a state sales tax, and you may not need a permit for most sales transactions in these states. Bear in mind, however, that cities or local governments in these states may impose sales taxes, and certain transactions in these states may be subject to something similar to a sales tax, although they call it by a different name. Again, the best way to find out all of the rules is to contact your state tax agency.

To obtain a seller's permit, contact your state agency that governs sales taxes to find out about the application process. Typically, you'll have to submit a simple application form and perhaps pay a fee. Your state agency should also have information on any special rules for nonprofits, including how to apply for any exemptions to which you may be entitled.

**TIP**

**To find your state sales tax agency's website,** either search the IRS website at www.irs.gov for its list of state tax sites (use the search term "state links"), or do an online search with Google or Yahoo! using your state name along with the words "sales tax agency" as your search terms.

## Funding From Grants

Besides asking individuals to contribute to your organization, your group can raise funds by applying for funding from foundations, government agencies, private businesses, and other groups. Grants from funding institutions are typically much larger than donations from individuals—often totaling hundreds, thousands, tens of thousands, or even millions of dollars—so getting even just one or two grants can make a huge difference in your nonprofit's budget.

While grant money is, of course, attractive to any nonprofit, you'll have to meet the grantor's eligibility criteria to throw your hat in the ring. Most grants are available only to nonprofits with 501(c)(3) status, for example. In addition, the process of finding and applying for grants takes some effort and forethought. Thankfully, the basics of the process are pretty easy to learn.

### Researching Available Grants

Half the battle of getting a grant is finding one that is available to your group for the activities that you plan to pursue with the money. Grant givers provide money for only those projects and activities that fall within the givers' funding priorities. For example, one funder might give money for programs helping disabled children; another funder might give money for activities related to arts education. You need to find grant givers with funding priorities that match your mission and activities.

With so many funding institutions out there, the process of researching grants can be intimidating. A good place to start is by consulting resources published by the Foundation Center, a nonprofit dedicated to promoting philanthropy with resources for grant givers and seekers. The Foundation Center has several publications in print and online, with tens of thousands of listings of foundations and specific grants.

Many Foundation Center publications are quite expensive, so consulting them at a public library is usually the best option. The Foundation Center's online directories are more affordable but can also usually be accessed for free at public libraries. Check the Foundation Center's Cooperating Collections page at http://foundationcenter.org/collections to find a library near you that carries these resources:

- *The Foundation Directory* offers information on the 10,000 largest foundations in the United States, including private grant-making foundations, community foundations, operating foundations, and corporate grant makers.
- The *Foundation Directory Online* is accessible online for monthly or annual subscription fees, starting at approximately $20 per month for the Basic version, with access to 10,000 foundations. At the high end, the Professional version includes access to the full database of more than 100,000 foundations for approximately $180 per month. You'll find the *Foundation Directory Online* at http://fconline.foundationcenter.org.
- The Foundation Center also publishes several guides to grant givers and specific grants within certain subject areas, such as arts and culture, health, and education.

## Writing Grant Proposals

When you find a foundation with funding priorities that match your programs, the next step is to apply for funding using that foundation's guidelines. It's important to take careful note of the foundation's application procedures and deadlines and follow them closely. Many foundations have an initial application process where they ask for a preliminary proposal or letter of inquiry as a first step. After the letter of inquiry, the foundation may invite your nonprofit to submit a full proposal—and often will not accept any full proposals without such an invitation. Don't make the mistake of spending valuable time and resources developing a proposal until you understand the application guidelines and know that your proposal will at least be accepted by the foundation.

### Preliminary Proposals

Preliminary proposals and inquiry letters typically run two to four pages long and follow a format such as the following:

- **Cover sheet.** Include your group's name, address, contact name, title, telephone and fax numbers, email address, and website address.

- **Overview of your nonprofit and your funding request.** Outline the basic facts about your group and the funds you are requesting. Include important details such as your group's mission, the amount and purpose of funds being requested, a statement of how your request matches the grantmaker's funding priorities, your tax-exempt status, and a proposed schedule for the grant and the programs it would support.
- **Description of the program in need of support.** Briefly but persuasively describe the nature of the work you plan to do with the grant, focusing on the community need it will address and whom it will affect.
- **Financial information.** While financial information sometimes isn't necessary at the preliminary stage, you may need to submit an operating budget and possibly program budgets.

### Full Proposals

When submitting a full proposal, you must follow the instructions provided by the funder in its call for grant applications or request for proposals (RFP). Many groups offer a streamlined application process using what's sometimes called a "common application form," allowing nonprofits to save time by using the same format for multiple grant applications. Even if a foundation does use a common application form, you need to be aware of any additional requirements, such as deadlines or preliminary application rules.

Most grant proposals are ten pages or less in length, single spaced, and include the following components:

- **Cover letter.** Include a brief, positive letter from a board officer on the nonprofit's letterhead, introducing the nonprofit and the proposal.
- **Cover sheet.** As with a preliminary application, include a summary of important information about the nonprofit and the request for funds.
- **Description of organization.** Offer a brief summary of your nonprofit, including its mission and goals, current programs and activities, and any significant accomplishments. Also note how many board members, staff, and volunteers your nonprofit currently has.

- **Needs assessment.** Describe the needs or issues facing your nonprofit, and how you plan to meet or resolve them. Also offer information on how this grant fits into your long-term funding strategies.
- **Program goals and objectives.** Outline specific ways your nonprofit plans to achieve its overall goals, including the activities it plans to undertake and a timeline. Also explain how you will measure performance and evaluate whether goals and objectives have been achieved.
- **Financial information.** Include a realistic and detailed budget, including the proposed grant and any committed matching funds.
- **Conclusion.** Wrap up your proposal with a concise and compelling summary.
- **Appendices and attachments.** Include important documentation, such as a copy of your 501(c)(3) determination letter, corporate documents, and financial reports. Also include lists of your board members and staffers, and any letters of support from the community. Finally, it's always helpful to include press clips showing positive mentions of your group in local or national media.

RESOURCE

**The Foundation Center offers a wealth of information on how to write and assemble winning grant proposals.** Besides offering authoritative databases of foundations and other grant providers, the Foundation Center also has free online tutorials on grant writing. Check out its website at www.foundationcenter.org.

## Corporate Sponsorships

Besides applying to organizations with established grant-giving programs, your nonprofit can also raise funds from local businesses, banks, or other institutions. Simply approaching these institutions and asking them to sponsor the organization can sometimes be enough to generate a large contribution.

Unlike foundations or government sources, corporate sponsors often get some sort of recognition in return for their contribution, which gives them valuable exposure to desirable audiences. But there are two important and potentially troublesome issues you'll need to understand about offering recognition for corporate sponsors. One is that giving recognition to sponsors might subject the income from those sponsors to tax. As discussed above, some nonprofit income may be subject to unrelated business income tax (UBIT). According to IRS rules related to sponsorships, if you "acknowledge" your sponsors, the money they give you will not be subject to tax. But if you provide your sponsors "advertising," their contribution may be subject to UBIT. The line between an acknowledgment and advertisement is not that clear, so you may want to consult an accountant or lawyer to determine whether your plans for recognizing sponsors will subject you to unrelated business income tax.

Second, if a 501(c)(3) nonprofit offers sponsors recognition that has commercial value (such as an advertisement at your website or in your newsletter), only a portion of the sponsor's contribution will be deductible by the sponsor. As discussed below, if you give something of value to a contributor in exchange for any gift of more than $75, you must:

- tell the donor that he or she can deduct only the difference between the value of the donation and the value of any gift premium he or she received, and
- provide a good-faith estimate of the fair market value of anything given to the contributor in exchange for the donation.

Refer to "The Law of Fundraising," below, for detailed information on deductibility and disclosure rules.

**EXAMPLE:** The Shawnee Independent Business Alliance develops a sponsorship program that offers varying levels of sponsorship benefits to businesses and institutions that contribute $500 or more to its group in any year. The sponsorship guidelines provide that:

All sponsors who contribute $500 or more in a calendar year will be recognized as SIBA Community Sponsors and receive the benefits listed below for one year. The benefits for varying levels of sponsorship are as follows:

| | |
|---|---|
| **$500** | • 150 × 75 pixel online ad at SIBA website home page |
| | • Print and verbal recognition at every SIBA event |
| | • Mention in SIBA's press releases to the media |
| **$1,000** | • Same as $500 level, but larger online ad (150 × 175 pixels) |
| **$2,000** | • Same as $1,000 level, plus Featured Sponsor popup at website for three (3) months |
| **$5,000** | • Same as $2,000 level, plus top banner ad (450 × 75 pixels) at SIBA website |

Because it plans to offer advertising-type recognition for its sponsors, SIBA realizes that the sponsorship income will probably be subject to unrelated business income tax. It is willing to accept this trade-off because so many potential sponsors want advertising in return for their contributions. The SIBA board plans to ask its accountant to explain the tax rules that will apply to this income and help set up its sponsorship program to minimize taxes. It also prepares thank you cards with the necessary disclosures regarding the tax deductibility of sponsorship funds.

## The Law of Fundraising

Before your nonprofit starts asking for or accepting contributions, you'll need to have a clear understanding of the legal rules that govern charitable donations. The IRS has several rules regarding the information a 501(c)(3) nonprofit must provide to donors, depending on the amount they contribute and whether the nonprofit gives them any benefits in exchange for their contributions. In addition, many states require nonprofits to register with a state agency before beginning any fundraising campaign. This section introduces key fundraising rules and offers guidance on how to comply.

### Disclosures to Donors

Considering the favorable tax treatment bestowed on 501(c)(3) nonprofits and those who donate to them, it's no surprise that the IRS imposes requirements on nonprofits that receive these benefits.

**SKIP AHEAD**
**The disclosure rules discussed in this section apply only to nonprofits with 501(c)(3) tax-exempt status.** If you haven't applied for or received this status, you don't need to worry about these rules and can skip ahead to "Charitable Solicitation Registration and Reporting," below.

Nonprofits must disclose certain information to contributors who give a "quid pro quo" contribution of more than $75 ("quid pro quo" means the donor receives something in return for his or her donation) and additional information to contributors who give $250 or more. The rules for each of these situations are discussed below.

**RESOURCE**
**Need more information on disclosures and donations?** The IRS has several publications on charitable contributions, including: Publication 526, *Charitable Contributions*; Publication 561, *Determining the Value of Donated Property*; and Publication 1771, *Charitable Contributions—Substantiation and Disclosure Requirements*. All are available free at the IRS's website, www.irs.gov. You can also get them by calling 800-TAX-FORM.

**SEE AN EXPERT**
**You may want to consult an accountant or a lawyer familiar with nonprofit fundraising issues.** Many of the rules regarding donor disclosures and charitable contributions are fairly straightforward. But, as with most things tax related, some rules can be hard to decipher. If you are planning a major fundraising campaign, check with

a professional to make sure you comply with all necessary requirements.

## Quid Pro Quo Contributions of More Than $75

If your nonprofit receives a contribution of more than $75 and gives the donor goods or services in return (often called a "gift premium"), you must provide the donor with a written disclosure statement that includes two pieces of information:

- a statement that the donor can deduct only the difference between the value of the donation and the value of any gift premium he or she received, and
- a good-faith estimate of the fair market value of any gift premium given to the contributor in exchange for the donation. The nonprofit may use any reasonable method to estimate the fair market value of the premium as long as it does so in good faith.

You must disclose these two items, but you do not have to take the additional step of calculating the donor's deduction.

**EXAMPLE:** A donor gives your nonprofit $100 and receives two tickets to the symphony worth a total of $40 as a thank-you gift. Your nonprofit provides the following disclosure statement to the donor:

> Thank you so much for your generous contribution of $100. Please note that only the portion of your contribution that exceeds the value of any gifts you receive is tax deductible. The estimated fair market value of your gift, two symphony tickets, is $40 total.

You could add that, as a result, $60 is tax deductible, but you do not have to do so.

Under this rule, the disclosure must be provided either when the nonprofit solicits a donation from a contributor or when the contributor makes a donation. If the nonprofit provides the statement when it solicits the potential donor, it does not have to provide the statement again when the donor contributes.

There are some exceptions to the written disclosure requirement. The most significant exception is that no disclosure is required for gifts that qualify as an "insubstantial benefit"; in these cases, the donor can deduct the full amount of his or her contribution. For tax year 2012 the IRS defined "insubstantial benefit" as a premium worth less than 2% of the contribution or $99—whichever is less. (Check the IRS website at www.irs.gov for more details and updated limits.)

**EXAMPLE 1:** Your nonprofit gives a coffee mug worth $5 to a donor who contributes $500. Because the gift is worth only 1% of the donation, you are not required to provide a written disclosure to the donor, because the gift is an "insubstantial benefit." The donor can deduct the full $500 donation on his or her income tax return.

**EXAMPLE 2:** Your nonprofit gives a tote bag worth $40 to the $500 donor. The tote bag does not fall into the "insubstantial benefit" exception because it is worth more than 2% of the donation ($10, which is less than the alternate IRS limit of $99). You must provide a disclosure stating that the donor's tax deduction is limited to the difference between the contribution and the value of the goods received, and that the fair market value of the tote bag is $40.

**RESOURCE**
**For more information on disclosure and substantiation rules,** see IRS Publication 1771, *Charitable Contributions—Substantiation and Disclosure Requirements.* You can get a free copy from the IRS by visiting www.irs.gov or by calling 800-TAX-FORM.

## Contributions of $250 or More

Donors may deduct a charitable contribution of $250 or more only if they have a written acknowledgment of the donation from the nonprofit. Although it is the donor's legal responsibility to ask for the acknowledgment, a wise nonprofit will always provide the necessary statement to its donors.

To help your donors comply with this rule, include a written statement along with the prompt thank-you note you should routinely provide to contributors. The donor must obtain this acknowledgment by the due date, including extensions, for filing a tax return for the year in which he or she donated, or by the date he or she actually filed the tax return, whichever is earlier.

## Charitable Solicitation Registration and Reporting

Most states have laws that govern nonprofit fundraising; these rules are generally known as "charitable solicitation regulations." Most states require nonprofits to register with a state agency—usually the state attorney general—before engaging in any fundraising efforts. In addition, the nonprofit may need to provide annual financial reports that may be made available to the public.

While you may feel frustrated by yet another paperwork requirement, these laws serve to protect the public from scams involving phony charities. In turn, the laws help reputable nonprofits because they help to instill public confidence that charitable donations are actually going toward good causes—not into the wallets of con artists.

Registration requirements vary considerably from state to state. Some require the nonprofit alone to register; others require all paid professional fundraisers and solicitors to register as well. In addition, states apply different rules to determine what constitutes fundraising. In some states, you may not be required to register if you are collecting only small amounts of money; in others, simply having a donation page on your website will trigger the registration requirements. Fees vary by state, and you may be required to post a bond. To find out more about your state's rules, contact the office in your state that regulates charitable solicitations. (You'll find a state-by-state list of website addresses for these offices on the Nolo website. See the link to this book's companion page in Appendix A.)

In an effort to streamline the registration process, the National Association of Attorneys General and the National Association of State Charities Officials jointly developed a standardized registration form, called the "Unified Registration Statement" (URS). Of the states (and the District of Columbia) that require charitable solicitation registration, most accept the URS in place of their own forms. In Colorado, Florida, and Oklahoma, you must use the state's own form. Also, in some states that accept the URS, you may need to submit some additional material.

You can download the URS as a PDF file at www. multistatefiling.org. This site also offers extensive, up-to-date information about charitable solicitation requirements by state, including any supplementary forms that may be required in addition to the URS. The chart below summarizes these basic requirements.

Registration will not fulfill any annual reporting requirement your state may impose—and the URS is usually not accepted for annual reporting. For annual reporting requirements, check with the agency that governs charitable solicitations in your state.

**RESOURCE**

**Comprehensive guide to the fundraising registration rules in each state.** See *Nonprofit Fundraising Registration: The 50-State Guide*, by Stephen Fishman and Ronald J. Barrett (Nolo) for detailed advice on state rules for initial and annual filing requirements, exemptions, Internet fundraising, and more.

## Working With Professional Fundraisers

The bigger your fundraising campaigns become, the more you may need professional help. If necessary, you can bring fundraising consultants in to answer specific questions or to handle major components of your campaign. In established nonprofits, consultants might even run a fundraising campaign from beginning to end.

Most fledgling nonprofits will use consultants sparingly (if at all), however, because their fees can add up quickly. Keeping a consultant's work focused in one area—for example, developing printed materials or expanding your prospect list—is the key to keeping your costs down. When you hire a consultant or

## State Registration Requirements for Charitable Solicitation

| State | Requires Registration? | Accepts the URS Form? | State | Requires Registration? | Accepts the URS Form? |
|---|---|---|---|---|---|
| Alabama | Yes | Yes | Montana | No | |
| Alaska | Yes | Yes | Nebraska | No | |
| Arizona | Yes | Yes | Nevada | No | |
| Arkansas | Yes | Yes* | New Hampshire | Yes | Yes* |
| California | Yes | Yes** | New Jersey | Yes | Yes |
| Colorado | Yes | No | New Mexico | Yes | No |
| Connecticut | Yes | Yes | New York | Yes | Yes |
| Delaware | No | | North Carolina | Yes | Yes |
| District of Columbia | Yes | No | North Dakota | Yes | Yes* |
| Florida | Yes | No | Ohio | Yes | No |
| Georgia | Yes | Yes* | Oklahoma | Yes | No |
| Hawaii | Yes | No | Oregon | Yes | Yes |
| Idaho | No | | Pennsylvania | Yes | Yes |
| Illinois | Yes | Yes* | Rhode Island | Yes | Yes |
| Indiana | No | | South Carolina | Yes | No |
| Iowa | No | | South Dakota | No | |
| Kansas | Yes | Yes | Tennessee | Yes | Yes* |
| Kentucky | Yes | Yes | Texas | No | |
| Louisiana | Yes | Yes | Utah | Yes | Yes* |
| Maine | Yes | No | Vermont | No | |
| Maryland | Yes | Yes | Virginia | Yes | Yes* |
| Massachusetts | Yes | Yes** | Washington | Yes | Yes* |
| Michigan | Yes | Yes | West Virginia | Yes | Yes* |
| Minnesota | Yes | Yes* | Wisconsin | Yes | Yes |
| Mississippi | Yes | Yes* | Wyoming | No | |
| Missouri | Yes | Yes | | | |

\* with supplemental information
\*\*Nonresident nonprofits only

Source: Multi-State Filer Project (www.multistatefiling.org) and state websites.

another type of fundraising expert, make sure to define clear expectations and a precise scope of work for the expert to handle.

While you should trust and feel comfortable with any consultant you hire, this is especially important with a fundraising expert. Be sure to check the consultant's references and work history, and talk to past clients. Most states regulate professional fundraisers, so you may be able to obtain information about the consultant from public resources, such as state or local government agencies. Also, make sure

that none of a consultant's past clients turned out to be bogus charities. You certainly don't want someone working for you who has been associated with any questionable nonprofits in the past.

It's always important to make sure that anyone representing your nonprofit is responsible, reputable, and ethical. This is particularly true when it comes to people working with sensitive financial matters, such as asking the public for money on your nonprofit's behalf.

---

## Checklist: Fundraising

☐ Focus on relationships with ongoing contributors. Relationships with supporters are the lifeblood of any nonprofit group.

☐ Fundraise from the inside out. Those closest to the nonprofit should be first on your prospect lists. Ask all volunteers, staffers, and board members to come up with ten or more prospective donors, and you'll be on your way to a solid donor base.

☐ Use early accomplishments to strengthen your appeals for support. Potential donors will be more inclined to give you money if they see what you have accomplished.

☐ Invest some time and money in an effective database program so you can keep careful track of whom you have asked to donate, who has given money, who asked not to be contacted again, and other important information.

☐ If you choose to solicit paid memberships, your members will expect to feel included in your group. Create ways to build a sense of community and involvement among your members, which can be a much more valuable benefit than a tote bag or coffee mug.

☐ Be thrifty. Don't model your fundraising materials on the expensive methods used by larger, well-established nonprofits. Keep your materials simple to show your potential supporters that you are counting your pennies.

☐ Train your fundraising team. Make sure your telephone or in-person solicitors are comfortable talking about your nonprofit and that they demonstrate enthusiasm for its mission. Robotic script readers do not reflect well on your group and will not inspire the public to contribute.

☐ Be sure you understand the tax rules governing unrelated business income, which is income you earn through activities not substantially related to your nonprofit mission.

☐ Comply with substantiation and disclosure rules. Provide your donors with all necessary notices, such as what portion of their donation is tax deductible.

☐ Your mother was right: Thank-you notes *do* matter! Recognizing your supporters and letting them know how much you appreciate their support helps build strong relationships. Thank-you notes are powerful tools—use them.

# Risk Management and Insurance

As discussed in Chapter 1, structuring your nonprofit as a corporation serves to protect the individuals who work on behalf of the nonprofit—particularly its board members—from personal liability for the nonprofit's judgments or debts. If the nonprofit corporation loses a lawsuit or otherwise finds itself in debt, only the nonprofit corporation—not the personal assets of its board members—will be on the hook for those costs. While an unincorporated nonprofit may not offer as much protection against personal liability as one that incorporates, a few state and federal laws protect people who work for unincorporated associations as well. Of course, lawsuits are no fun no matter who ends up liable—board members, staff, or the nonprofit itself—so it's best to take steps to avoid them whenever possible.

This chapter moves beyond incorporation to focus on broader strategies that will help you minimize the risk of a lawsuit against your nonprofit or its people, whether or not your group is incorporated. The first section in this chapter outlines the most common types of lawsuits you could face, including contract, employment, and personal injury claims. The next section explains who is at risk for certain types of claims, including when your nonprofit may be liable for the acts of those working on its behalf and what laws offer specific protection from liability.

With these risks laid out before you, the rest of this chapter explains how to manage your nonprofit's risks by implementing simple strategies that can minimize the chance that your nonprofit will be sued. Most nonprofiteurs are familiar with insurance as a risk management tool—and you should certainly purchase appropriate coverage, as explained in this chapter. However, there are other, better strategies that can help you avoid incurring liability in the first place. The good news is that many of these strategies can be remarkably easy, inexpensive, and effective.

In our litigious society, it's important to treat risks seriously and take active steps to protect your nonprofit and its people. The key is to use these strategies as preventive medicine by implementing them well *before* any legal issues arise for your nonprofit.

> **TIP**
>
> **Lawsuits can come from inside or outside your organization.** Your liability risks don't always come from the outside world, such as a visitor suing your nonprofit for an injury incurred at your office. Claims that originate within your nonprofit—such as a staff member suing because of a manager's sexual harassment or a volunteer suing over an injury at a special event—pose a significant risk to your organization as well. The more people who work or volunteer for your nonprofit, the more risks you face. It's essential to minimize the potential for both internal and external problems with risk management techniques.

> **SEE AN EXPERT**
>
> **See a lawyer if you're facing a lawsuit.** This chapter will help you understand legal liability issues and how best to minimize your risks in general. If you are threatened with a lawsuit, or are already involved in one, you'll need legal advice that applies to your specific situation—and you'll probably want to hire a lawyer. Liability issues often involve gray areas in the law that are best addressed by someone who understands your specific facts and has real-world experience in the field. See Chapter 13 for advice on finding and working with a lawyer.

## Common Legal Problems

To figure out how to minimize your risk of facing a lawsuit, you'll need to understand what types of legal claims could be brought against your group. After all, you can't avoid trouble unless you know what it looks like. This section explains the various types of legal claims that nonprofits (and for-profit organizations, too) face most often: contract disputes, employment claims, and personal injury lawsuits.

### Contract Disputes

One of the most common problems that can result in a lawsuit against a nonprofit is a dispute over a contract or an agreement of some sort. As discussed in Chapter 8, many everyday transactions—including hiring contractors, purchasing equipment, and renting commercial space—create legally binding contracts, whether you sign a lengthy document or just make an oral agreement that you execute with a handshake. When a contract exists, one party can sue the other for failing to hold up his or her end of the deal (in legal terms, for "breaching" the contract).

If you are hit with a lawsuit based on a contract claim, you can be forced to do what you promised to do in the contract and, in some cases, to pay additional money damages. To show that your nonprofit is legally liable, the other party has to prove that you had a valid contract and that you failed to live up to your end of the bargain. The other party must also prove exactly how it was harmed by your actions and set a dollar amount on its damages.

The best way to avoid a contract dispute is to consider all of the details carefully before you seal a deal; then put the final agreement in writing. Anticipating and addressing any potential points of confusion or conflict up front is always better than ignoring something until it comes back to haunt you later. (For more information on what makes a contract binding and how to draft solid contracts, see Chapter 8.)

## Employment Claims

Having employees—as helpful and wonderful as they may be—greatly increases your risk of being sued. Employment-related claims, such as for sexual harassment, wrongful termination, discrimination, and wage and hour disputes, make up a significant portion of lawsuits against nonprofits (and for-profit businesses, too).

To avoid employee lawsuits, all nonprofits need to understand the employment laws that apply to them. Then, they need to hire and fire carefully, train thoroughly, supervise adequately, implement solid personnel policies, maintain safe working environments, and purchase appropriate insurance. ("Managing Your Nonprofit's Risks," below, describes these and other techniques for reducing your legal risks in greater detail.)

The topic of employment law has filled countless books and is far beyond the scope of this chapter.

For a thorough discussion of employment law matters, including how to prevent employee lawsuits, consult one or more of the books listed in "Nolo Resources on Employment Issues," below. For now, here is an introduction to the most common types of employment-related suits and the workplace situations that might trigger them:

- **Wrongful termination.** Most employees are hired "at will," which means that they can either quit or be fired by the employer at any time, for any reason that's not illegal. In some cases, however, firing an employee could leave you vulnerable to a wrongful termination lawsuit. An employer may not fire someone for an illegal reason, such as his or her race, gender, or other characteristic protected by law (discussed in "Discrimination," below), or in retaliation for union organizing, complaining about discrimination, or reporting an employer's wrongdoing to a government agency (known as "whistleblowing"). Also, if an employee has an employment contract, he or she could argue that you need "good cause" to fire. If you terminate one of these employees without a solid, work-related reason, you could be in legal trouble.

- **Sexual harassment.** As you probably know, failing to prevent or to respond appropriately to an employee's claim of sexual harassment can expose a nonprofit to liability. Sexual harassment is unwelcome sexual conduct on the job that creates an intimidating, hostile, or offensive work environment for one or more employees. One type of sexual harassment is "quid pro quo" harassment (literally, "do this for that"), in which a worker is asked to comply with some sex-based request or face a negative consequence. Even in the absence of such demands, a sexual harassment claim may be successful if the workplace is deemed a "hostile environment" in which sexual jokes, pictures, innuendoes, or comments are allowed to persist.

- **Discrimination.** Federal law prohibits discrimination in employment based on race, color, gender, national origin, religion, disability, citizenship status, or age. In addition, state and local ordinances sometimes protect other characteristics as well, such as sexual orientation or marital status. If you rely on any of these factors in making such employment decisions as hiring, firing, pay, job or shift assignments, promotions, or access to training opportunities, you could be subject to a discrimination lawsuit.

- **Retaliation.** It is also illegal for an employer to take a negative employment action (for example, denying a promotion or giving a bad performance review) against an employee because that employee has filed a harassment or discrimination complaint or has supported another employee in making such a complaint— for example, by serving as a witness. Doing this could open you up to a retaliation claim in addition to the original discrimination or harassment claim.

- **Wage and hour claims.** Another area in which employers are often vulnerable to lawsuits is wage and hour disputes. Employers can be subject to wage and hour claims for such things as misclassifying hourly workers as salaried workers, failing to pay their workers overtime, or improperly handling an employee's vacation time. Nonprofits are not generally exempt from these laws. Because there are complicated rules that determine which workers—and which employers—are subject to certain wage and hours laws, you may want to consult a knowledgeable attorney for specific questions.

- **Defamation.** If you make false, damaging statements about someone, you may be subject to a defamation claim. In the employment context, defamation claims come up most often in the context of references—for example, if another nonprofit calls to ask about a job applicant who used to work for your group. Some state laws protect employers from defamation claims based on references. Whether or not your state has such a law, however, the best way to avoid these claims is to always be scrupulously honest when speaking about former employees—and to follow strict procedures when providing

references (for example, put one person in charge of providing references, and require prospective employers to request a reference in writing). These procedures are discussed in detail in *Dealing With Problem Employees*, by Amy DelPo and Lisa Guerin (Nolo).

---

### Watch Out for Implied Contracts

It's easy to figure out whether an employee has a written employment contract; just check your personnel files. However, an employment contract doesn't have to be in writing to be valid. An employee can claim to have an oral contract of employment—a spoken promise that he or she would only be fired for certain reasons, would have a job for a particular period of time, or would be kept on as long as the nonprofit is doing well. To figure out whether this type of contract exists, you'll have to talk to the people in your organization who do the hiring and supervise the employees.

Even more difficult to pinpoint is an implied employment contract—a contract that was not written or stated explicitly but was created by the statements and actions of the parties. Typically, employees who claim to have an implied contract point to various documents and statements that led them to believe they would be fired only for good cause. Statements by supervisors or managers, language in an employee handbook, comments in a performance evaluation, and much more have been used to create evidence of an implied contract. Not every state will allow an employee to sue based on an implied employment contract, however. What's more, there are many steps you can take to avoid these claims in the first place—including making very clear, in your employee handbook and elsewhere, that you reserve the right to fire at will. For detailed information on implied contracts, see *Dealing With Problem Employees*, by Amy DelPo and Lisa Guerin (Nolo).

---

## Personal Injury Lawsuits

Another type of lawsuit—not commonly filed against nonprofits, but still potentially devastating—is a personal injury claim (or, in legal speak, a "tort").

---

### Nolo Resources on Employment Issues

Nolo's website, www.nolo.com, offers free information on employment law (select "Employment Law" from the home page to get started). In addition, Nolo publishes numerous titles on employment law, including one book specifically for nonprofits. Check out the following titles to help you with your employment law questions:

- *The Nonprofit's Guide to Human Resources*, by Jan Masaoka. Focuses on human resource and employment issues unique to nonprofits.
- *The Essential Guide to Federal Employment Laws*, by Lisa Guerin and Amy DelPo. A desk reference that explains what each of 20 federal employment laws requires and prohibits.
- *Create Your Own Employee Handbook*, by Lisa Guerin and Amy DelPo. Guides you through the process of making a readable, legally sound employee handbook.
- *Dealing With Problem Employees*, by Amy DelPo and Lisa Guerin. Offers techniques for reducing problems in the workplace and dealing with issues as they arise.
- *The Performance Appraisal Handbook*, by Amy DelPo. A practical guide that will help anyone who supervises employees conduct effective—and legally safe—performance evaluations.

- *The Job Description Handbook*, by Margie Mader-Clark. A step-by-step guide to drafting and using job descriptions.
- *Hiring Your First Employee*, by Fred S. Steingold. This focused guide will help you decide whether it's time to hire, then lead you through all of the legal and tax requirements you'll need to follow when you bring on your first employee.
- *The Essential Guide to Workplace Investigations*, by Lisa Guerin. Step-by-step instructions for investigating and resolving employee complaints and problems.
- *The Progressive Discipline Handbook*, by Margie Mader-Clark and Lisa Guerin. Instructions for coaching and disciplining employees to improve performance and remedy misconduct.
- *The Essential Guide to Handling Workplace Harassment & Discrimination*, by Deborah C. England. The complete guide to addressing and preventing harassment and discrimination problems in the workplace.
- *The Essential Guide to Family & Medical Leave*, by Lisa Guerin and Deborah C. England. Provides information and forms employees need to comply with the FMLA.

---

Personal injury claims arise when someone in or around your nonprofit gets injured, either financially or personally, and the injury is not related to a contract. Such claims can stem from a physical injury, property damage, emotional distress, or damage to a person's reputation. In general, the person who causes an injury is financially liable for the damages suffered by the victim of the injury, even if the wrongdoer didn't mean to harm the victim; both intentional injuries and injuries caused by carelessness can result in liability.

For example, if one of your employees leaves an extension cord in front of a doorway, where a visitor trips on it and breaks an ankle, the visitor might file a personal injury claim against the nonprofit seeking compensation for medical bills, plus pain and suffering. Or, if your nonprofit's website contains

false and damaging information about someone—say, an article about the local art scene accuses a gallery owner of fraudulent activity that turns out to be untrue—the gallery owner might file a personal injury claim against the nonprofit based on the damage to his or her reputation.

While people file countless personal injury lawsuits each year, they don't always win. An injured person needs to prove certain things before a court will find another person or entity responsible for those injuries. At a minimum, the injured person must prove that he or she did, in fact, suffer an injury; that the person or organization being sued acted "negligently" (that is, carelessly); and that those negligent actions were a direct cause of the injury.

This is, of course, a very brief summary of a complex body of law—most law students spend an entire year learning the ins and outs of personal injury claims! While the world of potential personal injury lawsuits may be limited only by the imagination of lawyers, you can protect yourself by adopting some simple risk management strategies, discussed below.

---

### No More "Charitable Immunity"

A few decades ago, nonprofit organizations enjoyed broad protection from liability under a doctrine known as "charitable immunity." While the exact rules varied by state, charitable organizations were generally protected ("immune") from many types of lawsuits. Today, most states have done away with charitable immunity, leaving nonprofits vulnerable to lawsuits of all types.

In a few states, however, some remnants of charitable immunity remain and can protect nonprofits from certain legal claims. According to the Nonprofit Risk Management Center's publication *State Liability Laws for Charitable Organizations and Volunteers* (available through its website at www.nonprofitrisk.org), the states that still recognize some degree of charitable immunity for nonprofits include Alabama, Arkansas, Georgia, Maine, Maryland, New Jersey, Virginia, Utah, and Wyoming.

Even in these states, however, the doctrine may be significantly limited. In Maryland, for instance, charitable immunity applies only if the nonprofit's assets are held in a trust and the nonprofit has no liability insurance. In Alabama, immunity applies only to claims brought by beneficiaries of the nonprofit.

The bottom line is that charitable immunity no longer provides much protection to nonprofits or their workers. Other laws, such as the federal Volunteer Protection Act (discussed below), have been enacted to shield those who work at nonprofits from liability, but the nonprofits themselves don't enjoy the same protection. As a result, it's more important than ever to protect your nonprofit's assets using risk management strategies (including insurance).

---

**TIP**

**Employees' on-the-job injuries are covered by workers' compensation.** An employee who is injured on the job usually cannot sue the employer or a coworker for his or her injuries. Instead, on-the-job injuries are generally covered by workers' compensation insurance. A handful of states also have programs for state or private disability insurance to help compensate injured employees. Most employers are required to participate in such programs; contact your state labor department for more information on these requirements.

## Who Is at Risk?

In addition to understanding the types of lawsuits your nonprofit could face, you also need to know who in your nonprofit could be held legally responsible in those suits—board members, staff, volunteers, and/or the nonprofit itself. This question will likely be raised by those working with your organization, who may be concerned about whether they could be held personally liable for legal or financial mishaps involving the nonprofit. For example, if someone mismanages the nonprofit's funds, resulting in creditors suing for payment and the IRS imposing fines, could individual board members or others be held liable for the nonprofit's debts?

Nonprofits need to be especially concerned about personal liability, because people who sue always aim for the "deepest pockets"—in other words, the entity or person with the most money. In the for-profit world, the business itself, not its employees, is usually the target of lawsuits, because it usually has more money than the individuals who work for it. In the nonprofit world, however, the nonprofit's workers may have significantly more assets than the nonprofit itself, so someone filing a lawsuit may set his or her sights on an affluent board member, volunteer, or staff person.

The good news is that, in most cases, people who work for nonprofits don't have to worry about personal liability, unless they act with extreme carelessness, recklessness, or bad intentions.

<table>
<tr><td>

**State Laws May Protect Participants in Unincorporated Associations**

Board members, employees, and volunteers of nonprofits that have not incorporated may be protected by the Uniform Unincorporated Nonprofit Association Act (UUNAA)—a model law adopted in a handful of states. The general rule is that owners of unincorporated entities, such as partnerships and sole proprietorships, are personally liable for any debts or liabilities their businesses incur. The UUNAA changes this rule for unincorporated entities that are nonprofits, so that board members and others working for the nonprofits are not automatically liable for the debts and liabilities of those nonprofits.

The UUNAA does not protect a nonprofit's workers from being sued directly, based on their own actions — instead, it prevents liability based solely on their association with the nonprofit. For example, say someone sued a nonprofit for injuries suffered when the stage collapsed at a benefit concert the nonprofit sponsored. That person would not be prevented from suing a board member who erected the stage. However, if the injured person sued the nonprofit, he or she could not name the board member and other nonprofit workers as defendants in the lawsuit just because they are associated with the nonprofit. (Other laws, such as the Volunteer Protection Act, offer fuller protection, as discussed below.)

The provisions of the UUNAA apply to both paid and volunteer workers, but only in the states that have adopted this model law. The UUNAA has been adopted by Alabama, Arkansas, Colorado, Delaware, District of Columbia, Hawaii, Idaho, Illinois, North Carolina, Texas, Wisconsin, and Wyoming. As of 2012, two states have adopted a version of the UUNAA: Iowa and Nevada. (The revised version is referred to as the RUUNAA.)

Chapter 1 discusses the UUNAA in greater detail, including provisions not related to liability issues. For even more information on the UUNAA and any recent state adoptions, visit the National Conference of Commissioners on Uniform State Laws online at www.uniformlaws.org.

</td></tr>
</table>

## Liability for the Nonprofit

Whether incorporated or not, nonprofits generally are legally responsible for the acts of their workers. This is true of all employers, and nonprofits are no exception.

An employer is usually liable for everything its employees do within the course and scope of their employment. This includes both things the employer directly tells an employee to do (for example, a supervisor asks a staffer to mop the hallway entrance, where a visitor then slips and falls on the wet floor), and things that the employee does independently, without being told to do so, as long as it's within the scope of his or her work duties (for example, the staffer's duties include cleaning, and the staffer mopped the dirty hallway without being asked by a supervisor).

While it may seem unfair for employers to take the fall for employees' actions, the reasoning is simply that the buck stops with the employer: Because the employee is working for the benefit of the employer, it's considered fair to hold the employer responsible for any accidents that might occur in the process. This rule gives employers a strong incentive to hire carefully, train well, supervise appropriately, and ensure that their employees don't cause harm.

An employer is not liable, however, for actions that fall outside the scope of an employee's work duties. If the activity in question is simply unrelated to the worker's job (say, an employee takes his or her dog for a walk during lunch hour and the dog bites someone), or if the employee recklessly or even intentionally causes harm while at work (for instance, an employee of a nonprofit nature center flies into a rage and assaults a visitor), a judge would likely decide that the employee, not the nonprofit, should be responsible for the damages.

## Liability for Board Members

Board members won't usually be personally liable for a nonprofit's legal or financial woes, as long as they fulfill their duties to the nonprofit. As discussed in Chapter 4, board members have a "fiduciary duty" toward their nonprofit—a legal obligation to act carefully and in the nonprofit's best interests. To fulfill this obligation, board members must act with reasonable care and good faith in doing their work and must avoid conflicts of interest—in particular, situations where they stand to gain personally at the expense of the nonprofit. A board member can face personal liability by failing to meet these responsibilities.

If, for instance, a board member chronically misses meetings during which important financial decisions are made, that member has failed to act with reasonable care and could possibly be held liable for any misuse of funds or other fiscal mismanagement. Or, if a board member ignores persistent rumors for months that the executive director has engaged in lewd conduct toward some employees, that board member could become subject to personal liability if the employee files a sexual harassment lawsuit against the nonprofit. A board member might also face liability for engaging in self-dealing (by pocketing earnings from nonprofit-related services, for example).

As these examples illustrate, board members can do much to protect themselves against liability simply by doing a conscientious job. This typically involves:

- **Attending meetings.** Missing meetings is one of the most common ways board members fall short of their duty to act with reasonable care. Missing a meeting or two per year is sometimes unavoidable and generally will not expose a board member to liability. But the less involved a board member is, the greater the possibility that he or she could be held liable for the nonprofit's woes.

- **Staying informed.** Board members should always understand what the nonprofit is doing. This means reading reports, paying attention to the budget and other key financial issues, and, where necessary, asking questions. If a member is overwhelmed by the workload and cannot stay on top of important matters, he or she should let the other board members know and find a solution—whether it means recruiting additional board members, transferring work to staff or volunteers, or stepping down from the board.

- **Keeping the nonprofit on track toward its mission.** It's the board's job to make sure that the nonprofit is carrying out its stated mission. The state grants the privileges of nonprofit status— and the IRS gives tax exemptions—based on the nonprofit's stated mission. If the organization strays from its mission, the nonprofit could lose its federal tax-exempt status, its state nonprofit status, or both. Obviously, this could be devastating to a nonprofit, resulting not only in ineligibility for grants and other funds but possibly a hefty tax bill, as well. It's the board's responsibility to make sure this does not happen.

- **Understanding and complying with workplace laws.** As mentioned above, lawsuits alleging wrongful termination, harassment, or discrimination are a serious risk to nonprofits. Board members typically aren't personally liable for these types of claims. If, however, board members knowingly allow these laws to be broken or personally violate them, they could face personal liability. To help avoid this, board members should make sure that the nonprofit has solid policies in place for employees and volunteers—ideally in a written handbook. (For specifics on preventing employee lawsuits, see "Focus on Prevention," below.)

- **Making sure the nonprofit stays in compliance with local, state, and federal requirements.** While the executive director or another staff person is usually responsible for handling important bureaucratic tasks such as filing corporate reports, paying taxes, and complying with other regulations, the board should exercise sufficient oversight to responsibly conclude that the nonprofit is in compliance. An out-of-touch board that fails to ensure that bureaucratic requirements are met might face liability down the road if the mismanagement results in legal action or fines.

**RESOURCE**
**For detailed information on the bureaucratic tasks a nonprofit faces,** see *How to Form a Nonprofit*

*Corporation*, by Anthony Mancuso (Nolo). This title offers step-by-step instructions on the state and federal paperwork involved in starting and running a nonprofit.

Besides performing their duties responsibly, board members can also protect themselves by purchasing directors and officers (D&O) insurance. This type of coverage is discussed in more detail below.

State or federal laws may also protect your board members from liability. The federal Volunteer Protection Act (VPA) shields board members who are working for nonprofits on a volunteer (unpaid) basis. If your nonprofit is not incorporated and your state has adopted the UUNAA, board members cannot automatically be held liable for the actions of the nonprofit just because they run and/or work for it. See "State Laws May Protect Participants in Unincorporated Associations," above, for more on the UUNAA.

### Is a Nonprofit Liable for the Acts of Independent Contractors?

An independent contractor is someone who works for you on a freelance basis, not as a regular employee. (For more on this distinction, see Chapter 5.) If you hire an independent contractor, someone may try to sue you for an injury caused by the contractor's work. For example, if you hire a contractor to set up lighting for a special event and a light falls from the ceiling and injures someone, the injured person might sue your nonprofit rather than the contractor.

While employers are typically liable for the acts of their employees, the rules about an employer's liability for the acts of an independent contractor are not as clear-cut. The answer will depend heavily on the facts of the situation and on the language of the contract between your nonprofit and the contractor. If you are sued and found liable, you may be able to sue the independent contractor to reimburse you for the damages you suffered—the money you were forced to pay because of the contractor's mistakes.

For more information on liability for the work of contractors you hire, see *Working With Independent Contractors*, by Stephen Fishman (Nolo).

## Liability for Employees

In rare cases, employees of a nonprofit can be held personally liable for injuries they cause, but this doesn't happen very often. As long as employees act with "reasonable care" toward the nonprofit, they will not be responsible for damages. Unless an employee acts with recklessness or total disregard for others or intentionally causes harm, the nonprofit itself—rather than the employee personally—will be on the hook for any injuries.

For example, if an employee brings her attack-trained pit bull to the office and the dog seriously injures a visitor, the employee could be held personally liable for damages. The same is true if the employee causes damage through intentional acts, such as vandalizing the office or assaulting someone. Sexual harassment and illegal discrimination also may expose an offending employee to personal liability—especially if the nonprofit has solid workplace policies in place prohibiting such behavior.

**TIP**
**When individuals avoid personal liability, the nonprofit may still be on the hook.** Even if board members and staff are not liable, the nonprofit itself may still be legally responsible for a personal injury claim, an employee discrimination claim, or a breach of contract lawsuit—and could lose all or most of its assets in the bargain. Although board members and staff won't lose their personal wealth, they could very well lose their jobs, their cause, and the organization they've fought so hard to sustain. The bottom line is that no matter who foots the bill, being on the losing end of a lawsuit will cause great harm to everyone involved in the nonprofit's work (including the communities the organization exists to serve). The only way to avoid the problem is to reduce your risks from the outset.

If your nonprofit is not incorporated and your state has adopted the UUNAA, your employees will not automatically be liable for judgments against the nonprofit. See "State Laws May Protect Participants in Unincorporated Associations," above, for more on the UUNAA.

## Liability for Volunteers

Employers are generally liable for the acts of their employees, but state laws are less clear on the question of nonprofit liability for the acts of volunteers. A federal law, the Volunteer Protection Act, resolves this issue to some degree by protecting volunteers in all states from liability for certain types of lawsuits.

### State Laws

Every state has enacted one or more laws to address whether volunteers are personally liable for mishaps that happen during their volunteer work. Unfortunately, these laws differ greatly from state to state, so there are no general rules when it comes to volunteer liability protection under state law. To find out what the law says in your state, you'll need to do some research. See "Researching the Law in Your State," below, for information on how to get started.

If your nonprofit is not incorporated and your state has adopted the UUNAA, your volunteers (like your employees) may be protected from personal liability for the nonprofit's problems—but they can still be sued for their own misconduct. See "State Laws May Protect Participants in Unincorporated Associations," above, for more on the UUNAA.

CAUTION
**Volunteers may still be liable for certain types of misconduct.** Even when state laws shield volunteers from personal liability, the laws often make exceptions for certain acts. In other words, even if a state law protects nonprofit volunteers from liability, that protection won't exist if the injury occurred during one of these excluded circumstances. The most common exceptions to laws protecting volunteers from liability are for (1) willful or intentional actions (purposeful misconduct), (2) grossly negligent actions (acts committed with a total disregard for the safety of others), and (3) actions committed while operating a motor vehicle.

### Volunteer Protection Act

In 1977, Congress passed a federal law—the Volunteer Protection Act (VPA) (codified at 42 U.S.C. § 14501)—to establish more uniform liability protections for volunteers nationwide. Lawmakers enacted this statute to address the concern that people were less likely to volunteer for worthy causes because they were afraid of being exposed to liability. The VPA provides limited immunity to volunteers nationwide for any injuries or damages they cause in the course of their volunteer activities, regardless of the state in which they live and volunteer.

The VPA does not require a group to be incorporated or to have 501(c)(3) status to be covered. The VPA covers volunteers of all nonprofit groups that have 501(c)(3) status, or that are "organized and conducted for public benefit and operated primarily for charitable, civic, educational, religious, welfare, or health purposes." (42 U.S.C. § 14505(4)(B).) (Interestingly, the VPA excludes from the definition of "nonprofit organization" any group that engages in hate crimes, as defined by federal law.)

To qualify as a "volunteer" under the VPA, a worker must not receive compensation or anything of more than $500 value per year for his or her services. Directors and officers who meet this requirement also qualify as volunteers. Volunteers may be reimbursed their out-of-pocket expenses and still be protected by the act.

In addition, for a volunteer to be protected from liability under the VPA, his or her actions must meet all of the following conditions:

- The volunteer was acting within the scope of his or her responsibilities at the time of the act (or failure to act) that caused the harm.
- If appropriate or required, the volunteer was properly licensed, certified, or authorized to act.
- The actions causing the harm were not intentional, criminal, reckless, or grossly negligent (that is, they were not committed with a total disregard for the safety of others).
- The volunteer was not operating a motor vehicle, vessel, or aircraft. (Congress apparently wanted these risks to be addressed by insurance coverage.)

The general rule is that the VPA overrides any state law on personal liability for volunteers unless the state law offers more protection to volunteers than the

VPA. However, there are exceptions—some state laws that *limit* protection to volunteers will still have legal force despite the VPA. In other words, certain state volunteer protection laws will *not* be overridden by the VPA. State laws that continue to apply despite the VPA include the following:

- any state law that limits protection to nonprofits that have adopted policies to manage their risk of liability, including mandatory volunteer training. In other words, if a state law says that volunteers are protected only if the nonprofit has adopted risk management policies, then volunteers for a nonprofit that has *not* done so will *not* be protected by state law or the VPA.

- any state law making nonprofits liable for the acts of their volunteers to the same extent that private employers are liable for the acts of their employees. If a state has such a law, the VPA will not do anything to change it.

- any state law saying that volunteers are not protected from liability if a state or local government officer brings the suit against the volunteer. If such a state law exists, then the VPA will not provide immunity if a district attorney or other public official files suit against the volunteer.

- any state law that protects only those nonprofits that offer a source of compensation for those who are injured—for example, an insurance policy. If state law includes this type of limitation, then the VPA won't help a volunteer at a nonprofit that doesn't have insurance or another source of financial relief for those it may injure.

Another notable exception to the VPA is that a volunteer who commits a violent crime, hate crime, sexual offense, or violation of civil rights law against someone or who injures someone while under the influence of alcohol or drugs will not be protected from liability under the VPA. Also, the VPA does not prevent a nonprofit from suing a volunteer for injuries he or she caused; it just protects volunteers from lawsuits by third parties for actions the volunteer took during his or her volunteer work.

---

### Researching the Law in Your State

To find out about the laws on personal liability in your state, you may have to do a little digging. Start by contacting the office that oversees nonprofits in your state—often the secretary of state or other corporate filing office. (For a list of secretaries of state nationwide, visit the website of the National Association of Secretaries of State at www.nass.org.) Ask them to direct you to information on liability statutes for nonprofits in your state—for example, charitable immunity or volunteer liability laws. They may have a publication summarizing your state's laws, or they might be able to direct you to a specific section of your state's statutes.

The Nonprofit Risk Management Center is another excellent resource for information on nonprofit liability issues. This group has put together an informative, free publication, *State Liability Laws for Charitable Organizations and Volunteers*, which you can download from its website at www.nonprofitrisk.org. This publication is updated regularly and offers an impressive summary of liability laws in each state.

If you still need more information, you may have to do some basic legal research on your own. For simple tasks like finding state statutes, doing your own legal research is not as complicated as you might think. Chapter 13 offers tips on how to do legal research yourself. For a more thorough reference, see *Legal Research: How to Find & Understand the Law*, by Stephen R. Elias and the Editors of Nolo (Nolo).

---

CAUTION

**Nonprofits are not shielded from liability.** The VPA does nothing to prevent lawsuits against nonprofit organizations—it protects only the volunteers working for those nonprofits. But because nonprofits often have little or no assets, it's often the volunteers and their deeper pockets (if they have them) who need protection from those suing for money damages.

## Managing Your Nonprofit's Risks

So far, this chapter has looked at the (often intricate) rules that determine who may be on the hook for any harm that occurs during the course of a nonprofit's activities. As discussed, there are many gray areas when it comes to who will be liable; often, the only definitive answer is the one that's handed down by a judge or jury. Despite the legal complexities, however, one thing is crystal clear: Taking sensible steps to minimize your risk of being sued in the first place is the best way to avoid liability. Your primary goal is not to win a lawsuit brought by someone who has been injured by your nonprofit—or to rely on state and federal protections as a shield—but to avoid the lawsuit altogether.

The term "risk management" refers to the practice of actively addressing, managing, and minimizing your risk of causing injuries or being sued. It's a rapidly growing field, in no small part due to the perfectly sensible fear that a lawsuit will drop out of nowhere and wreak havoc on your nonprofit. Purchasing various types of insurance is a part of a risk management program but that's not all there is to it. Sometimes, insurance provides adequate protection; in other cases, insurance may be either too expensive or simply unavailable for particular activities. (Insurance is discussed below.)

A basic risk management strategy will address the following questions:

- What can go wrong in our organization?
- How can we prevent these events from happening?
- If, despite our best efforts, things still go wrong, how will we control the damage?
- If we do get sued, how will we pay for lawyers, court judgments (if we lose), or out-of-court settlements?

 **TIP**

**Focus on what you are trying to protect.** Keep in mind that your risk management efforts are all geared toward protecting your assets—financial and otherwise. Most organizations will have similar lists of things they want to protect: their people, their physical and financial assets, and their reputations. It's a good idea to put a little thought into what assets your risk management efforts are designed to protect. Knowing which assets are most important to you will help you identify potential threats to those assets more effectively.

### Anticipate What Can Go Wrong

Start your risk management program by outlining the operations and activities your nonprofit plans to undertake. This will help you identify your potential risks. For example:

- If your office will be open to the public, you'll need to make sure that your office environment is safe.
- If you plan to have a lot of employees or volunteers, you'll need to take steps to avoid workplace-related lawsuits.
- If you want to engage in potentially risky activities, such as horseback riding trips, kayaking lessons, or art classes with potentially hazardous materials, you'll need to take steps to avoid injuries and legal claims.
- If you intend to hold special events, you'll need to plan for dealing with large sums of cash, which can get lost or stolen.
- Any driving done in the course of nonprofit activities raises the risk of auto accidents—and the expensive lawsuits that can result.

In addition to identifying the risks that arise from your specific activities, you should brainstorm to come up with other possible problems. Talking with an insurance agent who is familiar with nonprofits—or, better yet, with your type of nonprofit activities—can help identify risks that you might not have considered. It's also useful to talk with other local nonprofits about their risk management strategies and to read trade magazines and other media to keep abreast of the kinds of lawsuits being filed against nonprofits. Don't forget to ask your employees what risks and problems they see lurking, as they may be one of your best sources for ideas that will help you reduce your risks.

Finally, it should come as no surprise to you that your nonprofit can get in trouble for violating government requirements or breaking criminal laws. Failing to pay federal or state taxes is a common way that nonprofits find themselves in trouble. Less commonly, nonprofits discover that an employee or board member has committed theft or fraud. While these may seem like remote possibilities, it's best to think broadly when assessing potential risks.

## Focus on Prevention

Once you've identified the main risks facing your nonprofit, it's time to think about ways to protect yourself against these risks. There are many ways to minimize potential problems, including ensuring adequate supervision, implementing and communicating clear policies, and getting insurance. In some situations, however, you may have to consider the possibility of changing or eliminating certain activities that you deem too risky (or that involve prohibitively high risk prevention costs). Of course, what is too risky may depend on the law and the availability of insurance in your state.

### Run a Tight Ship

It goes without saying that you should operate your nonprofit conscientiously. Besides ensuring a quality operation, solid management also helps prevent legal problems. Proper management includes:

- filing all required papers and getting the necessary permits
- being truthful and accurate in your paperwork and personal dealings
- keeping track of nonprofit funds, inventory, and important documents
- paying your debts
- delivering what you promise
- maintaining safety standards, and
- complying with all applicable laws, especially by paying taxes on time.

As mentioned earlier, even if an executive director, a manager, or another employee is in charge of filling out and filing the paperwork, ultimately it's the board's responsibility to make sure the nonprofit complies with all applicable laws. Your board should check in regularly to make sure that the necessary paperwork is getting done on time.

### Establish Workplace Policies

The key to minimizing the significant risks of workplace-related lawsuits is to be proactive—to implement policies and trainings designed to avoid such claims in the first place. It's essential to understand the employment laws that apply to your organization and to hire and fire carefully, train thoroughly, supervise adequately, implement solid personnel policies, and maintain a safe working environment. If you don't, any employees you hire pose a significant risk to your nonprofit—and possibly to its board members, managers, and other employees who could be sued personally. For more on potential employee lawsuits, see "Employment Claims," above.

Particularly with employment-related legal issues, one of the best risk management techniques is to implement effective policies and training programs from the get-go. For example, straightforward hiring and firing policies, including a written policy stating that employment is at will, can help protect you against claims of wrongful termination. A clear policy prohibiting sexual harassment and identifying what an employee should do to make a harassment complaint is essential to protect you from losing a sexual harassment claim. Including these crucial policies in an employee and/or volunteer manual and posting them in common areas (particularly effective with a sexual harassment policy) will help get everyone on the same page and avoid misunderstandings that can lead to legal conflicts.

In addition to having clear policies in writing, it's also smart to conduct orientation and training programs on important policies to make sure your employees and volunteers understand them—for example, sexual harassment, antidiscrimination, and workplace safety policies. Actively teaching your staffers what behavior is expected and what will not be tolerated will significantly reduce your liability exposure in those areas.

Beyond establishing and communicating personnel and other policies to your staff, you need to make sure that your management structure ensures that the policies will be enforced. Even the most airtight written policy on sexual harassment or workplace safety won't protect a nonprofit from being sued if complaints go uninvestigated or the organization doesn't take effective action to deal with violations. An "open door" or other reporting policy through which an employee or volunteer can launch a complaint is an absolute must. Employees who understand that their employer is taking care of their concerns are less likely to become frustrated and sue, and an employer who makes sure to follow all applicable workplace laws is less likely to be found at fault if sued.

If you are unsure which laws apply to your organization or which employment policies you should put in place, check the Small Business Resources section of the U.S. Department of Labor website (www.dol.gov), and check with your own state's department of labor. (Use Google or Yahoo! to do an online search with your state name and "department of labor" as your search terms.) You can also find helpful information on Nolo's website (www.nolo.com), as well as in books such as *Create Your Own Employee Handbook: A Legal & Practical Guide,* by Lisa Guerin and Amy DelPo (Nolo). You may wish to review other employers' personnel manuals to see what they cover, and/or hire a personnel specialist or an HR consultant.

RESOURCE

**Want more information on employment law?** Nolo publishes many different titles on a wide array of employment law, human resources, and workplace-related topics. For a complete list, see "Nolo Resources on Employment Issues," above.

## Obtain Appropriate Insurance

Another powerful risk management tool is insurance coverage. All businesses and nonprofits should consider purchasing standard property and liability insurance. In addition, there are some types of insurance designed specifically for nonprofits and the people who work for them.

### Alternative Dispute Resolution

One good way to avoid lawsuits—and ensure that workplace problems are resolved quickly, with input from everyone involved—is to steer disputes towards alternative methods of resolution, such as mediation and arbitration. One option is to include a provision in your personnel manual that workplace-related complaints will be referred to a mediator and then, if they can't be resolved within a reasonable time, to an arbitrator. A mediator is someone who helps people come to an agreement, while an arbitrator makes a binding decision. Some states automatically refer civil lawsuits to a mediator to see whether the parties can settle before a judge will hear the case.

To encourage employees to use the system—and to make sure that a court will uphold its validity—the nonprofit should pay the costs of mediation and arbitration. These can range from $500 to $3,000 per day, depending on the nature and complexity of the dispute. Some community mediation groups will take on nonprofit or small business claims free or for a nominal cost.

Bear in mind that agreements between employers and employees that make arbitration the employees' exclusive remedy are not always binding. Judges do not like to see employees give up their rights to complain to government agencies or to bring lawsuits, especially if the employees have to agree to arbitrate future disputes as a nonnegotiable condition of employment. The law in this area is changing rapidly, so you should find out what is legal in your own state. You can find information on alternative dispute resolution in *Dealing With Problem Employees*, by Amy DelPo and Lisa Guerin (Nolo).

CAUTION

**Employers are subject to special state and federal insurance rules.** If your nonprofit hires employees, it will be subject to a number of additional insurance requirements. Typically, employers must pay for workers' compensation insurance and unemployment insurance; a handful of states also require employers to pay into a state disability insurance fund. These insurance programs are specifically set up for employers and are regulated by state or federal agencies. See Chapter 5 for more on the rules that govern employer and employee contributions to these insurance programs.

 **TIP**

**Caring for your policy.** Treat your insurance policy like the precious, and possibly irreplaceable, document that it is. Store it carefully. Keep copies of old policies for your records, even if you change insurance providers. Claims can arise from long-ago events, and that document may be your only way to track down an insurer you had in the past. If the insurance company or its successor is still in business and you have a copy of the old policy to prove that it covered that event, the insurance company should provide the protection you paid for at the time.

## General Liability Insurance

General liability coverage insures you against the classic slip-and-fall situation: Someone is injured on your premises and sues you for damages. A general liability policy (sometimes called a "commercial general liability" or CGL policy) will cover damages that your nonprofit is ordered to pay to someone (such as a visitor, a customer, a supplier, or an associate) who was injured on your property. Injured employees are covered by worker's compensation insurance, so employees aren't a concern here.

For instance, if a visitor breaks a hip after tripping on an electric cord, or gets hurt when a shelving unit falls over, he or she might sue. In this age of fast and furious personal injury lawsuits, one accident like this can wipe out your organization's assets. For this reason, any operation—for profit or nonprofit—that has even minimal contact with the public should obtain liability insurance.

Most general liability policies do not cover certain employment law claims such as harassment, discrimination, and wrongful termination. Coverage for these claims (sometimes called "employment

practices liability" or EPL) must usually be purchased separately or as part of directors and officers insurance (as discussed below).

## Product Liability Insurance

Product liability insurance protects you from lawsuits by customers claiming to have been hurt by a product you provided—for example, a parent who sues the maker of a toy that injured his or her child, or a person who sues McDonald's after claiming to be burned by its extremely hot coffee. Most nonprofits are not in the business of selling products to the public—but if yours is, you might consider this type of insurance. It can be expensive, but it's better to pay a high premium than a multimillion dollar award to someone who sues you and wins.

## Property Insurance

While this chapter has focused on legal liability issues, there are, of course, other types of risks that can be devastating to a nonprofit. You can protect yourself from loss of property to theft, fire, or other causes with a property insurance policy. There is wide variation from policy to policy on what property is covered, what risks are covered, and how much the policy will pay out; be sure you're absolutely clear on these issues when choosing a policy.

When considering what property to cover, make sure that your policy covers the nonprofit's premises as well as any assets kept there, including:

- fixtures to the property, such as lighting systems or carpeting
- equipment and machinery
- office furniture
- computers and accessories, and
- inventory and supplies.

Most basic policies will cover these items.

**CAUTION**

**Renters may have to purchase property insurance.** If your nonprofit rents its space, your lease may require that you obtain a specific amount or type of property insurance coverage. Be sure to check your lease for any insurance requirements before you purchase a policy.

Besides establishing what property will be covered under your property insurance policy, you'll need to understand which types or kinds of losses will be covered. Ask your agent or broker to explain what kinds of property damage or loss your policy covers, and make sure you understand all of the details.

Most property insurance policies provide either "basic form," "broad form," or "special form" coverage. A basic form policy will commonly cover fires, explosions, storms, smoke, riots, vandalism, and sprinkler leaks. A broad form policy typically includes the above, plus damage from broken windows and other structural glass, falling objects, and water damage. Both basic and broad form policies, however, usually exclude certain risks from coverage—for example, many policyholders are surprised to learn that theft is not typically covered under either basic or broad form policies. Special form coverage offers the widest protection, usually covering all risks—including theft—unless they are specifically excluded. While premiums for special form policies will be more expensive, it may be worth it if your nonprofit faces several or unusual risks, or if theft is a big concern for your group.

Also bear in mind that some policies may not cover property owned by others that is lost, destroyed, or damaged while on your nonprofit's premises. For instance, if a volunteer's personal laptop is destroyed in an office fire, the computer may not be covered under some policies. If you expect to rely on the personal equipment of staffers at your nonprofit office, make sure that your property insurance covers their property. As an alternative, you could advise staffers that any personal equipment used at the nonprofit's office should be protected under their own homeowners' or renters' coverage.

If the policy you're considering excludes one or more items that you want covered, find out whether you can get it included and at what cost. You may have to purchase what's commonly called a "rider" or an "endorsement" that adds special coverage to your

policy. For example, standard property insurance policies often exclude accounting records, cash, and deeds, but these can usually be covered by adding a rider to the policy—and paying an additional premium.

There may be other ways to bring additional property under the scope of your policy, too. For example, if you keep your personal stereo at your office but the policy excludes personal property, you could transfer ownership of the stereo to the nonprofit.

> **CAUTION**
>
> **If you run the nonprofit out of your home, you may need to adjust your homeowner's or renter's insurance policy.** Some homeowners' or renters' policies exclude coverage of business-related claims, while others forbid business use of the home—meaning that if you run a nonprofit out of your home, your coverage could be limited or rendered void altogether. Make sure that this doesn't happen to you: It's better to come clean with your insurance company about your activities—even if it means spending some more on your premiums—than to find out after a catastrophe that your homeowners' coverage has been voided by your nonprofit activities.

Make sure that you understand the dollar limits on your policy and any deductibles or copayments the nonprofit will have to make. Make sure the policy covers the cost to replace the property, not merely its current (usually much lower) value. For example, if your four-year-old computer is stolen, you want the insurance company to pay you enough to buy a new computer, not to reimburse you for the negligible value of the one that was stolen.

## Auto Insurance

Auto liability insurance, which pays for injuries a driver causes to other people or property, is a must if your staff or volunteers use any vehicles (including their own cars) for the activities of the nonprofit. As mentioned above, your general liability insurance will not provide auto liability coverage, which is required by law in the vast majority of states. Even if it is not required in your state, you'd be foolish not to protect yourself against the common and potentially devastating risk of an auto accident.

In addition to auto liability insurance, some states require drivers to have other types of auto insurance, including personal injury protection (PIP) coverage and uninsured/underinsured motorist (UM/UIM) coverage. And, if your state requires certain *types* of coverage, it will usually also require you to purchase a certain minimum *amount* of coverage. Check with your state's department of motor vehicles to find out the insurance requirements for drivers in your state.

To get coverage for the personal cars that your employees or volunteers use for business purposes, your nonprofit will have to obtain "nonowned auto liability insurance." This will protect the nonprofit if an employee or volunteer hurts someone or damages property while driving a personal car for nonprofit business. If your employees or volunteers will use their own cars for nonprofit activities, you should get this type of coverage even if your state doesn't require it. Many nonowned auto liability insurance policies do not protect workers, however—they just protect the nonprofit itself. To protect themselves, workers generally need to get their own coverage as well (which they should have, anyway).

## Directors and Officers Insurance

As their name suggests, directors and officers insurance policies (often referred to as "D&O insurance") cover claims against a nonprofit's directors and officers. Unlike general liability insurance, which protects the nonprofit against personal injury suits, traditional D&O coverage focuses on lawsuits against a nonprofit that allege fraud or financial mismanagement and name the directors or officers personally in the lawsuit.

Even though board members are not usually personally liable for their work on behalf of a nonprofit, it's not uncommon for them to be personally named in lawsuits. For example, if a board member invests the nonprofit's assets unwisely and loses everything, a creditor might sue the nonprofit as well as its directors and officers. In such cases, D&O insurance would cover the cost of defending the directors and officers in the lawsuit as well as any money damages they are ordered to pay.

As with any insurance coverage, it is important to understand what types of claims are and are not covered by a D&O policy. D&O insurance typically covers a broad range of "wrongful acts," with specific exclusions. Claims that are usually excluded from D&O coverage include those arising from criminal or fraudulent behavior and "insured vs. insured" claims—lawsuits brought by one director against another.

Personal injury claims and employment claims (such as wrongful termination, sexual harassment, and discrimination) are also usually excluded from D&O insurance policies, unless the policy includes employment-related claims coverage (sometimes called "employment practices liability" or EPL coverage). While a policy that excludes employment claims will usually save you money on your insurance premiums, you probably shouldn't go this route if you have employees—the most common claims filed against directors and officers are employment related.

The premium costs for D&O insurance vary a great deal depending on the nature of the nonprofit's activities and the number of employees (if employment-related coverage is included), as well as the benefits offered and claims covered. Be sure to shop around, ask a lot of questions, and make sure you understand the policy's deductible and out-of-pocket limits before making a decision.

## Professional Liability Insurance

Professional liability coverage—also sometimes called "errors and omissions" (E&O) or malpractice insurance—is similar to D&O coverage in that it protects against liabilities resulting from mismanagement (or alleged mismanagement) of a nonprofit. Unlike D&O insurance, liability insurance doesn't cover just directors and officers, but also staff, volunteers, and the nonprofit itself. It aims to protect both the organization and the people working or volunteering for it from judgments resulting from poor management of the nonprofit or from workplace-related lawsuits, such as discrimination or sexual harassment.

As with D&O insurance, some professional liability policies may exclude workplace-related claims from coverage. Generally speaking, if you're going to pay for professional liability coverage, you should include protection from workplace-related lawsuits, because they are among the most common claims brought against nonprofits and their workers.

### Investigating and Purchasing a Policy

The key to making an intelligent and cost-effective insurance purchase is to do your homework. Understanding the fine print is absolutely essential in order to compare policies and find one that meets your needs. For example, you can't really compare the cost of different policies unless they cover the same types of property, the same risks, and up to the same dollar amounts of coverage. You need to research and understand all of these details fully to make an informed decision.

Insurance brokers who gather information from different insurance companies can be a big help when you're trying to decipher policies and come up with the best deal. Make sure your broker understands any special issues facing nonprofits and the risks that are, or may be, involved with your particular activities. If possible, use a broker who specializes in policies for nonprofits.

To do your own research, one good resource is the Alliance of Nonprofits for Insurance (ANI), a 501(c)(3) tax-exempt nonprofit insurance company (www.ani-rrg.org). ANI's mission is to be a stable source of reasonably priced liability insurance for 501(c)(3) nonprofits, and to assist them in developing and implementing effective risk management programs. In addition, many state nonprofit associations are affiliated with insurance firms and organizations that offer nonprofit-specific products and services. To find your state nonprofit association, visit the National Council of Nonprofits at www.councilofnonprofits.org.

## How to Deal With Problems Effectively and Minimize Risks

No matter how much preventive risk management you do, problems can still arise. The key to protecting your nonprofit and its people is to respond to problems promptly and appropriately, in a fair and thorough manner. When a problem arises, stay as calm as possible while you get the information you need to decide what to do. You won't do yourself or your nonprofit any good by making an unconsidered response.

If a problem comes up involving a written contract, start by reviewing the contract to pinpoint where things went wrong, whether the contract addresses the problem, and what solutions (if any) are available under the contract. After you've clarified the dispute as best you can in your own mind, a calm meeting or phone call with the other party is usually a good idea, followed up by a letter summarizing the meeting or conversation. If a problem arises with an employee, be sure to follow your established policies and keep employment matters confidential. If necessary or appropriate, or if you simply feel that you are in over your head, contact an expert such as a lawyer, a mediator, an employment law specialist, or another professional. (See Chapter 13 for more information on finding and working with lawyers.)

Keep in mind that if someone sues your organization, you may decide—or be required—to pay something to settle the claim or to defend yourself, whether or not you feel responsible for what went wrong. If you have insurance, the insurance company will generally pay for an attorney to defend you against claims covered by your policy. It will also likely pay some, if not most, of any eventual settlement or judgment against you if the claim is covered by your policy.

If you don't have insurance, you may have to get creative to adequately address your costs or losses in an emergency. Some nonprofits will be fortunate enough to have some extra money in the bank for emergencies. Others may choose to hold a special event to raise money in an unexpected emergency, such as a fire or natural disaster. While special events aren't cheap, you may find that local businesses, individuals, or other nonprofits might be willing to pitch in (in an emergency) to help or offer a venue, food, music, or other things for free. Flexibility and creativity will be your best assets for dealing with this type of crisis.

## Checklist: Risk Management and Insurance

- ☐ Treat liability issues seriously. Take active steps to protect your organization and its people.
- ☐ Understand the common types of lawsuits—contract disputes, employment claims, and personal injury lawsuits—in order to recognize where your nonprofit might be at risk.
- ☐ Understand who can be held liable in different situations: your board members, staff, volunteers, and/ or the organization itself.
- ☐ Use risk management strategies to minimize the possibility of a lawsuit against your nonprofit. Anticipate what can go wrong, and focus on prevention.
- ☐ Operate your organization conscientiously and implement effective workplace policies.
- ☐ Obtain appropriate property, liability, automobile, and other types of insurance for your nonprofit.
- ☐ If seriously threatened with a lawsuit, obtain legal advice specific to your situation.

# Understanding Contracts and Agreements

Regardless of its size, mission, or activities, your nonprofit will eventually have to enter into agreements with others, including other nonprofits, for-profit businesses, and individuals. For example, if you book a venue for an event, hire a consultant, order a set of printed brochures, or rent office space, you will have to reach an agreement with the other party about the details: the price of using the venue, the number of printed brochures, and so on. While some of these transactions may be simple enough to complete with a handshake, some will be sufficiently detailed, long-term, or financially important to require a written contract that clearly states the essential terms of the deal.

Thankfully, most contracts are relatively short, simple documents. You probably won't need a lawyer to complete many of the contracts your nonprofit will execute. However, there are some situations in which lawyers can be helpful or even essential. For example, if there's a type of contract you expect to use over and over again—such as a consulting agreement to use when you hire independent contractors—you might want to have a lawyer look over your contract and make any necessary refinements so that you'll have a solid template to use for years to come. And if you're entering into a complicated, high-stakes agreement, you should certainly get a lawyer either to help you draft the contract or to review any contract that is presented to you to sign. But you should be able to handle the majority of day-to-day transactions and agreements on your own, without bringing in a lawyer.

This chapter explains contract basics, including what makes a contract enforceable and how to decipher common contract clauses.

## Contract Law Basics

A contract doesn't have to take any particular form or contain any magic words to be legally binding. What "legally binding" means is that if you fail to live up to your end of the contract, you can be sued and forced to pay money damages to the other party or, in some circumstances, to do the things you promised in the contract. Some contracts are 50-page documents filled with Latin phrases and legal boilerplate; others are two- or three-sentence agreements scratched out on a napkin. Regardless of its length or formality, a contract will be legally binding if it meets these two requirements:

- The parties have reached an agreement—that is, an offer has been made by one party and accepted by the other.
- Promises or other things of value have been exchanged, such as money, merchandise, or a promise to perform services.

Generally, a contract is legally binding whether or not it is in writing. However, there are some situations when a contract must be in writing to be valid—these are covered in "Oral Versus Written Contracts," below.

! CAUTION
**Nonprofits must honor their contracts, just like other businesses.** The legal rules covering contracts apply to nonprofits just the same as any other entity. As long as the contract is valid under the rules of contract law (as described in this section), it binds a nonprofit just as it would a for-profit business or any other entity.

## Agreement Between Parties

Although it may seem obvious, a contract is valid only if all parties really do agree on every major issue. Sounds simple enough, but in real life it can often be hard to tell the difference between a preliminary discussion and a true agreement. To help bring the dividing line into clearer focus, the law has developed rules that define when an agreement has been reached.

The basic rule is that an agreement exists when one party makes an offer and the other party accepts it. If the acceptance of the offer is followed by an exchange of promises or other things of value (discussed next), a binding contract has been created. For most types of contracts, an offer and acceptance can be made either orally or in writing. In a few cases, however, the offer and acceptance must be in writing (these are discussed below). In any case, it's always a good idea to put your agreement in writing, to avoid future misunderstandings.

To illustrate the steps of offer and acceptance, let's say that you're shopping around for a print shop to produce brochures for your nonprofit. One printer says (by phone or by fax) that he'll print 1,000 two-color brochures for $400. This constitutes his offer. If you tell him to go ahead with the job, you've accepted his offer. This constitutes an agreement between the parties in the eyes of the law. But if you tell the printer you're not yet sure and want to continue shopping—or you don't respond to his proposal at all—you haven't accepted his offer and no agreement has been reached.

In the day-to-day world of business transactions, the seemingly simple steps of offer and acceptance can sometimes become quite convoluted. For instance, you might make an offer and then decide that you want to withdraw or change it before the other party accepts. Or, the other party might propose a change of terms, such as a higher price or a different end product. Delaying acceptance of an offer, revoking an offer, and making a counteroffer are common situations that may lead to confusion or even conflict. To minimize the potential for dispute, here are some rules that will help you figure out whether you've reached a valid agreement.

### Duration of an Offer

Unless an offer includes a stated expiration date, it remains open for a "reasonable" period of time. What's reasonable, of course, is open to interpretation and will depend on the particular situation. The law in this area is vague, so it's best to act quickly and be clear about your intentions. If you want to accept someone else's offer, do it as soon as possible, while there's little doubt that the offer is still open. If you made an offer but haven't received a response for a while, you should revoke the offer explicitly rather than letting it hang out there.

**EXAMPLE:** A nonprofit emails a Web developer to ask if she will create a new feature for its website for $300. The Web developer does not reply for three months; in the fourth month, she sends an email accepting the offer. In the meantime, the nonprofit has already found someone else to do the job and is now worried about whether it has any legal obligation to the first, slow-to-respond developer. A board member with a legal background advises the group that most courts would probably say three months was not a reasonable amount of time for the Web developer to expect the offer to remain open. But, of course, there's no guarantee that a particular judge will agree.

The nonprofit sends a polite, carefully worded letter to the Web developer explaining that the job is no longer available because she took so long to get back to them. Thankfully, the Web developer responds by apologizing that she took so long in responding to the offer and stating that she would be interested in future work. Her response makes it clear that she's not considering legal action to enforce any perceived agreement, and the nonprofit realizes it dodged a potential bullet. From now on, it plans to revoke any offer that doesn't receive a response after two weeks.

If you are making the offer, you can avoid potential confusion by being very clear about how long your offer will remain open. The best way to do this is to include an expiration date in the offer. In the above example, the nonprofit might have included the following text in its offer to the Web developer: "If we do not receive a response within two weeks, this offer automatically expires."

### Revoking an Offer

The person who makes an offer can revoke it as long as it hasn't yet been accepted. (Options—offers that can't be revoked for a period of time—are an exception to this general rule; see below.) If the other party wants to accept an offer after you've revoked it, it's too late—no agreement will have been reached because the offer is no longer open. But if the other party accepts your offer before you revoke it (and before any expiration date or a "reasonable" time has passed), an agreement will exist and you'll be well on your way to establishing a binding contract.

It's a good idea to state explicitly in your offers that you have the right to withdraw the offer prior to acceptance. A simple statement such as "We may revoke this offer at any time before acceptance" should suffice.

**TIP**

**Always revoke an offer in writing.** Although you are not legally required to put your revocation in writing, it's a very sensible idea. Revoking an offer in writing will help prevent misunderstandings about exactly what was said (and when). If the other party later tries to shade the truth, you'll have a written document to back you up.

## Options

Sometimes the party making an offer agrees that it will remain open—that it cannot and will not be revoked—for a stated period of time. This type of contract is called an option. Usually, the offeror requests a fee in exchange for keeping the offer open, to compensate for the fact that he or she cannot revoke the offer and make a deal with someone else while the option is in effect.

Say someone offers to sell a pickup truck to your nonprofit for $8,000, and you want to think the offer over without having to worry that the seller will revoke the offer or sell the truck to someone else. You and the seller could agree that the offer will stay open for a certain period of time—say, 30 days—in exchange for a nonrefundable payment of $50. Once the option is in place, the offeror cannot revoke the offer for 30 days.

## Counteroffers

Often, a person responds to an offer not by accepting the terms immediately, but by bargaining or proposing different terms (such as a lower price). In this situation, the original offer hasn't been accepted

and there is no agreement. In most instances, the law will treat a modified proposal as a "counteroffer," which must then be accepted by the other party (the original offeror) in order for the parties to reach an agreement in the eyes of the law. In other words, when a counteroffer is made, the legal responsibility to accept or decline shifts back to the person who made the original offer.

For instance, say your printer offers to print 1,000 brochures for you for $400. If you respond by saying you'll pay only $300 for the job, you have not accepted his offer (no contract has been formed) but instead have made a counteroffer. It is then up to your printer to accept, decline, or make another counteroffer (perhaps to charge $350). However, if your printer agrees to do the job for $300, he has accepted your counteroffer and an agreement has been reached.

## Exchange of Promises or Things of Value

Even if the parties reach an agreement, they haven't made a contract unless they exchange something of value in anticipation of the completion of the contract. The "thing of value" being exchanged—called "consideration" in legal-speak—is most often a promise to do something in the future, such as a promise to pay a fee, perform services, or provide a product. The purpose of this rule is to distinguish enforceable contracts from one-sided promises—such as a promise to give someone money as a gift—which are not legally enforceable. The legal reasoning here is that you shouldn't be able to enforce a promise unless you've given something in return.

For example, say a printer agrees to print free business cards for your nonprofit. If you make no promise in return, such as to put the printer's logo at your website or to use the printer for another job, then the consideration requirement hasn't been met. Because you and the printer didn't exchange promises (only the printer made a promise), there's no contract—the printer could change his mind and refuse to provide the free business cards, and you would have no legal right to force him to do it. But if your printer promises to print brochures and you promise to pay for them, then you have exchanged promises to do things of value, which creates an enforceable contract.

Although the consideration requirement is met in most transactions by an exchange of promises ("I'll promise to pay money if you promise to print my brochures"), actually doing the work or paying the money can also satisfy the rule. If, for instance, you leave your printer a voicemail message that you'll pay an extra $50 for the brochures to be folded, the printer can create a binding contract by actually doing the folding. And, once he does so, you can't get out of the deal by claiming that you changed your mind.

## Oral Versus Written Contracts

Before explaining which contracts have to be in writing to be legally enforceable, here's some simple advice: All contracts that are of more than minor importance should be written out and signed by both parties. Here's why:

- Writing down terms tends to make both parties review them more carefully, which helps eliminate ambiguities, misunderstandings, and other fatal flaws right from the start.
- An oral agreement—no matter how honestly made—is hard to remember accurately. A few months later, the parties could well have some differing recollections about the agreement. If you have a written contract, you can easily refresh your memories by pulling out your document and reading it. In the absence of a written agreement, you may end up in a potentially relationship-killing argument—which, in the worst case, might have to be conducted in front of a judge.
- Oral agreements are subject to willful misinterpretation by a not-so-innocent party who wants to get out of the deal.
- Oral contracts are often difficult (and commonly impossible) to prove, which makes them hard to enforce if you do end up in court.

**EXAMPLE:** Samantha, the executive director of a nonprofit, wants to run an ad in the local weekly paper for her nonprofit's upcoming event. She asks Leandro, an acquaintance who is a graphic designer, to create the ad. Because Samantha needs the ad right away, and because the two have known each other for a couple of years, they make a quick oral agreement that Leandro will create the ad for $100.

The finished ad contains a beautiful image that Samantha loves—so much, in fact, that she wants to use the image on T-shirts, mugs, mouse pads, and other types of merchandise to promote the nonprofit. When she tells Leandro of her plans, Leandro realizes that he and Samantha never discussed how the ad could be used. Leandro's agreement to create the ad for $100 was based on his understanding that the ad would be used just once in the weekly newspaper. As is standard in the graphic design business, Leandro would have charged significantly more to create an image that Samantha's nonprofit could use in unlimited ways.

If Samantha and Leandro had used Leandro's standard agreement for graphic design work, there would have been no misunderstanding—Leandro's contract would have clearly outlined the allowed uses for the work and stated that all other rights were retained by Leandro's graphic design studio. Now, after the fact, Leandro finds himself in the uncomfortable position of having to tell Samantha that she cannot use the image freely and that they must renegotiate a fee if Samantha wants to use it for other purposes.

Thankfully, when Leandro explains the situation to Samantha, she agrees that they hadn't talked about other uses when she asked Leandro to create the ad. They work out a new fee, giving Samantha's nonprofit unlimited use of the image. They also agree that they'll use a written agreement for all future work.

With that good advice in mind, here's what the law says: While many oral contracts are enforceable, a variety of state and federal laws require certain types of contracts to be in writing. These laws are often called "statutes of frauds" and are quite similar from state to state. In addition, most states have also adopted some version of the Uniform Commercial Code (UCC), which applies to certain sales of goods. These laws typically require the following types of contracts to be in writing:

- An agreement that by its terms can't be completed in a year or less. For example, a contract for a Web developer to maintain your nonprofit's website for two years must be in writing. On the other hand, if the contract might take longer than a year to complete but could be completed within a year, it doesn't have to be in writing. For example, a contract for a consultant to overhaul your nonprofit's management structure would not have to be written, because it is quite possible that the consultant would finish the work within one

year. Similarly, a contract for a Web developer to do specified site revisions with no time period stated would not have to be in writing.

- A lease for a term longer than one year, or an agreement authorizing an agent to execute such a lease on your behalf.
- Any sale of real estate (or of an interest in real estate), or an agreement authorizing an agent to purchase or sell real estate (or an interest in real estate) on your behalf.
- An agreement that by its terms will not be completed during the lifetime of one of the parties.
- A promise to pay someone else's debt.
- A promise to sell goods for $500 or more. A full-blown contract is not necessary here, only a brief written note or memo setting forth two essential terms of the agreement: that an agreement

---

## How Formal Should You Be?

It can be tricky to figure out how formal you need to be with various transactions. While the table below doesn't address every possible situation, it offers some examples to give you a general idea of which agreements need to be taken more seriously than others. As you gain more experience, you'll undoubtedly develop your own inner compass.

If you're making a simple agreement with another party and feel that the situation falls in the gray area between "simple enough for a handshake" and "better put it in writing," it's a good idea to send a letter or at least an email confirmation of the important terms of your agreement.

| Handshake Probably OK | Put a Contract in Writing, Using a Template or Your Own Draft | Put a Contract in Writing, and Consider Getting Assistance From a Lawyer or Another Professional |
|---|---|---|
| Scheduling a community leader to come speak to your organization at an informal lunch | Hiring a consultant to revamp your nonprofit's website | Merging with another nonprofit |
| Assigning volunteers to help set up and break down an event | Renting a hotel or another venue for a nonprofit event | Holding a major event, such as a film festival, a trade show, or another gathering, with many sponsors and/or participants |
| Having a local business donate free coffee and doughnuts for your board meetings | Hiring a caterer to supply meals for 200 guests at your annual dinner | Buying real estate |

was reached, and the quantity of goods to be sold. Other items that are typically covered in contracts, such as the price of goods or the time and place of delivery, don't have to be included to satisfy this rule (from state UCC statutes). This written memo usually has to be signed. However, if one party doesn't object to the memo within ten days of receiving it, then his or her signature isn't required.

 **CAUTION**

**Additional laws may apply to your situation.** While the rules outlined above are the most common laws that require contracts to be in writing, other laws at the state or federal level may apply to specific types of contracts. For example, under the federal Copyright Act, a contract to sell all copyrights in a creative work (known as a copyright assignment) or to grant an exclusive license to a creative work must be in writing. These miscellaneous laws apply much less often than state statutes of frauds and UCC laws, but they might come up in a given situation. The good news is that you won't have to worry about these laws if you put all of your important agreements in writing.

## Using Contracts in the Real World

Now that you understand how important it is to put your contracts in writing, you may wonder exactly how to go about it. The good news is that you probably won't have to draft anything from scratch. Standard, fill-in-the-blanks contracts are readily available that cover many types of business transactions. Even if you need to make modifications to a standard contract, it'll be much easier than writing one from scratch.

This section explains how to use (and, if necessary, modify) a standard contract or review a contract provided by the other party. It also covers practical issues, such as signing the contract and making changes after it's been executed.

### Are Email Agreements Enforceable Contracts?

Two parties can create a legally binding agreement through a series of email messages. For example, imagine an email chain between a nonprofit event organizer and a catering company regarding catering an event. Say the nonprofit emails details to the caterer such as the date, time, and location of the event, the number of people to be served, and desired menu, and requests a price quote. If the caterer emails back a price and the nonprofit emails back saying "Great! Let's consider it a go," it's likely that a legal agreement has been reached.

Remember, if (1) the parties are in agreement, (2) an offer and acceptance have been made, and (3) the parties each promise to do something (usually to provide a product or service in exchange for payment), a legal contract generally exists whether it is in writing or not. Email correspondence is definitely better than a purely oral agreement and can serve to document an oral agreement in the absence of a written contract.

Still, email messages aren't an ideal way to document important agreements for a number of reasons: They encourage informality rather than careful consideration, they can't easily be "signed" in a verifiable way, they are prone to being accidentally deleted, and they lack the sense of importance that formal contracts inherently carry. Still, it's far better to quickly list the fundamental terms of your agreement and email them to the other party than to rely on all-too-fragile human memory.

When sending an email message that indicates acceptance of any type of agreement, it's wise to include a statement at the end that you'd appreciate a reply indicating the other party received your message. Also indicate that if you don't receive a reply, you'll presume that the other party agrees with your recitation of the terms. If the other party emails you back saying, "The agreement you emailed looks fine," you've got a fairly solid record of your agreement. If you print out these messages and keep copies of them on your computer, you'll have some written proof of your agreement in case there's a dispute.

Finally, note that the question of whether a series of emails can constitute a binding contract is separate from the question of how to create a digital signature to sign a document electronically. This topic is discussed under "Electronic Contracts." below.

## Using Standard Contracts

Standard contract templates are readily available for many types of business transactions. Contracts to provide services, rent property, hire independent contractors, sell goods, and license intellectual property are just a few of the blank-form agreements you should be able to find easily. Standard rental agreements, for example, are widely available at office supply stores, through landlords' associations, at most public libraries, and from many other sources. Nolo also publishes standard contracts to use when hiring various types of independent contractors. Keep in mind that even though you're running a nonprofit, the contract you need may exist in the for-profit world.

**RESOURCE**

**Nolo publishes standard contract forms.** Nolo offers many standard forms for sale, including independent contractor agreements, nondisclosure agreements, releases, and more. Go to Nolo's website, www.nolo.com, to see the complete list.

Here are a few sources for standard contracts, in electronic and/or hard copy form:

- Nolo books and software offer many different blank-form agreements. For general business contracts, a great resource is *Quicken Legal Business Pro*, a software program that provides more than 140 business contracts, forms, and worksheets.
- Trade associations are excellent resources for fill-in-the-blanks contracts.
- Other nonprofits may be willing to share their contracts with you. If local groups aren't eager to let you in on their secrets, try nonprofits nationwide.
- The Web has oceans of information about various business transactions, including sample contracts. Try searching for terms particular to your needs, such as "events contracts" or "contractor agreements."

Once you find a contract covering the subject matter of your transaction, you'll probably have to modify it at least slightly to meet your specific needs. It's entirely appropriate and often necessary to change clauses of a standard contract. If you're working with a hard copy, it's okay to make minor changes by simply crossing out language and filling in new language directly on the contract itself. Both parties should initial any such changes to show that they weren't made after the fact without one party's knowledge. In today's world, however, you'll probably be working with an electronic copy of the contract either on your computer or the other party's. If so, it's a good idea to make the necessary changes to the electronic file and then print out a clean copy for both parties to sign.

Of course, you shouldn't make any changes to a standard contract unless you understand what you're doing. Don't just strike a clause because you don't understand what it means or add a clause without fully knowing the consequences of including it. You can find information on common contract clauses in "Typical Contract Terms," below.

## Using the Other Party's Contract

Sometimes you won't need to worry about finding a standard contract or drafting your own, because the other party will present you with a contract. While this might save you some time initially, you'll have to review the contract's terms very carefully to make sure you understand what you're signing and to figure out whether any changes are in order.

You may be hesitant to propose changes to the other party's contract, but you shouldn't be. If a clause is poorly written, is hard to understand, or doesn't accomplish your key goals, you should suggest changes to make it clearer or to better suit your needs. Of course, the other party might not accept your proposed changes, but you should still give it a try. Your success in convincing the other party to accept your proposed changes will largely depend on how much bargaining power you have—that is, on how much the other party wants what you have to offer or wants to do business with you.

As discussed above, when you propose changes to a contract, you're making a counteroffer. Contracts are commonly negotiated back and forth (offer and counteroffer) several times until both parties accept all the terms. If the parties don't reach an agreement, there's no contract—no matter how many discussions, drafts, or proposals go back and forth.

## Signing a Contract

Before you enter into any written agreements, you'll need to know who is authorized to sign contracts for your group. The answer can often be found in the nonprofit's bylaws, which outline the powers and authorities held by members and officers of the board of directors. Most standard bylaws state that the president of the board of directors is responsible for executing (signing) contracts and that the board can extend this power to any officer or agent of the nonprofit by issuing a board resolution. Assuming your bylaws adopt this policy, you should pass a board resolution listing any board or staff members besides the board president whom you want to have contract-signing authority.

Besides figuring out who can sign for your group, you should also make sure that whoever signs the contract for the other party has the legal authority to do so. If the signer isn't authorized to take on legal obligations for the other party, the contract may be declared invalid. Usually, common sense will tell you all you need to know. If a project manager, senior employee, department head, or other high-level worker signs the contract for the other party, you're probably fine. If in doubt, ask a manager or supervisor at the other business or nonprofit to make sure that the signer is authorized to enter into contracts on its behalf.

## Modifying a Signed Contract

After it has been signed and has gone into effect, a contract can be amended at a later date with a separate document called an addendum. The addendum should state that its terms prevail over the terms of the original contract, especially if the terms are in direct conflict, as would be the case if the price or completion time for a job were changed. Both parties should sign an original copy of the addendum and keep it with the original contract.

## Typical Contract Terms

This section explains some basic terms that appear in most contracts. The information here will help you understand, edit, or draft clauses of standard contracts, contracts presented to you by the other party, or ones you draft from scratch. You'll also find sample language for common contract terms (which you can certainly reword or refine).

There are many ways to organize a contract. The sections and titles suggested below correspond to the common issues and terms that most contracts include, but they certainly aren't written in stone. If you feel that it makes more sense to combine terms into one section, break a section into two or more sections, or otherwise arrange your contract differently, feel free to reorganize.

> **TIP**
>
> **Remember your goals.** If you feel stuck when reading over a contract or contemplating what it should include, remember that every contract aims to accomplish certain things. These include:
> - to clearly outline what each party is agreeing to do (including timelines and payment arrangements)
> - to anticipate areas of confusion or points of potential conflict, and
> - to provide for recourse (remedy) in case the agreement is not followed through to completion.

## Contract Title

Generally a contract will have a simple, descriptive title like "Contract for Consulting Services" or "Agreement for Sale of Computer Equipment."

## Names and Addresses of Parties

You should identify each party by name at the beginning of the contract. If using full names throughout will be too burdensome, introduce the shorthand you'll consistently use, such as "Client," "Consultant," or "Vendor."

Some contracts include the addresses of the parties at the beginning; others list them at the end of the contract, in the section that includes each party's signature.

---

> Business Mentor Network Inc. ("BMN"), a nonprofit corporation, desires to enter into a contract with MediaWeb LLC ("MediaWeb") for website consulting and development services.

## Brief Background Description

While not included in every contract, it can be useful to draft a brief description of the background of the agreement, often called "recitals." This type of information may be necessary to frame the contents of the agreement. Typically, this section includes a brief description of what the parties do and the nature of the transaction covered in the contract.

> Background of Parties
>
> BMN is an organization that aims to encourage entrepreneurship in disadvantaged communities. BMN's main activity is providing experienced business mentors for new and prospective business owners in target communities and offering classes and seminars on entrepreneurship and business management to members of these communities. MediaWeb offers website consulting and development services, helping businesses and organizations create or restructure their websites.
>
> The subject of this contract is an agreement ("Agreement") that MediaWeb will provide specific consulting, Web development, and related services (collectively, "Services") to BMN in exchange for payment.

## Description of the Services or Products

This section describes the terms of the deal. If a service is to be performed, describe the job in detail, clearly explaining exactly what each party is promising to do. If a product is to be sold, describe the product, price, and delivery date. If a meeting site is to be rented, describe the site, price, date, and time of the rental, as well as any items to be provided with the rental (catering services, audio equipment, or tables and chairs, for example).

For bigger or more complicated projects, you may want to outline the project timetable on a separate document and attach it to the contract. (See "Including Attachments," below.) Attachments may also include site maps for a website project, flow charts, scale drawings, formulas, or similar types of detailed information that would otherwise significantly interrupt the flow of your contract.

In many service agreements, one or both parties must submit reports, memos, sketches, drawings, outlines, or the like. Items like these (often called "deliverables") should be identified in the contract, either along with the description of services or in a separate section. If any deliverables have due dates, include those dates in the next section, "Schedules and Deadlines."

---

**Project Description**

MediaWeb will create a new website for BMN, which will include information about BMN's organization as well as helpful consumer information on entrepreneurship generally. Details regarding the site content, organization, and features are covered in Attachment A, which is attached to, and incorporated into, this contract.

**Deliverables**

MediaWeb will provide the following Deliverables as part of its services:

1. a preliminary, detailed site map ("Preliminary Site Map")
2. a final, detailed site map ("Final Site Map"), and
3. approximately 50 pages of final content ("Content").

---

## Schedule and Deadlines

Deadlines are a common source of conflict. To help head off disputes before they arise, make sure that your contracts clearly outline project schedules and deadlines for both parties, including any intermediate deadlines that must be met before the final completion date.

If strict compliance with deadlines is necessary, be sure to include the phrase, "Time is of the essence." This language conveys the parties' agreement that deadlines are important—and that missing a deadline could ruin the deal. If your contract states that "time is of the essence," and one party is even slightly late, a court is likely to find that party to have breached the contract. If you don't include this phrase in your contract, a court might be a bit more lenient.

---

**Project Schedule and Deadlines**

MediaWeb will deliver the Preliminary Site Map to BMN no later than June 1, 2013.

BMN will provide feedback to MediaWeb within three weeks of receiving the Preliminary Site Map.

MediaWeb will deliver a Final Site Map by August 1, 2013.

MediaWeb will deliver the Content to BMN no later than September 1, 2013. Time is of the essence with regard to the September 1, 2013 deadline.

---

### Including Attachments

If your agreement includes any detailed descriptions— say, the specifications of a creek restoration project, the details of a children's inoculation program, or architectural blueprints—it's often best to include them as attachments to the main contract. To do this, you must prepare and label your attachment and state in the main contract that the attachment is part of the agreement. For example:

"The timeline of the project is outlined in Attachment A, which is a formal part of this contract." (Or, "which is incorporated into this contract.")

"The detailed specifications for the Logo drawing are set out in Attachment B, which is a formal part of the contract." (Or, "which is incorporated into this contract.")

## Price

This section states the price or fee to be paid for the goods or services in the contract. If any future circumstances may affect the price—for example, changes in the amount of product or services needed—be sure to clearly describe how future adjustments will be calculated. You can include these details in the price section or put them in a separate section.

---

**Project Fee**

BMN will pay MediaWeb a project fee ("Project Fee") of $10,000 for on-time completion of the Services outlined in this Agreement, which include about 50 pages of Web content, as set out in Attachment A.

**Scope of Work; Additional Fees**

If the parties agree that the services necessary for this project significantly exceed the Services as described in this contract, the parties agree to make a good-faith effort to negotiate additional project fees ("Additional Fees"). Any Additional Fees will be based on a rate of $50 per hour for MediaWeb's additional work, not to exceed $2,000. An estimate of the Additional Fees must be submitted by MediaWeb and approved by BMN's Project Manager for this project before any work is performed that will result in Additional Fees. If the Additional Fees are estimated to exceed $2,000, BMN's Board of Directors must approve the estimate before any work is performed that will result in Additional Fees.

For the purposes of this section, if the parties agree that 60 or more pages of Content should be produced, this will qualify as "significantly exceeding the contract," and additional project fees will be negotiated.

---

## Payment Arrangements

Besides stating the price or fee to be paid, your contract should spell out how payment will be made,

including due dates. For example, state whether the fee will be paid all at once or in installments, when each payment is due, whether interest will be charged if payments are late, and any other special requirements (such as whether payment must be made by certified or cashier's check). If strict compliance with payment deadlines is necessary, use the phrase "Time is of the essence."

---

**Terms of Payment**

BMN will pay MediaWeb $4,000 upon execution of this Agreement, $3,000 within two weeks of delivery of the Preliminary Site Map, and $3,000 within two weeks of delivery of the Content.

---

## Warranties

A warranty is essentially a guarantee made by one party to another that a product or service will meet certain standards. This section is usually called "Warranties" but is sometimes called "Representations"; the two terms are often used in conjunction or interchangeably. While most contracts include warranty provisions, they are not absolutely essential. It's up to you and the other party to decide whether to include them in your contract.

If you do include warranty provisions, you should consider whether failure to live up to the warranties should constitute a serious violation of the contract that would effectively terminate the agreement, triggering its termination provisions (discussed below). In legal lingo, a deal-breaking violation of the contract is known as a "material breach," and you should include this term in your contract if violation of a warranty would cause such significant problems that you would want out of the deal.

---

**Warranties and Representations**

MediaWeb represents and warrants that it has the skills, professional experience, and technical capabilities to complete the Services in a professional and satisfactory manner. MediaWeb represents and warrants that it possesses any and all licenses and governmental approvals required for it to perform the Services. MediaWeb represents and warrants that the Content will not violate, invade, or infringe on any copyright, trademark, right of privacy, right of publicity, or other proprietary or personal right of any person or entity. Failure to satisfy any of the warranties and representations in this section shall constitute a material breach of this Agreement.

---

**Indemnification**

MediaWeb indemnifies BMN and will defend BMN against, and hold BMN harmless from, any claims and damages, including legal costs and attorneys' fees, arising out of any breach or failure of MediaWeb to perform any representations, warranties, or agreements contained in this Agreement.

BMN indemnifies MediaWeb and will defend MediaWeb against, and hold MediaWeb harmless from, any claims and damages, including legal costs and attorneys' fees, arising out of any breach or failure of BMN to perform any representations, warranties, or agreements contained in this Agreement.

---

## Indemnity

Another common contract term is an indemnity clause. "Indemnity" is legal lingo for one party's obligation to pay for any damage it does to the other party. Often, indemnity clauses obligate one party to pay for any legal claims that are brought against the other party by outsiders as a result of the first party's wrongdoing.

For example, consider a contract between your nonprofit and a database consultant in which both parties indemnify each other. Let's say the database consultant creates a faulty, bug-ridden database that crashes the computer systems of everyone who uses it—including your freelance fundraising consultant, who sues your nonprofit for the damages to her computer and for the business she lost because her system crashed. Because your contract included an indemnity provision, the database consultant would be legally responsible for any damages your nonprofit suffers as a result of the fundraising consultant's lawsuit.

Like warranty provisions, indemnity provisions are common, but not essential. If indemnity provisions are included, make sure they apply at least as much to the other party as they do to your nonprofit. In other words, don't agree to indemnify the other party unless the other party also agrees to indemnify you.

## Duration of Contract

All contracts should state how long the agreement will last, known in legal speak as the "term" of the contract. Generally speaking, contracts should last until the events covered in the contract have occurred—for example, when the services or products that are the subject of the contract have been completed and paid for. The contract term establishes the "natural" expiration date for the contract.

---

**Contract Term**

The term of this Agreement ("Term") shall be for a period from March 1, 2013 until September 1, 2013. This Agreement shall automatically terminate on September 1, 2013 or on the completion of the Services, unless extended in a written agreement signed by both parties.

---

## Terminating the Contract

Besides specifying the contract term, most contracts also indicate how a contract may be ended midstream—for example, a contract might terminate if one party fails to live up to its agreement or decides that it wants out. These provisions, usually called "termination" provisions, are generally included separately from the contract term provisions.

## Reasons to Terminate

Broadly speaking, there are two types of termination provisions: clauses that allow either party to voluntarily end the contract for any reason, and clauses that allow termination for specific reasons, also known as termination "for cause."

A typical voluntary termination provision allows either party to end the agreement by giving a written termination notice. A common example is a month-to-month lease agreement: Both parties often have the right to terminate the agreement by giving the other party written notice at least 30 days in advance.

Another type of termination provision says that the contract will automatically end if certain things happen. The situations that commonly trigger termination include a party breaching the contract, a party selling or dissolving its business or nonprofit, or a party going bankrupt.

Contracts often include provisions for both voluntary termination and termination for cause.

## Payment Provisions

Besides specifying the permitted reasons for terminating the contract, your contract should also state whether payments will be made in the case of termination. In other words, if the contract ends early, what payments will the contractor be owed? A common solution is to establish that the contractor will be paid for work performed prior to the termination.

---

**Contract Termination**

MediaWeb or BMN may terminate this Agreement for any reason upon 30 days' written notice to the other party.

This Agreement terminates automatically upon the occurrence of any of the following events: (1) bankruptcy or insolvency of either party, (2) the sale of MediaWeb's business or dissolution of BMN's nonprofit corporation, or (3) material breach of contract by either party.

If this Agreement is terminated by either party for any reason, BMN will have no further obligation to make any payments to MediaWeb, except for Services already done but not yet paid for prior to the termination, calculated at the rate of $50 per hour.

---

## Resolving Disputes

Despite all your careful planning and contract drafting, you may not be successful in heading off a dispute with the other party. You can, however, take steps to minimize the time and expense of dealing with these disagreements by including language in your contract to channel any dispute toward resolution methods other than a lawsuit.

One effective and popular approach to resolving disputes is mediation. In mediation, a neutral third party (the mediator) works with the parties to try to come up with a mutually satisfactory resolution. Unlike a judge, a mediator does not have the power to impose a judgment upon the parties, so a solution will be reached only if both parties agree to it.

If the parties can't resolve their dispute in mediation, they have an additional option short of taking it to court: arbitration. In arbitration, a neutral third party (the arbitrator) hears arguments and takes evidence from both parties, then makes a decision about what should happen. The arbitration process is more like a lawsuit in that the person overseeing the process (the arbitrator) has the authority to make a decision regarding the dispute, even if the parties aren't happy with the decision. But many prefer arbitration to litigation because it is generally more streamlined, quicker, and less costly than regular civil court.

Contracts often state that the parties will try mediation and then, if that fails, use arbitration to settle a dispute as an alternative to going to court.

---

**Dispute Resolution**

If any dispute arises under the terms of this Agreement, the parties agree to mediate the dispute. The parties will choose a mutually acceptable mediator and will share the costs of mediation equally. If the parties are unable to resolve their dispute in mediation, the parties agree to choose a mutually acceptable arbitrator to arbitrate the dispute. The costs of arbitration will be assigned to the parties by the arbitrator. The results of any arbitration will be binding and final.

---

## Applicable Law

Lawyers worry about which state's law will apply if a contract is breached. Because contract law is very similar in every state, it won't make that much difference in how your contract is interpreted. But if you enter into a contract with an out-of-state entity, you'll probably want your state's law to govern—otherwise, you may have to travel to another state to bring or defend a lawsuit over the contract. But for the fairly simple contracts most nonprofits sign with local people and organizations, it's safe (and sensible) to leave this clause out.

---

**State Law**

This contract shall be governed by and interpreted in accordance with the laws of Illinois.

---

## Signatures and Dates

Your signature section should ask the parties to enter their mailing addresses, the names and titles of the person signing the contract (the "agent"), and the date(s) on which the contract is signed. Also, make sure to obtain the tax identification number of contractors for your tax purposes. As discussed in Chapter 5, you are required to report payments you make to independent contractors if you pay them more than $600 in one year, and you'll need their tax ID number for your report.

**RESOURCE**

**More on business contracts.** For detailed advice on how to write contract provisions, find out what a particular contract term such as indemnity, means, or make sure you can enforce important business agreements down the road, see *Contracts: The Essential Desk Reference,* by Richard Stim (Nolo.)

---

**Signatures**

Business Mentor Network, Inc.

Mailing address: _____

Name of agent: _____

Title: _____

Signature: _____

Date: _____

MediaWeb LLC

Mailing address: _____

Tax ID or SS #: _____

Name of agent: _____

Title: _____

Signature: _____

Date: _____

---

## Electronic Contracts

While the basics covered so far generally apply to any contract regardless of form—whether the contract is printed in a formal document, scratched on a cocktail napkin, or just spoken and sealed with a handshake—there are new and emerging rules that apply specifically to contracts created online. Before you read this general overview of the special issues involved in electronic contracts, keep in mind that law in this area is rapidly evolving—scrambling, in fact—to catch up with fast-evolving technology.

### What Is an Electronic Contract?

An "electronic contract" is essentially any agreement that is created and executed in electronic form—in other words, no paper or other hard copies are used. Typically, electronic agreements are created either via email or on interactive Web pages. For instance, many companies use interactive forms at their websites that users must complete to purchase goods or software, join a membership organization, participate in a listserv, or do whatever else the company is offering. In addition to asking the user to enter various items of personal information, these forms typically display the terms of the contract between the company and the user, and ask the user to agree to the terms by clicking on a button such as "I Accept."

Here's another example of an electronic contract: Someone emails your program director that they would like your nonprofit to put on an educational workshop, on certain dates, and for a named price. If you email back that you agree to all the proposed terms, you've probably just entered into a legally enforceable electronic contract. Why the "probably"? Because emails can't be signed with pen and ink, and states vary in how they treat digital signatures. Read on.

## Taking Traditional Contract Principles Online

As mentioned above, contract law is only beginning to grapple with the details of these types of paperless agreements. When electronic contracts have been challenged, courts have had a difficult time determining whether an actual binding contract existed, since it can be unclear whether all the traditional elements of contract formation were met.

## Electronic and Digital Signatures

One of the stickier issues involving electronic contracts has to do with whether agreements executed in a purely online environment have been "signed." For many centuries, the traditional way to indicate your acceptance of contracts (and most other binding documents) has been to sign with your unique signature. But electronic contracts can't be signed this way. Instead, people use other means to indicate they accept the terms of a contract, such as simply typing their names into the signature areas of the documents.

Increasingly, better technological approaches to the problem of signing contracts online are being developed, such as certificate-based signatures (used, for example, by Acrobat to sign PDF documents) that use a cryptographic technology known as Public Key Infrastructure (PKI). The broad collection of methods

people use to sign electronic documents is typically referred to as electronic signatures. The term "digital signature" refers specifically to cryptographic signature methods such as PKI.

Until relatively recently, most states didn't have any laws stating which of these ways to "sign" an electronic document was legally acceptable. In response, the National Conference of Commissioners on Uniform State Laws (NCCUSL) drafted another model law, the Uniform Electronic Transactions Act (UETA), which specifically addresses electronic signatures. In a nutshell, the UETA provides that electronic signatures (in all their forms) and contracts are just as valid and legally binding as their paper counterparts. As of late 2012, all states except Illinois, New York, and Washington had enacted the UETA.

## Federal Law on Electronic Signatures

Fortunately, as the states were mulling over whether to adopt the UETA, the U.S. Congress forged ahead and passed federal legislation establishing the validity of electronic signatures nationwide. This bill, known as the Electronic Signatures in Global and National Commerce Act, became effective on October 1, 2000. The law applies to all states that had not already adopted the UETA or a similar electronic signature law by mid-2000. In this way, the law finally gave some much-needed consistency to the way states treat electronic signatures in online transactions.

This law is similar to the model UETA in that it makes electronic signatures and contracts just as valid as paper ones. While certain transactions are exempted from this law and must still be completed on paper (wills, cancellation of utility services, court orders, and other official court documents, among others), the law allows an enormous range of business and consumer transactions to be completed totally online. In essence, it throws the door wide open for all types of e-commerce, allowing nonprofits, businesses and consumers to create (in theory, at least) reliable, binding contracts online, without the inconvenience of shuttling paper documents back and forth.

## Special Contract Issues for Booking Venues

Nonprofits often have to deal with contract issues when they make arrangements with venues for meetings and events. Hotels or convention centers often use their own, fairly complicated, agreements, sometimes titled "Terms and Conditions" or "Booking Agreement." Understanding some common terms and issues will help you stay out of legal trouble when entering into one of these agreements:

- **Deadlines.** There will often be deadlines for reserving the space, posting your deposit, telling the venue how many people you expect, and canceling your reservation without losing your deposit. You need to be on top of these deadlines in order to avoid penalties and other consequences—such as losing your reservation or having to pay for the space even though your event was canceled.

- **Reservation.** Perhaps the most important effect of signing a contract with a venue is that the space will be reserved for you. However, this reservation often depends on your living up to your end of the contract. If you fail to pay deposits on time or meet other requirements of the contract, the venue may cancel your reservation.

- **Fees.** Some venues will quote you a price over the phone that turns out to be only a base fee, to which other charges will almost certainly be added. Make sure the contract is clear about any extra charges, such as a fee for help setting up, technical assistance, power usage, a DSL line, overtime compensation for the venue's staff, parking, or cleaning up afterwards.

- **Deposits.** Most venues will require your nonprofit to put down a deposit well ahead of your event. Make sure the contract clearly outlines when deposit payments are due, as well as the total amount you'll have to pay. Manage your nonprofit's cash flow carefully to make sure you meet these deadlines.

- **Cancellations.** The contract should clearly outline the venue's cancellation policy. It's typical for a venue to refund 100% of your deposit if you cancel by a certain date—30 or 60 days before the event, for example. If you cancel later, you may only receive a partial refund —and you could lose your entire deposit if you cancel at the last minute. If you do cancel, make sure you put it in writing and obtain some sort of confirmation of delivery; certified mail is best.

- **Head counts.** If your fee will be based on attendance, the venue's contract will likely have a deadline by which you must indicate how many people you expect to attend. In this situation, it's important to have a confirmed attendance number *before* the venue's deadline. If the deadline approaches and you haven't finalized your reservations, you may be forced to give a high estimate and pay for people who don't actually attend.

- **On-site costs.** If you will need equipment for your event, such as a public address (PA) system, slide projector, or lighting equipment, you may be able to rent it from the venue—but keep in mind that hotels and convention centers almost always charge very high rates. Food and beverage costs are usually similarly inflated at these venues. You'll almost always be better off renting equipment or hiring a caterer separate from the venue. If the venue won't allow you to do this, consider holding your event elsewhere. If you decide that the convenience of using the venue's equipment or food services is worth the higher price, make sure that everything you'll need is listed in the contract, along with the costs.

- **Technical services.** If you'll be using extensive electrical equipment, networked computers, or other technology at your event, you may need a venue employee to help you set up. If so, find out whether you'll have to pay extra for a technician's services or whether the general fee includes this cost. Again, make sure your contract includes every service you'll need—and doesn't subject you to charges for items or services you can do without.

- **Liability.** Make sure the contract addresses whether the venue will assume liability for injuries that occur during the event. Venues usually will assume liability. If they don't, however, they'll often ask you to show proof of liability coverage, which could be a general liability policy or a certificate showing coverage specifically for the event. (See Chapter 7 for a full discussion of liability issues, including risk management and insurance.)

Note: These issues may not come up at all if you use smaller or nontraditional venues for your events. For example, if you can hold your art education seminar in a library, an art gallery, or another nonprofit's conference room rather than at a hotel, you'll not only save money, but you also may be able to avoid many of the numerous contractual rules set out in typical hotel rental agreements.

## Checklist: Understanding Contracts and Agreements

☐ Familiarize yourself with the legal basics of contracts, especially the rules for what makes a contract valid and binding.

☐ Put all your agreements into writing whenever possible.

☐ When you need to create a contract, start by looking for a standard form contract. Modifying a standard contract will be much easier than drafting one from scratch and will likely yield a more solid contract.

☐ Keep your contract language clear and to the point, and don't be tempted to use legalese.

☐ Be detail oriented in your contracts. Make sure that any points of potential conflict are spelled out clearly.

# Marketing Your Nonprofit

No matter what its mission, every nonprofit needs to market itself. Spreading the word about your organization's work and accomplishments is an indispensable part of running a nonprofit. When you do this successfully and consistently, you'll create a favorable buzz about your organization, greatly improving your ability to attract potential funders, volunteers, and other supporters.

Despite what you might think, marketing your nonprofit does not have to be terribly time-consuming or expensive. For example, encouraging good word of mouth and networking in your community will cost you little (if anything) and will greatly help your group develop name recognition and forge productive relationships. Other inexpensive marketing methods, such as sending out press releases and fostering media coverage, can generate far better exposure than spending a fortune on advertising.

This chapter outlines a simple, affordable approach to marketing your nonprofit. The strategies and tips described here will help you get your marketing machine up and running—and expand your marketing efforts as your nonprofit's resources grow. You'll also find information on how to do basic market research, which will allow you to tailor your offerings and message to your target audience. Using the tools and information in this chapter will help you get the word out to those whom you hope to serve, potential supporters, and the larger universe of influential people, organizations, and public agencies interested in your mission.

**RELATED TOPIC**

**Websites, online marketing, and social media are discussed in Chapter 11.** That chapter describes how to spread the word and connect with potential supporters online, including strategies for using social media like Facebook. This chapter focuses on traditional offline marketing methods. Online and offline marketing definitely overlap to some degree—for example, while media relations traditionally involves sending press releases to journalists, these days it also might involve sending your press release over an online news wire. The best approach is to do both types of "real-world" and online marketing.

---

### Marketing and Publishing Can Overlap

While this book covers marketing and publishing in separate chapters, they are not mutually exclusive. "Publishing" means conveying substantive information to the public—for example, producing a newsletter with articles about water conservation or creating a website with photos and detailed instructions on self-defense techniques for women. "Marketing" means conveying information about your organization, with less emphasis on substantive issues. Examples of marketing include distributing brochures with basic information about your nonprofit, running ads in a local paper to promote an event, or putting up a one-page website with your mission statement and information on how to donate.

Publishing efforts usually create marketing opportunities. For example, if your ecological organization publishes a quarterly newsletter with articles on land preservation policy, you can (and should!) also include promotional information asking for volunteers and financial support. The same strategy applies to publishing a website: If your nonprofit creates a website with detailed, educational content on self-defense techniques for women, the website should also include some pages with marketing-driven content, such as how to donate, the history of the organization, or a request for volunteers.

Publishing efforts are covered in the next chapter, which explains how to decide whether to publish, different types of publications, what resources you'll need, and how to get started. Websites are discussed in Chapter 11.

## Marketing and Public Relations in a Nutshell

There's no denying that we live in a world saturated by marketing messages. As annoying as it is to be relentlessly courted by thousands of companies each day, constant exposure to marketing messages offers one benefit you can put to use for your nonprofit: Whether you've studied marketing or not, you've unwittingly absorbed a basic understanding of how marketing works. As you review the marketing strategies in this section, keep in mind that as an experienced marketing target, you probably know more about marketing than you think you do. Use this knowledge to turn the tables—to think like a marketer, rather than a "marketee."

Marketing is not synonymous with advertising. Paid advertising can be part of a marketing strategy, but it seldom makes sense for a new nonprofit to invest precious resources on ads. Paid advertising is much more expensive—and less effective—than many cheaper (or even free) methods of getting exposure.

More efficient ways to promote your nonprofit include:

- coaching board members and other influential supporters to spread the word
- networking with other nonprofits, government agencies, and community leaders
- creating a website and promoting it
- distributing brochures, flyers, or other literature
- pitching stories about your nonprofit to local media
- listing your organization or events in local calendars and directories, and
- organizing or participating in conferences, seminars, or other events.

## Common Marketing Terms

Because so many terms are bandied about when referring to marketing efforts, it can be hard to understand the distinctions among specific types of marketing, such as publicity, public relations, and media relations. Truth be told, there's often only a fuzzy line among these categories. This section defines some of the most common marketing terms as they are used in this chapter.

**Marketing.** This general term refers to just about any promotional activity: advertising, special events, direct mail, online discounts and promotions, and the like. "Marketing" means any and all ways of promoting your nonprofit. This chapter uses more specific terms to refer to individual types of marketing activities.

---

### Effective Marketing Starts With a Solid Organization

Lots of nonprofits (and even for-profit businesses) fail to understand the importance of having an efficient, organized operation in place before they start their marketing efforts. After all, you'll want to be ready to handle the heightened attention your marketing will bring to your organization. For example, a restaurant should not start a big marketing campaign without already having a good chef and enough waitstaff in place to handle a surge of diners. Otherwise, the unprepared restaurant's marketing efforts would likely result in unhappy diners and bad publicity.

The same holds true for a nonprofit. If you're not ready to manage volunteers or accept donations, sending out a press release with a plea for support could easily lead to disaster. If dozens of potential volunteers and donors call your nonprofit in response, only to learn that your group has no clear volunteer opportunities or system to handle donations, your nonprofit will lose credibility and suffer a blow to its reputation.

Before you decide *how* to market, pay attention to *what* you're marketing. Make sure your group's house is in order before you worry about how to call attention to it.

---

**Advertising.** "Advertising" means buying space or airtime to deliver a promotional message designed to reach the general public, usually through print media, television, radio, or the Internet. Of course, just about anything can carry an advertising message, including the sides of buses, billboards, and park benches.

**Listings or directories.** These terms refer to phone books, online directories, classified ads, or other specialized publications designed to reach a self-selected group of people, as opposed to the general public. As with advertising, you must pay for a listing. But, unlike most ads, directories often serve as valuable resources that are used again and again, which means that they can be very effective marketing tools if they get to the right audience.

**Public relations.** "Public relations" is another broad term that can refer to many different types of outreach efforts. In this chapter, public relations means a coordinated, multifaceted effort to get your nonprofit's message out to the public. Public relations might include advertising, paying for listings, pitching stories to the media, inviting key people to participate in conferences, and making speeches.

**Media relations.** This term refers to contacting the media and pitching story ideas in hopes of obtaining editorial coverage (coverage in articles or feature stories not tied to advertising). Most commonly, media relations involves sending press releases to newspaper editors, reporters, and television producers to announce an event or provide information that could be the subject of a news story. Another media relations technique is to hold a press conference at which your organization conveys a specific (and newsworthy) message to invited members of the press.

**Publicity.** Although the term "publicity" is often used loosely and sometimes interchangeably with the term "public relations," in this chapter, publicity means event-related marketing efforts. Examples include making speeches, sponsoring seminars, and participating in conferences.

> **RESOURCE**
>
> **Nolo's *Marketing Without Advertising*, by Michael Phillips and Salli Rasberry, offers useful marketing ideas.** Although *Marketing Without Advertising* is tailored more to profit-driven businesses than nonprofits, it provides helpful information about how to build positive recognition without spending a dime on traditional advertising. Its insights into effective marketing techniques are especially valuable for budget-minded enterprises.

## Know Your Audience and Your Field

To plan your nonprofit's communications with the public—whether through marketing, publishing, a website, or programs—you'll need to know who you're trying to reach and what they're looking for. You'll also want to find out about any nonprofits doing similar work: If there are other organizations in the same field, you should find out about their work and make sure your group offers something new under the sun.

### Who Is Your Nonprofit's Audience?

In the for-profit world, an early step in business planning is developing a clear vision of the business's target customers—in other words, the people most likely to buy what the company plans to sell. This step is essential both to ensure that the business has a niche and to enable the business to market itself effectively to its potential customers.

While your nonprofit may not have customers per se, you should still think carefully about exactly whom you want to reach—instead of "customers," think of these people as your audience. These are the people to whom you want to address your outreach efforts, including your marketing, publishing, and website. The better you understand who your audience is and what is important to them, the more effective your work will be.

The target audience for every nonprofit is its potential supporters: people who may be willing to support the nonprofit in some capacity, such as by volunteering, donating money, or participating in other ways. Some nonprofits have a second target audience as well: people whom the nonprofit aims to serve (for example, poor children, disabled veterans, young artists, or residents of a particular neighborhood), often through the nonprofit's programs such as classes, clinics, or other direct services. Not every nonprofit has this type of audience. For example, an environmental nonprofit aiming to reduce pollution in a city neighborhood may focus its efforts on cleanup weekends conducted by volunteers and not have any program activities that directly serve individuals. A nonprofit aimed at health care for the homeless, on the other hand, would definitely want to reach out to the homeless population and get them involved in its vaccination clinics, blood pressure evaluations, and other services.

Whether your nonprofit plans to have supporters, beneficiaries, or both, knowing key details about them will help your group plan effective outreach. By knowing your audience well, you'll be able to better physically target your marketing efforts (for example, by knowing where to distribute flyers, post information, and plan events and speaking engagements). And you'll be able to craft your marketing messages appropriately—using the right media, tone, language, and attitude to appeal to your audience.

When developing a profile of your audience, start by identifying specific characteristics of the people who you believe are most likely to actually support your group or need its services. These characteristics are sometimes called a demographic profile. Common characteristics used to classify a target audience include:

- age
- gender
- income level
- occupation or industry
- marital status
- family status (children or no children)
- geographic location
- ethnic group
- political affiliations or leanings, and
- hobbies and interests.

Deciding how narrowly to define your target audience is more of an art than a science, but in general, it helps to err on the side of being more specific. Envisioning an audience too broadly can make it difficult to engage in effective marketing efforts. Remember: A solid definition of your target audience serves as a foundation for all your marketing activities. The more carefully you've defined your audience, the better you'll be able to craft a targeted, specific message that really resonates with that group, and the more likely your marketing efforts—even simple, low-cost methods—will bear fruit.

### Learning About Your Field

Besides learning about your nonprofit's audience, it's important to know about other nonprofits doing similar work. Depending on the scope of your operations, you might be concerned only with local nonprofits, or you might need to know those working at a national level as well.

Once you know what other nonprofits are doing, your nonprofit can carve out its own unique niche and make sure it's serving needs that are not otherwise being served in the community. Unfortunately, funding can be very competitive between nonprofits, so it's essential to demonstrate that your programs and services don't duplicate the work of other nonprofits. (For more on making a compelling case for support, see Chapter 6 on fundraising.)

Also, researching other nonprofits will help your group keep up on trends and developments in the areas central to its mission. The best marketing efforts reflect an understanding of real-world issues and concerns, which are in constant flux. If your nonprofit seems behind the times, its appeals for support will not be as strong. For example, a nonprofit fighting mining and oil drilling operations in a particular area would obviously want to stay current on legislative efforts for or against its position. If the nonprofit sends out a mailer to its supporters with outdated information—for example, failing to mention some significant legislative proposal for drilling in the region—its credibility could seriously suffer and the outreach campaign won't be as effective as it would have been with up-to-date information.

## Market Research

Doing market research is an important and effective way to test your assumptions and answer any questions you may have about your audience or other players in your field. For example, if you want to raise money by offering paid memberships in your organization, you may not be sure about what types of benefits would most interest your target audience. Market research will help you find out what your supporters value and help you craft your membership drive.

The term "market research" tends to scare some people, who might equate it with hiring a pricey firm to conduct complicated demographic studies. In fact, market research can be much simpler and just as effective. Most nonprofits can do their own market research with a very limited budget. Large nonprofits might hire a firm to do more extensive market research studies, but the simpler approach usually makes more sense for small to medium groups, especially when they're just starting out.

Market research can include primary and secondary research. Primary research involves doing studies with your target audience to find out how they feel about your nonprofit's activities, other nonprofits' offerings, and other topics of interest to your group. Secondary research involves studying what others have learned about your audience or field; typically this involves reading newsletters, trade journals, other publications, or reports generated from studies that others have commissioned.

Nonprofits often focus on secondary research because they find primary research intimidating. But, by following the steps described below, nonprofits can easily and inexpensively tackle primary research—and there's no substitute for the information you get directly from your target audience.

## Clarifying Your Research Objectives

The first step in doing market research is to figure out exactly what questions you want answered. In other words, what do you want to learn? A good way to come up with research objectives is to separately consider what you want to learn about your audience, other nonprofits in your field, and the field in general that's related to your mission.

The table below offers a breakdown of the types of questions and research methods that would be appropriate for each group. As you can see, your research methods will depend on what you want to know.

With a clear outline of the questions you want answered, you'll be in a good position to choose the best research methods. The best approach is to conduct both primary research—getting information from actual or prospective members of your audience—and secondary research—reading what others have to say.

| Market Research Questions and Methods | | |
|---|---|---|
| **Subject** | **Questions to Answer** | **Methods** |
| Supporters and beneficiaries | • Who is your target audience?<br>• What services do they need or want?<br>• What issues do they care about?<br>• What motivates them to take action? | Primary research methods:<br>• Surveys and questionnaires<br>• Focus groups<br>• One-on-one interviews or inquiries of trusted contacts<br>Secondary research methods:<br>• Magazine or trade journal articles<br>• Reports from previously conducted studies |
| Other nonprofits | • What are their missions?<br>• What is the scope of their work?<br>• What programs do they offer?<br>• What do they charge?<br>• How do they provide the products/services?<br>• Who is their audience? | • Primary sources (marketing materials, websites, and so on)<br>• Trade shows<br>• Networking<br>• Magazine or trade journal articles |
| General field | • What are the issues getting the most attention and funding?<br>• What are the trends?<br>• What does the future hold? | • Magazine or trade journal articles<br>• Trade shows<br>• Books |

## Primary Research Tools

Though primary research may not be quite as easy as reading a trade magazine, it's manageable even for smaller nonprofits—and will generally yield much more valuable information because it's coming directly from your prospects. How you'll ask your questions will depend on your situation. Generally, there are three options: surveys and questionnaires, interviews, and focus groups.

### Using Surveys and Questionnaires

Presenting your target audience with surveys or questionnaires is a great way to gather information. Start with your research objectives, as discussed above. Based on the questions you want answered, you'll draft the actual survey questions. Your research questions are not exactly the same as the survey questions. Typically, research questions are more general and wouldn't necessarily yield the most useful information. Instead, the survey questions should be specific, tailored to gather the details that will help you answer your broader research questions.

For example, if an arts nonprofit is trying to determine how to get the largest audience for its experimental film screenings, one of its research questions might be "Where should we show our films?" Rather than asking this fairly general question on its survey, the group might include the following more specific questions: "Would you like to have food and beverages available for sale during screenings?" "Would you prefer outdoor or indoor screenings?" "Would you be likely to attend outdoor screenings if it required you to bring a folding chair?" "In what neighborhood would you ideally like us to present our screenings?"

You can send surveys in hard copy via mail, in plain text format via email, or—even better—by using a Web-based service, many of which are free. At sites such as SurveyMonkey (www.surveymonkey.com) and Zoomerang (www.zoomerang.com), you can create professional-looking online surveys, invite your prospects by email, and tabulate the results in useful ways, all for free. More features are available if you upgrade to a paying account, but the excellent free versions are a great place to start.

### Interviewing Prospects One on One

There are a few different ways to get information directly from your audience. For example, you could simply set up interviews with people whom you trust and who may have relevant opinions. For example, if your nonprofit is focused on arts education for teens, you could meet with people you know who are high school teachers, parents of teens, and teens themselves, and ask them about their opinions. Or, if your nonprofit is focused on developing technology support services for people with visual impairments, you could set up lunch meetings with people you know in the software industry and pick their brains about their accessibility challenges.

Another way to conduct interviews is to canvass people at locations where you are likely to encounter people within your target profile. For example, you could attend a trade show related to your mission—say, a green energy convention—and stand in a high-traffic area, asking people to answer a few short questions. The key here is to have just a few short questions that passers-by can answer quickly with concise answers ("yes" or "no" or a numerical answer, for example) that you can easily record on a clipboard or laptop computer.

### Working With Focus Groups

Focus groups are a great way to gather information from a number of people, all at once. A focus group is simply an event at which you provide a presentation or demonstration to your target audience and solicit its feedback. Often, feedback is gathered via a survey or questionnaire prepared in advance. Feedback can also be obtained though oral question-and-answer sessions and discussions among the group, often led by a moderator, which are recorded either on video or by someone taking careful notes. For example, a health-care-related nonprofit might invite a group to watch its informational webcast explaining how to apply for certain Medicare benefits, then ask them whether they understood the webcast, what the webcast did well, and any areas where improvements could be made.

While there's nothing inherently complex or expensive about conducting a focus group, it will require some time and energy. If you don't have an office or other space where you can hold the focus group, you may need to rent an appropriate venue (though you should usually be able to find someone in your network willing to donate space). You'll also need to figure out whom to invite and where you'll find them. Because of the preparation and possible expense involved, be sure to start the invitation process early enough to ensure that you get enough confirmed participants to justify the time and expense of doing the focus group.

### Getting Started: A Basic Approach to Primary Research

Now that you know some of the basic tools for doing primary research, here's a simple approach to help get you started:

1. **Start by identifying the questions that you want answered—your research questions.** Why are you conducting primary research? What do you want to find out?

2. **Decide the best way to get those questions answered.** As described above, the basic methods include surveys, interviews, and focus groups (often in conjunction with a survey or questionnaire). The methods you choose will largely depend on the types of questions you want answered and the nature of your nonprofit's work.

3. **If you'll be using a survey or questionnaire, draft the questions.** Your goal is to craft specific questions that will yield responses that will help you answer your research questions.

4. **Identify and invite your study's participants.** Start with your list of contacts and include people who fit your target audience. Build and expand your list by asking trusted contacts to suggest others who would be appropriate. Developing your list of contacts—particularly before you've started your nonprofit—may require networking, which is discussed below.

5. **After conducting the study, compile the results.** Doing market research is all about obtaining data, so don't neglect the essential task of assembling and analyzing your results. Once this is done, you'll be poised to make decisions based on the information you've learned.

### Secondary Research Tools

Doing secondary research is generally as simple as reading trade journals and other publications in your field. At a minimum, staying current with news and issues is important for all nonprofits. Other nonprofits may have newsletters or other informational publications covering the issues relevant to your mission. Mainstream magazines and newspapers can also be good sources of information. Identify the media outlets that are most relevant for your nonprofit's field and read (or view or listen to) them as often as you can. Also, particularly if your nonprofit will mostly have a local focus, read your local newspapers and other media to keep an eye on local trends and issues.

In addition to keeping up with the issues in your field, secondary research will help you decide where to target your marketing efforts. Are there particular newspapers, websites, or other publications that specialize in your nonprofit's issues? If so, they might be good prospects for a press release. Are there prominent people whose names are mentioned in connection with your issue? If so, they could be good contacts for networking, prospects for your board, or even fundraising targets. Secondary research will give you a good sense of which people and media will be most receptive to your nonprofit's message.

## Fundamental Marketing Tools

Once you've defined your target audience, figured out what types of programs, benefits, and information will be most meaningful to them, and done some research on the people and media outlets who might be interested in your nonprofit's issues, it's time to use that data to market your group.

New nonprofits often worry that they don't have the budget or resources to market themselves. This worry is usually unfounded. Not only are there many low-cost ways to effectively market your nonprofit, but many nonprofits also overestimate how much information they need to provide to potential supporters.

In truth, most nonprofits don't need a marketing blitz; instead, they simply need to provide timely, clear information about specific events or programs and how the public can participate. Newer non-profits will do better to promote specific events—it's easier to tell the public about an event than it is to explain your nonprofit in the abstract. Focusing on an opportunity for the public to take a class, attend an event, or participate in a rally is often a great way to cut through the media clutter and reach potential supporters.

While there are loads of ways to market your nonprofit, a few tried-and-true methods are particularly effective—and won't break the bank: networking, media relations, and listing your organization in directories. This section explores each of these strategies in detail.

## Networking

Those in the for-profit business world understand that networking is one of the best ways to build a business. This is even more true in the nonprofit sector, where money is tight and credibility is crucial. Through networking, you actively cultivate relationships with key contacts. With these relationships established and nurtured, you'll stand a better chance of being able to motivate these contacts at crucial times to help further the goals of your organization.

Nonprofit-minded people often fear that successful networking requires unsavory schmoozing or pandering. These concerns are unfounded. In fact, if you adopt a sleazy wheeler-dealer approach, you risk alienating the very people whom you want to make your allies. Instead, successful networking flows from your sincere desire to create relationships that further the honest and laudable goals of your organization.

**EXAMPLE:** Main Street Reborn is a nonprofit dedicated to preserving historical main street districts in Florida's small towns. One of its board members, Melissa, attends a city council meeting in the town of Arcadia that was called to discuss the problems of Arcadia's blighted old downtown area. Melissa testifies to the council about the nonprofit's work in other small towns and the positive impact of its education and preservation efforts. After the meeting, Melissa introduces herself to members of the city council, a local reporter, and the head of the local historical society. After some conversation, she exchanges contact information with each person with whom she speaks, gives out Main Street Reborn's website address, and promises to keep in touch.

A few days later, Melissa sends an email to each contact from the meeting, stating how much she enjoyed meeting them and learning more about the issues facing Arcadia's downtown. In the email messages, she also mentions a couple of suggestions about how Main Street Reborn could help start an educational campaign about Arcadia's downtown and help with ongoing efforts to preserve some of the area's older buildings.

The following month, one of Arcadia's city council members contacts Melissa to ask if she would be willing to meet with a historical preservation committee to exchange ideas and suggest strategies. Melissa is delighted to do so and soon thereafter becomes involved in the city's plans to save Arcadia's downtown. Later, when trying to prevent the scheduled demolition of Arcadia's oldest building, Melissa calls the local reporter she met at the initial city council meeting, who writes an article letting the public know how they can oppose the demolition.

Far from sleazy, the networking efforts in the above example show that good networking is little more than sincere interest and communication with others who share your nonprofit's interests or can help expand the scope of your nonprofit's work. You are "networking" every time you attend an event held by another nonprofit, get to know community leaders and activists, write a letter to the editor, participate in an online discussion group, or communicate your nonprofit's mission to others who may be interested.

To network successfully, you need to know who in your community may be interested in your cause. For instance, if your nonprofit supports music education for children, you would want to know about any similar groups in the area or any prominent individuals (such as local musicians or educators) who have demonstrated an interest in the issue. You probably already know of other groups and individuals who share your organization's mission; if not, you need to take the time to find out who they are. Once you identify these contacts, get in touch with them and let them know about your nonprofit's work.

Think broadly about who might be interested in your cause. Don't restrict your networking efforts to those whom you already know or those closest to your field. Some of your best resources may be people from other walks of life who share an interest in your cause, including:

- other nonprofit leaders
- community activists and local clergy
- local politicians, such as city council members or alderpersons
- state politicians, such as legislators or the governor
- members of government agencies, boards, or commissions
- prominent businesspeople, and
- members of print, radio, or television news media.

While it may be easiest to meet someone at an event, introducing yourself to a potentially useful contact can be as simple as picking up the phone, writing a letter, or sending an email. In making your initial contact, you should be as formal or informal as is appropriate for the person with whom you are making contact. A letter of introduction on attractive letterhead might be best for an influential politician, for example, whereas a phone call might be fine to introduce yourself to a local business owner. In your letter, email, or phone call, explain who you are, what your organization does, and why you thought that person might be interested in your activities. Try to conclude by encouraging further communication in the future, such as inviting the contact to an event or asking if he or she would be interested in receiving email updates from your group. If you talk to someone on the phone, a follow-up email or letter thanking the contact for his or her time is always a smart idea.

**TIP**

**Forge relationships with contacts before you need help from them.** For example, if you need the support of a local politician on an upcoming ballot measure, you'll have a better chance of getting the politician's vote if he or she already knows you and thinks favorably of your organization than if you place a call to his or her office out of the blue.

## Media Relations

Another excellent—and inexpensive—way to promote your nonprofit is to generate free media coverage in newspapers or magazines or on radio, television, or the Internet. Your goal is to get "editorial" coverage, meaning some mention of your group or event in news or feature stories (as opposed to paid advertising). Because editorial coverage is far more credible than advertisements or paid publicity, it will have a greater impact. For example, a local newspaper article about your nonprofit's upcoming seminar will almost always attract more attendees than any advertising you purchase for the same event. And editorial coverage costs you nothing but time.

The term "media relations" means the process of attempting to obtain editorial coverage. It is a fairly simple process: You contact the media on behalf of your nonprofit and encourage an editor, producer, or reporter to write or produce a story about your particular subject. As with most marketing efforts, the more specific and targeted your message, the more impact it will have. For example, you'll be more likely to get editorial coverage of your nonprofit's River Clean-Up Day than of the very general fact that your nonprofit exists.

The basic steps for conducting media relations are:

1. **Write a press release.** A press release is a key tool to use when pitching a story idea. Typically, a press release is a one-page announcement outlining the information you want the media to cover. You have two main goals in writing a press release: (1) to capture the journalist's attention, and (2) to make it easy for the journalist to write the story you want published. Stylistically, press releases are usually written like news stories, offering journalists an example of the story you want them to produce. (See "Elements of a Strong Press Release," below, for more details on how to put together a winning pitch.)

2. **Make initial contact with the journalist by phone.** Make a preliminary phone call before sending a press release, so your release doesn't get lost in the shuffle. If you haven't identified the person at the news outlet who would cover your story, call the news department, briefly describe the nature of your press release, and ask who might be the best person for you to contact. Once you have a name of a reporter, editor, or producer, give that person a call to introduce yourself and your nonprofit, briefly explain the nature of your news story, and tell the person you will be sending a press release. If you can't reach the journalist by phone (as is often the case), don't let it hold you up: Leave a message and send out your press release. While you could make this initial contact by email, a phone call makes a stronger impression. And creating lasting relationships with individual reporters is the best way to get positive coverage over the long term.

3. **Send the press release by email, fax, or both.** Years ago, press releases were sent by mail. This practice has long since given way to delivery by fax and email. When sending via email, it's best to send it both as a PDF attachment and as plain text in the body of the email. Emailed press releases work because reporters like having an electronic copy from which to cut and paste when writing their stories; faxes work because

they don't get lost or buried as easily as email. The best approach is to ask journalists or editors how they prefer to receive press releases, and use that method.

4. **Follow up after you send the press release.** Shortly after sending your press release—a few hours or a day later, depending on the timing of your announcement—follow up with another phone call or email to make sure your press contact received the release and to answer any questions he or she may have.

An example of a press release is shown below.

Some people feel timid about contacting the media and asking them to cover a specific story. While you shouldn't be a pest, you also shouldn't feel shy about pushing your story idea persistently. To do their jobs, journalists must come up with a constant stream of interesting new story ideas. Just as you need their help, they need yours. Because you will often know more than reporters do about a particular story, you can offer valuable information that they can use when writing stories. If you are honest and reliable, you will usually be treated with respect.

If you don't get a response after an introductory phone call, a press release via email and fax, and a follow-up call, let the particular story idea rest; this will help you preserve your reputation as a pleasant, professional person to deal with the next time you want to pitch a story. A journalist may not cover your story because he or she does not think it is newsworthy or because there are other stories that take precedence. A few months later, when you try again, you may be pleasantly surprised to find that you've pitched the right story on the right day.

The most effective media relations come from relationships you build with reporters, editors, producers, and other media contacts. Because you are more likely to get news coverage from a reporter with whom you've worked before than from someone who's never heard of you, you should always treat your relationships with people in the media as the valuable resource they are.

## Sample Press Release

FOR IMMEDIATE RELEASE

Shawnee Independent Business Alliance Kicks Off With Launch Lunch

SHAWNEE, Oklahoma—The Shawnee Independent Business Alliance (SIBA) will hold its inaugural event, the SIBA Launch Lunch, on May 13, 2013 at the Outpost Community Space. Attendees will be introduced to SIBA by its founders and learn more about the organization's activities and membership benefits. The event will also feature a presentation by Sara Berger of the Small Business Institute about the benefits of alliance building. A box lunch will be included. Those who wish to attend should call 405-555-1234 by May 7 to reserve a space. (See time, location, and cost details below.)

Founded in 2013, SIBA is dedicated to supporting Shawnee's local, independent businesses through programs such as cooperative marketing, networking, and branding the "indie" business image. Benefits for members include a listing at SIBA's online directory of local businesses, joint advertising opportunities, and a window decal identifying them as a local, independent Shawnee business. SIBA also aims to educate consumers about the impacts of their spending decisions and to encourage them to shop local and independent businesses.

SIBA is part of a nationwide movement that recognizes the connection between a healthy, local economy and strong, vibrant communities. Betty Breitbard, SIBA President and owner of North Valley Day Spa, says, "Shopping at local, independent businesses is the best way to nurture a healthy, local economy and make Shawnee a great place to live."

SIBA supporters include its community sponsor, First State Bank, and its founding members, North Valley Day Spa, Clarity Media, and Page Turner Bookstore.

EVENT INFORMATION:
SIBA Launch Lunch
May 13, 2013, 11 am to 1 pm
Outpost Community Space
1250 N. Harrison Ave., Shawnee
Cost: $10 for members; $15 for nonmembers
To reserve space: Call 405-555-1234 by May 7

MEDIA CONTACT:
Polly Harvey, SIBA Treasurer
Owner/Director, Clarity Media
405-555-1234
polly@shawneeiba.org

SIBA
135 Main St.
Shawnee, OK 74801
405-555-9876
www.shawneeiba.org

## Elements of a Strong Press Release

The better your press release, the more likely a journalist will write about your nonprofit, giving you valuable exposure in the press. Reporters, editors, and producers are chronically busy and squeezed by deadlines; they need good story ideas and clear information to get their jobs done. The easier you can make it for them to cover your story, the more likely they are to oblige. If you write a strong, clear press release, they may even use parts of your release verbatim. But because most media people are flooded with press releases and story pitches, you'll need to keep your press release as succinct as possible.

Here are some tips on how to construct a compelling press release that is likely to generate media placements:

- Start with a news hook. Like a news story, your press release should have a strong first sentence, known in the news biz as the story's "lead." What is the most important point you want to get across? Write it in a clear, straightforward style and you will have your lead. Compare the following examples:
  - Weak lead: "The mission of the Shawnee Independent Business Alliance is to help local, independent businesses compete with big-box stores."
  - Strong lead: "The Shawnee Independent Business Alliance will host a free marketing workshop on May 6 to teach local business owners how to compete with big-box stores."
- Date, time, and location information should be easy to find. If your press release is promoting an event, don't bury important information deep within long paragraphs. Include important event details, such as date, location, and registration deadlines, in the first sentence or two, in the last sentence (perhaps in bold text), or summarized in bullet points at the end of the press release.

- Include the most important information first. Like stories in the newspaper, your press release should include all important details up front, then work toward more general or background information in later paragraphs. You could even put background information at the end of the release, in a separate section.
- Include quotes from board members or prominent supporters. Reporters like to include quotes from real people in their stories, so include at least one or two catchy quotes in your press release. If you are writing the release and you are the best person to offer a quote, don't be shy about quoting yourself! It may feel strange but it's perfectly appropriate. Remember, you're offering the media a sample of the story you want them to write, so include a quote as if an outside reporter interviewed you.
- Include a separate section with contact information. The journalists who receive your release may have additional questions to ask you or others in your group. Choose a point person who will be available to field any such questions, and include his or her contact information clearly at the end of the release.
- Create a news angle. If it is appropriate and possible, tie your release into a topic that's currently in the news. For example, if your press release announces your nonprofit's services assisting uninsured people in accessing health care at county and community centers, you'd certainly want to include a reference to the nationwide problem of people lacking health insurance—perennially a hot news topic.
- Use statistics. Reporters love statistics that show how prevalent a problem is or how many people are affected by an issue. Using the previous example, you could include recent statistics that 20% of people nationwide lack health insurance.

## Listings or Directories

Getting your group listed in appropriate directories is a great way to connect with your audience. Listings work so well because consumers who consult a particular information source have already determined that they want this type of information. In addition to every city's phone books and classified ads, most communities have other types of directories—for example, a directory of local arts organizations, environmental groups, or social service agencies. Some directories are published in hard copy, though many directories are posted online. And many different entities publish community directories, including local government offices, trade associations, nonprofits, or other organizations.

Many directories—particularly those online—may give your nonprofit a free listing. Other directories may charge a modest fee, which may well be worth it if the price is reasonable and the directory exposes your group to the right audience. Some directories, however, are prohibitively expensive; these are not worth considering unless the audience you're trying to reach is extremely narrow and desirable and the directory is highly targeted to that audience.

To find all of the directories in which you should list your nonprofit, you'll have to do some homework. Looking online is a good start, but you should also check with local resources, such as local government offices, trade associations, and other nonprofits. Don't limit yourself to nonprofit-only directories; your organization might fit well in a directory that lists both for-profit and nonprofit groups. A directory of local film organizations is a good example: It might list for-profit businesses, such as production companies, camera repair shops, and film stock companies, as well as nonprofit groups, such as film preservation societies and artist advocacy organizations.

---

### Checklist: Marketing Your Nonprofit

☐ Focus on marketing strategies other than advertising—such as networking, media relations, and listing your organization in directories—that are usually less expensive and just as effective.

☐ Have an efficient, organized operation in place before you start your marketing efforts.

☐ Learn basic marketing terminology, approaches, and goals.

☐ Conduct some primary research—through surveys, interviews, and/or focus groups—to gather information about who your target audience is and what's important to them.

☐ Do secondary research about issues in your field and about other groups that are pursuing goals similar to yours.

☐ Focus on getting the word out about your nonprofit's events and activities, rather than about the nonprofit in the abstract.

☐ Network by cultivating relationships with other nonprofits, community leaders, and others interested in your mission.

☐ Develop relationships with reporters and editors and pitch newsworthy stories about your nonprofit to them.

# Publishing Informational Materials

Publications are a great way to communicate substantive information to your constituency and the public. Newsletters are the most common way to make information available, but nonprofits also publish books, guides, pamphlets, how-to manuals, training materials, content-rich websites, blogs, CD-ROMs, instructional videos, and many other types of media, both in print and online.

Besides providing information, publications and other media can also help your nonprofit in other ways, such as:

- forging a closer bond with your constituency
- motivating readers to take action on certain pressing issues, and
- broadening your audience by reaching new members of the public.

If you decide to publish, you'll need a plan to help you manage the many resources required for even the smallest newsletter or pamphlet. Developing story ideas, writing articles, designing graphics and text, laying out a publication, printing it, and distributing it will all take valuable time—and usually also cost money. If you don't do some planning at the outset to clearly define what you intend to publish and how you will get the work done, you may find yourself either completely overwhelmed by your publishing operation or simply unable to pull it off (or both).

This chapter covers many important issues you will need to consider before your nonprofit starts any sort of publishing project. First, it will help you make the most important decision: whether your nonprofit should undertake a publishing operation or not.

If you decide that publishing is appropriate for your group, you need to think through and make decisions about a number of issues—from broad concepts, such as what your publishing goals are, to specific items, such as what media you'll use and where you'll distribute your information. This chapter explains these issues and describes the nuts and bolts of how to get articles, reports, and other important information out to the world, whether in print or online.

This chapter also covers copyright law—the legal rules that set forth who owns text, graphic art, video, and other original materials, including who can use or copy those works and under what circumstances. Nonprofits need to know this basic information to make sure that they don't inadvertently create publications that violate someone's copyright and risk exposing their groups to lawsuits for copyright infringement.

**TIP**

**Your publishing efforts can help market your nonprofit.** As discussed in Chapter 9, pure marketing materials differ from publications in their content and purpose. Marketing materials focus solely on promoting your group, while publishing focuses on conveying substantive information on topics of interest to your group. However, this doesn't mean that you can't use your publications to market your nonprofit. If you create articles, statistics, studies, or other informational materials on topics of interest to your group, use them to demonstrate that you are experts in your field—and that you are using this expertise to help people. Consider including excerpts from (or copies of) recent publications in your marketing and fundraising materials. And, of course, include marketing messages within your publications—for example, an ad for an upcoming event or an appeal for contributions. (For more information on marketing, see Chapter 9.)

## Decide Whether to Publish

Many new nonprofits jump into publishing projects without first considering whether publishing makes sense for their group at all. Although this kind of initial enthusiasm might yield a few interesting articles written by board members or volunteers, failing to plan ahead will inevitably lead to a misguided publishing effort fraught with stress, confusion, and wasted resources.

With this in mind, one of the first questions your nonprofit leaders should ask is whether to publish at all. The answer to this question will largely depend on two factors: whether you have any substantive information to convey and, if so, whether you have (or can obtain) the necessary resources to publish that information in some form.

 **SKIP AHEAD**

**If information is at the heart of your work, publishing may be essential to your goals.** Many groups—particularly those with scientific or educational missions—specialize in generating, analyzing, and presenting data. These groups may need to publish in order to achieve their missions. If your group falls in this category, feel free to skip ahead to "Create a Publishing Plan," below. Starting with that section, the rest of this chapter will outline publishing basics and explain how to use your existing resources to create a realistic publishing plan.

## Do You Have Substantive Information to Convey?

Even if you have all the money and resources in the world, your nonprofit shouldn't jump into publishing unless it can generate some substantive information that will interest its intended audience. Remember, unlike marketing, publishing efforts should go beyond merely promotional materials to feature informative content related to your nonprofit's focus.

While the essence of a publishing operation is putting out substantive material, this information doesn't have to take the form of lengthy, footnote-heavy reports or dry, academic articles. Anything that can be presented in articles, reports, books, or videos might fit the bill, such as:

- an article on the environmental effects of a proposed river dam
- a feature story about the efforts of a women's health activist in the community
- results of a study examining the negative effects of cuts in arts education
- a legal FAQ for victims of spousal abuse
- a book-length manual explaining the latest techniques of wilderness rescue and emergency medicine, or
- a short video examining the negative effects of acid rain on the environment.

Start by considering what type of content your publication or other type of media should logically feature. In the publishing world, determining your content is often referred to as defining an editorial mission or an editorial focus.

Some nonprofits will have an obvious editorial focus for their publishing efforts. For example:

- A nonprofit aimed at educating the public about the history of the Zuni tribe in Arizona would focus its editorial content on Zuni history and culture in Arizona.
- A nonprofit focused on finding a cure for pediatric leukemia could publish analyses of recent research studies, information on available treatments and therapies, and articles about the latest medical breakthroughs in the fight against pediatric leukemia.

Other nonprofits, however, might have to stretch to come up with an editorial focus for a publishing venture. For example:

- A nonprofit dedicated to delivering home-cooked meals to AIDS patients may have trouble coming up with ideas for articles or a publication because its activities are totally focused on delivering meals, not on any substantive topics.
- A nonprofit that offers day care services for low-income single parents might not know what it would feature in a newsletter or website, other than basics about its day care services (such as hours of operation, costs, policies, and so on), which would be better suited for marketing materials, not a publishing venture.

Some nonprofits may simply not have much substantive information to pass along. If you have a hard time coming up with an editorial focus, it may mean that publishing isn't the best way for your nonprofit to spend its time and money.

## Do You Have the Necessary Resources?

Even if your group can easily come up with a compelling editorial concept, you may find it difficult to marshal the resources necessary to start publishing. Even small publishing ventures require a decent commitment of time and money, which are always in short supply in your early days. You'll simply need to evaluate your priorities and your resources and then decide where publishing fits into the bigger picture. If your resources are thin and publishing isn't vital, you may want to put off your publishing plans until you're better prepared. (If you decide to move ahead after all, you'll have to devise a strategy that works with the resources available to you, a process covered in "Create a Publishing Plan," below.)

When evaluating how important publishing is to your group, start by considering whether and to what extent publishing helps to achieve your mission. If publishing is a central or an important way to further your mission, then it should bump upward on your priority list. If publishing is not directly tied to your mission, other activities should probably come first.

Even if publishing isn't directly tied to your mission, it can offer several benefits, including forging stronger ties with your members or gaining exposure for your group. But if you're short on resources, publishing won't be the most cost-effective way to achieve these goals. You can bond with members and get publicity through other methods (such as special events or media relations) and save the significant resources that would go into a larger publishing project.

**TIP**

**Consider forming a publishing alliance.** Before you launch your own publishing venture, search existing literature—both in libraries and online—to see whether any similar publications are already in print. If so, perhaps you could periodically contribute articles to that publication instead of starting your own. If you don't find an existing publication, you might approach another nonprofit to discuss joining forces to create one. For example, if your organization provides donated computer equipment to low-income children, it might make sense to approach another group—say, a computer department at a local college—to author a series of how-to manuals for the computers, rather than trying to publish them on your own.

## Create a Publishing Plan

If you decide to go forward with a publishing project, you've got some planning to do. You'll need to sketch out big-picture issues, such as your publishing goals, the information you want to convey, and your intended audience. You'll also have to consider practical matters, such as what resources you'll have available, what publishing vehicles you'll use, how often you'll publish, and how you'll distribute your publications.

Lots of details, large and small, go into every publishing project. But figuring out these issues doesn't have to be a complicated affair. The most important step is to take the time to think things through and make a plan. Doing so will yield a big payoff in efficiency and will help maximize your resources when you put your plan into action.

**RESOURCE**

**Recommended reading on planning and executing a publishing venture.** *Every Nonprofit's Guide to Publishing*, by Cheryl Woodard and Lucia Hwang (Nolo), is an excellent resource for new and experienced publishers alike.

## Define Your Editorial Mission and Features

The best way to start your planning is to home in on exactly what you want to achieve with your publishing operation. Start with your broadest ideas about your goals and audience. Do you aim to educate your audience about a certain topic? Inform them about late-breaking developments in your area? Motivate them with stories about inspiring people? With your fundamental goals clarified, you can turn to the task of defining your editorial mission.

### Editorial Mission

Much like a nonprofit needs to have a well-defined mission that guides its activities, a publication needs an editorial mission to shape its content. When planning your publishing operation, you should put careful thought into the topics your publication will cover and draft an editorial mission statement reflecting this editorial scope. While your editorial mission statement will undoubtedly be similar to your nonprofit mission statement, it should speak directly to the focus of the publishing venture, not the focus of the nonprofit in general.

| Sample Mission Statements | | |
|---|---|---|
| **Nonprofit** | **Nonprofit Mission Statement** | **Newsletter's Editorial Mission Statement** |
| Artists Rights Alliance | The mission of Artists Rights Alliance (ARA) is to help artists understand copyright and other arts-related legal and business issues. | The editorial mission of ARA's newsletter, *Copy—Right!* is to offer the latest news and information about copyright laws, informative articles on specific copyright issues, and entertaining stories about artists and their work. |
| Robots Care | Robots Care's mission is to help disabled people live independently with the help of robotic technology. | The editorial mission of Robots Care's newsletter, *Robots Helping Today*, is to inform readers about the latest developments in robotic technology, show how this technology improves the lives of disabled people, and profile the inventors and engineers pushing the industry forward. |

## Regular Features

Besides outlining the topics your publication will cover, it's also a good idea to identify the specific features it will offer. For example, a short eight- or 12-page newsletter might contain the following regular features:

- letters from readers
- a current events column with short news blurbs
- two feature stories
- a question-and-answer column, and
- one editorial/opinion article.

Planning and executing each issue will be much easier if you identify in advance regular features such as the ones listed above. Of course, you can always deviate somewhat from your list—for example, sometimes you might not have room for two features, or you might need to add an extra editorial piece to fill up space. But having an outline of regular features will help everyone plan their time and workloads more effectively—and create a consistent product for your readers.

## Evaluate Your Resources

An important step in planning your publishing venture is to make a realistic assessment of the resources you can commit to it. Obviously, the publishing strategy of a large, well-funded nonprofit will be quite different from the strategy of a scrappy young nonprofit with a few committed founders and a three-digit bank balance.

When assessing resources, don't think just in terms of money—you'll also need people with publishing skills on board. This includes people who can write, edit, and do graphic design, as well as folks who understand how to market and distribute a publication. If you don't have these people on staff, you'll need to hire them as employees or freelancers or seek out able volunteers. Bear in mind that the more you outsource your publishing operation to an outside contractor, the more money you'll spend and the less control you'll have over the final product. The more you can do with your existing board, staff, and volunteers, the better.

If you have to bring in outside help, consider starting by hiring a consultant to help you plan your publishing program, from overall strategies to specific steps. If your board, staff, and volunteers possess even just a few publishing skills, this plan may be all you need from the outside consultant. With a clear plan in place, it may be possible for your own people to execute the writing, editing, production, and distribution of your publications. If not, you can hire contractors for only those tasks that you can't handle in-house.

## Finding Volunteer Designers

David Dabney is a graphic designer and principal of Red Rooster Creative, a graphic design firm in Santa Fe, New Mexico. He offers the following advice for nonprofits that need graphic design work but are short on funds:

*Depending on the size of the project, design and printing can quickly eat up project funds. To stretch your dollars, see if a design school or class might be willing to do the work you need as a class project. For example, a student might be assigned your project as his or her main project for the semester. Schools commonly match students with local nonprofits in order to give the students real-world knowledge about working with clients and to help build the students' portfolios. Remember, even if your town doesn't have a design college, most community and technical colleges offer print and Web design classes. For print jobs, your nonprofit will usually have to pay for the costs of paper and ink, but you will save the considerable costs of hiring professional designers.*

In addition, many design firms and individual designers aim to do a few projects per year in which they donate their time for worthy causes. The key is to find out who they are and let them know about your nonprofit's needs. Try going to local meetings of the American Institute of Graphic Arts, the Graphic Arts Guild, or other design organizations in your area to get to know local firms and designers and put your nonprofit on their radar screens. Network in your community to find designers who might be willing to volunteer their services for your group.

You can also advertise on Craigslist, in your local weekly, or in other local media (both online and print), but networking and finding someone through your world of associates will usually yield better candidates than advertising for them.

---

$\textcircled{!}$ **CAUTION**

**Make sure you own your content (or have the right to publish it).** If contractors or volunteers create the content for your publications—for instance, articles, photographs, illustrations, or other graphics—you'll need

to pay special attention to copyright ownership issues and make sure that your nonprofit obtains ownership to the content or the right to publish it. Generally speaking, your nonprofit will automatically own copyright to the content created by employees, but not the content created by freelancers. The legal rules governing works created by volunteers are fuzzy, and your nonprofit may not automatically own their work. To obtain ownership to content created by freelancers (and possibly volunteers), you should put an agreement in writing. Copyright and intellectual property issues are covered below. For the full treatment, be sure to read *Getting Permission: How to License & Clear Copyrighted Materials Online & Off*, by Richard Stim (Nolo).

## Choose Your Media

With your goals and available resources sketched out, it's time to choose the form your publishing venture will take. Common nonprofit publishing tools include newsletters (both print and electronic versions), blogs, websites, guidebooks, pamphlets, and videos. It's common to use a combination of publishing methods—for example, a website that includes a blog, plus an informational guidebook and a few respected peer-reviewed studies.

 **RELATED TOPIC**

**Need more information on websites?** This chapter covers only publishing-related online media, such as blogs, articles, guides, and other editorial content. For information on nonprofit websites in general, see Chapter 11.

Generally speaking, the media you use should depend in large part upon the nature of the information you want to convey, which will depend, in turn, on your publishing goals and editorial mission. For example:

- If your nonprofit will regularly generate information that you want to communicate to the public, then a periodic newsletter (in print, online, or both) may be the best choice.
- If you want to distribute lengthy information or content that will be generated sporadically, the

material may be better suited for a guide, report, pamphlet, or website.

- If your nonprofit will constantly be generating new information that will rapidly go out of date, a website or electronic newsletter may be the best way to make it available. You can update these media as often as you want without incurring print costs.

Besides the information you want to convey, another important factor in choosing specific media is your budget. It costs money to produce printed materials, and periodicals like newsletters will need to be printed on a regular basis, usually at least quarterly. To keep print costs down, many nonprofits start their publishing efforts online or choose nonperiodical print formats like pamphlets or guides, which you don't have to publish on a regular basis.

### Print or Digital Format

Publishing online with blogs, e-newsletters, and other online methods of distributing information is the biggest thing to hit publishing since the invention of movable type centuries ago. Online publishing offers some major advantages over traditional print publishing—particularly the freedom from print and paper costs. In addition, distribution can be instant and worldwide, and updates (not to mention corrections) can be made easily and inexpensively. Interactive features allow you to obtain valuable feedback from your audience, which helps to build and strengthen bonds within your online community.

On the down side, people are flooded with online media these days, which can make it very hard to break through the clutter and get your audience's

---

### Should Your Nonprofit Blog?

As discussed in more detail in Chapter 11, a blog is basically a website format that consists of chronologically ordered posts (with the most recent entries at the top), much like an online journal. A number of characteristics make blogs valuable publishing vehicles: They are easy to update; they allow an informal, friendly voice and flexible coverage of topics; and allowing readers to comment and interact helps immensely in forging a connection between the blog and its readership.

Blogs are very effective in attracting traffic and readership. Because your nonprofit's blog will likely discuss your organization's goals and activities, as well as news and issues relevant to your nonprofit's mission, it will attract visitors searching for information on these topics. Information on driving traffic to your website is discussed in Chapter 11, but for now keep in mind that new and informative content regularly posted to a blog will help drive traffic to your website. Sites with blogs that are updated on a regular basis will always attract more traffic than sites whose content is purely marketing copy that never or rarely gets updated.

If you decide your nonprofit will maintain a blog, one or more people at your organization—perhaps the board president or the executive director—will need to add regular posts to the blog on topics related to your nonprofit's mission. (For example, the Sierra Club's former chairman Carl

Pope wrote a blog at the Sierra Club website called "Taking the Initiative," focusing on green issues and politics. Another Sierra Club blog, "The Green Life," offers a variety of practical green living tips from a range of staff writers and editors.)

The trick to a successful nonprofit blog is to offer information that's interesting to your audience and helps advance your nonprofit mission. At a minimum, don't overlook the following bottom-line realities if you're considering launching a blog:

- The blog needs to be regularly updated, ideally a couple of times per week or more. Don't start a blog unless you're sure you or someone at your nonprofit has the time to keep it updated.
- The blogger needs to be well-informed on the topic, and Web savvy. While the blogger doesn't have to be the world's top authority on your topic, he or she needs to know enough to create posts that are interesting and helpful to others seeking information on that topic. Part of this skill is the ability to ferret out useful information online and link to it.
- The blogger needs to have some basic writing skills. An informal, lively writing style is best on blogs. Avoid dry, academic writing. Humor is always an asset.

attention. If your readers have overloaded email boxes, they may barely read the subject line of your e-newsletter before clicking it into the trash. Unlike a print newsletter that readers can peruse on the couch, online media is usually read at the computer—often during the workday, when people are pressed for time. It can be a stretch to expect even committed members to take the time to read your blog or e-newsletter unless the information is truly compelling or practical.

With these pros and cons in mind, it's often a good strategy for a budget-pressed nonprofit to start with a blog or an electronic newsletter and later, once the nonprofit has funds for printing and distribution, add printed publications to the mix. Not only can online media be inexpensive to create, but they are also inherently malleable—an important factor in the early days when you'll still be refining your publishing strategy. You can tinker with your blog or your e-newsletter as you get a sense of what kind of information you want to publish. When you have settled on appropriate content and style, you can consider creating a print publication as well.

If you publish both in print and online, your print and online versions will almost certainly differ in some ways and should offer slightly different sets of information. Some content may be appropriate for one medium but not the other. Certain interactive features, for example, will be possible only at a blog, not in print. But another reason to vary your content between print and online versions is to achieve strategic goals. For example, your nonprofit may want to sign up readers for a print newsletter in order to obtain mailing address information for future fundraising efforts. If so, you might offer some information only in your print edition as an incentive for your online readers to sign up for a print subscription.

**TIP**
**Use material from online newsletters for a less-frequent print version.** Many nonprofits publish a monthly newsletter online and/or via email, then send a longer hard copy newsletter less frequently, say twice a year. The print copy typically includes a good amount of material from the monthly online versions—and an appeal for donations with a return envelope. Many nonprofits find these hard-copy appeals to be more successful than online appeals.

### Frequency

Lots of people assume that "nonprofit publishing" consists solely of putting out a newsletter. These folks forget that publishing isn't only about creating periodicals—publications that are issued according to some regular schedule. In fact, you don't have to commit to putting out a publication each week, month, or quarter to enter the publishing world. Instead of a newsletter, you could publish an occasional guide or report or a website that doesn't promise to be updated at any particular time. You should commit to a regular periodical only if you really want to—or, better put, if you actually have the information to fill it and the resources to put it out, issue after issue.

**TIP**
**A blog is another alternative to a newsletter—though it also requires a commitment.** While a blog doesn't involve a predictable schedule like a newsletter, blogs that aren't updated at least once or twice a week won't likely get very much traffic. Because most blogs are short posts, it is easier to get them done than more formal articles for newsletters. But on the flip side, new blog posts need to be added frequently. As with newsletters, don't start a blog if you don't have the resources to maintain it.

If you decide to publish a periodical, then you'll have to determine how often you'll put it out. This is called the publication's frequency. Most newsletters are published every month or every quarter, though some are done bimonthly (every other month) or twice a year. If you can't commit to a publishing schedule of some sort, you'd be better off considering a single-issue publication, like a guide, report, or white paper, so you don't create an expectation among your readers that another issue will come out on a particular date in the future.

Publishing even a small newsletter (whether in print or online) requires a fairly serious commitment. While you may think it's easy to write a couple of short articles every month or quarter, you'd be amazed at how many nonprofits dread their newsletter deadlines. It's not uncommon for a nonprofit to realize—only after putting out an issue or two—that it doesn't have the resources to publish a newsletter after all. It might decide instead to focus on one or two publishing projects a year, or even to abandon the idea of publishing altogether in favor of more basic marketing efforts. Rather than wasting time and resources—and risking losing some of your audience because you've failed to meet their expectations—it's much better to plan realistically from the start so you can choose a publishing schedule that works for your group.

When trying to determine how often you'll put out your newsletter, consider factors such as:

- **Staff resources.** Don't commit to putting out a newsletter every week, month, or quarter unless you're confident your staff and volunteers can pull it off.
- **Costs.** Costs are a real issue with print publications—the more often you publish, the higher the cost.
- **Type of content.** Some content has a longer shelf life than others. A publication that focuses on profiles of community leaders will remain fresh for a longer time than one based on breaking legal news.
- **Timing of subject matter.** If your publication will report on events that have their own schedule, you may want your publishing schedule to be similar. For example, a community garden nonprofit might time its newsletter to precede the planting season and harvest season.

## Distribution

Distributing nonprofit publications is somewhat simpler than distributing commercial newsletters and magazines, because most nonprofits start with a built-in readership base. Print publications are generally sent by mail to nonprofit members and supporters or distributed via racks at appropriate locations. Electronic publications are simply sent via email. The more members and supporters you already have in your databases, the easier it will be for you to get your publications into their hands and email boxes. That said, you may also want to expand your audience, in which case you should put some thought into your distribution strategy.

To reach a broader audience, use the marketing techniques discussed in Chapter 9 and think creatively about distribution methods. A great approach is to look for opportunities to link up with other like-minded groups. For example, if you know a fellow nonprofit is about to hold a well-publicized seminar, ask whether you can leave a stack of your publications at the event. Likewise, a neighbor nonprofit might be willing to swap advertising or editorial space in its newsletter for space in yours, which gives each of you an opportunity to promote your own publications to a new audience. As with any marketing efforts, the most effective outreach will be to a targeted group, rather than to the public at large. The more you can reach members of groups with similar inclinations to yours, the better.

Here are some more tips on how and where to distribute your publication:

- Most cities have libraries and public information centers where businesses and community groups can distribute their information.
- Nonprofits often have tables at their offices with literature from other groups.
- For-profit businesses may be willing to carry your publication, especially if your work overlaps with theirs.
- Universities and colleges are good places to distribute nonprofit publications. Check with individual departments that cover your subject area.
- Churches often distribute literature from community groups.

## Putting It All Together

With your goals clarified, resources identified, types of media chosen, and issues like format, frequency, and distribution nailed down, you'll have all the major components of a publishing plan in place. As with many of the planning tasks discussed in this book, it's a good idea to put your publishing plan in writing—you might even include it as an addendum to your strategic plan.

Ultimately, your plan will need to balance what you want to communicate with the resources you have available to get the job done. Whether in print, online, or both, the initial publishing efforts of many nonprofits are bite-sized—say, a four-page newsletter distributed quarterly or a basic website offering a few informative articles posted every other month. As long as you get out the information that you deem essential, taking a modest approach can work just fine.

As your nonprofit grows, your publishing ventures can grow along with it. Some large, mature nonprofits publish high-end magazines, sophisticated books, feature-length documentary videos, or cutting-edge websites with thousands of pages of information. It's not uncommon for educational or research-driven nonprofits to develop into publishing-intensive organizations. The bottom line is that the scope of your publishing efforts will depend largely on how they further your mission and on what you can afford.

EXAMPLE 1: Native Florida History Inc. (NFH), a nonprofit dedicated to educating the public about the history of Native Americans in Florida, decides that publishing is central to its goal of telling the story of native Floridians. The nonprofit plans to conduct four historical research projects each year and present the findings of the research to the public through seminars and printed materials. The group decides to post each report on its website. NFH also wants to publish the reports in print, so the group can make them available to people who don't have Internet access and use them as a tool in meetings with potential supporters and funders. A local print shop has offered to print NFH's

materials at half-price, allowing NFH to expand its print efforts beyond what it could otherwise afford.

The board discusses printing the report results in individual pamphlets whenever a research project concludes. However, they also want to convey other information to their readers, such as a calendar of events, grant announcements, and other NFH news that changes regularly. This leads them to decide to publish a regular newsletter instead of individual pamphlets. The board decides to publish the newsletter quarterly, to coincide with the research reports, which are concluded every three months.

As board members continue to discuss the newsletter, they quickly realize that they can't afford to include every report in full, which would push each issue into the 40-page range. Instead, they decide to print abbreviated two-page versions of the reports in each newsletter and publish the full versions on their website. The print version would refer readers to the website for the full reports and any other Web-exclusive content.

The board decides to mail its newsletter to all supporters on its mailing list, except for those who specifically ask that it not be delivered. They will also make free copies available at seminars and in the reception area of NFH's office. They also make plans to contact other local nonprofits to ask about leaving stacks of the newsletter in their offices, perhaps in exchange for allowing the other nonprofits to distribute their materials at NFH's office.

EXAMPLE 2: The president of the board of Critters Care, a nonprofit that provides companion animals for sick children, proposes that Critters Care publish information about the therapeutic benefits of companion animals so that the public understands the value of their nonprofit mission. But financial resources are very tight, and the board wants to make sure that pursuing a publishing program won't prevent the organization from accomplishing its key goals of matching pets with children, providing initial vaccinations for each pet, and equipping each pet with basic necessities, such as a leash and collar.

Because the board members understand the importance of keeping the public informed about their mission and accomplishments, they decide to create a blog where they will regularly post information about their activities and links to related groups. The blog will also include basic information about the nonprofit, its history, contact information, and an appeal for donations.

The Critters Care board decides to update the blog at least twice per week. It also decides that after one year of maintaining the blog, it will revisit the issue of publishing a print version of information relevant to Critters Care's mission.

## Copyright Basics for Nonprofit Publishers

Even simple publishing efforts can raise serious questions regarding ownership and rights to use text, artwork, or other content. This area of law is known in general as intellectual property law, and the specific area of intellectual property that publishers need to deal with is known as copyright. While copyright law can quickly become a complex topic, the basic rules are fairly straightforward. This section will introduce you to the fundamental issues you will need to understand if you decide to publish.

 RESOURCE

**Recommended reading on copyright and licensing.** For more information on licensing text, artwork, and other copyrighted materials, consult Nolo's *Getting Permission: How to License & Clear Copyrighted Materials Online & Off,* by Richard Stim. It's an excellent resource that will help you understand and figure out how to handle copyright and other intellectual property issues in both traditional media and emerging digital formats.

### What Copyright Protects

You're probably already aware that much creative work is protected by copyright. Generally speaking, when someone creates a work such as an article, story, song, painting, poem, photograph, or other original material, that person owns a broad set of rights to control how that work is used, known collectively as a copyright. Copyright laws prohibit others from reproducing, modifying, distributing, or selling such a work without the copyright owner's permission.

---

### Not All Content Is Protected by Copyright

Certain material, including works published before 1923 and works created by the U.S. government, fall into a category known as the public domain. If a work is in the public domain, anyone can use it without permission. If you want to use content from another site that falls into the public domain, you can do so without obtaining permission from, or entering into a contract with, the owner of that site. By the same token, if your website posts public domain material, other sites are also allowed to post that material without your permission.

Broadly speaking, there are four reasons why a creative work might be in the public domain:

- The original copyright of the work has expired.
- The original copyright of the work was not renewed according to specific copyright rules.
- The work was deliberately placed into the public domain by the owner.
- The work was not eligible for copyright protection in the first place; U.S. government works fall into this category.

Public domain rules are fairly complex; for detailed information, see *The Public Domain*, by Stephen Fishman (Nolo).

---

Copyright protects a broad range of creative work, not just fine art or literature. Materials subject to copyright include original text, photographs, drawings, computer graphics, Web design, multimedia works, videos, music, sculpture, and even architecture.

In legal terms, obtaining permission to use someone else's copyrighted content is known as getting a license. A content license is simply a contract that allows you to use copyrighted content according to whatever specific terms you've outlined in the agreement. The party that owns the content and gives permission for someone else to use it is called the licensor; the party that gets to use the content is called the licensee.

When you license content, you do not own it; you're simply obtaining the right to use it in specific circumstances. In contrast, buying the copyrights to a creative work (known in legal terms as a copyright assignment) gives you all the rights to the work as if you were the original copyright owner.

## Ownership and Works for Hire

When employees, contractors, or volunteers create content or other creative works for your nonprofit, you'll need to understand who owns the work. Your nonprofit will want to make sure it has unfettered rights to use any text, artwork, photos, logos, and other materials that are created by the people working for you. In some situations, you probably won't want or need to own the copyright to certain works, as long as you have permission to use them (a time-sensitive article for your website might fall into this category). In other situations, however, you will want full ownership—for example, to your nonprofit's logo and any other graphics or photos you use to identify your nonprofit. Before you hire anyone to create anything for your group, you should understand the rules regarding ownership of creative works.

The general rule is that the person who creates content owns the copyright. However, there is an exception for "works for hire"—such works are owned by the hiring party, not the creator. The rules regarding what constitutes a work for hire vary depending on whether the work is created by an employee or an independent contractor.

### Rules for Employees

When an employee creates any work in the course of employment, the employer—not the employee—owns copyright to that work. Having your content created by employees, not contractors (or volunteers, as discussed below), is the simplest and most straightforward way for your nonprofit to make sure that it owns copyright in the content.

### Rules for Contractors

When a contractor creates certain types of content, the hiring party owns copyright in the work only if the contractor and hiring party have made a written agreement stating that the work is a work for hire. Work-for-hire agreements are necessary whenever a nonemployee creates the work. Without a written work-for-hire agreement, the nonemployee creator owns copyright to the work.

However, you cannot turn every kind of creative work into a work for hire using a written agreement. According to copyright law, a work-for-hire agreement will give copyright to the hiring party only if the content falls into one of the following eight categories:

- part of a larger literary work, such as an article in a magazine or a poem or story in an anthology
- part of a motion picture or other audiovisual work, such as a screenplay
- a translation
- a supplementary work, such as an afterword, introduction, chart, editorial note, bibliography, appendix, or index
- a compilation
- an instructional text
- a test or answer material for a test, or
- an atlas.

If the content created by a contractor doesn't fit into one of these categories, then a written work-for-hire agreement won't be sufficient to give copyright to the hiring party. Instead, you'll have to execute a copyright assignment—an outright sale of the copyright from the contractor to your nonprofit. Unless you decide to hire the creator as an employee, you'll need to use one of these two types of agreements—a work-for-hire agreement if the work falls into the categories above, or an assignment agreement if it does not—in order for your nonprofit to gain ownership rights in work created by the contractor.

At the end of this chapter, you'll find a Contractor Work-for-Hire Agreement that also includes assignment provisions. You should be sure to execute this agreement with any contractors who create copyrightable work, such as text, artwork, graphic design, or other media. The agreement is structured to establish the work as a work for hire unless the work does not meet the applicable requirements, in which case a back-up provision converts the arrangement to an assignment.

### Rules for Volunteers

Nonprofits often use work created not by employees or contractors, but by unpaid volunteers. Unfortunately, copyright law doesn't even address this situation—it deals only with employees and contractors.

Because copyright law doesn't provide any guidance on ownership of works created by volunteers, the wisest legal course of action is to assume the worst—that is, to assume that you will not automatically own copyright of your volunteers' work but will have to obtain it through a work-for-hire agreement or a copyright assignment. Because some works won't fall into the categories required for work-for-hire agreements, many nonprofits simply ask all volunteers to sign an agreement assigning copyright to the nonprofit for any work they create in the course of their relationship with the nonprofit.

You'll find a streamlined Volunteer Assignment Agreement below. As in the Contractor Work-for-Hire Agreement, the agreement establishes the work as a work for hire if it meets the legal requirements. Otherwise, the agreement will act as a copyright assignment.

### Sample Contractor Work-for-Hire Agreement

You should use the sample agreement below whenever you hire contractors to create copyrightable material for your nonprofit. Enter the names of the nonprofit and the contractor in the appropriate blanks. In the Services section, describe the work that the contractor is supposed to perform, for example: "Shoot photographs to use at the Eco-Sud website." Insert the amount to be paid to the contractor in the Payment section.

The section titled Works for Hire—Assignment of Intellectual Property Rights establishes that the work is made for hire. However, if the work does not meet the requirements of copyright law, the agreement contains a back-up provision that converts the arrangement to an assignment. Businesses and nonprofits commonly use this type of provision to cover all of their bases and make sure that ownership rights have been acquired.

The Contractor Warranties provision establishes that the work is the contractor's original material and that it doesn't violate any intellectual property or other laws. This and the indemnification language serve to protect the nonprofit if the material proves to be legally unsound (for example, if the contractor copied the work from another source without permission). In the agreement's Miscellaneous provision, insert the nonprofit's home state, which will establish which state's law will govern the interpretation of the agreement in the event of a dispute.

**FORM**
A blank Contractor Work-for-Hire Agreement is included in the forms section (Appendix B) in the back of this book, and the Nolo website includes a downloadable copy of this form. See Appendix A for the link to the forms in this book.

### Sample Volunteer Assignment Agreement

If your nonprofit will use volunteers to create content for your publications or any other copyrightable material, make sure they fill out and sign volunteer assignment agreements such as the one below. It's very similar to the agreement for contractors but simplified and streamlined so as not to be intimidating to your volunteers. It also differs in that it covers ongoing work by the volunteer rather than a specific project, so you can simply have the volunteer fill it out and sign it once.

You can adapt this agreement by entering your nonprofit's name throughout. Then, simply have the volunteer enter his or her name and complete the signature portion. Also indicate what, if anything, the nonprofit is promising to do for the volunteer—for

## Contractor Work-for-Hire Agreement

This Work-for-Hire Agreement (the "Agreement") is made between _____
_____ ("Nonprofit"), and
_____ ("Contractor").

### Services

In consideration of the payments provided in this Agreement, Contractor agrees to perform the following services:

_____
_____ .

### Payment

Nonprofit agrees to pay Contractor as follows: _____
_____ .

### Works for Hire—Assignment of Intellectual Property Rights

Contractor agrees that, for consideration acknowledged in this Agreement, any works of authorship commissioned pursuant to this Agreement (the "Works") shall be considered works made for hire as that term is defined under U.S. copyright law. To the extent that any of the Works created for Nonprofit by Contractor are not works made for hire belonging to Nonprofit, Contractor assigns and transfers to Nonprofit all rights Contractor has or may acquire to all such Works. Contractor agrees to sign and deliver to Nonprofit, either during or subsequent to the term of this Agreement, such other documents as Nonprofit considers desirable to evidence the assignment of copyright.

### Contractor Warranties

Contractor warrants that the Works do not infringe any intellectual property rights or violate any laws related to libel, privacy, or otherwise and that the Works are original to Contractor. Contractor agrees to indemnify Nonprofit and hold it harmless in any action arising out of, or relating to, these representations and warranties.

### Miscellaneous

This Agreement constitutes the entire understanding between the parties and can be modified only by written agreement. The laws of the State of _____ shall govern this Agreement. In the event of any dispute arising under this agreement, the prevailing party shall be entitled to its reasonable attorneys' fees.

Contractor Signature: _____

Contractor Name: _____

Contractor Address: _____

Contractor Tax ID #: _____

Date: _____

Nonprofit Authorized Signature: _____

Name and Title: _____

Address: _____

Date: _____

## Volunteer Assignment Agreement

I, _____ ,

am a volunteer with _____ . It is my intent that any Work I create in my capacity as a volunteer

for _____ ,

will become the property of _____ ,

which will own full copyright in all such Work(s). To the extent that any Work(s) I create for _____

_____ is not a work for hire, I assign and transfer

to _____ all

worldwide copyright interests in the Work(s), for the life of such copyright interests.

In assigning all right, title, and interest in the Work(s) to _____ ,

I intend to transfer to _____

the full ownership in and of the Work(s), including all rights of reproduction, distribution, display, and adaptation, and

the right to create derivative work(s). All such rights apply without limitation to any print, electronic, multimedia, or

other formats including HTML format for websites, distribution online by email, and all other methods of creating and

distributing media. I agree to sign and deliver to _____ ,

either during or subsequent to the term of this Agreement, such other documents as _____

_____ considers desirable to evidence the assignment of copyright.

In consideration of this agreement, _____ agrees to (check all that apply):

☐ allow me to include the Work or a reproduction of the Work in my portfolio or other such compilation, to be shown

    to my prospective employers or clients, and no other commercial or noncommercial use. All such portfolio uses must

    include a notice of _____'s copyright ownership.

☐ acknowledge my transfer of the Work to _____

    as a charitable contribution.

☐ give full and complete credit in all versions of the Work(s).

☐ other: _____

_____ .

I warrant that any Work(s) I create pursuant to this agreement are original and do not infringe any intellectual property rights

or violate any laws related to libel, privacy, or otherwise. I agree to indemnify and hold harmless _____

_____ in any action arising out of, or relating to,

these representations and warranties.

Volunteer Signature: _____

Volunteer Name: _____

Volunteer Address: _____

Date: _____

example, to include credit for the volunteer's work or acknowledge the donated copyright as a charitable contribution. If you want to address credit and acknowledgments separately for each project, you could check "other" and enter "Terms will vary per project and will be outlined in attachments." Then, for each project, outline the credit and acknowledgment terms and include them with the main agreement as separate attachments labeled Attachment A, Attachment B, and so on.

**FORM**

**A blank Volunteer Assignment Agreement is included in the forms section (Appendix B) in the back of this book, and the Nolo website includes a downloadable copy of this form.** See Appendix A for the link to the forms in this book.

---

## Checklist: Publishing Informational Materials

☐ Decide whether to publish. Do you have substantive information to convey? Do you have the necessary resources?

☐ Create a publishing plan that defines your publishing goals, the information you want to convey, and your audience.

☐ Evaluate your publishing resources. Consider publishing alliances with similar publications or groups.

☐ Decide on publishing vehicles, formats, and distribution strategies that fit with your publishing plan.

☐ Become familiar with the basics of copyright law and copyright agreements.

# Spreading the Word Online About Your Nonprofit

These days, any nonprofit that wants to be taken seriously has to have at least a minimal presence online. If you don't have a website, a Facebook page, or some other way for the public to find out about your group online, people may think you're not credible. Worse, many may simply fail to learn you even exist. Looking at this in a more positive light, the benefits of establishing your nonprofit's online presence are major. Websites, blogs, email, and other methods of electronic communication can be highly effective marketing and fundraising tools for your nonprofit, allowing you to share crucial information about your group and its activities quickly, widely, and inexpensively. Best of all, the interactive nature of online communications facilitates relationships between your nonprofit and its supporters—something that one-way communications from your group outward can't do.

Establishing your online presence—which may include a website, a blog, social media activities, email or crowdfunding campaigns, and more—is a task that must be approached strategically. As explained in this chapter, figuring out how your online activities will serve your mission and how they fit into your overall strategy are crucial first steps. Without careful planning and thought, you might end up spending valuable resources with little to show for your efforts.

Even when your online strategy is clear, the question of how to go about developing a website, a blog, or an email campaign can be tricky. There's no question, it can feel overwhelming to figure out how to get your nonprofit online, to stay current with what's happening in online media, and to separate what's truly effective from over-hyped technologies.

The good news is that establishing your nonprofit online can be done simply, effectively, and inexpensively. This chapter will help you develop a realistic online strategy that truly serves your nonprofit and its mission. We'll look at:

- how to assess your overall strategy and ensure your online activities are compatible with each other

- the best methods and tools currently being used to promote nonprofits online, including email marketing, blogs, and social media
- how to drive traffic to your site through search engine optimization (SEO) and other means
- the process of planning and developing a website, including how to find, hire, and work effectively with a Web developer
- the basics of registering your domain name and setting up a hosting service, and
- legal rules governing ownership of and copyright to your site's content.

(For information on publishing substantive content on your site—and offline, too—see Chapter 10.)

---

**CAUTION**

**If you outsource the development of your website, blog, or other online communication vehicle, retain control of strategic decisions.** Unless someone involved with your nonprofit has technology expertise, it's generally best to outsource most aspects of technology development. Do not, however, give a consultant or Web development company complete discretion over your site or blog—particularly when it comes to defining strategy. Even if you know and trust the developer you hire, key nonprofit staff (paid or volunteer) or board members must be involved in these important strategic questions. This chapter describes the overall process of developing your online presence and can help you decide how much your nonprofit can handle in-house.

## Planning Your Online Activities

The key to effectively establishing an online presence for your nonprofit is to approach the process strategically, with a solid assessment of how your nonprofit will use its online activities to advance its mission. If you develop a website, for example, without careful initial thought and planning, you'll miss the opportunity to tailor the site to meet your nonprofit's real needs. Even worse, a poorly planned website may end up creating unanticipated site maintenance work for your nonprofit's staff or volunteers, creating a resource drain. Don't make this mistake!

## Web Jargon, Demystified

Besides the often bewildering technical jargon that's often used by Web developers and consultants, even nontechnical terms are sometimes used in confusing ways as the language of the Web continues to evolve. To help you understand what's what, some key terms are defined below as they'll be used in this chapter. Because the e-world is relatively new, definitions are still a bit fluid, and others might use these terms somewhat differently:

- **Blog** is short for "weblog," a website using a format of short posts, ordered in reverse chronological order (the most recent posts are at the top of the page), which often include links to other sites. Blogs are regularly updated—sometimes several times daily— with new information by one or more contributors, called bloggers. Blogs started out as largely personal communication vehicles, but they have been adopted by nonprofits, businesses, and online publishers.

- **Content management system, or CMS,** refers to software that allows a nonprogrammer to update and manage the content at a website. The user logs into the CMS using a regular Web browser and can add, edit, or remove content without special technical skills, such as knowing HTML (hypertext markup language, which is the language used to create Web content).

- **Crowdfunding** is a method of raising money online directly from your social media network and other supporters. Crowdfunding websites (also called "platforms") like Kickstarter or IndieGoGo make it easy for users to create fundraising campaigns that can easily be promoted among social media networks such as Facebook or Twitter. See Chapter 6 for more on crowdfunding.

- **E-commerce** refers to an online sales operation, generally via a website that is set up to take online orders and process credit cards or other types of payments. In the nonprofit world, an e-commerce operation might include sales of items such as T-shirts or tote bags, often as a way to raise funds.

- An **email list** is simply a list of email addresses of people who have expressed interest in receiving email from a specific sender or about a certain topic. For example, your nonprofit could send messages about special events to an email list—which should be composed of people who have clearly expressed interest in receiving your emails. (As you're probably aware, unsolicited marketing emails are known as spam.) Recipients on an email list cannot usually post their own messages to the entire group; communications are typically one-way from the administrator to the list. If the content of the email is substantive, the email would usually be called an e-newsletter.

- A **marketing website** refers to a basic website that features marketing-type information about an organization, such as a mission statement, descriptions of programs, contact information, and the like. Very basic marketing websites are sometimes called brochure-ware because they are analogous to an informational brochure. A marketing website might include enhanced functions such as online donation processing or online registration and payment for events. Even though these additional functions may involve payment processing, they wouldn't normally be considered e-commerce operations, a term that typically implies an online store environment.

- **Listservs** are email discussion groups about different topics, and they allow people who have signed up to share information with each other. Any subscriber can send an email to the listserv, and that email will automatically be sent to all other listserv subscribers. This differentiates a listserv from an email list, in which communications are typically only one-way from the site administrator to the list.

- **Online presence** refers to the collection of ways a nonprofit is represented in the electronic world. For instance, in addition to having a website, you could maintain a blog; be listed in numerous online directories; be a regular commentator on other blogs and online forums; have a monthly email newsletter; supply informative articles to other websites; or moderate a listserv. The sum of all these activities is often called your online presence.

- **Plug-ins** are small pieces of software that add to another application's functionality. You'll typically install a plug-in to expand your existing software's capability. For example, you can install various plug-ins that help your Web browser track various blogs and social media sites; with the plug-in installed, the browser will offer new buttons and functions. Or, you can install a calendar plug-in to your Web content management system to enable adding and editing events into a searchable calendar at your site.

## Web Jargon, Demystified (continued)

- **RSS**, which stands for "really simple syndication," is a technology that allows users to subscribe to frequently updated sources of information and read all the headlines (and sometimes a line or two of text) on one page. The RSS feed (the information you're tracking) will appear in an RSS reader, which is software that aggregates all your feeds onto one page. Many RSS readers/aggregators are browser based; you simply log into a certain Web page to read your RSS feeds.
- **Social media** includes sites like Facebook, YouTube, and Flickr, which focus on content that is submitted by users. These sites are "social" in that users typically identify friends within the system and create groups and communities.

- **Web 2.0** refers to the transition of the Web towards social media and user-generated content. Previously, websites tended to feature content created and maintained by the site owner; now, sites tend to feature content submitted by users, such as blog posts, comments (including customer reviews of businesses and nonprofits on sites like Yelp), videos, and photo albums.
- **Web developers** (also known as Web builders) specialize in all aspects of creating websites, including organizing the information, graphic design, and programming. The term "Web developer" is preferable to "Web designer" because graphic design is only one aspect of creating a website.

Start by carefully considering how your website, blog, or other online activities will fit into your strategic plan. The more specifically you can identify your goals, the better. Is it a priority to attract new members? To raise money? To educate the public? To streamline nonprofit operations? If you have multiple goals, identify the most important and use them to guide your online strategy. Here's a list of common goals for nonprofit websites:

- to build recognition and awareness of the nonprofit and its mission
- to reach the populations the nonprofit aims to serve and get them involved in its programs or events
- to streamline operations—for example, by allowing online class registration or online member management functions
- to reach new supporters and get them involved as volunteers, staff, or board members
- to raise money through online donations
- to publish information about the issues and topics related to the nonprofit and its activities in these areas, and
- to collect email addresses or other contact information for other outreach efforts.

By clearly defining goals, you'll be better able to decide what information you want to communicate to your audience. For example, if you rush to put together a website and fail to provide a prominent link to your "Donate" page, you probably won't get much traffic to that area. If, on the other hand, you outline your goals for the site and identify online donations as a top priority, you will be less likely to make that blunder. This advice may sound obvious, but an unbelievable number of websites are poorly designed to the point of uselessness. Don't join their ranks.

**EXAMPLE:** The mission of the Shawnee Independent Business Alliance (SIBA) is to educate its community about how locally owned, independent businesses are a cornerstone of a healthy local economy. The SIBA Shopper Network is one of SIBA's main programs. Local, independent businesses can join the network as SIBA Businesses, and people in the community can join as SIBA Shoppers. The SIBA Shoppers get a card they can present for discounts at any of the SIBA Businesses.

In its start-up days, SIBA's board members make a quick website displaying their mission statement on the home page. Other pages offer information about the organization, including its history and contact information for the board.

After a few months, SIBA's board members realize that the website isn't doing much for their organization. They decide that the website should focus on a specific goal that is important to the nonprofit: raising awareness of the SIBA Shopper Network. With this goal clarified, they revamp the website to feature the SIBA Shopper Network's logo and introductory information prominently on the home page. They add a link to the directory of SIBA Businesses to make it easy for shoppers to use the SIBA Shopper Network. In addition, they provide links to:

- membership information for businesses and individuals
- an online registration form for new members
- educational materials about the importance of supporting local, independent businesses, and
- a description of SIBA, including its history, a list of its board members, and mission statement.

Within a few months, the site traffic more than doubles, with most hits at the pages featuring the SIBA Shopper Network. For SIBA, featuring its main program on the home page is much more effective than offering general information about its mission. Its mission statement still appears on the site, but in a much less prominent position.

**TIP**

**Make strategic decisions in-house.** As stated earlier, clarifying strategies and goals are tasks your nonprofit should tackle. While you may get valuable advice from a Web developer or another expert, your nonprofit's key people should make the ultimate decisions.

## Understanding Your Options Online

Having an online presence can and should mean more than just having a website. While a website is often the centerpiece of a nonprofit's online presence, you need to consider the range of options for communicating with your constituency online.

Email outreach, blogging, and networking with social media are particularly effective ways to connect with your supporters online, spread your message, and further your mission.

### Email Outreach

As we discussed in Chapter 10, sending a newsletter via email (called an e-newsletter) is a great way to distribute information, which helps not only to keep your constituency informed, but to establish your nonprofit's credibility. Besides using email for newsletters, you can also use email for other kinds of communications, such as fundraising appeals (discussed in Chapter 6), inviting supporters to events, or putting out a call for volunteers.

To collect email addresses, include a form at your website. Email outreach services like Campaign Monitor offer ready-made forms (sometimes called "widgets") that streamline the task of collecting and managing email addresses. (Read more about using email outreach services in the sidebar below, "Ethical and Effective Email Outreach.") When registering people for your nonprofit's events, make sure to include an option to sign up for your email list. Also make sure to have a hard-copy sign-up form at any special event. If you have a physical location open to the public, include an email list sign-up sheet in your reception area. (For more details on managing your list and avoiding being a spammer, see "Ethical and Effective Email Outreach" below.)

Also consider moderating a listserv, which is slightly different than email outreach. A listserv is an email discussion group about a specific topic. Because nonprofits are issue oriented, listservs are particularly appropriate, allowing supporters to engage in an ongoing discussion about the nonprofit's subject area. For example, your nonprofit dedicated to educating the public on infectious disease control could create a listserv on the topic, using a service like Google Groups or Yahoo! Groups. Subscribers would discuss

## Ethical and Effective Email Outreach

When sending email to your supporters, keep in mind the following:

- **Make sure your audience wants your emails.** Don't automatically add supporters to your email list; add them only if they explicitly express an interest in getting your emails. Just because someone registered for one of your nonprofit's events doesn't mean they want regular (or even occasional) emails from you.

- **Don't promise an "e-newsletter" if your emails are fundraising oriented.** Many folks get peeved when they receive purely promotional or fundraising-related information, having originally signed up for a newsletter (which implies topic-based articles and other such substantive information). Fundraising outreach via email is fine, but don't mislead people who sign up for your email list into thinking that they will be receiving an informative newsletter if that won't be the case.

- **Use an email outreach service to help manage your email list scrupulously.** Managing hundreds or thousands of email addresses—including dealing with returned mail, address change requests, and unsubscribe requests—is no easy task. It's definitely best to use an email outreach service, such as Campaign Monitor (www.campaignmonitor.com), Constant Contact (www.constantcontact.com), or iContact (www.icontact.com), to help avoid mistakes that can be big turn-offs to your supporters.

- **Keep email outreach on the up-and-up with "double opt-in" systems.** Email outreach services use a double opt-in system, which helps ensure that the recipients of your emails actually want them and won't think you're a spammer. A subscriber opts in the first time by providing an email address to receive your email communications—perhaps he or she signed up for your list at your website or signed a sheet at an event. Then, an email is sent asking the requestor to confirm that he or she indeed wants to be included on your list. It's yet another reason to use an email service company like Campaign Monitor, which automates this process.

- **Make it easy for people to unsubscribe.** Services like Campaign Monitor always include clear links or buttons in every email allowing recipients to remove themselves from the list. If you don't use an email outreach service, make sure to include easy unsubscribe instructions and links in your emails.

- **Keep email addresses private.** If you don't use an email outreach service (and you really should), at the least, make sure to put all the addresses in your email list in the blind copy, or Bcc, field. This way, recipients will not be able to see all the other recipients' email addresses. Failing to do this risks irritating the members on your lists and making your nonprofit appear unprofessional.

and interact with each other by sending emails, which would be distributed to the whole group.

## Blogging

Blogs offer an easy, effective way to communicate with your supporters and forge stronger ties with them. For the uninitiated, a blog is a website format that consists of chronologically ordered posts with the most recent entries at the top, much like an online journal. Photos or images are often included with individual posts. Posts tend to be short (though this isn't always the case) and almost always include one or more links to related information at other websites. In addition, blogs typically allow readers to post comments. Inexpensive (often free) and user-friendly blog software makes it easy to add new posts, even for folks who have no clue about HTML or web development.

If your nonprofit is considering publishing news and information relevant to its mission, blogging can be a great option. Not only does it eliminate printing costs, but blog posts tend to be shorter than traditional articles, making it easier for your nonprofit to send out short bursts of information. For more on blogs as publishing vehicles, see Chapter 10.

Blogs also tend to attract site traffic and readership. Sites that offer a steady stream of current and informative content will always attract more traffic than sites whose content is purely promotional copy that never or rarely gets updated. Driving traffic to your site is discussed further under "Strategies for Promoting Your Site" below.

Some people find the distinction between a blog and a website confusing and wonder which one they should create for their nonprofit. The answer is that a blog is just one way that material can be presented at a website, and many websites include blogs. For example, your nonprofit could have a website with a page about your organization's mission, a page describing your programs, a donations page, and a page with information about your board and staff— *and* a page offering your nonprofit's blog, which (as described above) is essentially a page of journal entries with the most recent entries at the top. In short, it's important to understand that blogs and websites aren't mutually exclusive.

## Social Media: Facebook, Twitter, and More

These days, being online is all about being "social." If you've wondered what "social media" and "Web 2.0" mean exactly, these terms refer to a major trend online towards websites with user-generated content, such as Facebook, Twitter, LinkedIn, Flickr, or YouTube, to name just a few. In the broadest strokes, social media sites differ from traditional websites in that they consist almost entirely of content contributed by site users. After creating an account, a user can post all sorts of content including text, photos, videos, links to other sites, and other multimedia. These sites are "social" in that users typically create networks of friends or followers, and, in this way, build online communities within which they share information.

While many social media sites like Facebook and YouTube began as vehicles for largely personal inter-action among friends (Facebook started as an online network for Harvard students), these days they're used extensively by businesses and nonprofits to promote themselves and their brands. Very generally speaking,

a nonprofit engages in social media by creating an account on one of these social media sites in the name of the nonprofit, then networking in whatever ways are appropriate within its online communities. The ways to do this are virtually endless. While a comprehensive review of how your nonprofit can use social media is beyond the scope of this book, here are a few tips, ideas, and examples to get you on the right track:

- **Implement a comprehensive social media strategy.** Using social media to promote your nonprofit is best done with a well-thought-out plan and a clear idea of where you'll focus your efforts. Figure out which social media sites will work best for your group and what your communication goals are before jumping in. Keeping your strategy (and your audience) firmly in focus will also help you avoid being swayed by overhyped technologies that may not be a good fit.

- **Know your audience, and use social media sites that your audience uses.** For example, while seemingly everybody uses Facebook, there are tons of other social networks online that may be more closely aligned with your target audience. In fact, many experts predict that "niche" social networks online are poised to be the next big thing. Search for any networks that may cater specifically to your nonprofit's area of interest or geographical location.

- **Understand the ins and outs of any online community you're thinking about joining.** Create a user account for yourself personally to learn how the community operates. Learning the conventions and customs that others use will help you avoid making any faux pas—more than just embarrassing, these kinds of missteps can damage your nonprofit's reputation.

- **Don't just focus on your own Facebook page or blog.** Make sure to post on other nonprofits' Facebook pages or comment on their blog posts—of course, always remembering to offer helpful information that's not overly promotional or self-serving.

- **Be creative!** If your nonprofit produces an inexpensive yet clever or hilarious video that brings awareness to your nonprofit or the issues it works with, you can get a lot of exposure. Do your best to attract and nurture creative people who can develop fun ways of delivering your nonprofit's message.

## Planning a Website Project

After clarifying your strategy for your nonprofit's online activities, chances are you'll embark on creating a website. As mentioned earlier, a website typically serves as the central point of your online operations, so it's particularly important to approach a website project with care and planning.

Before contacting a Web developer, you should tackle some preliminary considerations. From defining who in your nonprofit will be involved with the project to scoping out a rough budget, doing a diligent amount of preparation will help you set priorities for your website, get the most out of your meetings with potential Web developers, and set the stage for an efficient workflow once you get the project underway. Of course, it's normal to have some unresolved questions when you contact a Web developer and to have the developer help you refine your overall goals. But doing some planning and preparation before meeting with a Web developer will help you get the most out of the working relationship.

The advice in this section assumes you will hire a Web developer rather than doing it yourself, which is almost always the best course unless someone in your nonprofit has a true command of Web-related technologies.

### Identify Participants

It may sound obvious, but it's important to decide who at your nonprofit will be involved in the project and who will have decision-making authority. More often than you might think, website development projects get seriously derailed after someone who was not involved in the project suddenly surfaces

---

### Does Your Nonprofit Need a Website?

While the rest of this chapter presumes that you want to create a website, some of you may be wondering whether you need one at all. My advice is that every nonprofit should have at least a simple website with basic information about its mission, programs, and contact information. Whether to create a more extensive site will depend on your nonprofit's mission, needs, and resources.

Even an ultra-basic site offers valuable benefits:

- It creates a permanent place where you can solicit donations and serves as a central base for online fundraising efforts.
- It allows you to communicate more information than you can typically fit in a brochure. When you include your nonprofit's Web address on your brochures, event announcements, or other printed materials, people interested in your work can go to your site for more in-depth information, such as how to volunteer or when and where your events will take place.
- It facilitates word-of-mouth awareness of your nonprofit's work, because your supporters will easily be able to share information about your nonprofit with their friends and family simply by providing your URL.
- It allows you to spread the word about your nonprofit without paying print costs. This can save you a lot of money if the information you want to communicate is lengthy or changes frequently, as might be the case with special event information, legislative updates, or time-sensitive reports. And of course, your website can use full color, which can be quite expensive to print.
- It allows you to develop and refine your messages before committing them to print. For example, you could create a simple three-page site with information about your mission, programs, and contact information, and refine these pieces of content for a month or two until you're satisfied with them. Then you could create a print brochure using the information from the website.

Keep in mind that a website might offer even more opportunities for your nonprofit, such as the potential for sponsor revenues, member management, and more. The bottom line is that even the simplest website will be an asset to your nonprofit.

with strong objections to how the site has been built. Needless to say, making major revisions to a website late in the development process is usually costly and results in a great amount of wasted work. You can avoid this problem by carefully identifying participants and roles at the outset of the project. Clarify who will be asked for their input and who will make the final decisions.

At fledgling nonprofits, participants usually include some or all board members and any key staff (paid or volunteer), such as an executive director or a program director. Participants generally help to set goals, review the site in various stages of development, and have approval authority. Some people might be included in the project in an advisory or feedback role only, without any decision-making authority; this can be an effective way to get a broader range of opinions about the site without having to obtain consensus from too many people. However you structure your team or committee managing the website development project, make sure everyone understands the timelines and how decisions will be made.

## Consider Desired Functions

Before approaching a Web developer and asking for a quote or proposal, you should develop a rough outline of the functions and features you want at your site. Besides the fundamental marketing function that is common to just about every site, sites often feature other functions. Common examples for nonprofits include:

- a blog
- online donations processing
- an events calendar
- a photo gallery or portfolio of images
- e-commerce
- registration forms (for membership, events, volunteer work, and so on)
- a subscription form for e-newsletters or other announcements, and
- a directory that users can browse, search, or both.

It's important to identify the extra functions you want at the outset because they will usually (though not always) require additional technology, and therefore more money, to implement. The more specifically you can identify functions that you want, the more accurate the price quotes you'll get from Web designers.

Don't go overboard with functions. When developing your list of desired functions, stay focused on how the site will help your nonprofit achieve its mission. Even if money is no object (which is rarely true), it's a bad idea to implement functions just because they are cool or flashy. Instead, include only those functions that will help streamline your operations, facilitate your programs, raise funds, or otherwise advance the nonprofit's mission. For many small nonprofits, a simple, well-organized site with clear text about programs, along with some professional-looking images, is all that's needed.

To help you understand the functions that make sense for your site, browse the Web and look for examples. When reviewing other sites and assessing which features might work for your site, you'll need to distinguish form from function. You'll also want to identify site functions as specifically as possible. If you aren't particularly tech savvy, this might seem difficult at first, but the more you evaluate sites, the better you'll be able to identify specific functional elements and see them as separate parts of a whole.

## Develop Design Direction

Besides identifying the functions you want at your site, you should also put some thought and research into how you want your site to look. The critical elements in site design—also called the "look and feel" of a site—are colors, fonts, and page composition (how images and text are organized on the screen).

Because design is so inherently subjective, most Web developers will ask you to provide examples of site designs that you like and don't like. Even if your developer does not ask for examples, reviewing other sites is the best way to get a sense of design trends and figure out the look and feel you want for your site. When reviewing sites for design elements, remember again to keep form separate from function. Sites that have entirely different functions from those envisioned for your site might have design elements that yours can use. Make particular note of color schemes you like (some developers call them "color palettes"), typeface styles and sizes, and how images, such as photographs or illustrations, are used at a site. The more you can point to things you like or don't like, the better your developer will be able to design the site according to your vision.

## Learn About Technology Options

Assuming you use a professional Web developer, at some point the developer will recommend the kind of technology—generally called a development platform—to use to build the site. To help you understand what your developer is talking about, here's a quick overview. In very broad terms, a development platform is a kind of "prefab" website kit. Instead of writing code from the ground up, the developer applies a design template then configures various elements within the development platform to meet your specific needs and the design specifications you've agreed to use.

Development platforms can be either proprietary (requiring annual licensing fees paid to the platform owner) or open-source platforms (free). The clear trend these days is to use open-source platforms that are not only free to use, but—in the case of popular platforms—are supported by an extensive community of developers who constantly test and enhance the platforms. The most popular open-source platform as of this writing is WordPress; in the world of proprietary platforms, ExpressionEngine is fairly popular.

All common development platforms have a crucial feature: a content management system, or CMS, that makes it easy to add, edit, and manage content, even for non-technical people. Especially if you plan to update your site's content regularly, having a CMS (sometimes called a "content-managed site") will be essential.

 **TIP**

**WordPress isn't just for bloggers anymore.** Originally, the WordPress platform was developed as a CMS specifically for blogging. It offered clean templates and an exceptionally easy to use back-end interface making it incredibly popular off the bat. Over the years as more and more features and customizations options have been added to the WordPress platform, businesses and nonprofits of all sizes are increasingly turning to WordPress as the platform for their websites. People have discovered how easy it is to use the WordPress CMS to create a robust site that doesn't look anything like a blog, but like a "regular" nonprofit or business site. While sites built with open-source platforms like Joomla or Drupal used to be the norm, most folks prefer WordPress these days.

Development platforms continually release upgraded versions, which means that you'll need to upgrade yours (and pay for the upgrades) at least occasionally. As the upgrades come along, your developer can tell you which are essential and which you can skip. For example, if you built your site using WordPress and six months later WordPress releases a new version of the platform, your developer might tell you that upgrading is a low priority because the new version contains few changes from the previous version. Six months later, however, there might be yet another version that your developer tells you is essential to implement, because it addresses important bugs and site security issues. In that case it might cost you a few hundred dollars to hire the developer to upgrade your WordPress installation to prevent your site from succumbing to errors or hackers.

## Set a Realistic Budget

Before you hire or even start contacting Web developers, you should come up with at least a ballpark idea of your budget, including cash and other resources. When assessing your resources, be realistic—don't include donations or grants that you aren't sure you will be able to get or help from board members, staff, or volunteers who are already stretched too thin.

Bear in mind that you need to consider not only resources to create the site but also to maintain the site over time. Don't make the mistake of creating a site that promises up-to-the-minute news about your field of work unless you know that you will be able to keep the site updated. Ongoing site maintenance absolutely must be considered before you plan and build the site in the first place. Create a website that needs frequent updating only if you are sure you will have the resources to handle it.

Very generally speaking, the cost to build a content-managed website that you can update yourself will usually start at around $2,000. To build additional features—say, a photo gallery, a graphical calendar, or an event registration system, for example—the price will go up. Remember also that there may be third-party fees beyond what a Web developer charges, such as payment processing and security certificate fees for sites that process sales or donations. Don't forget domain name registration (roughly $10 per year) and hosting fees (which start at $10 or so per month.)

Assuming you create a site with a content management system, much of the ongoing maintenance will probably be easy enough for a board member, staffer, or volunteer to handle. But don't underestimate the time commitment required—you'll need to define an updating schedule, establish who will be doing the updating work, and make realistic estimates for the time it will take to get the updates done. The following maintenance tasks are typical:

- writing new content—for example, revising program descriptions as your programs evolve
- taking new photographs—for instance, for staff pages
- adding/updating event information and keeping a calendar up to date
- responding to emails from site visitors
- generating traffic and site analytic reports, and
- promoting and marketing the website.

Even with a CMS, you may occasionally need to hire a Web developer to make deeper technical changes—say, to add a calendar function or change the layout of a page. As mentioned earlier, you'll also need to update the underlying software of whatever development platform and plug-ins you're using, usually every year or so. With Web developer fees ranging from $50 to $150 an hour, maintenance can get expensive. Do your best to anticipate your needs and develop realistic budget estimates for these ongoing tasks.

 **TIP**

**You get what you pay for.** Even simple websites require several components: information architecture, graphic design, content creation, and programming. To have all these done well, you'll generally need a bare minimum budget of $2,000. You are not likely to get a quality, professional site—even a simple one—for $500. Anyone charging a fee this low is likely to be either a total novice or someone doing your nonprofit a big favor, and favors like this often come at a price (delays or low quality). Paying a reasonable amount will allow your nonprofit to expect more from the developer, which will increase the likelihood that the site will look professional and will meet your needs.

## Outline a Schedule

For some nonprofits, the timing of their website launch is crucial—for example, you might absolutely need your site to go live before a membership drive or a special event. For others, it may not matter very much at all. During your planning, consider whether the timing of your website project is an important issue. If so, you'll need to schedule accordingly and make sure the Web developer you choose can meet your deadlines.

It typically takes at least two months from the start of a website project until the site's launch, and usually longer—for complex sites, considerably longer. For example, if a holiday food donation drive is an important program for your group, you'll need to get the ball rolling in time to have your site up and running by early November. At a bare minimum, you'll have to get a contract signed with a developer by September, which means starting your search for a developer and making other preparations in the summer. Of course, even this is cutting it close, considering how long it can take to market a site and gain exposure for it. The point is to start the process well before your site absolutely must be launched.

Don't forget to factor in your own busy schedule when planning a Web project. Web developers typically need a fair amount of input from the nonprofit's project participants during the development process. For example, you'll likely need to review and approve several demos and provide guidance on site content. Don't assume that the Web developer will just run with your site project and finish it off; account for the time you'll need to spend reviewing progress and providing information to the developer.

Finally, your cash flow can be an issue when timing your Web project. Make sure you'll have the necessary cash or credit for any up-front deposits and other scheduled payments.

### Draft an Outline of Site Content

Drafting at least a rough outline of the content you want to feature at your site is a good idea for a few reasons. First and foremost, your site content should be closely related to your site strategy and goals. Because you know this information better than anyone, it's best not to turn site content entirely over to a developer. In addition, drafting the initial content outline may help reduce costs by minimizing the work that a Web developer will have to do. Finally, you know best what kind of content exists or can easily be created on the topics you want to feature. Your Web developer can (and likely will) help you refine your content outline, but you are in the best position to make the first draft.

A content outline is pretty much what it sounds like: It's not the content itself, but an organized list of topics and subsections that you envision for the site. It's helpful to think in terms of "modules" or "components." Each module may consist of one or more Web pages. For example, you could have an "About Us" module that's just one page of background information, or you could include three subsections on your mission, staff biographies, and biographies of your board of directors. At this stage of the game,

focus on what modules you'll include rather than what will go into each module.

When deciding what content to include, focus on content that will directly help you achieve your goals for the website. For example, if you are creating a simple marketing site with the goals of describing your mission and programs and attracting volunteers, effective content might include some well-written text about your work and a clear request for volunteers. If your goal is to educate the public on community health issues, informative articles (ideally, readable at the site and downloadable as PDFs) would be an obvious choice.

In addition to your substantive content, you'll certainly want to include easy-to-find contact information, including your phone number, email address, and, if you have a walk-in address, your location. Or, if a site goal is to reduce phone calls to your nonprofit, then include only an email address. Again, think about your nonprofit's goals for the website and include content that meets those goals.

## Choosing and Working With a Web Developer

Because your nonprofit's website should present its best face to the world, you should work with someone who has a decent amount of experience developing websites, rather than hand the job to a well-intentioned but inexperienced website novice. If cash is short, you might be tempted to try to do the job yourself or let one of your volunteers who is studying Web design take a stab at creating the site. Unfortunately, this approach more often than not results in an unprofessional-looking site that is difficult to navigate and fails to serve your organizational goals. A poor-quality website puts your nonprofit in a bad light and may lead potential supporters not to take you seriously. You may think you'll improve the site later when you have more resources, but in reality it is often more costly and time-consuming to revise an existing site than simply to start over with a clean slate.

Finding a qualified developer who is a good fit for your organization can be easier said than done. And once you've found a developer who appears well-qualified, you may find the process of working with the developer more complicated than you expected. This section offers tips for evaluating potential developers and describes the role you can expect to play in the project.

While the information in this section assumes that you will be using an outside developer to build your site, you can use the information to guide your own process if you do the work yourself.

## Criteria for Choosing a Web Developer

Even simple Web development projects involve a number of elements that require different skills. You'll need more than a good programmer; you'll typically need a team and a project manager that follows a methodical process. Include the following considerations in your evaluation process.

**Team of specialists.** You'll usually get a better result from a firm that assigns a team to each project, rather than asking one person to do it all. A solid team usually includes a graphic designer, a programmer, an editor/writer, and ideally a project manager who coordinates everyone's efforts (including yours). Sure, sometimes a talented graphic designer might also be a top-notch programmer, or the programmer might be an excellent editor—but this is not usually the case. The best approach is for each major task to be handled by a specialist.

**Project manager approach.** An important but often overlooked issue is how well a Web developer—specifically, the project manager, assuming the firm you're considering will include a project manager on the team—manages and coordinates all the various aspects of the project. The project manager should be able to articulate a clear process for the various tasks involved, such as defining the information organization, doing the graphic design, creating the content, and programming the site.

**Approvals-based process.** It's particularly important that the process be approvals based, meaning that the project participants at your nonprofit will be asked to approve the Web developer's progress at specific points in the project. If a Web developer does not follow a methodical process, and does not obtain your approval of early stages of site development, you may find yourself presented with a nearly finished site that has no resemblance to what you envisioned. If this happens, the developer may have to start all over again—a situation that could have been averted if approvals had been requested along the way.

**Ability to work collaboratively.** If you plan to handle certain aspects of Web development in-house or through other contractors with whom you have a relationship, you'll want to look for a Web developer who can work collaboratively with you and your team. For example, if you want to maintain absolute control over the design elements of your site (as may be the case if you have a solid relationship with a graphic designer), but want the developer to handle other technical issues, make this fact clear to the prospective developer and evaluate whether you will be able to work well together.

**Relevant experience.** Of course, be sure to visit other sites that the developer has created. Web developers' own websites will usually have online portfolios showing websites they've done. Visit those sites and poke around to make sure they work well. Ideally, the developer will have experience with nonprofit sites and features that are similar to what you want. The more your developer understands your nonprofit and the strategies driving it, the better.

**Use of technologies.** Some Web developers use specialized development platforms and other technologies that are proprietary or difficult for others to use. So if you end up parting ways with such a developer, you might get stuck with a website that is difficult or nearly impossible for others to maintain and update. Ask your prospects what technologies they use, whether they are widely supported, and what difficulties might arise for other developers in maintaining the site. You may feel uncomfortable asking this, but it's a perfectly legitimate question that the developer should answer clearly.

## Proposals, Quotes, and Contracts

When you have met with a few potential developers and narrowed your list down to a few prospects, ask them to give you a proposal and quote in writing. Generally speaking, it's best to get at least two or three proposals or quotes to compare. Some developers might give a bare bones quote focused on numbers; others will give a more detailed proposal that outlines their planned approach. While an exhaustive, novel-length treatment isn't necessary, a proposal is better than a strictly numbers-oriented quote; it will help you figure out whether the developer understands your needs and has come up with the right solution for you.

Watch out for developers who balk at putting a quote or proposal in writing, or who merely want to give you a total quote without a breakdown of services and fees. At the very least, you want the quote to show what services will be offered; ideally the cost will be broken down into an itemized list.

Once you choose a developer, it's essential that you both sign a contract that clearly outlines the project. At a minimum, your contract should cover the following terms:

- **An overview of the scope of services.** In particular, make sure you and the Web developer are on the same page regarding who will be responsible for content creation. Web developers typically will work with your text and photographs, but will not write text from scratch or take photographs without extra charges.
- **A list of deliverables.** The contract should specify anything the developer will deliver to you, such as a site map, a color mock-up, an HTML template, or anything else that's promised to be delivered as the project progresses and at the end of the project.
- **A schedule.** The contract must include a clear schedule of deadlines for various aspects of the project, often tied to deliverables.
- **Intellectual property provisions.** Make sure the contract indicates who will own the materials developed in the project, including graphic designs, templates, written content, photographs, software programming, and any other material subject to intellectual property protection (you'll find more information in "Intellectual Property: Who Owns What?" below).
- **Compensation and payment terms.** Include information on how fees will be calculated if work goes beyond the originally anticipated scope.
- **Termination provisions.** The contract should spell out what will happen if the working relationship falls apart and either party wants to end the project.

**RESOURCE**

**Need help with your contract?** Check out *Nolo's Legal Guide to Web & Software Development*, by Stephen Fishman. It's packed with useful information, including a sample website development agreement.

Written contracts are always a good idea when hiring independent contractors. In the case of website developers, contracts are particularly important so that you can address intellectual property issues. Do not work with a Web developer without a written contract; in fact, be wary of a developer who wants to get started without a contract in place. At the very least, this indicates that the developer does not have professional business practices.

As discussed in Chapter 10, you need to be careful to ensure that your nonprofit obtains ownership of or appropriate permission to use materials such as text, graphic designs, multimedia, and other materials developed by outside contractors or volunteers, including Web developers. The best way to do this is by using work-for-hire or assignment agreements, or similar clauses included in a general services contract. If you do not include such provisions in a contract with your Web developer, you may find that the developer owns the site content and can prevent you from making changes to it.

## Your Role in Developing Your Site

Even if money is no object, it is unrealistic to expect your Web developer to build your site without significant involvement from you or others at your nonprofit. Besides playing a major role in defining strategies, one or more people from your nonprofit will need to monitor the progress of the project. You should designate one person whom the developer can contact with questions. In addition, you will need to decide who at your nonprofit will have decision-making power and who will be involved in approving the developer's work at various steps along the way.

It's crucial that your developer use a methodical process that involves intermediate deadlines, milestones, and approvals. Typical milestones are described in more detail below. For now, keep in mind that you should identify in advance which people from your nonprofit will have a say in approving the developer's work at each stage of the project.

Don't underestimate the time commitment involved in website development, even if you hire someone else to do it. You'll need time to hold meetings with the board of directors and any website-oriented committees; time to develop consensus on the website's strategies and goals; time to review the developer's work, figure out what revisions your group wants, and provide approvals (this needs to be done a number of times in the process); and time to review the near-final site and give final approvals.

The next section describes in detail the overall process of creating a website. Consider the process described as a model workflow: Developers will have their own variations, but they should approach website development roughly as described below.

## Creating Your Site

After your nonprofit does its internal prep work and finds a developer to do the work, you'll be poised to start the project. Before getting your website project underway, it's very helpful to understand the typical steps involved in a well-managed website development project. Understanding a high-quality, carefully planned website development process will help in two ways:

- **You'll be better equipped to choose a developer.** A potential developer who does not follow a methodical process may not be a good candidate for the job. Of course, developers have different approaches to their work, but they should cover some of the fundamental steps, such as providing you proposed outlines of the site's information organization (also known as "information architecture"), giving you input into the site's aesthetic design (also called "look and feel"), and asking for your approval at various stages along the way.

- **You'll be able to interact more effectively with the developer you choose.** Communication helps to keep the process more efficient and increases the likelihood that you will be satisfied with the finished site.

This section outlines a simple, generalized approach that will help ensure an efficient workflow. Keep in mind these steps aren't written in stone, and that there's always a certain amount of fluidity in Web development projects.

In particular, be aware that it's common for Web projects to get a bit circular at times, and that you may need to revisit earlier steps to make modifications. For example, you may need to refine your site's information architecture after you create content, if some of that content does not fit into your original design. This is normal, as long as it's not chronic and extensive. The point here is to understand that following a methodical process will improve efficiency. Even if you're planning a small, simple site, following a process similar to what we describe will help you maximize your chances of success. The process will generally involve the following steps, many of which were discussed earlier in this chapter:

- defining strategy and goals
- defining content and organization (information architecture)
- defining design elements (look and feel)
- creating content, including text and graphics
- building the website
- testing, and
- training.

### Developing a Website on a Microbudget

Most nonprofits are not in a position to pay market rates for website development. If your website budget is tiny or nonexistent, here are a few ideas for how to proceed:

- Colleges, universities, and technical schools that offer courses in website development may offer their students to help local nonprofits develop their websites for free. While the students may not have loads of experience, they are usually supervised by a professor or someone knowledgeable about website development. Contact the schools in your area to see if they offer this kind of help.

- You might find a sponsor for your website—a local business that will cover the costs of site development, usually in exchange for being recognized on the site (and possibly in other materials) as a sponsor. (For more on using sponsors to support your organization, see Chapter 6.) Keep in mind that this sponsor might be the Web development company itself or a completely unrelated business that simply wants to help your nonprofit.

- Do-it-yourself sites based on templates are far more sophisticated in design and features than in years past. This category includes a range of options, from customizing a WordPress template to using a service like Weebly. The upside is considerable cost savings—for example, some template sites might cost as little as $50 or even $25 per month compared to a typical minimum $2,000 for a basic site built by a developer. The downsides can be major, however. For one, design and functionality options are still not likely to be nearly as robust as a website built by a developer. Most of these types of sites look awful at best. And using a do-it-yourself template often takes considerably more time, effort, and skill than is advertised. In short, proceed cautiously and fully explore the feature set of whatever service you're considering before committing to a product.

## Define Strategy and Goals

As explained above, all website projects should start with a clearly identified strategy and goals. Ideally, your nonprofit will have already put careful thought into these questions. If so, then this step should be focused on ensuring that the participants from your nonprofit and the developer are on the same page. This typically involves one or more meetings where you provide lots of information to the developer about your nonprofit, and the developer asks lots of questions to help ensure your strategy is sound.

Web developers use different approaches to gather this information from their clients at the outset of a project. Some use workshop-type meetings that involve your nonprofit's Web project participants and possibly other staffers or associates. This approach can be quite effective in generating input from a wide range of people in the early stage, even if those people won't be involved in the project as it progresses. Soliciting feedback from people who will be affected by the website (often called "stakeholders" by Web developers) helps to ensure that a wide range of perspectives are included, avoiding tunnel vision.

## Define Content and Information Architecture

At this stage, you and your developer will broadly outline the content your site will feature. You should focus on the types of information that will help achieve the goals you've set for your website and your nonprofit's mission. For example, if a charitable nonprofit plans to use its website primarily to raise funds and recruit workers, its content may consist largely of appeals to donors and volunteers. If, on the other hand, a scientific nonprofit will use its website as a crucial research tool to achieve its mission, its content may be heavy on in-depth scientific information of special interest to researchers who visit the site.

In addition, most nonprofit websites include basic background information about the organization, including its mission statement, a list of board members, and contact information. Other helpful information may include a calendar of upcoming events, an appeal for donations, and information on how to volunteer or get involved.

With broad content areas sketched out, the next task will be to establish how the content will be organized. This process is sometimes called information architecture or information design, and its importance should not be underestimated. Sites with solid information architecture are easy and intuitive to navigate, while poorly organized sites confuse visitors and make it hard for them to get to the information they want. Of course, a site that's hard to navigate usually results in visitors leaving the site in a hurry.

Web developers typically use visual representations of the website during the building process, much like architects use blueprints. Two common development documents are site maps and user interface diagrams:

- A site map is a diagram showing all of a website's content areas, focusing on identifying categories and subcategories of content.
- A user interface diagram (or "UI" diagram) is a rough sketch of how content will be organized and where it will appear on the screen. It's called a user interface diagram because it represents how site visitors (users) will interact (interface) with the site.

Web developers vary a lot in how they use site maps and UI diagrams. Some Web developers simply use content outlines instead of graphical site maps. Others like to diagram everything graphically. Diagramming can be time intensive, so your developer might just do a few to give you an idea of the organization before starting to build. If every last button and detail isn't included on the diagrams presented to you, don't

## Sample Site Map

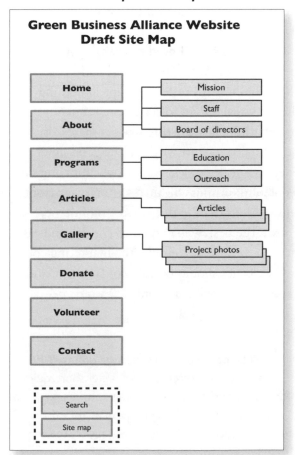

## Sample User Interface Diagram

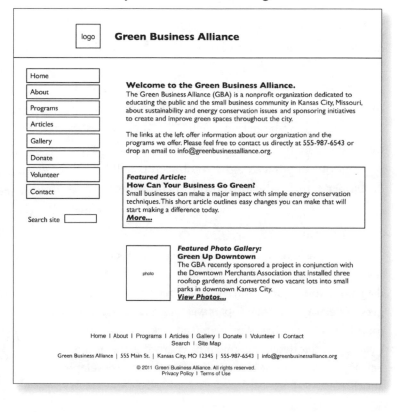

approve the diagrams without clarifying with your developer that those little details will be taken care of without extra charge. Asking for things to be done that weren't on the approved diagram may be considered a change order and subject to additional fees. Ideally, every element that you envision for your site will be on the architecture diagrams that you'll approve before the project moves to the design stage.

## Develop Graphic Design Elements (Look and Feel)

After your nonprofit approves the site architecture, your developer will begin to develop the graphic design elements of the site. This includes making choices for colors, typeface styles, images, graphic art, and other design elements. This task is often called developing the look and feel of the site. Your developer will typically show you color mock-ups of the site, sometimes called "color comprehensives," to allow you to identify the color schemes and other design aspects you want.

As explained above, it's a good idea to provide your developer with examples of other sites that you like. Perhaps you really like the colors used by one site and the way text is formatted at a different site. Show these examples to your developer and point out what you do and don't like about each. Visual examples are much more helpful to your developer than abstract descriptions of what designs you like and will help the developer achieve the look and feel you want.

**TIP**

**Be sure to clarify how many rounds of revisions the Web developer will do on your site map, UI diagrams, and color comprehensives before the project gets underway.** Web developers will typically do one or two rounds of revisions based on your feedback. If you're not clear about this detail, you might be charged extra for the developer's time to make more revisions than the developer anticipated.

**CAUTION**

**Banish bad clip art from your site.** "Clip art" refers to small illustrations and graphics—sometimes animated—that are available online, often for free. While some clip art is of high quality, the vast majority tends to look very amateurish. Do your nonprofit a favor and don't pepper your site with angels, teddy bears, or animated dragons because you think they look cute. There's nothing cute about an unprofessional-looking website.

## Create Content

With content, organization, and design elements established, you can begin creating and finalizing the content for your site. Remember, you'll need to create content to fill all the pages identified in your site map.

Writing and editing are time-consuming tasks (even for us professional writers), so content development often feels like a burden. To clear this hurdle, start with what you have. Chances are you've already spent time developing brochures, flyers, or other written information about your nonprofit. Don't reinvent the wheel: Use what you have as a basis for your website's content. You probably will need to rework your existing content to make it shorter and more concise for the Web, but it's still easier to adapt something that's already written than to start from scratch.

If you don't have any existing written materials, someone will need to start writing. The good news is that, generally speaking, less is more when it comes to online content. Nothing will turn visitors away from your website faster than multiple screens of dense, lengthy text. The best Web content is concise and easy to digest. As a very general guide, the marketing copy on most Web pages should be 150 words or less, and articles should be capped at about 400 words per page.

**TIP**

**Bullets make good ammunition online.** When reading from a computer screen, people prefer short, quick bits of information rather than long paragraphs of text. Keep this in mind as you create online content or adapt existing content for your website. As much as possible, try to keep information blurb-sized or broken down into bullet points. If you're adapting existing content, break down longer paragraphs in this manner.

If you publish longer material—for example, the text of a report your organization produced—either break it up into sections, with links between them, or provide the document in a downloadable format, such as a PDF (Portable Document Format) file. Better yet, offer both an HTML version navigable by section and a downloadable version, so that your visitors can read the document in whichever way they prefer. (Chapter 10 covers the ins and outs of online publishing in detail.)

Finally, make sure that at least two people are involved in creating the website's content. At a minimum, one person should write the material and another person should review it and edit. Even if the writer is experienced, a second set of eyes can really make a difference. Your content should be clear, concise, and free from errors. A little bit of care in these areas will go a long way toward making your site useful to visitors and enhancing the credibility of your nonprofit.

> **TIP**
>
> **Keep time-sensitive content fresh.** If you include time-sensitive information on your website, be sure to keep it up to date. To do this, plan for regular updates and budget appropriate resources before you commit to including the material on your site. Dated content on your site looks unprofessional to visitors, who may include potential funders and other important folks. If you know that you might not have the resources necessary to continually update your site, don't post information that will rapidly go stale (or downright rotten). Instead, concentrate on material that will have a reasonably long shelf life.

## Build Your Site

Often, while the content is being written and photographed, the programmer is busy building the site based on the approved site architecture diagrams and design mock-ups. When the build is complete, it will be ready for the content (both text and images) to be entered into the CMS. Depending on your contract, either the Web developer or you will do the content entry. If you do it, you'll likely need some guidance as to how to use the CMS, perhaps in the form of a mini training session in addition to the full training done at the conclusion of the project (see "Train the Site Managers," below).

Your Web developer will build the site on a test server or on the Web server where it will ultimately have its home. If the latter, you'll need to tackle domain name registration and Web hosting before the developer starts the build. (See "Domain Names and Hosting," below.)

## Test Your Site

When your site is complete, it should be thoroughly and methodically tested in multiple browsers to make sure links and features work, images load, and text displays correctly. The developer should fix any glitches or bugs. It's normal and not a bad reflection on the Web developer if the site contains some bugs. What's important is to find them and fix them before launching your site to the public. Professional Web developers should include a testing phase. It's not uncommon for a developer to ask your nonprofit to have its staffers participate in site testing. Once the testing phase is completed and all bugs reported and corrected, the site is ready to be launched.

## Train the Site Managers

When the site is finished, the Web developer will generally offer a one- to three-hour training to whomever at your company will be in charge of maintaining the site (the site managers or administrators). If you'll be outsourcing maintenance to the Web developer or an experienced outside contractor, the training may not be necessary.

## Domain Names and Hosting

Before your site can go live, you must register a domain name and sign up with a Web hosting company. Your domain name is part of the address visitors will use to access your site, such as artsforkids.org or cleanmilwaukeeriver.org. Your Web host is the company that keeps all the code, images, and other files associated with your website on computer servers that are connected to the Internet 24 hours a day, so they're always available for visitors to view.

### Register a Domain Name

Your first task is to choose an available domain name—that is, a name that is not currently registered to, or being used by, another group. (Chapter 1 explains how to do this.) Once you select an available name, you should register it online at a domain name registrar. One popular and inexpensive registrar is Namecheap at www.namecheap.com, but there are hundreds of options out there. Ask your web developer what registrar she uses; also ask colleagues and others you know who have been involved in website projects.

At the registrar's website, you will enter your proposed domain name to see if it has already been registered. If not, you will proceed and register the name yourself. Fees vary depending on the options you choose; all are generally affordable. The cost to register one name for one year ranges from about $10 to $25 and will be cheaper per year if you register for two or more years at a time. Once you've chosen your options, simply enter information about your nonprofit and provide credit card information (or if you prefer, call the registrar and do it by phone).

Although registering a domain name is pretty simple, there are a few pitfalls to watch out for. Your domain name is an asset, and the people or organizations listed in the domain name registration have varying degrees of authority over the asset. Be particularly careful about whom you list as the following:

- **The registrant.** The registrant is the legal owner of the domain name. Use your nonprofit's legal name.

- **The administrative contact.** The administrative contact should be someone in your nonprofit who has authority to make policy decisions, particularly with regard to the domain name.

- **The technical contact.** This is the person whom the registrar may contact with technical issues.

### Choosing a Web Host

A Web host is a company that maintains servers, which are simply high-performance computers that are connected to the Internet continuously, serving the Web pages stored on it to the world. When your Web pages are on the host's server and your Web host has configured your domain name correctly, your website will be live and all the information it offers will be available to visitors around the globe, 24 hours a day, 365 days a year.

Your Web developer will probably recommend a host that the developer regularly uses. If you want more options, ask around to get recommendations. Ultimately you'll want to find a Web host that supports any services your site will offer (such as e-commerce), has reliable servers, and above all provides good customer service. Make sure there are reasonable customer service hours during which you can talk to an actual human. More than a few host companies offer no live-person customer service, which can be infuriating if you're experiencing any problems.

Web hosts may charge by the month or by the year. Fees are based on how much data you need the server to store—that is, the size of your website in disk space—or how much data you transfer to and from your website each month. One popular host, BlueHost (www.bluehost.com), starts at about $7 per month for small, basic sites.

## Driving Traffic to Your Site

Promoting and driving traffic to websites has become a thriving industry—perhaps a bit too thriving, judging by the amount of junk email we all receive hawking traffic-building services promising millions of visitors. When considering website promotion and marketing approaches, it can be hard to separate reality from the hype.

Keep in mind that heavy site traffic is generally much less important for nonprofits (particularly small grassroots groups) than it is for profit-oriented businesses that are selling products or services online. While you obviously want your site to have decent exposure, it usually doesn't make sense for a small nonprofit to spend significant resources to lure website visitors. It's far more common for a nonprofit to use its site to offer information and resources to its existing supporters and to people who have heard of the nonprofit from a brochure, an event, or word of mouth. When you look at your website this way— as a great tool to communicate with your known audience and potentially to reach some new people, rather than as a mass marketing tool—you'll see that many of the heavily hyped website promotion services on the market today are simply unnecessary for your purposes.

To figure out what strategy your nonprofit should adopt regarding site promotion, start by revisiting the goals you identified for your site. If your website's main purpose is to keep your current supporters informed of news and events, then you'll want to focus on making sure those supporters know your Web address and not so much on whether the greater world knows it. On the other hand, if your site aims to educate the public or raise awareness about a certain issue, then wider promotion efforts might be appropriate.

The rest of this section looks at ways you can promote your site, including using social media, the practice of tailoring your site so that search engines find it and rank it as highly as possible (a practice called "search engine optimization," explained more fully below), and simple off-line methods. Choose the methods that best match your nonprofit's goals and available resources.

## Use Facebook and Social Media

As discussed earlier in this chapter, creating a Facebook page for your nonprofit is a great way to connect and interact with existing and potential supporters—not to mention donors, members, staff and volunteers, and more. Also use social media networks that are popular among your supporters. Do some research to find out where your people interact online. If you see lots of your audience using Twitter or LinkedIn heavily, you should aim to develop a presence in those places as well.

Interactions on Facebook and other social media sites tend to be quick, casual and informal, so it's generally fairly easy to maintain a presence—usually considerably easier than maintaining your own blog, for instance. Make sure to include the URL for your main nonprofit website in your profile information, and include links to it in your posts when appropriate to allow your social media network to click through to your main site, where you'll likely have much fuller information about your nonprofit's mission and programs.

## Optimize for Search Engines

Making your site as attractive and visible as possible for search engines such as Google or Yahoo! is known as search engine optimization, or SEO. The point of SEO is to have your site rank as highly as possible on a search engine results page (or SERP) for searches related to your nonprofit's topic. For example, suppose your nonprofit helps domestic abuse victims, and suppose someone types "domestic violence," "domestic abuse," "battered spouse," and related terms into a search engine query box. You'd want your website to appear high up on the list of results.

As mentioned above, nonprofits generally don't have to worry as much as for-profit businesses about driving traffic to their websites and, therefore, don't need to be overly concerned with how they rank with search engines. SEO services and techniques can get very complicated and expensive, so you absolutely need to be realistic about how important search engine rankings are for your nonprofit's website—otherwise, you could easily get sucked into an expensive or time-consuming SEO rabbit hole. That said, some of the basic ways to make a website attractive to search engines are so simple that it makes sense for all websites to use them.

Because SEO is such a complicated topic—and is of questionable value for small nonprofits—this section will offer a brief and broad overview of the factors affecting search engine results. In a nutshell, search engines base their results on internal and external aspects of a page, as described below.

**Internal aspects** include whether a site includes certain "keywords" (words likely to be used in a search). Generally, the more a site's text includes keywords that match the terms used by people using search engines, the better the site will rank in a search engine results page. Where the keyword appears on the site may make a difference, too. Including keywords in a site's title or in the text comprising a link (also called "anchor text" or "linked text") will provide better results than including keywords only in the body text of the site.

**External aspects** include how many other sites link to your site, or "link popularity" in SEO-speak. In general, the more sites that link to your site, the better your site will rank on search engines; these links are also called "inbound links." But not all inbound links are created equal, in the eyes of the search engine companies—quality sites rate higher. Through complex algorithms, search engines make a judgment as to the relevance and quality of the sites linking to your site. "Quality," of course, is a very subjective and mysterious determination; no one outside the search engine companies knows exactly how this determination is made. But very generally speaking, a quality site will contain useful editorial content—say, articles about environmental issues or educational material on music theory. Poor quality sites tend to be those that offer only sales-oriented information, or worse, they depend on spam or other questionable business practices (like a site that sells Viagra and sends out millions of junk emails a day). The more relevant, quality sites that are linked to your site, the better you will rank with search engines.

This is just the barest introduction to a large and evolving area. But all the complicated techniques used by SEO specialists and consultants essentially boil down to these two factors: keywords within your site and link popularity.

With that brief introduction to the primary factors affecting search engine rankings, keep in mind that most experts say that external factors are more important. In other words, having relevant, quality inbound links will do more good for your site than optimizing it with keywords. Of course, it's easy to include keywords in your site because you have control over this feature. Getting other sites to link to you can be more challenging. But working on your link popularity isn't rocket science, either. Here are some ways to develop inbound links from relevant, quality sites:

- **Develop content that others will want to link to.** This is a concept known as "link-baiting": You create content that will be attractive to other sites and hope they will bite. User-friendly articles tend to be popular online; think about creating articles featuring consumer tips or how-to guides that will have wide appeal.

- **Invite others to link to your site.** Contact other organizations or businesses that are related to your area of work and encourage them to include a link to your nonprofit's site. Sometimes, the other site will require you to link to their site as well—known as a reciprocal link. Providing a reciprocal link is okay if there is an appropriate area for you to do so at your site, but don't do it without careful consideration. Make sure that you're comfortable with the other site's content before including a link to it from your site.

- **Get listed in online directories.** Listing your nonprofit in online directories that include businesses and nonprofits in your city or region can be a great way to get the word out to your community. In many cases, local online listings are free.

 **RESOURCE**
**Want to know more about SEO?** Here are some resources:

- *The ABC of SEO*, by David George (Lulu), is essentially an extended glossary of terms used in the SEO field. The alphabetical organization of the entries makes this an easy-to-use reference book.

- *Search Engine Optimization*, by Jennifer Grappone and Gradiva Couzin (Sybex), offers in-depth information on how search engines work and how to tailor your site to them. The authors also maintain a companion website with up-to-date information at www.yourseoplan.com.
- *Search Engine Marketing, Inc.*, by Mike Moran and Bill Hunt (IBM Press), also explains SEO techniques, in excruciating detail.

 **TIP**

**Use your website for online publishing.** Publishing materials online rather than on paper is an effective way to convey information to your community. It saves printing costs and allows you to update the information more frequently. Some nonprofits begin publishing efforts online—for example, by creating an electronic newsletter—which allows them to work out the kinks before producing a print edition. For a discussion of online publishing, see Chapter 10.

## Use Off-Line Methods

Don't forget to promote your site in the off-line world. One of the simplest and most effective ways to raise the visibility of your website is to mention it in all of your nonprofit's materials and communications, such as:

- brochures, business cards, and on your letterhead
- merchandise such as stickers, T-shirts, or coffee cups, and
- press releases and event announcements and invitations.

When board members, staffers, and volunteers talk to interested people, they should encourage them to go to the website for more information. Similarly, any time you list the nonprofit in a directory (including the phone book) or purchase an advertisement, be sure to include the Web address.

## Intellectual Property: Who Owns What?

As mentioned earlier, it's crucial that your contract with a Web developer includes clear, detailed terms on ownership and permissions for any materials

developed for the website protected by copyright. (Other intellectual property laws, such as those for trademark or patent, also may come into play, though not as often.) Copyrightable materials include text, photos, artwork, and designs, as well as technology developed for your site, such as databases and programming.

Copyright basics are covered in Chapter 10, including the general rules of who owns what in specific situations. For the purposes of this chapter, just keep in mind that in the absence of a contract stating otherwise, the creator of content is the owner of that content. This means that if your website developer writes text, takes photos, creates programming code, or otherwise creates original material, the developer will by default own that content. A contract is essential in order to transfer ownership of those materials to the nonprofit, or at the very least to give the nonprofit an appropriate license (permission) to use those materials.

As you can imagine, serious trouble can arise if the ownership of any aspect of your website is in dispute. For example, if you fail to obtain the copyright to the site's text content from the Web developer, the developer could prevent you from making any changes to the text at the site. The same is true for images, graphic designs, and technologies created by the developer for the website. You might think this sounds far-fetched, but consider what might happen if you and the developer get into a conflict and decide to part ways. A developer with a bone to pick who owns any rights to your site can deal a serious blow to your nonprofit's operations online—or at least use that threat as a powerful hammer in any negotiations to resolve your differences.

 **RESOURCE**

**Nolo offers in-depth resources on copyright and intellectual property issues.** For the full treatment on copyright and the permissions process, check out *Getting Permission: How to License & Clear Copyrighted Materials Online & Off*, by Richard Stim. Also, check out Nolo's website at www.nolo.com for free information and other resources on intellectual property issues.

While it's obviously in your interest to obtain ownership of all aspects of your website, Web developers sometimes will not want to assign copyright ownership to your company for certain aspects of the site, for perfectly legitimate reasons. For example, your nonprofit might be able to save money by allowing the Web developer to retain copyright ownership of things like photographs taken for the site. And developers sometimes will not transfer ownership of technology they develop for your site, because that technology is the lifeblood of their business. Instead, they'll give your nonprofit permission (a license) to use the technology in specified ways.

When deciding what ownership or licensing arrangements will work for your nonprofit, keep in mind the following rule: The more important the content or technology is to your site, the more crucial it is that you get either ownership or a broad license to use and possibly modify those materials. This is true whether or not the Web developer has a valid reason to retain ownership. If it's essential that you retain copyright ownership in a database or other technology, don't enter into an agreement that won't confer the rights you need.

**EXAMPLE:** Krista, the executive director of a brain research nonprofit, is negotiating contract terms with the Web developer she chose to create the nonprofit's website. To keep costs down, Krista and the developer agree that the nonprofit will be responsible for taking photos. However, they also agree that if the developer takes photos for the site, the developer will retain the copyright to those photographs. To make sure she retains control over the website, Krista makes sure to get a provision in the contract granting the nonprofit a license to display any of the developer's photos at the website indefinitely. In addition, Krista asks the developer to include a license allowing her to modify the size and the brightness of the photos in case they ever need such adjustments. The developer agrees to a license to modify that is limited to size and brightness, but no other modifications.

---

### Checklist: Spreading the Word Online About Your Nonprofit

☐ Consider carefully how your online activities will help advance your nonprofit's mission and goals. Plan your website, blog, and any other online communication vehicles so that they are tailored to serving your nonprofit's specific goals.

☐ Plan for coordinated online activities, such as a website, blog, and Facebook page, that all have links to each other. You'll get the most exposure with a multichannel approach.

☐ When choosing a Web developer, make sure he or she has all the required skills necessary for creating a professional website and follows a methodical development process.

☐ Do not work with a Web developer without a contract. In particular, make sure that intellectual property terms in the contract clearly specify site ownership terms.

☐ Drive traffic to your finished site with quality, useful content and with savvy use of keywords in page titles and content. Don't use unsavory search engine optimization tactics, which can result in serious penalties from search engines like Google.

# Managing Your Finances

Implementing a good system of financial management is an essential part of running a nonprofit. You can't make wise financial decisions without having a clear understanding of how and when money comes in and goes out. And if that isn't reason enough, you also need well-organized bookkeeping and accounting systems because the tax advantages given to nonprofits come with a strict duty to manage funds properly.

The good news is that you don't need to be a financial whiz to manage your nonprofit's finances. When you're first starting out, just make sure that the person who serves as your nonprofit's treasurer has a comfortable working knowledge of the basics. As your nonprofit grows (or if you run into any complicated tax or accounting problems), you can—and should—hire an accountant or other financial professional who has experience with nonprofit finances to give you a hand.

This chapter explains how to manage your nonprofit's money, including what records your nonprofit should keep and how to keep them. This chapter also explains how to use the information in your financial records to measure your nonprofit's financial health and ensure that you will have enough cash to pay your important bills on time.

If you find yourself approaching this chapter with any discomfort or fear, you'll be pleasantly surprised to learn that managing your finances is a relatively straightforward task. Due to the availability of powerful and affordable software programs (such as *QuickBooks* and *MYOB*), the accounting process is much easier to handle than ever before. Once you enter your income and expenses into the program, you're only a few mouse clicks away from sophisticated financial reports that would have taken many hours and considerable skill to generate just a decade ago. In fact, these programs are so affordable (many under $300) and user-friendly that it makes little sense not to use one of them.

But while accounting software makes it much easier to keep records and generate informative financial reports, you still need a basic understanding of what the numbers mean so that you can make them work

for your nonprofit. It's especially important that the person in charge of managing your nonprofit's money and the people on any financial committees your nonprofit creates are able to communicate clearly regarding financial issues. This chapter offers the information you need, explaining financial basics and sound bookkeeping and accounting practices that will help keep your nonprofit on track.

### SEE AN EXPERT

**It pays to get help with bookkeeping and accounting tasks.** The information provided in this chapter will be valuable for anyone who is unfamiliar with accounting basics. Depending on the size and operations of your nonprofit, however, hiring experienced help may be a smart idea. This need not be prohibitively expensive: In an hour or two, an accountant with nonprofit experience should be able to suggest effective strategies for keeping records, selecting and configuring a computerized accounting system, and other ways of managing your nonprofit's money. At the beginning, a competent board member, staff person, or volunteer should be able to keep your system humming. But as the nonprofit's budget grows, you should consider hiring a part-time bookkeeper to maintain your books and an accountant to complete your taxes.

## Bookkeeping and Accounting Overview

While budgeting (discussed in Chapter 3) helps you create a realistic plan for raising and spending your nonprofit's money, bookkeeping and accounting allow you to keep track of the actual money that flows into and out of the nonprofit. Despite what you may fear, bookkeeping and accounting can be fairly straightforward—the key is to put some thought and planning into your system early on.

You have three primary goals when doing bookkeeping and accounting:

**Keeping track of income and expenses in order to run your nonprofit efficiently.** To make smart decisions about how to use scarce resources, avoid waste, pay bills on time, and plan to raise adequate funds, you must have an up-to-date and accurate accounting system.

- **Organizing financial information about your nonprofit to file tax returns and other financial reports required by government or other agencies.** If you don't have your finances in order, putting together tax returns and other financial reports (for a major institutional funder, for example) can be a real nightmare—one that you can prevent by putting the proper systems in place.
- **Avoiding the penalties and embarrassment that come from mismanaging nonprofit funds.** Even with the best of intentions, your nonprofit can get into real trouble and generate negative publicity if financial mismanagement is exposed through an audit or other examination.

Above and beyond these fundamental goals, well-organized finances will help your nonprofit:

- **Set appropriate fundraising goals.** Only by staying on top of your income and expenses will you know how much money you need to bring in to pay for your programs. This knowledge is essential for you to come up with a solid fundraising plan, including whether and how much to charge in fees for your programs or membership dues and how to generate income through grants, donations, and other sources.
- **Pace your growth effectively.** A good set of books will give you the information you need to decide when and how to expand your programs. Without meaningful financial numbers, making any decisions about growth can be a gamble. For example, just because your nonprofit has a lot of money in its checking account after a fundraising drive doesn't mean that you should spend it all on a new program. A well-organized set of financial records will give you an accurate and complete financial picture, including information on where your money is most needed.
- **Minimize taxes on unrelated business income.** As explained more fully in Chapter 6 and in "Tracking Income and Expenses," below, many nonprofits earn money from activities that are unrelated to their central missions—and that

## Common Financial Terms

The first step toward understanding nonprofit finances is to learn some commonly used financial terms. Unfortunately, many people use these terms imprecisely or even incorrectly—and if this happens in your organization, it can be almost impossible to have a meaningful conversation about the numbers. Once you're familiar with these terms, you'll be well prepared to make sense of basic written reports and better able to communicate with others about important financial information. Here are a few of the terms you should know:

- An **invoice** is a written record of a transaction, usually submitted to a customer or client when requesting payment. Invoices are sometimes called bills or statements, though the latter term has its own specific meaning (see below).
- A **statement** is a formal written summary of an account. Unlike an invoice, a statement is not generally used by itself as a request for payment but to clearly outline an account's transactions and to clarify what is owed to whom.
- A **ledger** or **register** is a collection of related financial information, such as revenues, expenditures, accounts receivable, and accounts payable. Ledgers used to be kept in books preprinted with lined ledger paper (which explains why a business's financial information is often referred to as the "books"). Checkbooks also come with a register, where you keep track of the checks you've written. These days, the terms "ledger" and "register" are also used to refer to the screens where you enter transactions into accounting software.
- An **account** is a collection of financial information grouped according to purpose. For example, if you have a regular supplier, the collection of information regarding purchases and payments to that supplier would be called its "account." A written record of an account is called a statement.
- **Accounts payable** are amounts that your nonprofit owes. For example, unpaid utility bills and purchases your nonprofit makes on credit are included in its accounts payable.
- **Accounts receivable** are amounts owed to your nonprofit but not yet paid. Accounts receivable includes sales your nonprofit makes on credit.

income is taxable under IRS rules, even with tax-exempt status. Keeping careful track of your expenses will help you spot deductions that can reduce your tax bill. If you are sloppy with your bookkeeping, you'll miss valuable opportunities to save tax dollars.

- **Avoid tax penalties.** Responsible bookkeeping can also help you avoid errors in your tax returns that can subject you to fines and other penalties. If your nonprofit is audited and its books are in bad shape, you risk harsh treatment by the IRS. Don't court this kind of trouble—make sure to maintain basic, accurate records.

## Bookkeeping Versus Accounting: What's the Difference?

Generally speaking, bookkeeping consists of entering data into a system—usually computer software—to track your income and expenses. Accounting refers to using those figures to generate reports that offer insight into your financial situation and to complete tax returns. Although people sometimes use the terms interchangeably, it's important to understand how they differ—particularly if you plan to hire a professional to help you with your finances. For example, you wouldn't want to spend a lot of money to hire a CPA just to enter routine data into your books. On the flip side, you also wouldn't want to ask your part-time bookkeeper to complete a complex tax return.

## Cash Versus Accrual Accounting

When setting up your financial record-keeping system, you'll need to choose one of two principal methods for keeping track of your income and expenses: the cash or the accrual method (sometimes called cash basis and accrual basis). These methods differ in the timing of when you credit or deduct transactions to your accounts:

- Under the more common accrual method, you record transactions when the transaction occurs, regardless of when you actually receive or pay the money.

- Under the cash method, you do not record the transaction until the payment (cash, check, or credit card payment) is actually received, and you do not record expenses until they are actually paid.

In other words, the cash method tracks the actual cash you have on hand at any given time, whereas the accrual method tracks transactions and obligations as they occur, even before you actually receive or pay out the money.

---

### Double-Entry Versus Single-Entry Bookkeeping

The terms "double-entry" and "single-entry" bookkeeping refer to two systems for keeping track of an organization's finances. In a single-entry system, every transaction is recorded once, either as income or as an expense to your nonprofit. In a double-entry system, each transaction is recorded (you guessed it) twice, as both a debit to (deduction from) one account and a credit to another.

Double-entry bookkeeping is intended to reflect the basic structure of financial transactions: Money is paid in exchange for something. Therefore, a cost to one account is always a benefit to another. For example, spending $1,000 on a computer would be a debit to your bank account (a loss of $1,000) but a credit to your assets (a gain of the computer as your property). On the other hand, selling a nonprofit publication for $50 would be a credit to your bank account (a gain of $50) but a debit to your assets (a loss of one book from your inventory).

Double-entry bookkeeping was developed as a way to catch clerical errors. Because transactions had to be entered twice (back when bookkeeping was done by hand in ledgers), entries could be compared to ensure that the books were accurate. It was more labor-intensive than single-entry accounting but resulted in more accurate books.

These days, most enterprises use bookkeeping software that automatically handles the double entry for you. Programs such as *QuickBooks* essentially do the double entry behind the scenes.

**EXAMPLE 1:** You purchase a new laser printer for $2,000 on a credit card in May and pay the $2,000 credit card bill two months later, in July. Using the accrual method, you would record the $2,000 debit in your books in May, as soon as you purchase the laser printer and become obligated to pay for it. Under the cash method, however, you would wait to record the $2,000 debit until the month of July, when you actually pay the $2,000 to your credit card company.

**EXAMPLE 2:** A foundation awards your nonprofit a $10,000 grant in November 2012, but you do not receive the award check until January 2013. You would record the $10,000 credit to your account in November 2012 under the accrual method, but you would wait until January 2013 under the cash method.

Nonprofits and for-profit businesses alike use the accrual method more often than the cash method, in large part because the accrual method is the standard used by accounting and financial professionals. Although you don't have to follow their lead when keeping your internal books, using the accrual method will help you when it comes time to generate reports for outside agencies, who will expect (and often demand) that you adhere to the standards of the profession. (See "Generally Accepted Accounting Principles," below, for more on these standards.)

Another good reason to use the accrual method is that it generally provides a more accurate picture of your nonprofit's financial health, because it reflects earning and spending activity as it happens rather than when cash changes hands—in other words, it shows you how much money you really have available to use, not including cash that you are already obligated to pay out. If, for example, you have $10,000 in the bank when you buy a $2,000 computer on credit, the accrual method would show that you only have $8,000 left to spend, despite the fact that your bank account balance would still show $10,000 until you pay your credit card company.

---

### Generally Accepted Accounting Principles

Professionals in the field of finance follow a set of standards designed to ensure consistency and accuracy in financial records and reports. These rules, called "generally accepted accounting principles" (GAAP), are intended to make it easier for the public to understand an organization's financial books—and to make it more difficult for an organization to hide financial problems from funders, auditors, and others with an interest in how the group makes and spends its money.

GAAP rules apply only to reports and statements generated for those outside your group, not to your internal books. For instance, government and private grant-giving agencies often ask grant applicants to submit an audited statement (discussed in "Audits, Reviews, and Compilations," below), which must be prepared by a certified public accountant in accordance with GAAP. Because you will virtually always hire an accountant to prepare these types of formal reports, you really don't have to worry about GAAP. As long as your internal books are accurate and complete (and you keep track of the information required by GAAP, as explained in "Tracking Income and Expenses," below), your accountant should have no trouble generating reports and statements that meet GAAP requirements.

For information on GAAP requirements for nonprofits, go to the website of the Financial Accounting Standards Board, the private organization that sets the standards, at www.fasb.org. See Statements 116 and 117, in particular, for rules that apply to nonprofit reports.

---

Because the accrual method is used by professionals and provides more accurate information, all but the smallest nonprofits would be well advised to use it—particularly for important reports such as quarterly or year-end financial statements. The accrual method isn't perfect, however. Although it shows the ebb and flow of income and debts as they occur, it may leave you in the dark about how much money you actually have on hand—which could result in a serious cash flow problem. For instance, your income records may show thousands of dollars in grants and contributions, while in reality your bank account is empty because your funders and donors haven't put their checks in the mail yet.

### Tax Years and Accounting Periods

All nonprofit and for-profit enterprises must use an accounting period called a "fiscal year." Also sometimes called a "tax year" or an "accounting year," this simply refers to the 12-month period for which you report your income and expenses for tax purposes. While you may choose the calendar year as your fiscal year, you may also choose a different period—say, June 1 to May 31—if it makes more sense for your organization.

While many nonprofits find it simplest to use the calendar year as their fiscal year, some nonprofits find that a different 12-month period works better for them. If your programs run on a schedule other than a calendar year—for example, you run an after-school program that mirrors the academic year, with most of your income arriving in August and most of your spending occurring between September and May—you might want to choose a different fiscal year. If you are unsure what fiscal year to use, you could start by using the calendar year and then see if any issues arise that warrant choosing a different fiscal year.

The bottom line is that no matter which system you decide to use, you will not be getting the whole story. To get a complete picture of your nonprofit's finances, you need to understand what the numbers mean and how to use them to answer specific financial questions, as discussed below.

## Tracking Income and Expenses

For your financial records to be useful, they must be based on accurate information about your nonprofit's income and expenses. To keep your books in shape, you'll have to develop good habits, like keeping all receipts so that you have a record of the amount, date, type, and other relevant information for each and every transaction. You will also need to be disciplined about having someone enter these transactions into your books on a regular basis.

### Creating Accounts in Your Bookkeeping Software

Bookkeeping software programs (such as *QuickBooks* and *MYOB*) allow you to track all the separate accounts that belong to your nonprofit—for example, your checking, savings, credit card, investments, and petty cash accounts. It's important to set up your accounting software to categorize each of these accounts separately, so you can easily reconcile your records with your bank, credit card, and other statements. Here's how to do it:

- Start by creating a checking account in your bookkeeping software. Enter all transactions from your bank checking account here. When you deposit checks into your checking account (or spend money from it), enter those totals into the checking account section of your bookkeeping software.
- If you use a credit card, set up a separate credit card account in your bookkeeping software. When you make purchases on credit, enter those expenses in the credit card account of your bookkeeping—not the checking account. Similarly, enter payments to your credit card and any finance charges in the credit card account.
- Repeat this process for all other accounts your nonprofit has, always taking care to record every transaction.
- When you get your bank, credit card, and other statements, it will be easy to reconcile them against your bookkeeping records one account at a time. Go through each account statement—from your bank, credit card company, and so on—and make sure each item in those statements is also recorded in the appropriate account in your bookkeeping. Of course, you should also make sure that the totals match.

### Recording Income

It goes without saying that you must carefully document all income your nonprofit earns. This section explains some practices to follow when tracking and categorizing your income.

## Restricted and Unrestricted Income

As explained in Chapter 3, some funders may give your nonprofit money on the condition that it must be used a certain way—for example, a grant might stipulate that your nonprofit must use the money for a certain educational program or that it may not use the money for administrative expenses. Income that's subject to these types of conditions is known as "restricted income," while income that you can use as you wish is known as "unrestricted income."

You must clearly identify restricted and unrestricted income in your financial records for several reasons. If you have to create any formal financial reports, your accountant will have to verify that you kept track of the nature and details of any restrictions on your income, as well as whether those conditions were met. (This requirement is a GAAP standard—see "Generally Accepted Accounting Principles," above, for more information.) Practically speaking, it is important to distinguish income that is restricted so that you know which income you can use for which purposes.

The easiest way to track restricted income is to make a notation, such as "RESTRICTED," plus a description of how that income must be used, in the "memo" or "notes" area of the bookkeeping entry. For example, when entering information about a conditional grant in your books, you might note, "RESTRICTED: May not be used for administrative expenses." Also note how you ultimately used the income so you can show that you met the condition.

## Categorize Your Income

You should create categories for the different types of income you receive. These categories will help you plan and forecast, showing you clearly which fundraising activities are the most productive and which are falling flat. Categorizing your income will also help you at tax time, because different tax rules may apply to different types of income. Even nonprofits that have federal or state tax-exempt status may have some income that is taxable—known as "unrelated business income" (discussed below).

The income categories you create will depend on your nonprofit's activities and sources of income. Some common income categories include:

- individual contributions
- membership fees
- grants
- corporate sponsorships
- program revenues
- publication and subscription sales
- advertising income (e.g., from selling advertisements in your newsletter or event programs), and
- loans.

## Track Unrelated Business Income

As discussed in Chapter 6, a nonprofit with 501(c)(3) tax exempt status (or another type of federal or state tax exemption) may still have to pay income tax on revenues it earns from activities that are not substantially related to its nonprofit mission. Income derived from such activities is known as "unrelated business income," and the tax on this income is known as unrelated business income tax, or UBIT.

The basic rule is that income derived from business activities that you conduct regularly and that are not substantially related to your mission is taxable, unless a special IRS exemption applies. For example, if a nonprofit dedicated to pollution awareness has an ongoing business selling topographic maps of national parks at retail prices, the income from that activity is probably taxable, because it's not substantially related to the group's mission of pollution awareness. As you can probably imagine, the IRS has many rules to determine what income is taxable. For more details, see Chapter 6.

### CAUTION

**Income earned from selling advertisements is taxable.** Many nonprofits are surprised to learn that revenue from selling ad space in their newsletters or event programs is taxable. Similarly, if you offer ad space on your website or in your newsletter to businesses that sponsor your group, some or all of the sponsors' contributions may be taxable. The IRS rules here are fuzzy, so you may want to consult an accountant or lawyer to determine whether your income from sponsors is subject to unrelated business income tax.

**RESOURCE**

**Do your homework before pursuing income that may be taxable.** If you are considering any business activities that are not substantially related to your mission, be sure to read IRS Publication 598, *Tax on Unrelated Business Income of Exempt Organizations.* You can get this and other IRS publications online at www.irs.gov or by calling the IRS at 800-TAX-FORM (800-829-3676). Consult an attorney or accountant if anything remains unclear.

### Track Sales Tax Separately

In addition to tracking categories of income, you also need to keep track of income that is subject to state sales tax. Whether a sale is subject to state sales tax is an entirely separate issue from whether the income you make from the sale is subject to state or federal income taxes. Sales tax is money you collect from those who purchase items from your group, then pass along to the state. Income tax is money you pay to the IRS out of your nonprofit's own pocket.

Not all states impose sales tax. Of those that do, many offer a sales tax exemption to nonprofits. States that offer exemptions usually limit them to certain types of nonprofits—for example, only groups with 501(c)(3) status or only groups with particular nonprofit purposes, such as nonprofit hospitals or religious organizations. Even if you meet the state's criteria for an exemption, you will still have to submit an application—the exemptions don't apply automatically. If your group receives an exemption, you won't have to collect sales tax from your customers, so you won't have to worry about remitting that money to the state.

If you are not exempt from state sales tax and you engage in taxable sales, you'll need to keep track of the income you earn from your taxable sales and the amount of sales tax you collect on the sales separately. For example, if you sell books for $10 each and collect a 5% sales tax on each sale ($0.50), don't just enter $10.50 for each sale into your records. Instead, record each sale as $10 in sales income and $0.50 in sales tax collected.

**RELATED TOPIC**

**Chapter 6 offers more detailed information about sales tax requirements.** Refer to that chapter for information on how to figure out and comply with sales tax requirements in your state. You can find your state sales tax agency's website by searching the IRS website at www.irs.gov (use the search term "state links"), or searching online using Google or Yahoo! with your state name and the words "sales tax agency" as your search terms.

### Track Pledges and Donations

Special rules apply to pledges and donations— categories of income that only nonprofits receive. These are GAAP rules (see "Generally Accepted Accounting Principles," above), so you will have to follow them in your records to allow your accountant to prepare formal reports and statements. The rules for these categories are:

- **Pledges.** A pledge is a promise by a contributor to give a certain amount to your nonprofit at some point in the future. You must record all unconditional pledges in your accounting records, even if the pledge has not been received. A pledge is unconditional if it is not contingent on some other event, such as the nonprofit implementing a certain program or receiving a matching grant.
- **Donated goods.** You must record most contributions of goods (also known as "in-kind contributions") in your books, just like monetary contributions. You must record the value of all goods donated to your nonprofit, with a few exceptions—for example, galleries, museums, and other groups with collections of art and other artifacts are generally exempted from recording the value of donated works.
- **Donated services.** Certain types of volunteer time need to be recorded in your books. The volunteer time must be recorded if either of the following is true:
  - The volunteer work creates or enhances a nonfinancial (physical) asset—for example,

your volunteers help build a homeless health care clinic.

- The volunteer work involves specialized skills—for example, lawyers, accountants, electricians, or other professionals volunteer their services to your nonprofit.

**RESOURCE**

**The IRS has several publications on charitable contributions and related issues.** They include Publication 526, *Charitable Contributions*; Publication 561, *Determining the Value of Donated Property*; and Publication 1771, *Charitable Contributions—Substantiation and Disclosure Requirements*. You can get these and other IRS publications online at www.irs.gov or by calling the IRS at 800-TAX-FORM (800-829-3676).

## Recording Expenses

Of course, your nonprofit won't just bring in money—it will spend money as well. Every time your nonprofit spends money or buys something on credit, you need to record that expense in your books. This includes wages to employees, rent, printing costs, office supplies, computer equipment, and every other cost of running your nonprofit. Make sure to get a written receipt for every transaction, then enter the expenses into your records on a regular basis. If you have very few transactions, you may be able to get away with entering receipts into your books once a month; otherwise, enter them weekly (or even more often if you have a lot of expense transactions).

### Expense Categories

You should organize your expenses by category, just like your income, for several reasons. First of all, it will help you prepare your taxes. Even tax-exempt nonprofits must pay income taxes on any unrelated business income they earn, so carefully categorizing expenses will help you claim all of the tax deductions to which you are entitled. Also, being able to see your expenses summarized in categories—such as rent,

marketing, office supplies, utilities, and so on—will help you understand your spending patterns and make it easier for you to adjust your expenses when necessary. And carefully tracking your expenses will help you complete all tax returns and other necessary financial reports accurately.

### Regular Expenses Versus Capital Expenses

As discussed in Chapter 3, tax laws and standard accounting practices treat regular, day-to-day expenses differently from capital expenses, which are expenses for things that have a useful life of more than one year. These items are called "assets" or "capital assets." Common regular expenses include salaries, rent, utilities, postage, and office supplies. Computers, furniture, and vehicles are common examples of capital assets.

When categorizing expenses, you should enter capital expenses into their own subcategories, separate from regular expenses. In other words, you should have a number of subcategories for regular expenses such as rent, salaries, postage, office supplies, and so on, plus subcategories for capital assets such as computers, office equipment, and furniture. Most bookkeeping software have built-in categories and subcategories for regular expenses and for assets, which makes it simple to keep them separate.

**TIP**

**Multiple receipts can confuse your bookkeeping.** Sometimes, you'll receive a number of receipts for just one purchase—a credit card slip, a register receipt, and an itemized statement, for example. If you throw all three receipts into your files to be posted later, you run the risk of counting them as three separate transactions. You might think that you'll remember the transaction or catch the duplication, but when dealing with dozens of receipts at the end of a long day, week, or month, it's all too easy for mistakes to creep into your paperwork. To avoid counting transactions more than once, either discard multiple copies of receipts immediately after the transaction or staple them all together.

## Creating Basic Financial Reports

Financial reports bring together key pieces of information about your nonprofit's income and expenses, to reveal its overall financial health. Two of the most commonly used reports are income statements and cash flow forecasts, both of which combine data from your income and expense records to show you whether you are bringing in enough income to meet your expenses. This section takes a closer look at these two important reports.

### Income Statement

An income statement compares your revenues to your expenses on a monthly basis. If you've ever seen a profit and loss statement—ubiquitous in the for-profit world—you will recognize the function of an income statement in the nonprofit world. An income statement shows, month by month, whether your revenues are higher or lower than your expenses and by how much. At the year's end, you can total the monthly results to obtain your annual net revenue or loss.

Once you've entered income and expense transactions, most accounting software will generate an income statement with just a few clicks of the mouse. (Your software may call this statement something else, like a "profit and loss report" or something similar.) You can also easily create an income statement by hand, using spreadsheet software such as *Excel*. Starting with the income and expense data that you've entered into your books, enter the amount you earned or spent in each category in each month. Then, enter and subtotal your income, and do the same for your expenses. Finally, subtract the expenses from the income for each month. It's common practice to indicate negative figures by putting them in parentheses.

Below is a sample income statement for a nonprofit that has been in existence for six months.

Your income statement is an absolutely crucial tool to help you identify what operations, if any, your nonprofit needs to adjust to stay on budget. Seeing the totals for all of your expense categories over the course of several months or quarters allows you to quickly pinpoint areas in which you may be overspending—or at least have some room for belt-tightening. Similarly, accurately tracking income totals by month is important so you can see whether you're bringing in the revenues you predicted in your budget—and so you can take quick action if you're falling short.

### Cash Flow Projection

Besides tracking your overall financial health with an income statement, it's also important for your nonprofit to know whether it has enough cash at any given time to pay for its costs of operation. Having a wealth of contribution pledges and promised grants is not the same as having money in the bank to pay your bills. If your cash flow is poor—in other words, if you do not have enough available cash when you need it—you can easily face a situation in which your income statement says you are in the black, but you cannot actually pay your rent, salaries, or other key bills on time.

A cash flow projection can help you predict a future cash shortage, giving you time to take steps to remedy the situation. A cash flow projection focuses on the actual dollars your nonprofit pays out and takes in—also known as cash-ins and cash-outs, or inflows and outflows. Cash-ins and cash-outs reflect the cash you actually have on hand, whereas the revenues and expenses shown in an income statement might not be paid right away. By tracking your cash-ins and cash-outs and then using that information to develop a forecast for upcoming months, you can predict when you might run short—and take action to avoid emptying your bank account. Unless you know when a cash shortage might occur, it may be too late to do anything about it once it hits, which could force you to pay bills late or even take drastic action such as cutting programs or staff.

### How to Do a Cash Flow Projection

Your cash flow projection uses most of the same numbers as your income statement, plus a few extras.

## Six-Month Income Statement

| | Jan | Feb | Mar | Apr | May | June | Total |
|---|---|---|---|---|---|---|---|
| **Income** | | | | | | | |
| Membership fees | $ 5000 | $16,250 | $ 2,500 | $ 8,750 | $ 6,250 | $ 7,500 | $46,250 |
| Event revenues | 0 | 12,050 | 0 | 0 | 0 | 0 | 12,050 |
| Sponsorships | 15,000 | 0 | 5,000 | 0 | 5,000 | 0 | 25,000 |
| Total Income | $20,000 | $28,300 | $ 7,500 | $ 8,750 | $11,250 | $ 7,500 | $83,300 |
| **Expenses** | | | | | | | |
| Salaries | $ 5,000 | $ 5,000 | $ 5,000 | $ 5,000 | $ 5,000 | $ 5,000 | $30,000 |
| Website costs | 3,000 | 0 | 0 | 0 | 0 | 0 | 3,000 |
| Marketing costs | 0 | 0 | 2,750 | 0 | 0 | 0 | 2,750 |
| Office supplies | 1,050 | 0 | 850 | 0 | 350 | 400 | 2,650 |
| Postage | 0 | 0 | 0 | 0 | 1,110 | 0 | 1,110 |
| State filing fees | 250 | 0 | 0 | 0 | 0 | 0 | 250 |
| Telephone service | 250 | 250 | 250 | 250 | 250 | 250 | 1,500 |
| Event costs | 0 | 8,000 | 0 | 0 | 0 | 0 | 8,000 |
| Professional services | 5,000 | 0 | 0 | 0 | 0 | 0 | 5,000 |
| Insurance | 3,000 | 0 | 0 | 0 | 0 | 0 | 3,000 |
| Miscellaneous | 500 | 350 | 500 | 350 | 500 | 350 | 2,550 |
| Total Expenses | $18,050 | $13,600 | $ 9,350 | $ 5,600 | $ 7,210 | $ 6,000 | $59,810 |
| **Total Income/Expenses** | $ 1,950 | $14,700 | $(1,850) | $ 3,150 | $ 4,040 | $ 1,500 | $23,490 |

The big difference is that your cash flow projection includes not only contributions, grants, and the like, but other sources of revenue as well, such as loans, interest from investments, and transfers from your personal accounts. That's because when it comes time to pay the landlord, the utility company, and other creditors, the crucial issue is whether you have adequate funds at the time you need to pay the bill—not where the money comes from. For the same reason, your cash flow forecast will include only income that you've actually received—not, for example, pledges of future contributions or grant checks that haven't arrived. Finally, your cash flow projection must include all money you'll pay out of the nonprofit, whether for important program costs or for things like supplies, taxes, credit card payments, and so on.

The simple formula for a cash flow analysis is:

Cash in the bank at the beginning of month
+ Actual cash received during the month
− Actual cash disbursements during the month
= Cash in the bank at the end of month

Each month's cash flow projection starts with the dollar figure you have in the bank, which should be the same amount you had when the previous month ended. Next, add any cash that comes in during the month in all relevant categories, such as grants, contributions, loans, interest earned, and any personal money you put into the nonprofit. These are your total cash-ins for the month. Next, subtract all the money you spend during the month—your cash-outs.

The result is the cash left at the end of the month. Enter that figure into the beginning of the next month's column, and do the same process for the next month. Accounting software makes generating a cash flow spreadsheet a snap once you've entered figures for income and expenses.

### How to Predict Future Cash Flows

Now that you know the basic formula behind cash flow analysis, you can see that the real power of this tool is not in tracking actual cash-ins and cash-outs, but in predicting future cash flows. Periodically— once a month or every few months—you should use your actual figures to help you make estimates for upcoming months and complete a cash flow projection for the future, for a time period of up to one year. Hopefully you will see that your nonprofit will have adequate cash to cover your expenses each month, plus a cushion to handle unexpected bills. If not, don't panic. First, pat yourself on the back for doing a cash flow analysis and figuring out ahead of time that you may soon find yourself in a crunch. Then come up with a plan: Make some cuts, put off some expenses, or raise more money, perhaps through a quickly arranged special event or fundraising drive.

Accurately predicting cash-ins and cash-outs for future months is not easy, especially when you're in the early stages of running your nonprofit and don't have much of a financial history on which to base your projections. Cash-outs tend to be easier to predict than cash-ins because, with good planning and tight financial discipline, you have more control over what you spend than what you bring in. But there's no escaping the fact that you'll need to make estimates

of how much income will come in—a task that may seem only slightly easier than reading tea leaves.

The key to making useful cash-in projections is to be moderately conservative. Accept the fact that your income estimates will likely be somewhat optimistic, and discount your estimate by a third or so. For example, if you have firm pledges totaling $15,000, you might choose to enter $10,000 in your cash flow projection. As the months tick by and the flow of cash into and out of your nonprofit settles into daily, weekly, and monthly patterns, making estimates will inevitably become easier and you'll find them becoming increasingly more accurate. And, as the months and years go by and you gain experience with your community of funders, you'll be able to trust that your estimates will be closer to reality.

Above is an example of a cash flow projection you can do on a simple spreadsheet. In this fictional example, "real" figures were used for April through June, and the rest of the figures are projections based on what happened in those first few months and on best estimates of future activity. As you can see, arranging income and expense information into a cash flow projection reveals a lot about the financial workings of a nonprofit. For example, the sample cash flow forecast below shows that cash will be tight in several months. The most pressing concerns are the projected cash shortfalls in July and September.

Knowing a few months in advance that a shortfall is likely will help the board or executive director figure out what to do while there's still time to take action. Board members could contribute personal money to the nonprofit (note that the cash flow didn't include any loans or personal transfers to the group's coffers), get on the phone and recruit additional contributions, or decide to pare down the less essential expenses, at least until December when the nonprofit expects to reap some special event revenue.

To stay on top of cash flow issues, replace your projections with actual results from your accounting system each month. It's a good way to see how accurate your projections have been, which will help you make even more accurate estimates in the future.

## Cash Flow Projection

| | April | May | June | July (projected) | Aug (projected) | Sep (projected) | Oct (projected) | Nov (projected) | Dec (projected) |
|---|---|---|---|---|---|---|---|---|---|
| **Cash at beginning of month** | $ 6,550 | $ 6,700 | $ 1,750 | $ 5,650 | $ (2,200) | $ 1,500 | $ (900) | $ 3,550 | $ 950 |
| **Cash-ins** | | | | | | | | | |
| Membership fees | $ 6,250 | $ 5,000 | $ 6,250 | $ 6,250 | $ 5,000 | $ 6,250 | $ 6,250 | $ 5,000 | $ 6,250 |
| Event revenues | 0 | 14,550 | 0 | 0 | 0 | 0 | 0 | 0 | 12,050 |
| Sponsorships | 5,000 | 0 | 5,000 | 0 | 5,000 | 0 | 5,000 | 0 | 5,000 |
| Loans and transfers | 0 | 0 | 0 | 0 | 0 | 0 | 0 | 0 | 0 |
| Total Cash-ins | $17,800 | $26,250 | $13,000 | $11,900 | $ 7,800 | $ 7,750 | $10,350 | $ 8,550 | $24,250 |
| **Cash-outs** | | | | | | | | | |
| Salaries | $ 5,000 | $ 5,000 | $ 5,000 | $ 5,000 | $ 5,000 | $ 5,000 | $ 5,000 | $ 5,000 | $ 5,000 |
| Website costs | 0 | 0 | 0 | 3,000 | 0 | 0 | 0 | 0 | 0 |
| Marketing costs | 0 | 0 | 1,000 | 0 | 0 | 1,000 | 0 | 0 | 1,000 |
| Office supplies | 850 | 350 | 400 | 850 | 350 | 400 | 850 | 350 | 400 |
| Printing costs | 0 | 9,250 | 0 | 0 | 0 | 0 | 0 | 0 | 2,500 |
| Postage | 0 | 1,500 | 0 | 1,500 | 0 | 1,500 | 0 | 1,500 | 0 |
| State filing fees | 0 | 350 | 0 | 0 | 0 | 0 | 0 | 0 | 0 |
| Telephone service | 250 | 250 | 250 | 250 | 250 | 250 | 250 | 250 | 250 |
| Event costs | 0 | 6,750 | 0 | 0 | 0 | 0 | 0 | 0 | 6,550 |
| Professional services | 4,500 | 0 | 0 | 0 | 0 | 0 | 0 | 0 | 0 |
| Insurance | 0 | 0 | 0 | 3,000 | 0 | 0 | 0 | 0 | 0 |
| Miscellaneous | 500 | 1,050 | 700 | 500 | 700 | 500 | 700 | 500 | 1,050 |
| Total Cash-outs | $11,100 | $24,500 | $ 7,350 | $14,100 | $ 6,300 | $ 8,650 | $ 6,800 | $ 7,600 | $16,750 |
| **Cash at end of month** | $ 6,700 | $ 1,750 | $ 5,650 | $ (2,200) | $ 1,500 | $ (900) | $ 3,550 | $ 950 | $ 7,500 |

## Nonprofit Financial Management: Some Resources

Many, many people are intimidated by anything with the word "financial" in it, so if the idea of financial management stresses you out you're in good company. Fortunately there are lots of resources online to help people understand basic financial concepts, and develop a comfort level and proficiency with maintaining financial records. Here are a few of the most helpful online resources.

- The Resources area of the **Nonprofits Assistance Fund** (www.nonprofitsassistancefund.org) offers an impressive range of articles, worksheets, and templates all related to financial issues facing nonprofits. From articles on how to use a finance committee effectively, to budgeting and cash flow templates, the resources here are extensive and extremely practical. As part of its mission "to build financially healthy nonprofits that foster community vitality," the Nonprofits Assistance Fund also offers many services such as consulting, trainings, and webinars, many for no charge.
- **All About Financial Management in Nonprofits** by Carter McNamara (http://managementhelp.org/nonprofitfinances) is a website-based guidebook organized into sections such as "Basics of Financial Management" and "Understanding and Setting Up Your Nonprofit Bookkeeping and Accounting." The sections and subsections contain substantive information as well as links to other sites with more information.

- **The Nonprofit Risk Management Center** (www.nonprofitrisk.org) offers several articles on the topic of minimizing risk to your organization through sound financial practices. Articles discuss issues such as how to implement internal controls to prevent fraud and theft, and using audit committees to minimize risks to the organization's finances.
- **The National Council of Nonprofits** (www.councilofnonprofits.org) includes information and links on financial management within its resource section on "administration and management."
- **Blue Avocado** (www.blueavocado.org), the magazine of American Nonprofits, regularly reports on topics related to financial management, budgeting, financial controls, and more.
- If you or someone in your organization wants to dive in headfirst, consider signing up for a **degree program in nonprofit management**. There are more such programs now than ever before, and many of them are quite affordable. U.S. News and World Report ranks graduate schools offering degree programs in nonprofit management at this URL: http://grad-schools.usnews.rankingsandreviews.com/best-graduate-schools. Look in the public affairs section and you'll find a link to the "specialty" of nonprofit management.

## Audits, Reviews, and Compilations

While keeping your books in order is always a good idea, nonprofits sometimes need to prepare official financial statements for a funder, a tax agency, or another entity upon request. Fledgling nonprofits might not need to deal with these statements in their early days, but may need to create them in the future.

Generally speaking, what sets these more official statements apart from your regular bookkeeping is that an outside accountant (generally a certified public accountant, or CPA) should prepare them and give them some level of review. The types of statements that you should have a CPA or another appropriate

professional prepare include audited statements, reviews, and compilations. (For detailed information about CPAs and other types of accountants, see Chapter 13.) These are described below:

- The most formal document you may need to prepare is an *audited statement*, also known as an audit, in which a CPA closely examines the nonprofit's books, conducts an independent investigation to verify that your numbers are reliable, and creates reports based on his or her findings. (Don't confuse this with an IRS audit, in which the IRS investigates your nonprofit to make sure its tax returns have been accurate.) The CPA often contacts the nonprofit's key associates, such as independent contractors and funders. If the nonprofit sells a significant amount of goods, the CPA will actually go to the warehouse and count the inventory. Audited statements must conform to Financial Accounting Standards Board (FASB) guidelines, which include rules on how to record contributions, classify assets, and format financial reports. Government and private grant givers often require audited statements from groups applying for funding; exceptions are sometimes made for nonprofits with very small budgets.

- Substantially less formal than an audit is a *review*, in which a CPA conducts a more limited analysis of your records and prepares briefer financial statements. Instead of independently investigating your operations, the CPA relies on reviewing your records to verify that the reports are accurate. A prospective funder might request a review, or a nonprofit might decide to conduct a yearly review once its budget grows to $10,000 or more, to ensure that the books are in good shape.

- Least formal is a compilation, in which a CPA puts the nonprofit's financial data in a standard financial reporting format but makes no statement about the accuracy or reliability of the financial information. In a compilation, the accountant does not review supporting documents.

As you probably can guess, an audit is the most expensive option and a compilation costs the least. Most nonprofits choose the least expensive option that meets their needs, whether it be assuring the board or nonprofit members that the financial house is in order or satisfying a funder or another entity that you are accurately keeping track of the money you spend and bring in.

## Reporting Requirements

In addition to any financial reports they may need to provide to funders or other private entities, most nonprofits will also have to file one or more reports, returns, or other financial documents with state and federal tax agencies. Detailed instructions on completing your tax forms are beyond the scope of this book, but half of the battle is knowing what forms you need to file. Here's a quick overview:

- **Form 990:** *Return of Organization Exempt From Income Tax.* This form—your nonprofit's annual tax return—is due on the 15th day of the fifth month after the end of your fiscal year. If your nonprofit is required to file this return, it also has to maintain a copy of it for public inspection. Tax-exempt public charities with gross receipts of less than $200,000 and total assets of less than $500,000 can use the short form, Form 990-EZ. Nonprofits that normally have gross receipts of $50,000 or less per year must complete a short online form, 990-N, commonly called the "e-postcard."

**RESOURCE**

**Advice on completing Form 990.** For more information on the Form 990, including line-by-line instructions for the Form 990-EZ, see *Every Nonprofit's Tax Guide,* by Stephen Fishman (Nolo).

- **Form 990-T:** *Exempt Organization Business Income Tax Return.* You need to file this return if your nonprofit earned $1,000 or more in gross receipts from an unrelated business. Like the annual return, it's due on the 15th day of the fifth month after the end of your fiscal year.

- **Form 1099-MISC:** *Miscellaneous Income.* If your nonprofit paid any single independent contractor $600 or more in a year, you need to file a 1099-MISC for that contractor. An independent contractor is anyone you hire to do work for your nonprofit who is not an employee of the nonprofit—for example, a database consultant or the CPA you hire once a year to complete your taxes. For more information on determining whether a worker is an independent contractor or an employee, see Chapter 5.

- **Form 941:** *Employer's Quarterly Federal Tax Return,* **and Form W-2:** *Wage and Tax Statement.*

Nonprofits with employees must withhold federal income taxes and FICA taxes (Social Security and Medicare taxes) from employees' paychecks and must periodically report and send these taxes to the IRS. This requirement applies only for employees—not for independent contractors, unpaid directors, or others who volunteer for the nonprofit. If you have to withhold and pay payroll taxes for employees, you will also need to report their wages and tax withholdings to them (and to the IRS) on Form W-2.

- **State payroll taxes.** Nonprofits with employees usually are also required to withhold state income taxes from employees' paychecks and deposit them periodically with their state's income tax agency. Find your state income tax agency's website by searching the IRS website at www.irs.gov (use the search term "state links") or doing an online search with Google or Yahoo! using your state name along with the words "tax department" or "tax agency" as your search terms.

- **Form 940:** *Employer's Annual Federal Unemployment Tax Return.* Nonprofits that have employees and do not have 501(c)(3) status must report and pay federal unemployment insurance taxes on wages paid (also known as FUTA taxes). If you have 501(c)(3) status, you are exempt from these taxes.

**RESOURCE**

**Download IRS forms.** You can obtain IRS forms and informational publications from the IRS website at www.irs.gov or by calling the IRS at 800-TAX-FORM (800-829-3676).

---

## Checklist: Managing Your Finances

- ☐ Gain an understanding of financial management fundamentals, such as the difference between bookkeeping and accounting and between the cash and accrual methods of accounting.

- ☐ Choose bookkeeping software, learn how to use it, and set it up to track all of your nonprofit's accounts, including your checking, credit card, petty cash, investment, and other accounts.

- ☐ Keep all receipts of income and expenses and enter these amounts into your bookkeeping software regularly.

- ☐ Create categories for income and expenses. Some expense categories will be "regular" expenses like office supplies and rent, while others will be "capital" expenses for assets like computers, furniture, vehicles, and real estate.

- ☐ Periodically use the information you've entered into your books to create income statements that compare revenues to expenses and cash flow projections to ensure that the nonprofit can always pay its bills.

- ☐ Hire an accountant to help if your nonprofit is asked to provide an audited statement, review, or compilation to a funder or another entity.

- ☐ Become familiar with the tax returns and other reports your nonprofit may have to file with governmental and other agencies.

# Hiring Lawyers, Accountants, and Other Professional Help

f you're reading this book, you're probably a do-it-yourself type who isn't usually inclined to hire pricey professional help. While your can-do spirit is as commendable as it is sensible, you should recognize the value in using professionals judiciously. Hiring a professional—such as a lawyer, tax adviser, or bookkeeper—for advice or other services is often the most efficient way to handle particular tasks or problems. Even though you'll undoubtedly be able to cope with most nonprofit tasks and problems on your own, tackling issues with a steep learning curve may not be the best use of your time. And, of course, some situations—for example, a lawsuit by a former employee—will clearly call for professional help.

Even when things are running smoothly, virtually every nonprofit should consult an accountant or other tax expert at least once a year for help in getting financial records in order and preparing any necessary tax returns. Making contact with a lawyer early in your nonprofit's life is also a sensible step, even if you don't have any pressing legal issues. Establishing a relationship early on will serve you well if you find yourself in the kind of legal trouble that requires immediate help.

Once you decide you want to hire a professional, your next question very likely will be, "How can I find someone I can trust?" This chapter offers strategies that will help you find and develop relationships with competent professionals.

## Relationships Are Critical

The key to working well with any professional is to develop an ongoing relationship. The more familiar a professional is with your nonprofit and its activities, the better he or she will be able to advise you. You'll generally get better quality services—often at better rates—from a professional you've worked with before, rather than one you hire out of the blue to handle a problem.

Sometimes, you'll simply need some basic advice or coaching from a professional, to make sure that you're handling day-to-day nonprofit tasks correctly. Other times, you'll need more extensive services, such as help preparing a tax return or performing a financial audit. Ideally, you'll develop relationships with professionals who are willing and able to take on both roles: to act as your coach when asked for advice, and to handle more comprehensive services when you need them.

## Working With Lawyers

Even though the attorney section of the yellow pages always takes up a good portion of the phone book, a good lawyer can be hard to find. This section discusses how to find a lawyer who meets your needs—and how to make sure you're getting the most for your hard-earned money.

### What to Look for in a Lawyer

There are a number of qualities that are important for your lawyer to have. You'll want to find an attorney who has some experience with nonprofit issues, preferably for your type of nonprofit. You'll also want someone who's intelligent and competent—two qualities that don't necessarily go hand in hand with having a law degree. And, of course, you'll want a lawyer whom you can trust and work with comfortably. Ideally, you'll find a lawyer with all of these qualities and establish a working relationship.

In **today's** world of ever-increasing specialization, lawyers often focus their areas of expertise rather narrowly. For example, an expert negotiator may not be an effective courtroom lawyer, and vice versa. Most lawyers also specialize in particular areas of law, such as tax, business law, or employment issues. There are also a handful of lawyers, primarily in major metropolitan areas, who focus solely on nonprofit law, and regularly handle legal issues unique to nonprofits (for example, involving board members and bylaws). Make sure that your lawyer can handle the particular type of problem you're facing, in terms of both its subject matter and the type of work involved.

In addition to finding a lawyer with the skills and experience relevant to your situation, it's important that you and the lawyer get along on a personal level. If an otherwise qualified lawyer is condescending or rude, you might as well keep looking for someone with better personal skills. You won't be able to develop a good, long-term relationship with a lawyer unless you can work well together.

You may have to look a bit harder to find a lawyer who is willing to work with you collaboratively on matters that you can handle at least partially on your own. Tackling some routine legal issues, such as amending your bylaws or executing a contract for services, may be well within your abilities, though you may be more comfortable having a lawyer review your work or give you limited advice. While lawyers traditionally offered their services on an all-or-nothing basis (and charged fees accordingly), some lawyers are now more willing to act as coaches for their clients, giving only as much service as the clients want. If you'd like to be more involved in your nonprofit's legal matters and minimize your attorney's fees, be sure to ask the lawyer directly whether he or she is willing to have this kind of working relationship with you. Legal coaching is discussed in more detail below.

## How to Find a Lawyer

Unfortunately, the easiest and quickest ways to find a lawyer are usually the least effective. Sure, you'll find hundreds of lawyers' names in the yellow pages, but how will you choose among them? You'll have the same problem if you look in legal newspapers for attorney ads. Flashy, aggressive advertising is definitely not a good indicator of quality legal services.

Believe it or not, one good place to start looking for inexpensive legal help is at large law firms. Nonprofits are often attractive clients for lawyers looking to do volunteer legal work (called "pro bono" work). State bar organizations encourage lawyers to do pro bono work, and many large firms require their lawyers to log a certain number of hours of pro bono work each year. Many law schools also provide free or low-cost legal services through community law clinics run by students, under the supervision of a law professor. Call any law school in your area and ask if they offer such services.

---

### Internet Legal Research

Some of your legal questions may not warrant an expensive consultation with an attorney but may be beyond the scope of a self-help book. For instance, you may need to look up your state's rules on fundraising or learn more about the unrelated business income tax. If you don't want to call your lawyer every time you have a question, you might consider doing a little legal research.

The good news is that finding basic legal information is usually not too difficult, and plenty is available free online. The following resources are a good place to start:

- Most states make their statutes available online. To find laws governing nonprofits, look in the corporations code of your state's statutes. Bear in mind that some sites are markedly better than others in terms of searching and navigating statutes. If your state statutes aren't easy to navigate online, you may be better off just going to a law library.

- Besides the actual statutes, official state sites often offer valuable information for nonprofits, including incorporation procedures, forms, state tax rules, summaries of the law on volunteer liability issues, and much more. You'll usually find this information as part of the corporations section, which is sometimes (but not always) part of the secretary of state's website. States vary greatly in how much information they make available online, but most states have been rapidly improving their online information systems and making their sites more useful and accessible for citizens.

- For specific citations to nonprofit codes in each state, see *How to Form a Nonprofit Corporation*, by Anthony Mancuso (Nolo).

- For general rules and issues regarding nonprofits, Nolo offers extensive free information and resources at its website, www.nolo.com. You'll also find state-specific articles on nonprofit corporation laws on the Nolo website.

- For more information about legal research both online and off, a thorough reference is Nolo's *Legal Research: How to Find & Understand the Law*, by Stephen R. Elias and the editors of Nolo.

Besides exploring pro bono and law school clinic options, perhaps the most effective way to find a good lawyer is to get a personal referral, preferably from someone involved in running a nonprofit. Even better is a referral from a similar type of nonprofit, such as an arts or scientific group.

If you can't come up with a personal referral, try to find out which lawyers work with nonprofits in your area. Keep your eyes and ears open for names of attorneys who have worked on cases in your field. For example, a local environmental magazine might run an article about a current lawsuit that mentions the names of the attorneys involved. Visit websites that focus on nonprofits, or contact organizations directly. A good place to start is your state association of nonprofits. Find yours and lots of other resources at the National Council of Nonprofits' website (www. councilofnonprofits.org). They may be able to direct you to lawyers who have worked in the nonprofit sector. Once you get some names, call these lawyers and ask if they're available for the type of services you need. If not, they can probably refer you to someone else who might be able to help.

**TIP**

**Speak with the lawyer personally, not just the receptionist.** You can probably get a good idea of how the attorney operates by paying close attention to the way your call is handled. Is the lawyer available right away? If not, is your call promptly returned? Is the lawyer willing to spend at least a few minutes talking to you to determine if he or she really is the best person for the job? Do you get a good personal feeling from your conversation? The way you're treated during your initial call can be a good indicator of how the lawyer treats clients in general.

## Using a Lawyer as a Coach

In a traditional attorney/client relationship, a client hires an attorney to take care of a legal problem and then hands over all responsibility for—and control over—the matter to the lawyer. While some clients like it this way, many would rather be more involved in their legal affairs, both to maintain some control

and to save money on legal fees. But, until recently, getting limited legal help from a lawyer wasn't really an option. Most lawyers wouldn't take on a legal matter unless they could handle it on their own, from start to finish.

But a new model of legal services is finally emerging. In this approach, sometimes called "legal coaching" or "unbundled legal services," a lawyer provides only the services that a client wants, and nothing more. For example, a client who wants legal help in drafting a contract can arrange a short consultation with a lawyer to get answers to general questions, go home and draft the contract, and then fax it to the lawyer, who will review it and suggest changes.

For people running nonprofits, using a lawyer as a coach can be especially useful. More often than not, the legal issues that arise in the course of day-to-day business are relatively simple, and—with a bit of good legal advice—within the capabilities of most people to handle. Rather than hiring an attorney for upwards of $1,000 to deal with an issue, using a coach might cost $100 and enable the nonprofit manager to proceed on his or her own.

While getting limited help from a lawyer has become an increasingly popular approach to legal problems in recent years, it still can take some effort to find a lawyer who is willing to act as a coach. To find one, use the same strategies discussed above (personal referrals, for example), but take the extra step of asking the lawyer directly whether he or she is willing to help you in your efforts to solve your own legal problems. If not, or if you sense that the lawyer wouldn't really embrace a coaching arrangement, keep looking. In today's increasingly competitive legal marketplace, it shouldn't take you too long to find a lawyer who is willing to offer flexible services, including coaching.

**RESOURCE**

**Find a lawyer at www.nolo.com.** You can check out Nolo's Lawyer Directory, which offers comprehensive profiles of the lawyers who advertise there, including each one's education, background, areas of expertise, fees, and practice philosophy. Lawyers also indicate whether or not they are willing to review documents or coach clients who are doing their own legal work. You can also submit information about your legal issue to several local attorneys who handle business issues, and then pick the lawyer you'd like to work with.

## Dealing With Bills and Payments

One area in which most lawyers have some expertise is billing for their services. Before you hire any lawyer, make sure you fully understand how your fees will be calculated. All too often, clients are unpleasantly surprised by their bills because they didn't pay enough attention to the billing terms when they hired the lawyer. Make sure you understand who's responsible for items like court fees, copy fees, transcription costs, and phone bills. These costs aren't trivial and can quickly send your otherwise affordable bill into the keep-you-awake-at-night range.

As described below, lawyers generally use one of four methods to calculate fees for their services: hourly fees, flat fees, contingency fees, or retainers.

**Hourly fees.** This arrangement is fairly straightforward: You pay the attorney's hourly rate for the number of hours he or she works on your case. Simple as this system is, there are some details to consider. For example, you'll want to find out what hourly increments the lawyer uses for billing. For instance, if an attorney bills in half-hour increments, then you'll be charged a full half-hour even if you talk for just five minutes. That can easily total $100 or more for a five-minute phone call. You'd be better off if your lawyer uses ten- or 15-minute periods, though not all attorneys break down their time into such small increments.

Another issue to ask about is whether all time spent on your legal work is billed at the attorney's regular rate—even if the attorney isn't doing the work. For example, it's reasonable to expect a discounted rate for time the attorney's administrative staff spends making copies or organizing paperwork. Make sure that the hourly fee for the attorney applies only to the work of the actual attorney.

Hourly fees for attorneys range from $100 or so to more than $400 per hour. Very generally speaking, lawyers that specialize in nonprofit clients often have rates toward the lower end of that range. High rates may reflect a lawyer's extensive experience—or they might reflect the lawyer's lavish lifestyle. Don't pay the highest rates unless you feel the lawyer's expertise—not his Armani suit—is worth it.

**Flat fees.** In some situations, attorneys will charge a flat fee for a specific task, such as negotiating a contract, filing articles of incorporation, or drafting bylaws. As long as the job goes as expected, you'll pay only the price you and the lawyer negotiated, regardless of how long the job takes. If the lawyer hits a snag, however, or if the case becomes convoluted for some other reason, the price may go up. Be sure you and the lawyer are on the same page regarding the situations that may result in a higher fee—a clear written agreement is essential. Also, find out if any charges such as copy fees or messenger costs will be added to the flat fee.

**Contingency fees.** In a contingency fee arrangement, you pay an attorney's fee only if the lawyer wins money for you through a court judgment or a negotiated settlement. In that case, the fee is a set percentage of the monetary award, usually one-third to one-half. In contingency fee arrangements, you need to be especially careful of costs like travel expenses, transcription fees, and phone bills. If you lose your case, you won't owe any attorneys' fees, but you will often be responsible for the lawyer's out-of-pocket expenses on your case.

Nonprofit issues don't typically require contingency fee arrangements. This payment method is usually used in personal injury cases and other situations in which a plaintiff sues someone in hopes of winning a large money award.

**Retainers.** Sometimes you can hire a lawyer to be more or less "on call" by paying a regular fee (usually monthly) called a retainer. This type of arrangement is useful when you have regular, ongoing legal needs such as contract review or negotiation. Based upon your expected needs, you and the lawyer settle on a mutually acceptable monthly fee. Then, you simply have the lawyer take care of any routine legal matters that arise. If you run into a sudden, complex legal dispute, or if your problems escalate greatly, you'll likely have to make additional payments. For this type of arrangement to work, you and the lawyer must have a clear understanding of the routine services that you expect. Unless your legal needs are regular and predictable, a retainer arrangement is probably not your best option.

State laws may require a fee agreement to be in writing in some cases, such as if your lawyer estimates the total cost of legal services to be more than $1,000 or if you have a contingency fee arrangement. Even if it's not legally required, it's always a good idea to get your fee agreement in writing. A written agreement will help prevent disputes over billing and is the best way to avoid unpleasant surprises.

**RESOURCE**
**Useful nonprofit law blog.** Check out the Nonprofit Law Blog (www.nonprofitlawblog.com), run by the San Francisco-based NEO (Nonprofit and Exempt Organizations) Law Group, and includes posts on a wide variety of legal topics of interest to nonprofits.

## Working With Accountants and Other Professionals

Many of the issues nonprofits face can be solved by professionals other than lawyers. In particular, accountants and tax professionals are often indispensable in helping you deal with tax laws, which can have a big impact on your nonprofit. Every nonprofit should consult with an accountant occasionally, at least once a year. While complicated tax troubles may call for a tax attorney, many questions can be answered by an accountant.

### Bookkeepers Versus Accountants

For routine maintenance of your books, you don't need the experience—or expense—of an accountant (certified or otherwise). An experienced bookkeeper will be able to implement an effective system of tracking your income and expenses and help you stay on top of your important bills and reporting requirements, including the various taxes your nonprofit will owe. Depending on the complexity of your nonprofit's finances, you may even decide to do your own bookkeeping—a job that's undoubtedly easier these days with the availability of accounting software. As your nonprofit grows, however, paying for an experienced bookkeeper will likely become worthwhile.

If you find yourself needing specific tax advice or facing a tricky financial problem, you may have to go up a step on the professional ladder and hire an accountant. The top dogs of the accounting field are called "certified public accountants" (CPAs) and are licensed and regulated by the state. Uncertified accountants, called public accountants, also may be licensed by your state. The licensing requirements for CPAs are more stringent, so they are often the most experienced and knowledgeable type of accountants—and, accordingly, the most expensive.

In addition to bookkeepers and accountants, there are other professionals out there who specialize in tax preparation. Some are licensed and some are not. An enrolled agent (EA) is a tax professional licensed by the IRS who can answer tax questions and help you prepare your returns. Others who simply use the title "tax preparer" or "tax return preparer" may not be licensed at all. If a tax professional doesn't have a license as an enrolled agent or as a public or certified public accountant, it may mean that the "professional" has no official qualifications whatsoever.

The best strategy in choosing among these various professionals is to pay for only as much expertise as you need. Obviously, you shouldn't pay a CPA to do simple bookkeeping, but you also shouldn't use a bookkeeper to prepare complex tax returns. You'll need to decide for yourself what kind of professional is appropriate for your situation.

## Finding Prospects

Finding a tax professional is a lot like finding a lawyer: Your goal is to find someone both competent and trustworthy. The strategies discussed above for finding a lawyer are equally useful in finding other professionals. Getting a personal referral is the best way to find someone you can trust. Referrals from other nonprofits are particularly valuable. Virtually every nonprofit will have to consult a tax pro at one point or another, so it shouldn't be too hard to get a decent list of names.

As with attorneys, choose your tax professional carefully, with an eye to developing a long-term relationship. Don't be shy about asking lots of questions. Find out about the person's experience with nonprofits and about his or her knowledge of bookkeeping methods, the tax code, the IRS, or anything else that's relevant to the work you want the professional to do for you.

Make sure you understand the professional's fee structure up front, before he or she does any work for you. Most professionals charge hourly fees, which vary a great deal depending on what kind of qualifications the professional has. Like your attorney fee agreement, your fee agreement with a tax professional should be in writing—written fee agreements minimize the possibility of disputes over the bill.

---

### Checklist: Getting Professional Help

☐ Aim to develop relationships with lawyers, accountants, and other professionals so that they can help you on an ongoing basis.

☐ Ask associates and friends for recommendations for lawyers, accountants, and other professionals. Also check trade magazines and other industry sources.

☐ Try to find a lawyer who is willing to work as a legal coach.

☐ Understand how you will be billed, and get your fee agreements in writing.

☐ Familiarize yourself with online sources of legal information, such as www.nolo.com, the IRS website, and your official state website.

# How to Use the Interactive Forms on the Nolo Website

This book comes with eforms that you can access online at:

**www.nolo.com/back-of-book/SNON.html**

You can open, edit, save, and print the RTF files provided by this book using most word processing programs such as *Microsoft Word*, *Windows WordPad*, and recent versions of *WordPerfect*.

> **TIP**
>
> **Note to Macintosh Users.** These forms were designed for use with Windows. They should also work on Macintosh computers; however Nolo cannot provide technical support for non-Windows users.

## Editing RTFs

Here are some general instructions about editing RTF forms in your word processing program. Refer to the book's instructions and sample agreements for help about what should go in each blank.

- **Underlines.** Underlines indicate where to enter information. After filling in the needed text, delete the underline. In most word processing programs you can do this by highlighting the underlined portion and typing CTRL-U.
- **Bracketed and italicized text.** Bracketed and italicized text indicates instructions. Be sure to remove all instructional text before you finalize your document.
- **Optional text.** Optional text gives you the choice to include or exclude text. Delete any optional text you don't want to use. Renumber numbered items, if necessary.

- **Alternative text.** Alternative text gives you the choice between two or more text options. Delete those options you don't want to use. Renumber numbered items, if necessary.
- **Signature lines.** Signature lines should appear on a page with at least some text from the document itself.

Every word processing program uses different commands to open, format, save, and print documents, so refer to your software's help documents for help using your program. Nolo cannot provide technical support for questions about how to use your computer or your software.

> **CAUTION**
>
> **In accordance with U.S. copyright laws, the forms provided by this book are for your personal use only.**

## List of Forms Available on the Nolo Website

Go to **www.nolo.com/back-of-book/SNON.html**

The following files are in rich text format (RTF):

| Form Title | File Name |
| --- | --- |
| Contractor Work-for-Hire Agreement | Work-for-Hire.rtf |
| Volunteer Assignment Agreement | Volunteer.rtf |
| Nonprofit's Initial Budget | InitialBudget.rtf |

The following file is in portable document format (pdf):

| Form Title | File Name |
| --- | --- |
| State Charitable Solicitation Registration Offices | StateReg.pdf |

# Forms and Budget

**Contractor Work-for-Hire Agreement**

**Volunteer Assignment Agreement**

**Nonprofit's Initial Budget**

# Contractor Work-for-Hire Agreement

This Work-for-Hire Agreement (the "Agreement") is made between _____
_____ ("Nonprofit"), and
_____ ("Contractor").

## Services

In consideration of the payments provided in this Agreement, Contractor agrees to perform the following services:

_____

_____ .

## Payment

Nonprofit agrees to pay Contractor as follows: _____

_____ .

## Works for Hire—Assignment of Intellectual Property Rights

Contractor agrees that, for consideration acknowledged in this Agreement, any works of authorship commissioned pursuant to this Agreement (the "Works") shall be considered works made for hire as that term is defined under U.S. copyright law. To the extent that any of the Works created for Nonprofit by Contractor are not works made for hire belonging to Nonprofit, Contractor assigns and transfers to Nonprofit all rights Contractor has or may acquire to all such Works. Contractor agrees to sign and deliver to Nonprofit, either during or subsequent to the term of this Agreement, such other documents as Nonprofit considers desirable to evidence the assignment of copyright.

## Contractor Warranties

Contractor warrants that the Works do not infringe any intellectual property rights or violate any laws related to libel, privacy, or otherwise and that the Works are original to Contractor. Contractor agrees to indemnify Nonprofit and hold it harmless in any action arising out of, or relating to, these representations and warranties.

## Miscellaneous

This Agreement constitutes the entire understanding between the parties and can be modified only by written agreement. The laws of the State of _____ shall govern this Agreement. In the event of any dispute arising under this agreement, the prevailing party shall be entitled to its reasonable attorneys' fees.

Contractor Signature: _____

Contractor Name: _____

Contractor Address: _____

Contractor Tax ID #: _____

Date: _____

Nonprofit Authorized Signature: _____

Name and Title: _____

Address: _____

Date: _____

# Volunteer Assignment Agreement

I, _____ ,

am a volunteer with _____ . It is my intent that any Work I create in my capacity as a volunteer

for _____ ,

will become the property of _____ ,

which will own full copyright in all such Work(s). To the extent that any Work(s) I create for _____

_____ is not a work for hire, I assign and transfer

to _____ all

worldwide copyright interests in the Work(s), for the life of such copyright interests.

In assigning all right, title, and interest in the Work(s) to _____ ,

I intend to transfer to _____

the full ownership in and of the Work(s), including all rights of reproduction, distribution, display, and adaptation, and

the right to create derivative work(s). All such rights apply without limitation to any print, electronic, multimedia, or

other formats including HTML format for websites, distribution online by email, and all other methods of creating and

distributing media. I agree to sign and deliver to _____ _____ ,

either during or subsequent to the term of this Agreement, such other documents as _____

_____ _____ considers desirable to evidence the assignment of copyright.

In consideration of this agreement, _____ agrees to (check all that apply):

☐ allow me to include the Work or a reproduction of the Work in my portfolio or other such compilation, to be shown
  to my prospective employers or clients, and no other commercial or noncommercial use. All such portfolio uses must
  include a notice of _____ 's copyright ownership.

☐ acknowledge my transfer of the Work to _____
  as a charitable contribution.

☐ give full and complete credit in all versions of the Work(s).

☐ other: _____

_____ .

I warrant that any Work(s) I create pursuant to this agreement are original and do not infringe any intellectual property rights

or violate any laws related to libel, privacy, or otherwise. I agree to indemnify and hold harmless _____

_____ in any action arising out of, or relating to,

these representations and warranties.

Volunteer Signature: _____

Volunteer Name: _____

Volunteer Address: _____

Date: _____

# Nonprofit's Initial Budget

| | Program 1 | Program 2 | Program 3 | Administration (Unrestricted) | Total |
|---|---|---|---|---|---|
| **INCOME** | | | | | |
| Individual contributions | | | | | |
| Membership revenues | | | | | |
| Grants/Institutional donors | | | | | |
| Special events revenues | | | | | |
| Sponsorships | | | | | |
| Income-producing activity 1 | | | | | |
| Income-producing activity 2 | | | | | |
| **TOTAL INCOME** | | | | | |
| **EXPENSES** | | | | | |
| **Program costs** | | | | | |
| Program costs type 1 | | | | | |
| Program costs type 2 | | | | | |
| Program costs type 3 | | | | | |
| Program costs type 4 | | | | | |
| Program costs type 5 | | | | | |
| Program costs type 6 | | | | | |
| Program costs type 7 | | | | | |
| Miscellaneous | | | | | |
| **Program Costs Subtotal** | | | | | |
| **Fixed costs** | | | | | |
| Office rent | | | | | |
| Salaries | | | | | |
| Utilities | | | | | |
| Telephone service | | | | | |
| Office supplies | | | | | |
| Postage | | | | | |
| Website hosting | | | | | |
| Fundraising costs | | | | | |
| Insurance | | | | | |
| Professional services (accountant, etc.) | | | | | |
| Other fixed costs | | | | | |
| Other fixed costs | | | | | |
| Other fixed costs | | | | | |
| Miscellaneous | | | | | |
| **Fixed Costs Subtotal** | | | | | |

# Nonprofit's Initial Budget

| | Program 1 | Program 2 | Program 3 | Administration (Unrestricted) | **Total |
|---|---|---|---|---|---|
| **CAPITAL EXPENSES** | | | | | |
| Computer equipment | | | | | |
| Telephone/fax equipment | | | | | |
| Office furniture | | | | | |
| Vehicle | | | | | |
| Capital Expenses Subtotal | | | | | |
| **START-UP COSTS** | | | | | |
| Printing—brochures, business cards, etc. | | | | | |
| Website development | | | | | |
| Telephone set-up | | | | | |
| State fees (incorporation, etc.) | | | | | |
| Other fixed costs | | | | | |
| Other fixed costs | | | | | |
| Startup Costs Subtotal | | | | | |
| | | | | | |
| **TOTAL INCOME** | | | | | |
| Program Costs Subtotal | | | | | |
| Fixed Costs Subtotal | | | | | |
| Capital Expenses Subtotal | | | | | |
| Start-up Costs Subtotal | | | | | |
| **TOTAL EXPENSES** | | | | | |
| **NET ANNUAL REVENUES** | | | | | |

# Index

 **Keep Up to Date**

 Go to Nolo.com/newsletters to sign up for free newsletters and discounts on Nolo products.

- **Nolo's Special Offer.** A monthly newsletter with the biggest Nolo discounts around.

- **Landlord's Quarterly.** Deals and free tips for landlords and property managers.

 Don't forget to check for updates. Find this book at **Nolo.com** and click "Legal Updates."

## Let Us Hear From You

 Register your Nolo product and give us your feedback at Nolo.com/customer-support/productregistration.

- Once you've registered, you qualify for technical support if you have any trouble with a download (though most folks don't).

- We'll send you a coupon for 15% off your next Nolo.com order!

SNON5

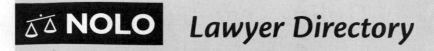